Moving Home

NEXT WAVE: New Directions in Women's Studies
A series edited by Caren Kaplan, Inderpal Grewal, and Robyn Wiegman

Moving Home

GENDER, PLACE, AND TRAVEL WRITING

IN THE EARLY BLACK ATLANTIC

Sandra Gunning

Duke University Press Durham and London 2021

© 2021 DUKE UNIVERSITY PRESS

Printed in the United States of America on acid-free paper ∞
Designed by Courtney Leigh Baker
Typeset in Whitman and Helvetica Neue by Westchester Publishing Services

Library of Congress Cataloging-in-Publication Data
Names: Gunning, Sandra, [date] author.
Title: Moving home : gender, place, and travel writing in the early Black Atlantic / Sandra Gunning.
Other titles: Next wave (Duke University Press)
Description: Durham : Duke University Press, 2021. | Series: Next wave | Includes bibliographical references and index.
Identifiers: LCCN 2021000522 (print)
LCCN 2021000523 (ebook)
ISBN 9781478013624 (hardcover)
ISBN 9781478014553 (paperback)
ISBN 9781478021858 (ebook)
Subjects: LCSH: Travel writing—History—19th century. | African diaspora in literature. | American literature—African American authors—History and criticism. | American literature—African influences. | Great Britain—Colonies—Description and travel. | Atlantic Ocean Region—Description and travel. | BISAC: SOCIAL SCIENCE / Black Studies (Global) | SOCIAL SCIENCE / Gender Studies
Classification: LCC PN56.T7 G86 2021 (print) | LCC PN56.T7 (ebook) | DDC 809/.93352996—dc23
LC record available at https://lccn.loc.gov/2021000522
LC ebook record available at https://lccn.loc.gov/2021000523

ISBN 9781478092636 (open access)

Cover art: (Top) *Refugees on levee, photo by Carroll's Art Gallery.* Mississippi, ca. 1897. Photograph. (Bottom) Robert K. Griffin, *Fish Town at Bassau, Liberia.* Watercolor, ca. 1856. Both images courtesy the Library of Congress Prints and Photographs Division, Washington, DC.

This book is freely available in an open access edition thanks to TOME (Toward an Open Monograph Ecosystem)—a collaboration of the Association of American Universities, the Association of University Presses, and the Association of Research Libraries—and the generous support of the University of Michigan's College of Literature, Science & the Arts and the Provost Office. Learn more at the TOME website, available at: openmonographs.org.

For Hannah
and in memory of
Marguerite

Contents

Preface ix
Acknowledgments xvii

Introduction 1

1. Mary Seacole's West Indian Hospitality 23

2. Home and Belonging for Nancy Prince 55

3. The Repatriation of Samuel Ajayi Crowther 86

4. Martin R. Delany and Robert Campbell in West Africa 120

5. Sarah Forbes Bonetta and Travel as Social Capital 160

Coda 197

Notes 205
Bibliography 227
Index 251

One of my earliest memories is of a cloudy day (around 1965), when I watched my father stuff crumpled newspaper into a broken windowpane, in anticipation of "spraying." Not long after, a truck drove slowly up and down our street, releasing a fine mist into the air. Years later, I learned that that mysterious mist was DDT. As part of its campaign to eradicate malaria from the tropical Americas, the World Health Organization had doused my island with a chemical no Jamaican at the time knew to be a carcinogen. In those early years of self-government, the administering of a "harmless" insecticide must have seemed an appropriately forward-looking measure. While this advancement put a nail in the coffin of Jamaica's ecosystem, there was a sense, too, in the 1960s and 1970s that the postcolonial condition was already poisoning our new nation. For example, because Jamaica exported bauxite and alumina, as opposed to aluminum, the ore's end product—or better yet, *finished* aluminum products such as cooking utensils, vehicle parts, and metal sheeting—we were far, far away from reaping the full benefit of our natural resources. If you threw in OPEC and the global oil crisis, in addition to the ever-growing national debt, Jamaica's foreign currency reserves rapidly verged on *empty*—or, to borrow my father's favorite metaphor, it was as if we were subsisting on fumes. The only question seemed to be, When would we finally come to a standstill?

Don't get me wrong—there were wonderful things about growing up in Jamaica in the years under Prime Minister Michael Manley: fantastic, if brutally strict, teachers who gave me an outstanding primary education; the amazing National Dance Theatre Company; wonderful, locally produced music by people who were not international reggae stars; Sangster's Bookstore; and the tingling down my spine every time I stood to sing the national anthem. But even with these precious gifts, there was no escaping the sense that the nation was in an economic free fall. Crippled by predatory loans from the International Monetary Fund (IMF) and the World Bank, Jamaica could afford next to nothing. When the price of petrol and kerosene went up, condensed milk, flour, and cooking oil moved beyond the reach of the poorest Jamaicans. During periods of drought, water shutoffs were a way of life. At home, a steady supply of matches and candles got us through regularly scheduled blackouts. School textbooks from overseas vanished from bookstore shelves. Crucial car parts went from being horrendously expensive to entirely unavailable. When a vehicle owner parked on the street overnight (particularly if they owned a Volkswagen Beetle), by morning the headlamps were missing. But the black market in car parts was merely the benign edge of a horrific crime wave marked by countless armed robberies and home invasions, frequently accompanied by beatings, rape, and murder. Depending on your income, you fought back with an angry dog chained up in clear view, a firearm, a fancy alarm system, or all of the above. Everyone who could afford it welded iron bars and gates across not just doorways and windows, but indeed *any* crack or crevice that might admit even the smallest human being. And everywhere there were guns, guns, and more guns. On call-in radio talk shows, political commentators and members of the public bemoaned the debt, the government, the criminals, the United States, OPEC, the IMF, and on and on.

In search of relief, my parents, my sister, and I regularly made the two-hour winding drive across the Blue Mountains to Port Antonio, home of my mother's aging Lebanese-born parents. Despite the political and economic chaos, my grandparents' shotgun-style house seemed peaceful and constant. Every room emitted the comforting smell of mahogany and bay rum. To accommodate an ever-expanding family (eight children in all), my grandparents had tacked on rooms wherever, so that exterior French doors in the living room creaked open into a large, high-ceilinged guest room. The terrazzo-tiled kitchen sat just beyond a set of dining-room sash windows that once opened onto a side yard. A bathroom trip in the middle of the night required tiptoeing through Grandma's room to access the house's central hallway. The house's two bathrooms were really one gigantic room, partitioned by an ancient beadboard divider. Since the divider had regular gaps where it met the floor, as children my sister and I passed notes and comic books back and forth, while we pretended to take our showers.

Right on the water, where the northeastern foothills of the Blue Mountains ended in the Caribbean Sea, Port Antonio bore the brunt of every weather system coming in from the Atlantic, taking the prize as the wettest spot on the island. To foreign tourists passing through, the town's mold-stained concrete walls and ramshackle brown zinc roofs must have seemed quaint and bucolic. If they entered my grandparents' country store and saw that all purchases were wrapped in pages of the *Gleaner* and tied with cotton string, they marveled that Jamaicans had the wherewithal to produce a daily paper. One summer while I took a turn helping out in the store, a skinny white American with long hair and a struggling beard ran his hand across the newspaper sheets laid out at the wrapping station. With wide-eyed astonishment, he asked if he could take one of the sheets with him. "Ahmm, we do know how to read and write, you know," I said, with quiet indignation.

None of these strangers had the least interest in the dark secrets of slavery and colonial atrocities behind the breathtakingly green landscape; nor did they care to know how the rich racial and cultural diversity of Jamaica came to be. But it was in Port Antonio that I supplemented my father's family stories of African slaves, Scots-Irish immigrants, and British Baptist missionaries with the much more recent history of my mother's Catholic Lebanese parents, a pair of Arabic-speaking first cousins from turn-of-the-century Choueifat (pronounced *Sch-why-fate* by my mother), who grew up in what was still the Ottoman Empire. Just before World War I, they migrated first to Haiti and then to Jamaica, where they learned to master the local patois, albeit with a very thick Arabic accent. Eventually, as shopkeepers, they began supplying small farmers and town locals with pots and pans, nails by the pound, cloth by the yard, shovels, kerosene lamps, coal stoves, Dutch ovens, handmade brooms, schoolchildren's exercise books, rubber work boots, and, occasionally, dress shoes, both secondhand and new.

Neither British nor of African descent, my grandparents would have learned early on that in Jamaica's complex class- and color-obsessed society, they would never achieve anything akin to racial equality with European whites. Consequently, as with many newly arrived groups bent on success, they took every opportunity to put themselves above the island's Black population: the modestly dressed market women, the ragged small farmers, the United Fruit Company pickers on whom their living depended. However, my grandparents did have several things in common with the people they looked down upon. As with a number of their customers, they could neither read nor write English. And they ate the same food. Indeed, over time their Eastern Mediterranean cuisine merged with local dishes rooted in the experiences of African slaves and Chinese and South Asian indentured workers. To be sure, my grandmother went on making kibbeh, *labnah*, and cabbage-leaf *meshi*, but more often than not we ate rice, yams, avocados, curried goat, roasted breadfruit, boiled green bananas, escovitch fish, and fried plantains. With seven daughters and one son, they at first hoped to orchestrate marriages among the handful of other Christian Lebanese families on the island, but as happened to successive waves of English, Irish, Scots, Portuguese, German, Chinese, South Asian, and Ashkenazi Jewish immigrants, their children and their children's children married across color, class, and religious lines, the obvious consequence of life on a small island.

To a Jamaican, there is nothing odd about being the product of two or three different ethnic histories. And regardless of how far back you trace your lineage, the journeys embarked upon by your ancestors had much to do with imperial profit seeking and territorial domination. Though at first glance the ability to reinvent yourself would seem to rest with those who were European and free, regardless of race there were limitations, especially with respect to class, ethnicity, and place of origin. Though they were Christian and had always worn Western-style clothing, my grandparents were still regarded by the British as Arabic-speaking "Orientals." As with everyone else trying to fit into Jamaica's colonial society, they had to learn the appropriate colonial script and rub shoulders with Port Antonio's tiny mixed-race and Black colonial elite, while also working hard in their business to establish a class identity that put them above their Black housekeepers and yardmen, from whom they expected perfect obedience, despite paying miniscule wages. If they were upset that their grandchildren ended up being racially mixed (Chinese and Black) it was hard to tell, since all of us had the run of their small garden and the whole house, especially that airy and light-filled guest room, with bay windows looking out onto one of Port Antonio's two natural harbors.

As one of these grandchildren, I witnessed contradictions in terms of class and race long before I had the words to describe them. But none of that prepared me for the moment when I spied a peculiar photograph in an aunt's family album. Black and white and probably dating back to the 1920s, the image featured a short, unsmiling, and apparently white man in a pith helmet, staring defiantly into the camera, his light eyes overhung by thick dark brows that almost met in the middle of his forehead. With thin lips tightly pressed together, he wore a very wrinkled khaki jacket with pleated breast pockets, a pair of shorts, and puttees. Off to his left side and slightly behind him stood a small-boned, bare-breasted Black woman, fabric draped around her waist, as she steadied a clay jar atop her head. She was equally blank-faced, but her eyes were averted, and though tonally distinguishable from the darker tropical foliage behind her, her Black skin created a sharp contrast to that of the man, making him appear almost luminous.

The photograph reminded me of an early silent film still, or an illustration cut from an ancient issue of *National Geographic*. I immediately asked my aunt for an explanation. She replied, "Oh, that's Uncle C in Africa." A little later on she added, "That C was a brute," with no further explanation. The quiet bitterness informing that last detail discouraged further questions. Going to my grandparents was out of the question, since broaching what seemed to be a difficult family topic would have meant a tongue-lashing from my mother. In the intervening years, and after a bit of digging, a few more facts surfaced. Apparently, C visited Jamaica from Lebanon, ending up in Port Antonio, where he fell in love with my grandparents' oldest child, sixteen-year-old R. After they married, C took his Jamaican-born bride back to Lebanon. Having very little money to begin with, C had great difficulty finding employment back home. Perhaps driven to financial desperation, he left R in the care of his parents and set off for the African continent to pursue some moneymaking venture. Ironically, no one in the family seemed to recall where he went or if he made any money. Instead, there was an enduring sadness for years afterward because R had been separated from her Jamaican family, then essentially abandoned by her husband to an unfamiliar household. According to family reminiscences, R may or may not have suffered abuse at the hands of her in-laws, who may or may not have used her as their scullery maid. Looking at a teenaged photo taken on the eve of her wedding, I thought that to her in-laws, R's jet-black hair and alabaster skin must have seemed at odds with her West Indian food ways and her patois, and especially the hint of a Jamaican accent lacing her Arabic. However attenuated, the African diaspora had entered C's Lebanese home, even as he worked hard in Africa to acquire a racist colonial lexicon that might mitigate (at least within the figural boundaries of the photograph) his own nonwhite status.

During colonialism, countless European and American fortune hunters set out to make it in Africa, and Middle Easterners were no exception. Men such as C arrived as peddlers and small shopkeepers to operate as middlemen supplying more or less the same items sold in my grandparents' store, this time to petty white colonial officials and African and South Asian laborers laying railroad tracks or erecting bridges. As an antidote to his own poverty and alienation as an "Oriental" in colonial Africa, C *needed* that African woman to embody stasis, silence, and powerlessness, so as to highlight himself as akin to Richard Francis Burton or Henry Morton Stanley, producers of African "knowledge" and seemingly capable and commanding in any situation that arose on the backward continent. Of course, C could assert a white Western colonial manhood only within the safety of the photograph. And he had the image made not to convince a middle-class European viewer that he was of equal status but rather to update his family in Lebanon and his in-laws in Jamaica that he had "made it" in Africa. Therefore the photograph functioned as both an artifact of and a commentary on his sojourn abroad. To his two families he signaled that his sacrifice of a stable homelife in Lebanon had paid off because he had embraced imperial racism. Instead of revealing him as (to play on Homi Bhabha's phrase "almost the same, *but not quite*" from "Of Mimicry and Man") a not-quite-not-white Middle Eastern trader, C's photograph suggested that imperial travel had accorded him a new competency, a new freedom to remake his identity. In this way, he may have replicated the same racial maneuvers enacted by my grandparents when they arrived to the Caribbean in the first years of the twentieth century.

But what of the carefully posed African woman? Reduced to a colonial cliché, she functioned as the feminized continent ready for takeover. As the object rather than the subject of the image, she lacked the means of shaping and broadcasting her own story. However, though C's centrality depended on silence, that silence did not mean absence. As a teenager, I couldn't abide the suggestion that she had no story, so in her African face I imagined the Jamaican faces of my teachers, my public-school classmates, female cashiers in the local corner shop, elderly ladies in church, and women selling produce and household goods in the market. Having grown up in the violent context of early postcolonial Jamaica, I also wondered if C had done her any harm before or after the staging of the photograph. However, from my own temporal and geographical location, I was as much an outsider as C. And, as a part of the family to which C had directed the image, I too consumed her through the superficialities of race and gender. Even today, because of my own diasporic position as a Jamaican immigrant to the United States, and my fantasies of what long-dead Uncle C might have been like, I risk projecting a history of my own design onto who that African woman might have been. That projection assumes a colonial-era African woman automatically dispossessed and immobile, even as her presence helped C to prove his apparent social advancement.

It would be simplistic to make C the clear villain of this narrative because I, too, am entangled in a neocolonial script that highlights my education and agentive mobility as a "successful" immigrant to the United States and a privileged global traveler. Still, the thought of both individuals, and especially the unequal relationship staged in the image, continues to elicit a range of questions, not least of which are: Can travel be transformative for the racialized and sexualized Other? How do racial regimes change or shift for an immigrant versus a sojourner? What impact does the phenomenon of intersecting migratory patterns have on the individuals involved? What essential powers are gained or lost as the regimes of race, ethnicity, and class subtly shift and recombine, depending on location? How does gender identity shape strategies for agency in relation to stasis or mobility? What valence does national identification have, in the absence of the nation-state?

These early musings proved to be the seeds from which *Moving Home: Gender, Race, and Travel Writing in the Early Black Atlantic* has emerged. Writing as a scholar on a range of nineteenth-century Black American, West Indian, and West African travel literature, I still feel the imperative to provide a space for that African woman standing behind my uncle. This book marks a step, but it is certainly not a resolution.

Acknowledgments

The idea for this book first came to me in the mid-1990s, while I was working on an article on the Jamaican healer Mary Seacole. That burst of post-tenure energy was short-lived, however, since for the last decade and a half the particular turmoil of family life (in this case illness, and then more illness) threatened repeatedly to derail my writing and research altogether. Thankfully, the act of completing this project eventually became a refuge. Here and there I stole thirty minutes in a hospital waiting room to write a paragraph. On good days, that paragraph turned in a page, and despite long gaps of time, that page eventually became a chapter. As I look back now, I'm so very grateful for the help I received from family, friends, and home care staff: their collective contributions enabled me to carve out chunks of time to visit archives in the United States, Canada, and Britain. I especially want to thank my successive research assistants, including David Shih, Emma Garrett, Kyle Grady, Amanda Healey, and Latara MacLamore, for their assistance, in large and small ways, at different stages of my writing and rewriting of chapters.

This book would not have been possible without consistently generous funding from the University of Michigan, in particular the Rackham Graduate School; the College of Science, Letters, and the Arts (LSA); the University of Michigan ADVANCE Program; and the Departments of English, American Culture, and Afroamerican and African Studies. Words cannot express my gratitude as well to the many librarians and archivists in the United Kingdom at the University of Birmingham, the Royal Archives at Windsor, and the British Library's Newspaper Division. I owe a great debt as well to the Special Collections librarians at Dalhousie University (Canada) and to the staff of the microfilm reading room at the Library of Congress.

Without the direct help of Josiah Olubowale, my recovery work on Sarah Forbes Bonetta would have been impossible. Olubowale helped me locate crucial material at the Nigerian National Archives in Ibadan, and he became my eyes and ears on the ground, helping me verify the accuracy of typed copies of documents I had found in Dalhousie University's Special Collections. His Yoruba-to-English translations of key material from *Iwe Irohin* also helped me clarify details about Sarah Forbes Bonetta's firstborn child. I was honored to receive the invaluable help of the late writer Walter Dean Myers in piecing together Bonetta's biography. Ever protective of the heritage of people of African descent, Mr. Myers was nevertheless gracious enough to allow a perfect stranger into his home to view his collection of letters written to and by Bonetta.

At the University of Michigan and at other institutions, I have been extremely lucky to have colleagues who read my work, listened to my endless droning, and encouraged me when I thought this project would never end. My sincere thanks to Paul Anderson, Naomi André, Amy Carroll, Phil Deloria, Mamadou Diof, Frieda Ekotto, Frances Smith Foster, Jonathan Freedman, the late Rosemary Marangoly George, K. Ian Grandison, Arlene Keizer, Robert S. Levine, Kerry Larson, Carla Peterson, Adela Pinch, Yopie Prins, Elisha Renne, Marlon Ross, Xiomara Santamarina, Julius Scott, Sid Smith, Stephanie A. Smith, Abby Stewart, Richard Yarborough, Lisa Yun, and Magda Zabarowska. I am exceedingly grateful to both the late Nellie Y. MacKay and Marie Louise Roberts at the University of Wisconsin–Madison for allowing me to participate in various symposia, where participants—especially those in African studies—pushed me to answer hard and necessary questions. Other audiences that both encouraged and challenged me to be better include the English Departments at Rutgers University (New Brunswick), Michigan State University, and Emory University.

An earlier version of chapter 1 appeared as "Traveling with Her Mother's Tastes: The Negotiation of Gender, Race, and Location in *Wonderful Adventures of Mrs. Seacole in Many Lands*," *Signs* 26, no. 4 (Summer 2001): 949–81. An earlier version of chapter 2 appeared as "Nancy Prince and the Politics of Mobility, Home, and Diasporic (Mis)Identification," *American Quarterly* 53, no. 1 (March 2001): 32–69.

My particular thanks to Caren Kaplan and Inderpal Grewal for supporting the publication of this book and to Ken Wissoker at Duke University Press for his immense patience with the slow pace of completion. I am also grateful to the manuscript's two anonymous readers for their detailed engagement with my work and their encouragement to deepen and extend its arguments.

Danielle Lavaque-Manty absolutely deserves a paragraph of her own. She whipped me into shape toward the end of the writing process by pushing me to trim, cut, rewrite, reorganize, and then finally let go of the damn book so it could see the light of day. She pulled me out of the traps I set for myself, providing the clear voice of reason throughout. Though she modestly brushes aside all praise, this book definitely would have taken another fifteen years to complete if she had not come into my life at just the right time.

Marlon Ross and K. Ian Grandison continue to bless my life and that of my family. Numerous times they have opened up their home to my daughter and me, providing rigorous discussion, love, *lots of laughter*, and other supports both material and moral, especially during some very dark times. I am grateful to them for all they have taught me about gardening as well as academia: much of what they gave me went into the writing of this book, and I hope they enjoy reading it.

Sincere thanks are in order to my ex-husband Keith L. T. Alexander for working to keep our daughter alive and well in her early years, and especially for taking on childcare burdens during my trips for research. Specifically, his contributions allowed me to complete the research for chapters 3 and 5. Thanks as well to Dr. Irving Leon for his support through difficult times. Love and gratitude always and forever I send to Hannah, Jacqueline, Glen, Fulton, Wesley, Daniel Jr., and Janice. As I cherish close family and friends, I continue to mourn the loss of my parents, Rymund and Marguerite Gunning; my indomitable aunt, Victoria Touzalin; my brother, Trevor; and my mother-sister, Francene Rutlin. I think of them in everything I do.

I'm grateful to the Department of Afro-American and African Studies and to the Department of American Culture for helping to fund the open access edition of *Moving Home*.

Introduction

Qualities traditionally associated with travel writing include leisure, choice, curiosity, love of the exotic, and wanderlust. Indeed, the term *travel* suggests a world of cosmopolitan privilege where one is free to leave and return to a place called home or settle on a whim in some new location. Additionally, the credibility of travel writers rests on the public belief that they have actually been to the places described in their narrative, signaling once again the assumed power of class, personal agency, literacy, and access to publication, all in the service of captivating an audience by transporting them to "exotic" locales. Though travel narratives are, to some extent, semiautobiographical, the (usually white) narrator operates as a guide, becoming the eyes and ears of the (usually white) reader, transforming the latter, at least imaginatively, into something of a sympathetic companion. The luxury of travel writing for its own sake also gestures to the form's assumed unavailability to anyone deemed marginal to the nation—that is, the politically disenfranchised, the destitute, and the persecuted. Consequently, far from being an innocent pastime, travel writing has always been shaped by a specific political, social, and historical subject position, one that requires the objectification of a sexualized, classed, ethnic, and racial Other. How in the world, then, could such an exclusionary genre possibly have served the purposes of nineteenth-century African diasporic subjects in the age of transatlantic slavery, when the majority of these subjects were legally defined as someone else's movable property, rather than as human beings who might have traveled in their own right?

A leading figure in the critical demystification of European and American travel writing, Mary Louise Pratt has long argued that nineteenth-century European explorers saw with "imperial eyes" when they visited the continents of Africa and South America—and we might add the earth's polar regions, the Caribbean, the Middle East, the Indian subcontinent, the American West, the territories in and around the Pacific Ocean, and so on.[1] According to Pratt, as representatives of particular national interests, white male tourists, explorers, and ethnographers tended to belittle the presence of nonwhite populations, often by imagining them outside of modernity or removing them from the narrative altogether, so as to render the landscape completely available for imperial consumption.[2] To accomplish this goal, suggests Pratt, the Euro-American male writer might choose to represent himself as the disembodied omniscient narrator, or he might include himself in the larger plot of the narrative as the protagonist who survived to the end of the journey, managing to outlast the barbarity seemingly characteristic of undiscovered territory. One of her most effective examples is the late eighteenth-century Scottish physician and explorer Mungo Park, who in *Travels in the Interior Districts in Africa* (1799) represented himself as a figure deeply caught up in the action, enduring destitution, starvation, and even capture at the hands of hostile Africans, all for the sake of scientific knowledge. A sampling of narratives that in part or on the whole fall within Pratt's arguments include John Franklin's *Narrative of a Journey to the Shores of the Polar Sea* (1823), Dixon Denham, Hugh Clapperton, and Walter Oudney's *Narrative of Travels and Discoveries in Northern and Central Africa* (1826), Richard Francis Burton's *Personal Narrative of a Pilgrimage to Al-Madinah and Meccah* (1855), and David Livingstone's *Missionary Travels and Researches in South Africa* (1857).

Nonetheless, there were several nineteenth-century Black American, Afro-West Indian, Americo-Liberian, and Christianized Yoruba men—some freeborn, others ex-slaves—who wrote about their exploration of West African territory, revealing a relationship to both the land and its peoples that could be very different from the kind of dramatic contact articulated by their white counterparts. These men especially had to confront the meaning of "return" to an imagined ancestral homeland or, in the case of Christianized West Africans who were themselves former slaves, "return" to the geographical location of familial and physical trauma. Of particular interest to missiologists and to cultural anthropologists studying Yoruba ethnogenesis is the Yoruba slave turned Anglican clergyman, missionary, and early Nigerian linguist Samuel Ajayi Crowther. Indeed, Crowther's first published work was one half of the *Journals of the Rev. James Frederick Schön and Mr. Samuel Crowther: who, with the Sanction of Her Majesty's Government, Accompanied the Expedition up the Niger, in 1841, in Behalf* of the Church Missionary Society (1842). As a young catechist, Crowther and his senior white colleague, Schön, accompanied a royal naval expedition on the Niger River so as to assess the "heathen's" receptiveness to the establishment of Christian mission stations. So many sailors died of malaria and other tropical fevers that the project was aborted mid-journey, but Crowther's resulting narrative walked a perilous tightrope: as a Christianized ex-slave, he had to demonstrate his worth to the English men and women whose contributions were paying for his sustenance, even as he looked with new eyes upon populations and locales that were familiar to him during his pre-slavery boyhood. After the success of his first project, Crowther went on to publish *Journal of an Expedition up the Niger and Tshadda Rivers* (1855) and *Niger Mission: Bishop Crowther's Report of the Overland Journey from Lokoja to Bida, on the River Niger: and Thence to Lagos, on the Sea Coast* (1872).

The period of Crowther's missionary travels coincided with a journey of "return" made by American Black Nationalist Martin R. Delany, in search of land for Black American settlement in what is now Nigeria, among Africans whom he hoped would be unsullied by contact with whites. Delany's *Official Report of the Niger Valley Exploring Party* (1861) is rarely addressed, perhaps because he put his African adventure behind him once the American Civil War broke out, devoting himself instead to the recruitment of Black soldiers for the Union and later to Black American political engagement during and after Reconstruction.[3] Often overlooked, as well, is the work of Delany's traveling companion on the journey, the Jamaican Robert Campbell. Because of Campbell's ancestry, his sojourn in the United States, and finally his permanent move to Lagos, his *Pilgrimage to My Motherland: An Account of a Journey among the Egbas and the Yorubas of Central Africa, 1859–60* (1861) stands at the intersection of early African American, early Caribbean, and early West African literature. How did his combined identities shape his role as an African explorer, in the early years of an increasingly British colonial Nigeria? Meanwhile, the recently anthologized narratives of two Americo-Liberians—James L, Sims's 1858 *Scenes in the Interior of Liberia: Being a Tour through the Countries of the Dey, Goulah, Pessah, Barlain, Kpellay, Suloany and King Boatswain's Tribes in 1858* and Benjamin J. K. Anderson's 1870 "Narrative of a Journey to Musardu, the Capital of the Western Mandingoes"—shed light on how Black American settlers in newly created Liberia regarded their contentious relationship with the indigenous populations whose land they and the American Colonization Society had claimed. In contrast, as a late nineteenth-century Black American traveler to the Belgian Congo, George Washington Williams inserted himself within the controversial frame of European colonial expansion after 1884 in *An Open Letter to His Serene*

Majesty Leopold II, King of the Belgians and Sovereign of the Independent State of Congo (1890), in an effort to protest slavery and genocidal atrocities committed against indigenous peoples.

As representatives of different diasporic communities across the Black Atlantic, these men each wrote to achieve particular group agendas, but by virtue of being African and of African descent, as well as ex-slaves or the descendants of ex-slaves, they might just as easily have become the objects of study for white race scientists, ethnographers, missionaries, and protoeugenicists. Yet, by claiming the genre of the exploration narrative for themselves, they fruitfully complicate Pratt's insightful theses and the very question of what constituted early narratives shaping the perception of the African continent. Writing as they did in the age of American and internal African slavery, and before the end of the transatlantic slave trade, each traveler witnessed and in many ways participated in American and European colonial expansion on the continent of Africa. Though they came from vastly different backgrounds and fell into exploration for a variety of reasons, all were concerned on some level with a sense of loss—a sense of displacement and disenfranchisement in the land of their nativity, in the organizations that might have employed them, and in the communities on whose behalf they traveled. Ironically, their narratives discuss West Africa in registers tinged by a poignant desire to find a resting place, a refuge-as-antidote that might overcome the soul-crushing legacies of slavery and discrimination, especially for those born in the United States. At the same time, regardless of their nativity, these Western-educated Christians necessarily reproduced some of the same Eurocentric assumptions about West African "heathens" that white male explorers exhibited. As such, these writers embraced Western notions of modernity, nation building, and territorial expansion.

Such complications require us to think carefully not only about oversimplified notions of "resistance" but also about the misleading dichotomy the term encourages against its opposite, "complicity." These men felt that their interest in the African continent was different from that of white Europeans. However, any oppositional stance they might have taken to white imperialism, any declaration they might have made that Africa should become the *home* of the formerly enslaved as opposed to being merely a resource for white acquisition, would have been conditioned by a broad range of intraracial, and at times dissimilar, cultural assumptions and allegiances. Additionally, their sense of themselves as male travelers and writers would have been in conversation with, rather than merely in opposition to, nineteenth-century Euro-American ideas of "masculine" pursuits such as scientific observation and discovery. After all, these men were products of the West, even as they were lifelong critics of and activists against the racially discriminatory practices of majoritarian American and European societies. Consequently, an analysis of their African exploration narratives reveals their challenges to and deep entanglements with nineteenth-century imperialist discourse.

Thus far I have used the example of travel writing by early African diasporic men. Now I shift to a discussion of writing by their female counterparts and, consequently, the difference made by thinking about not just women's writing but gendered subjectivity for men and women. Indeed, in *Moving Home* I argue that Christianized African, British West Indian, and African American women were as deeply invested in travel writing as their male counterparts.[4] Tim Youngs defines travel writing as "predominantly factual, first-person prose accounts of travel that have been undertaken by the author-narrator."[5] Youngs's definition allows us to observe ever more closely how the literary landscape changes with the inclusion of Black and African women as nineteenth-century traveling subjects within the Atlantic African diaspora. As we have known for some time, early Black and African women reworked traditional forms to tell their own unique stories in an age when Blackness synonymized both immorality and captivity. Concerned primarily with freeborn and ex-slave female subjects of the African diaspora hailing from vastly differing social circumstances, the following chapters explore women's travel writing from the United States, the British West Indies, and Anglophone West Africa. Travelers discussed include the American reformer and small-businesswoman Nancy Prince, the Jamaican sutler and hotelkeeper Mary Seacole, and the West African ex-slave Sarah Forbes Bonetta, who became Queen Victoria's ward. The published works of both Seacole and Prince are by now well known as both Black female autobiography and travel texts. Nevertheless, the lack of similarly published material from Anglophone West African women in this period requires an examination of alternate materials, including unpublished letters and diaries. Such materials reveal that mission-educated African women throughout the period of European empire were often traveling writers and interlocutors. Only through archival materials, then, is it possible to see Bonetta as both a representative of the Anglophone West African elite and a unique female voice who assigns meaning to her own subjectivity as she travels between Lagos, Freetown, and the south of England.

ENSLAVEMENT, ESCAPE, AND THE FUTILITY OF "HOME"

Even though Crowther, Delany, Campbell, Seacole, Prince, and Bonetta appear in their writing to be free from any nation-based constraint, their travel has to be gauged against transatlantic slavery, which in both its practice and its aftermath appeared to fix Blackness as a state of physical immobility and intellectual and moral deficiency. Though various West European nations, along with the United States, eventually banned their citizens from engaging in the Atlantic slave trade, captive Africans still made the Middle Passage to Cuba and Brazil until the 1860s. Before the American Civil War, the Fugitive Slave Law of 1850 extended the authority of slaveholders to northern states, while the 1857 US Supreme Court ruling on *Dred Scott v. Sandford* declared American citizenship off-limits to anyone of African descent. In the nineteenth-century Black Atlantic, then, freedom to travel from place to place without threat of violence or capture would have been a crucial, constitutive element of personhood and self-ownership. Among others, Lisa Brawley, Michael A. Chaney, and Stephen Lucasi have argued that African American runaway slaves indexed the theme of flight in their autobiographies as they sought to characterize the agonizing separation from family in bondage, the risk of torture or death if caught, and the challenge of running in extreme heat or cold with nothing to eat and in fear of any white person claiming to be a friend.[6] These horrific conditions require a redefinition of the word *travel* to include not just "the action of traveling or journeying" but especially the term's original Middle English meaning of *travail* or work, as in "labor, toil, suffering, trouble."[7] Thus, whether for nineteenth-century slaves, or for free Black people in settings that still denied them political, economic, and social self-determination, the ability to seize and exercise the right to physical mobility was often equated with self-protection, with the ability to keep oneself alive.

Key African American slave texts that, in one way or another, thematize physical escape along a North-South trajectory include Frederick Douglass's first two narratives, *The Narrative of the Life of Frederick Douglass, an American Slave* (1845) and *My Bondage and My Freedom* (1855); Josiah Henson's *The Life of Josiah Henson, Formerly a Slave, Now an Inhabitant of Canada, as Narrated by Himself* (1849); Henry "Box" Brown's *Narrative of the Life of Henry Box Brown, Written by Himself* (1851), so called because he managed to mail himself in a wooden crate from Richmond, Virginia, to abolitionists in Philadelphia; and, of course, Harriet Jacobs's *Incidents in the Life of a Slave Girl* (1861). Perhaps one of the best examples of how an American slave narrative could transform the themes and purpose of a genre traditionally associated with white writers is William and Ellen Craft's 1860 *Running a Thousand Miles for Freedom; or, The Escape of William and Ellen Craft from Slavery*.[8] Written by William Craft, the narrative describes how the light-skinned Ellen used men's clothes and extensive bandaging around her face to pass as a white male invalid traveling north from Georgia in 1848. Cross-dressing and racially passing as a well-to-do white man, Ellen received no resistance from white travelers for being accompanied by an enslaved body servant played by William. The Crafts disguised themselves to take advantage of socially acceptable, upper-class, white male privileged mobility to achieve their flight to freedom. Thus, their ability to plan a successful escape depended on a keen understanding and manipulation of the gendered proprieties of public travel for whites. Their ruse confirms that travel in the nineteenth century was completely shaped by the politics of gender, race, and power and that when it came to millions of enslaved Black Americans, agentive mobility was a significant right denied. Seizing that right would mean danger and possible death. Ironically, even if a slave escaped north, the 1850 Fugitive Slave Law required anyone who failed to reveal information about or was caught assisting a runaway slave to be punished with fines and a jail sentence. Consequently, simply crossing the Mason-Dixon Line did not make one safe. How, then, might *escape* function as a tool of resistance and self-making, if runaways were unable to control the conditions and direction of their journeys?

According to the Crafts' narrative, they faced intense racism in Boston, ironically the cradle of American resistance to British imperialism and the heart of the American abolition movement. Traveling across the US-Canada border to Halifax in hopes of catching a transatlantic Cunard steamer, they were further rebuffed, this time by a white ticket agent. When the Crafts finally boarded a Britain-bound vessel, Ellen fell gravely ill from sheer anxiety. At the very end of their narrative, William Craft writes, "It was not until we stepped upon the shore of Liverpool that we were free from every slavish fear. We raised our thankful hearts to Heaven, and could have knelt down, like the Neapolitan exiles, and kissed the soil."[9] Here William draws a parallel to a well-publicized 1859 incident when the tyrannical Ferdinand II of Naples forced all would-be revolutionaries out of his kingdom, packing them off to Spain by ship. After the Neapolitans landed at Cadiz, the Spanish refused them permission to disembark, causing the exiles to remain virtual prisoners aboard ship for over three weeks. It was only after being transferred to an American frigate that the dispossessed were allowed to land in Ireland. Homeless and denied citizenship in their land of birth, the Neapolitans nevertheless set about making the best of things, as did the Crafts once they arrived in Britain. By creating a parallel between those Italian refugees and the repeated escapes he and Ellen had to engineer, first from Georgia, then from the United States, and finally from British Canada, William gestures to multiple displacements on an international scale that not only equaled that of the Neapolitans but surpassed them. The Crafts, after all, had escaped slavery and so literally marked every one of the thousand miles between their American enslavement and their freedom in Britain.

While their story brings attention to the larger issues of Black escape, refugee status, and exile in the age of slavery, there is something more to be said about Ellen Craft having to become a man in order for the couple to achieve their emancipation.[10] Her pale skin allowed her to pass for white, but if Ellen had escaped as a woman, she would have only courted disaster by traveling with her male "slave." In almost any era, as Gary Totten reminds us, both white and Black female bodies were policed differently from Black male bodies, such that the conditions and experience of escape were vastly different.[11] Likewise, the meaning of freedom gained could also be different for men versus women, as in the case of Harriet Jacobs in *Incidents in the Life of a Slave Girl*. For Jacobs, the literal, physical escape from slavery came with the requirement that to rescue herself and her children, she first had to hide for seven years in a tiny crawl space in the ceiling of her grandmother's cabin. By having letters sent from the North to her family in North Carolina, Jacobs tricked her master into thinking she had actually departed from the state, leaving her two enslaved children behind. Interestingly, the two times Jacobs left her crawl space and exited her grandmother's cabin she disguised herself as a Black sailor: first when she visited the young white lawyer who had fathered her children, to beg him to have them sent north, and second when she left for Philadelphia to join her son and daughter. Like Ellen Craft, Jacobs had to take on a male identity, in this case one tied to a legitimately peripatetic form of Black male labor, to move about town without attracting attention. Still, at the heart of Jacobs's narrative was the danger that she might never escape the slave mother's enforced stasis. Finally, after reuniting with her children in the North, Jacobs's definition of freedom took on a particularly female-centered emphasis:

> Reader, my story ends with freedom; not in the usual way, with marriage. I and my children are now free! We are as free from the power of slaveholders as are the white people of the north; and though that, according to my ideas, is not saying a great deal, it is a vast improvement in *my* condition. The dream of my life is not yet realized. I do not sit with my children in a home of my own. I still long for a hearthstone of my own, however humble. I wish it for my children's sake far more than for my own.[12]

In referencing "freedom" versus "marriage," Jacobs highlighted the complete inappropriateness for enslaved Black women of the traditional late eighteenth- and nineteenth-century plotline where, to reword Samuel Richardson, white female virtue would be rewarded with matrimony and domestic bliss.[13] Because she and her children had been legally purchased and her own bill of sale handed to her for safekeeping, Jacobs did not seek refuge in Canada or Britain. However, hers was a simmering anger that "home" for the runaway had to be continually delayed. Thus, her story registered a deep frustration at being denied a home that should have been hers in the first place. In the era of the 1850 Fugitive Slave Law and onward into the Jim Crow era, home as a place of belonging and as a symbol of self-protection and of local citizenship was repeatedly denied Black Americans.

The struggle for agency endured by the slave women Ellen Craft and Harriet Jacobs clearly articulates a complex set of issues when compared to the struggle of white women travelers who sought to compete with their male counterparts. Many nineteenth-century narratives of exploration by white men were commissioned by geographical societies, Christian evangelical groups, and interested governmental bodies. Some narratives were the work of white women travelers who sought to gain intellectual legitimacy, such as Mary H. Kingsley's *Travels in West Africa* (1897). Other white women wrote ostensibly to share the pleasure of being wholly iconoclastic among the seemingly exotic, as in the case of Lady Mary Wortley Montagu's Ottoman Empire letters (1763). The Englishwoman Frances Trollope published her scathing 1832 touristic observations of the United States in *Domestic Manners of the Americans*. Meanwhile the Yorkshire-born Isabella Bird proved she had the stamina for any trek in *The Hawaiian Archipelago* (1875) and *Unbeaten Tracks in Japan* (1880). Isabelle Eberhardt, the cross-dressing Swiss author of *In the Shadow of Islam* (1903), and the British aristocrat Gertrude Bell, the so-called modern architect of the Middle East, whose memoir *Amurath to Amurath* was published in 1911, made traditionally masculine roles their own, thereby challenging conventional norms of Victorian femininity. Yet, as revolutionary as all this sounds, sometimes the presence of these white women in "uncivilized" territory also encouraged readers to assume that said territory was already halfway toward domestication, the proof being the presence of the female traveler herself. For example, by the time Mary Kingsley showed up in West Africa, Britain was at the height of its imperial control of large territories that would later become Ghana and Nigeria. The success of her largely ethnographic *Travels* partly relied on her, as a woman, facing the "danger" of racial contamination, rather than being put to death by so-called savages. True, some of these middle- and upper-class white female travelers in the nineteenth century might have lost the respect of their polite middle-class societies, but many also reveled in their independence, their feats of daring, and their intellectual contributions. Many also had a sense of national belonging, based on a cultural citizenship granted at birth.[14]

In contrast, whether enslaved or free, Black women were automatically regarded by whites as the central measure of immorality. At the same time, for those who managed to win their freedom, "liberty" often came hand in hand with complete destitution. Such was the case for the Bermuda-born runaway slave Mary Prince, who in 1828 ended up in London with her physically and sexually abusive master, Mr. Wood. Since *Somerset v. Stewart* (1772) had confirmed the illegality of slavery on British soil, Prince sought refuge with local abolitionists. However, though she had literally reversed the Middle Passage by crossing the ocean from slavery to freedom, her pressing concern soon became finding a means of supporting herself. Though she initially went into domestic service, by 1833 she disappeared from public record.[15] This problem of financial survival after escape was a common one for both male and female runaways, but it was especially difficult for Black female fugitives who were paid less than men. To take an even earlier example, we have no record of what sixteen-year-old Sally Hemings was thinking in 1789 while she was in Paris with her master, Thomas Jefferson. Instead of walking away from her forty-six-year-old owner—who had already impregnated her—she returned with him to slavery at Monticello. As Annette Gordon-Reed has convincingly argued, in Paris Jefferson paid higher-than-average wages to both Sally and her brother James and appears to have allowed them some freedom to explore the city. According to Gordon-Reed, "The feeling of being paid for her work, in a place where she considered herself to be a free person, could only have been empowering to Sally Hemings. For the first time in her life, she had something that belonged to her that she had worked for. Work, and payment for it, tends to foster a sense of independence and encourages thoughts about the future."[16] Certainly, Sally would have been aware of a free Black community in Paris and that French revolutionaries had made it possible for slaves to petition for their freedom. But Jefferson's departure would have left her financially destitute, with few options beyond life on the street. In addition, staying in Paris would have cut her off entirely from her enslaved family at Monticello. Fear of poverty and the need to be with kin as her pregnancy neared its end were probably enough to force Sally Hemings to choose slavery over emancipation.

For freeborn Black women, the challenges might have been somewhat different, but no less difficult. To take another example from the nineteenth-century United States, when the widowed Jarena Lee set out to become a traveling preacher in 1820s New Jersey, she divested herself of all possessions, including her two children, whom she handed over to friends and relatives. Her goal was, no doubt, to make sure they had stable, loving homes since, given her unshakable conviction that she had been called by God to preach anywhere and everywhere, she would have little time for mothering. Lee's story also points to the fact that some free Black women in the Anglophone diaspora authorized their travel as acts of Christian sacrifice. Two other Black women preachers, Zilpha Elaw and Amanda Berry Smith, extended their missionary activities overseas. Lee, Elaw, and Berry all published autobiographies that included discussions of their itinerancy, but only and always in the context of their evangelical work.[17] Importantly, their travel brought them in contact with Black as well as white reformers who were traveling for the same reasons. In this sense, they were part of a much larger, interracial missionary circuit that allowed women's travel, as long as it was in the context of spreading the gospel. Sometimes these Black women preachers and evangelists traveled alone, which generated a negative response even from their own African American communities, as was the case with Jarena Lee. Regardless, the accounts of travel provided by these women focused on their interaction with converts and with the various missionary communities to which they belonged. For them, travel for the sake of adventure, fame, or scientific inquiry was simply unthinkable. Nor did their religious work make them financially stable or, for that matter, immune to racism and ill-treatment during their journeys. Despite setbacks, as evangelical Christians they accepted that travel was a practical way to reach unbelievers, and they thought nothing of relying on themselves to generate food and lodging wherever they landed. In a similar vein, though they also endured poor treatment as Black women, both the Jamaican hotelier Mary Seacole (who was a businesswoman rather than a missionary) and freeborn Black American abolitionist Nancy Prince (who was dedicated to mission) relied entirely on their skills to secure food and lodging in Panama and Crimea and in Jamaica.

BECOMING AFRICAN AND FREE IN THE AGE
OF THE ATLANTIC SLAVE TRADE

Free Black women such as Seacole, Prince, Elaw, and Berry, along with free Black men such as Martin Delany and Robert Campbell, and Americo-Liberians such as James L. Sims, traveled far and wide to conduct business, spread Christianity, or reconnoiter African land for future settlement. In so doing, these Americans crisscrossed the Atlantic Ocean, revising their enslaved ancestors' experience of the Middle Passage.[18] Often of humble circumstances, they were rarely able to make *Western* sense of what they saw, and they often believed before their arrival that their presence would uplift the African "heathen." The shock that Africans might not necessarily be welcoming, combined with the newcomers' Western worldview, sometimes made it difficult for them to see any connection with Africans beyond skin color. Therefore, the connection they sought had to be either imagined or, in the case of some Americo-Liberians, entirely tossed aside. In other words, they saw Africans as culturally unchanging over the centuries, in contrast to seeing themselves as the advance guard of Black "civilization." And yet, as numerous historical anthropologists and historians who study Africa in the precolonial and colonial eras have argued, populations on the African continent were often as *diasporic* in nature as their counterparts in the Americas. That is, Africans have always migrated across the continent to pursue trade opportunities and escape warfare, as soldiers in search of conquest, and as slaves. As a result of these migrations, creolization was a given by virtue of contact with other African cultures and with Europeans who had arrived for mission, trade, and the control of land.[19]

A key Black Atlantic text that demonstrates such African transformation is, of course, Olaudah Equiano's *The Interesting Narrative of Olaudah Equiano or Gustavus Vassa, the African* (1789). Written by the Afro-British abolitionist, entrepreneur, and ex-slave who helped turn British public opinion against the transatlantic slave trade, *The Interesting Narrative* covers Equiano's kidnapping from West Africa, his endurance of the Middle Passage, and his subsequent enslavement in the thirteen colonies, the Anglophone West Indies, and the Royal Navy during the Seven Years War (1756–63). Eventually buying his freedom, Equiano continued his peripatetic lifestyle for a while longer, until finally settling permanently in Britain. At the very end of his narrative, Equiano tells the reader of his ill-fated attempt to join the 1787 colonial expedition to Sierra Leone for the settlement of the so-called Black poor of London. (By 1796, these initial Afro-British settlers had been supplemented by Black loyalists from the new United States via Nova Scotia, followed by a contingent of Jamaican Maroons.) Equiano reveals that he has been dismissed from the project because of a false charge of theft. Nevertheless, he is steadfast in his support of Afro-British repatriation to Sierra Leone, both because of its potential to strike a blow against the African side of the Atlantic slave trade and because of his theory that if Europeans could only imagine Africans as consumers rather than objects of consumption, they could surpass the profits of the slave trade by selling "civilized" Africans manufactured goods from Europe. By the end of the narrative, and despite the charges of theft, Equiano the African comes full circle as the captive who rescues himself from the position of chattel to become the unlikely agent of capitalism in the Atlantic world's triangle trade.[20] If Equiano's text were just a slave narrative, the story could have ended simply with the purchase of his freedom in chapter 7. However, he goes on for five more chapters, detailing his time as a free man at sea, continually involved with a range of commercial enterprises. In between voyages, he picked up the skill of dressing hair, so that if all else failed, he at least had a trade that would have been viable anywhere in the British Empire. Thus, in addition to functioning as the urtext for the American slave narrative, *The Interesting Narrative* tracks Equiano's keen understanding of empire and the possibilities of travel to achieve his survival.[21]

More recently, though, scholars have been debating the difference it makes to see Equiano either as "African" or as someone born in the Americas. In the opening chapters of *The Interesting Narrative*, Equiano identifies himself as Igbo and provides an ethnographic account of his life before capture. At the same time, he calls himself "the African" on the title page, a European term for anyone from the continent. The literary historian Vincent Caretta has unearthed records that seem to confirm Equiano's birthplace not in West Africa, but in colonial South Carolina. This discovery has turned our attention somewhat away from what Equiano said about himself, about slavery, and about his life at sea, to whether he was "authentically" African. In a 2006 response to Caretta's findings, the historian Paul Lovejoy argues vigorously that, in fact, Equiano was born in West Africa: "I think that there is sufficient internal evidence to conclude that the account is essentially authentic, although certainly informed by later reflection, Vassa's acquired knowledge of Africa, and memories of others whom he knew to have come from the Bight of Biafra. The reflections and memories used in autobiography are always filtered, but despite this caveat, I would conclude that Vassa was born in Africa and not in South Carolina."[22] Regardless of where Equiano was born, this discussion illuminates the category *African*, especially within the context of traditional African American diaspora studies and in the context of early literature of what Paul Gilroy has famously called "the black Atlantic."[23] Generally, *diaspora* has come to mean populations dispersed *from* the African continent, rather than populations dispersed *within* the continent. Lovejoy's description of how Equiano utilizes *African* fits well with Ira Berlin's idea of the "Atlantic creole."[24] According to Berlin, trade, whether in commodities or in the human form of slaves, had necessitated the interaction of small groups of European and West Africans since the Middle Ages. Indeed, Berlin emphasizes the nature of West African slave-coast cultures, where African slave sellers and European buyers created working relationships that generated new languages, new mixed-raced people, and new cultural, political, and religious exchanges. Whether or not Equiano was born in West Africa, Lovejoy's larger point that Equiano's story was "informed by later reflection" and supplemented by an "acquired knowledge of Africa" that he would have picked up along the way, in addition to the "memories of others whom he knew to have come from the Bight of Biafra," is crucial. Essentially, by the time he published *The Interesting*

Narrative in 1789, Equiano's "African" identity signified his experience of an unending process of hybridization and creolization. These processes would have begun even before Equiano set foot on a slave ship, since he describes moving to the coast among peoples with habits increasingly distant and distinct from those of his own community.

A number of Africanists have argued that the invention of diasporic identity did not begin in the crowded hold of the slave ship, but well before that at the moment of capture in the hinterland.[25] This reading of dynamics internal to African communities on the continent should caution against simplistic romanticization of "African culture," since peoples on the coast and in the interior of the continent were continually assimilating, supplementing, reinventing, enforcing, and expanding, as expressed by the hybridity of their political, social, commercial, and religious practices. Building upon Berlin's idea of the Atlantic Creole is David Northrup's concept of the "Atlantic African," which I adopt within *Moving Home* to refer (as Northrup does) to individuals born in West Africa—whether they were free or enslaved, whether they left the continent or not—if, like Equiano, they participated in and were transformed by the creolization processes set into motion by the transatlantic slave trade.[26] While Berlin focuses on individuals he regards as neither European nor African, but rather "middle-men" who could move in the space in between, Northrup argues that Atlantic Africans were not necessarily a mixed-race population, and he takes into account the changes taking shape as nineteenth-century European colonization of West Africa took hold.

Though both Britain and the United States had abolished the slave trade in the first half of the nineteenth century, the practice persisted in the South Atlantic, especially with respect to Brazil, until the 1860s. Consequently, the complex processes whereby the transatlantic slave trade produced hybrid African identities on the West African coast did not suddenly cease to exist once white people decided the trade was immoral. Rather, the processes that had always created creolized African identities simply continued with the advent of colonialism. For example, by 1800 the private, antislavery Sierra Leone Company had engineered the "return" of Blacks born outside of Africa. Rather than perpetuating the cultural mix created by the intermingling of European and African slave traders, this strategy constructed a new vision of who "Africans" could be if they accepted Christianity and made themselves available to the so-called civilizing mission. To emphasize this immigration project's antislavery agenda, the British christened Sierra Leone's capital Freetown. In a parallel move, the American Colonization Society sent American ex-slaves and freeborn Blacks to found a similar beachhead in 1820 that was immediately christened

Liberia. If this were not enough, prior to 1841 ex-slaves from Brazil, Cuba, and even the Anglophone West Indies made their way back to West Africa, now fully Christianized but still seeking a nostalgic "return" to past homelands.[27] Essentially acting as vectors of European colonialism, these migrants moved increasingly eastward, ahead of British occupation, culturally and economically having an impact on the indigenous populations they encountered. Clearly, then, the dramatic effects of dispersal created by the transatlantic slave trade that began in the 1500s were now propelled by abolitionist "back-to-Africa" schemes that further transformed West Africans who would never leave the continent.

If reverse migrations from the New World were not enough, existing nineteenth-century African communities were further supplemented by thousands of displaced ex-slaves who had also never left the continent. In 1807 and 1808, respectively, the anti-slave-trading commitment on the part of the British and the Americans required the creation by each government of special naval squadrons which patrolled the West African slave coast so as to intercept slavers making their way to the Americas. Once the British and American naval crews captured and confiscated their human cargo, the latter were taken to Sierra Leone and Liberia, respectively, for "repatriation" among coastal peoples who regarded them as aliens and among American and Caribbean ex-slave migrants who introduced their particular Creole cultures. In Sierra Leone and Liberia, white missionaries set up shop to minister to newly arrived "recaptives," and when necessary, they solicited slave narratives to energize their lay supporters at home. Thus emerged in an 1837 issue of the *Church Missionary Record* the early narrative of the prolific ex-slave turned Anglican bishop Samuel Ajayi Crowther, albeit significantly shortened by a heavy-handed white editor. As with Equiano in *The Interesting Narrative* some thirty-two years earlier, Crowther recorded his life before capture, his journey to the coast, and the forced boarding of a Portuguese slaver bound for Brazil. But unlike Equiano, Crowther's slave ship was intercepted by the British, who "returned" him to the wholly unfamiliar environs of British Sierra Leone. Dazed and frightened, he and his fellow "liberated" Africans had to be whipped by their rescuers to get them to walk from the beach to the local Court of Mixed Commission. In Sierra Leone, the intersection of multiple diasporic populations created what many refer to as *krio* (as in *creole*) identity on the African side of the Atlantic.[28] Clearly, the processes that invented Sierra Leone's *krio* identity were not identical to the processes encountered by African slaves in the New World. However, in both cases, the direct impact of the transatlantic slave trade enabled new cultural frameworks on either side of the African Atlantic. Given these nineteenth-century developments, in *Moving Home* I extend the term *diaspora* to include both sides of the Atlantic Basin, pertaining not only to men and women from the Americas but also to those living on the African continent itself.

In the following pages, I highlight Anglophone writers whose texts emerged from the circuits of commerce, migration, and transatlantic abolition running throughout the Atlantic Basin, writers fostered by whites and Blacks in the Americas, by Anglo-Europeans, and by Africans on the continent. My goal, then, is to think about the slave trade as well as its aftereffects on both sides of the Atlantic, in the context of imperial expansion and the complex "contact zones" which consequently emerged.[29] Toward this end, I have drawn upon both published and unpublished nonfiction by the formerly enslaved Christianized West Africans Crowther and Bonetta. Overall, each individual discussed in this book retained allegiances to the local, even as they engaged the wider Atlantic World, though *local* was itself often a fluid and highly permeable idea even as it appeared to be bounded. These men and women wrote to give personal meaning to their experiences on the road and to create public identities for themselves, in a literary form that in the hands of whites usually cast them as the objects of touristic obsession. These African diasporic figures wrote variously for financial gain, for a communally important purpose, and to accrue valuable social capital that might allow them to move freely within, between, and among different social and geographical contexts. As a result, the dynamics of region, class, gender, and culture at once connected and divided them. Additionally, since their writing was by definition semiautobiographical, they sought to inhabit public personae to which they were normally not granted access; as such, they wrote self-consciously for multiple transatlantic audiences. And, since they lived in the age of slavery and a transoceanic slave trade, their travel writing almost always turned upon questions of exile, citizenship, and belonging. Even though they were all free, they inhabited a world plagued by a brutalizing racism that put their claim to personhood in doubt and exposed them to multiple forms of humiliation and discrimination.[30] To one extent or another, each writer endured conditions of economic privation and political disenfranchisement, and their texts became sources of personal power as they responded to detrimental forces.

Regardless of their birthplace, Seacole, Prince, Crowther, Delany, Campbell, and Bonetta had complex and deeply fraught relationships with the multiple worlds they inhabited, worlds constructed through the interconnection of transatlantic slavery and European and American empire. For example, Martin Delany was both a product of his Victorian age and a proud Black Nationalist. He entertained romantic ideas of a Black empire and a Black version of the civilizing mission, even as he devoted his life to formulating resistant and expansive ideas to defeat racism and improve the status of Africa and people of African descent in the world.[31] Repeatedly, Delany threatened to cut ties with the United States for good: first he moved temporarily to Canada, and then he made short-lived plans to relocate to what is now Nigeria. In the end, he returned to the United States to support the Civil War and participate in the changes that he hoped would come with emancipation. Meanwhile, the Jamaican Mary Seacole seemed to turn her back on the struggles of ex-slaves at home and instead embraced her imperial subjectivity, using her service to British troops in the Crimean War as the argument for apotheosis as national heroine. Robert Campbell also exiled himself from Jamaica, though more openly as an avowed enemy of racism. Indeed, as a migrant to the British Crown Colony of Lagos, Campbell joined a "new" population resisting the same imperial heavy-handedness he had encountered as a West Indian youth. Finally, as African slaves who were spared the Middle Passage, the early Nigerians Crowther and Bonetta were characteristic of elite Atlantic African populations who were heavily influenced by British Christian missionaries. Indeed, as was the case with Delany, both Crowther and Bonetta embraced the so-called civilizing influences of Christianity, even as they challenged white attempts to curtail the self-determination of their respective West African communities. Regardless of their birthplace, then, what these writers had in common was their contingent, complex negotiation of class, gender identity, place, nation, and empire, as they strove to create stable lives and communities in locations where populations, economies, and the balance of power were perpetually in flux.

In selecting writers for this study, I have chosen individuals who might properly belong to Caribbean, African American, and African studies as well as the study of nineteenth-century empire formation, so as to engage both the limitations and possibilities of defining African diaspora. The travel texts generated by each writer also encourage us to engage the distinctive features of the nineteenth century directly, rather than merely seeing "the past" as precursor to a twentieth-century flowering of more sophisticated Black Atlantic exchanges. I take as a given, then, that in the nineteenth-century Atlantic World, the African diaspora had its own conflicts and conditions; its own particular philosophical, economic, cultural, and technological challenges; and its own discourses of change and progress. These features created possibilities and trajectories that were necessarily different from those of the twentieth century, though no less important. Indeed, this book pushes back against arguments for an intellectual and activist genealogy toward more sophisticated political action in the present.[32] Since academic knowledge making relies on the creation of canons and traditions, there is always the risk that the need for forefathers and foremothers encourages a celebration of the present by way of flattening the past.

Moving Home engages crucial analytical categories, including *gender, class, color, race, ethnicity, home, citizenship, nation,* and *empire.* Throughout any century, these categories mean different things to different people, at different historical moments and under varying conditions on the ground. As a group of categories, these terms all gesture to intersecting social processes, each of which are at once nuanced, contradictory, and continually being reinvented in response to changing social, economic, and political conditions. By exploring how and why the travel writers in this book assigned particular meaning to their travel, and how and why they enacted particular public selves through their texts, I engage the unique ways that Seacole, Prince, Crowther, Delany, Campbell, and Bonetta articulated a set of experiences, even as they shared a great deal with the communities they inhabited.[33] Collectively, their work confirms the vitally important connections between and among African American, Caribbean, and African studies. In their differently nuanced complexities, these writers also allow us to work toward a new appreciation of not just Black feminist studies, but also a transnational, Black gender studies.

IN CHAPTER 1, I EXPLORE the travel writing of Mary Seacole, who is usually treated as an early Anglophone Caribbean figure. Born in Jamaica, Seacole worked to cultivate her own special relationship to imperial Britain for the purposes of economic prosperity, exploiting while also reworking colonial stereotypes to her advantage. Seacole deliberately set her path along the trajectories of empire, escaping an economic depression in 1840s Jamaica by relocating her restaurant–cum–boarding house from Kingston to Panama during the period of the California gold rush. When the Crimean War broke out, Seacole picked up and set off across the Atlantic Ocean to the theater of war in Turkey, both to capitalize on an alternate market of male clientele and to help nurse Britain's wounded soldiers. Lest we romanticize Seacole as saintly and self-sacrificing, as some recent biographers are wont to do, her commercial concerns had to be in the forefront of her thinking, since she was responsible for her own survival. Seacole did not simply make money to give it all away in the form of bandages and homemade medicines to sick British soldiers. Rather, she was just as interested in capitalist accumulation as any good colonial subject of the period. Though the general facts in *Wonderful Adventures of Mrs. Seacole in Many Lands* (1857) are not in dispute, the impoverished Seacole deliberately used her travel narrative to elicit gratitude for her war service in the form of English pounds, so she could pay off debts incurred in the Crimea and then retire. Thus, Seacole's writing has an unmistakably financial motivation wedded to the establishment of herself as a bona fide Crimean heroine on the order of Florence Nightingale.

Chapter 2's Nancy Prince—the American domestic servant turned land-lady, seamstress, and later missionary—could be viewed as something of an American analogue to Mary Seacole, in that her *Life and Travels of Mrs. Nancy Prince* (1850) is also a narrative of foreign travel, published with the hope of generating much-needed income. Emerging from crushing poverty and a trou-bled homelife in Newburyport, Massachusetts, Prince had no choice but to go into service, as her siblings were scattered to the four winds. After struggling to redeem a sister who had fallen into prostitution, Prince eventually opted to save herself by marrying a Black sailor employed in, of all places, the mid-nineteenth-century Russian court. Such a drastic escape from the hopeless cir-cumstances of Newburyport to Saint Petersburg would not have been possible for a single and cash-strapped nineteenth-century Black woman who wanted to preserve her good name. So, Prince chose marriage to enable redemptive travel as well as domestic refuge. Indeed, Prince's "home" in Russia was a boarding-house she ran for schoolchildren away from home, the income from which she supplemented with dressmaking. As with Seacole, Prince took on the trappings of domesticity in order to survive and even thrive financially, jettisoning na-tional and regional identity as needed to accomplish her independence. But while Seacole relied upon an imperial loyalty that (according to *Wonderful Ad-ventures*, anyway) required perpetual itinerancy as part of a larger strategy to gain the British reader's support, Prince returned to the United States, opting to become a selfless missionary to newly emancipated slaves in Jamaica. Part of her motivation to travel to the West Indies rested in the hope for some kind of racial solidarity, even as she saw herself as the superior of the uneducated ex-slaves. However, both the pressures of economic survival and her alien status as an American in Jamaica made it difficult for her to establish herself. After returning to the United States, Prince continued to make use of her travels via lectures and the publication of her 1850 narrative, which she managed to have reprinted at least twice. Additionally, she engaged with Black American emigra-tion debates, penning a separate newcomers' guide to Jamaica, since the abolition of slavery in the British colonies now opened up new relocation possibilities for Black Americans who could no longer abide life in their native United States. As a woman alone, Prince proved that the African American debate on emigra-tion was as much an issue for Black women as it was for their men.

Chapter 3, "The Repatriation of Samuel Ajayi Crowther," explores writing on African repatriation by a former Yoruba slave turned Christian missionary. Samuel Ajayi Crowther had been rescued from a Portuguese slaver in 1822 by a warship assigned to the Royal Navy's Anti–Slave Trade Squadron. As was the case with slavers intercepted close to the West African coast, Crowther and his fellow captives were disembarked at Freetown, Sierra Leone, where a Court of Mixed Commission determined their status as kidnapped Africans. In the end, Crowther was released to agents of the Church Missionary Society (CMS), who in turn immediately began the Christianization process. This included literacy for all ex-slaves, so that the latter could begin reading the Bible, and the mastering of a trade, which in Crowther's case meant becoming a carpenter. Very quickly, however, CMS agents realized that he was intellectually gifted, especially with languages. Given the policy championed under the CMS secretary, Henry Venn, Crowther received a careful education, which later enabled him to became a prime candidate for the native pastorate, then in its infancy. As something of a poster child for successful African conversion, Crowther rose to celebrity status among white Britons who were the financial backbone of the CMS. First as a catechist and later as an ordained Anglican minister, Crowther traveled with various British expeditions deeper and deeper into the Nigerian hinterland. Eventually he was assigned the task (along with several white colleagues) of creating a Niger mission, and by the time of his death in 1891, he had become the bishop of all of Anglican West Africa. Crowther's rise occurred in spite of palpable racism from white missionaries in the field and was due in large part to Henry Venn's faithful support. However, after Venn's period of leadership ended, a younger generation of white missionary executives took charge, stripping Venn's native pastorate—and Bishop Crowther—of any real power.

Still, Crowther authored numerous translations of the Gospels into various West African languages, including his native Yoruba. Additionally, he penned a short slave narrative, describing his rescue by the Royal Navy from Portuguese slavery, as well as three narratives describing his subsequent travel with three later expeditions into the Nigerian interior. The focus in chapter 3 is on Crowther's narrative covering the tragic 1841 Niger expedition, reprinted in the *Journals of the Rev. James Frederick Schön and Mr. Samuel Crowther* published a year later. My focus on this text has to do with the fact that it is one of Crowther's earliest representations of himself as an African convert to white CMS supporters in Britain, and it combines not only an eyewitness, observational perspective on the failed expedition but also a self-construction as the obedient and loyal African propagator of Christian mission, who retraces his steps back to the region of his preslavery origin. In a sense, this text becomes Crowther's first public articulation of an "Atlantic African" identity.

Chapter 4 continues the theme of African exploration with a combined discussion of Martin R. Delany's *Official Report* and Robert Campbell's *A Pilgrimage to My Motherland*, both published in 1861 as part of a joint effort to report on the economic, political, and geographic possibilities for Black American relocation to what later became southeast Nigeria. For his part, Delany's exploration narrative followed the stringent lines of a scientific inquiry. Rarely referring to himself in the *Official Report*, he matter-of-factly made note of everything from wood-eating ants to early morning mists, from malaria to the presence of European missionaries. In many ways, Delany used his narrative not only to democratize for his African American audience bodies of knowledge about their ancestral homeland but also to demonstrate his deserving ownership of said knowledge. Though at the end of his narrative Delany declared his desire to return to Lagos with his family, the final effect of his *Official Report* was less to rehearse the idea of African repatriation than to affirm a Black American right to "knowing" the continent, something that had hitherto been the prerogative of only white explorers.

As was the case with Seacole, Robert Campbell left a financially depressed Jamaica in the late 1840s hoping to make his fortune in Panama. Trained as both a schoolmaster and a printer, Campbell did not fare well in Central America, and by the 1850s he and his family had moved to New York and then Philadelphia, where he gained valuable science training and teaching experience at the Quaker-run Institute for Colored Youth. Still, hemmed in at every turn by American racism, Campbell finally set out in 1859 for southeast Nigeria, coordinating his travel with Delany's to explore possibilities for resettlement in and around the city of Abeokuta. Campbell may have meant *A Pilgrimage to My Motherland* to serve as an ethnographic guide, but the text also articulates his own experience among Yoruba-speaking Africans, both non-Christian and Christian, who seemed to effortlessly take charge of their own destiny in what appeared to be the absence of any substantial white presence. As if anticipating his own eventual move to Lagos, Campbell wrote as a participant-observer and then finally transformed himself into an African adoptive son.

Chapter 4 ends with a discussion of the response to both Campbell's and Delany's narratives by none other than Richard Francis Burton, one of the premier African explorers of the Victorian era. A notorious racist and anti-Semite, Burton attacked both men on racial grounds and in terms of their credibility as explorers. However, the fact that he felt obliged to engage their work at all suggests that both Campbell and Delany had indeed compelled his attention.

Moving Home concludes with chapter 5's exploration of the life and travels of the African ex-slave Sarah Forbes Bonetta, who as a child became the ward of Queen Victoria. Drawing on records from the Church Missionary Society archives, the Royal Archives at Windsor, and the family archives of her husband, James P. L. Davies of Lagos, this chapter provides the fullest biographical portrait of Bonetta currently available, within the context of multiple arrivals and departures that spanned her lifetime. Literally given to Queen Victoria as a young girl by the king of Dahomey (modern Benin), Bonetta was, of course, freed by her abolitionist benefactor. However, as a royal ward, Bonetta found herself under strict management by a range of paternalist figures who had her journeying from Britain to Sierra Leone and then back again, in the service of imparting "civilization" in the form of the three Rs, piano playing, and Christian devotion. Giving in to royal pressure to accept a marriage proposal from the older Yoruba widower James P. L. Davies, Bonetta moved with him among the Christianized West African elite society of Lagos, Britain's newest crown colony. With a wealthy husband and her royal connections, Bonetta enjoyed a position of affluence and social prestige unavailable to most white Britons. In this chapter, I argue that travel, particularly if overseas, became a hallmark of the West African social class into which Bonetta had married. As she traveled between Britain and Lagos to build and consolidate social and familial ties, she wrote many letters and kept a travel diary. Consequently, in line with feminist arguments that demand a rethinking of genres and archives in order to make women's lives and work more visible, I explore her unpublished writing and the world of colonial travel in which she was vitally engaged.[34] The questions in this chapter are less about the formality of a single genre and more about how Bonetta's required itinerancy speaks to the subtle class dimensions of being simultaneously the index of Davies family respectability and the embodiment of the queen's personal largesse. "Home" for Bonetta was both Lagos and the small Kentish town of her white foster family. However, in Britain and West Africa, different audiences enabled or forbade particular practices, such that Bonetta's agency as a colonial tourist would always be somewhat provisional. Though they differ from the other kinds of writing addressed here, Bonetta's informal letters and diary entries engage questions of persona, place, belonging, race, and gendered agency on a subtle and important scale.

Ultimately, in *Moving Home* I offer a perspective informed by both African and African American studies, from all points of the Anglophone Atlantic diaspora, with a particular emphasis on exploring the subtle impact of gender norms on nineteenth-century Black identities. In many ways, this book decenters the United States not to diminish Black American experiences but rather to highlight the coeval nature of Afro-Caribbean and West African life under colonialism at the moment when Blacks in the United States grappled with slavery, abolition, and territorial expansion. Throughout, for each writer I reveal the twists and turns enabled and foreclosed by Victorian gender norms, as well as the necessity these writers felt to construct transformative and ever-evolving identities for themselves, through the act of writing about travel.

1. Mary Seacole's West Indian Hospitality

An itinerant Jamaican entrepreneur and "doctress," the colored Creole Mary Jane Grant Seacole (1805–81) (figure 1.1) ran combination lodging houses and taverns throughout the Caribbean and Central America during the first half of the nineteenth century.[1] While in Jamaica, Seacole had always counted British soldiers among her most esteemed clients: as a result, she relocated mid-career to Turkey during the Crimean War (1854–56) to be of service to the British Army. Setting up her "hotel" near the battlefield, she sold food and beverages to the soldiers while also treating their wounds, medicating their fevers, and providing comfort to the dying. Ironically, when the war ended sooner than expected in 1856, Seacole had to sell her Crimean business entirely at a loss. Now faced with bankruptcy, she moved to London and set about publishing in 1857 what she hoped would be a financially lucrative life story. Already universally acknowledged for the nursing care she provided to British troops away from home, she must have been further gratified by the popularity of *Wonderful Adventures of Mrs. Seacole in Many Lands* (it went into a second printing), as well as by the numerous efforts of officers and soldiers to stage fundraising events in her honor. However, even with her efforts and those of her supporters, it was not until the establishment in 1867 of the royally sanctioned "Seacole Fund" that she finally escaped poverty.[2]

Inevitably, Seacole had her detractors. Writing in 1870 to her brother-in-law, the politician Sir Henry Verney, no less a figure than Florence Nightingale disputed Seacole's contributions to nursing, arguing that in the Crimea, the

FIGURE 1.1. Mary Seacole after the Crimean War. (Mary Evans Picture Library, UK)

latter had kept a "bad house," and that wherever Seacole served she was bound to "introduce much kindness—[but] also much drunkenness and improper conduct."[3] If sentiments such as these were shared by others at the time, they had little impact on Seacole's overall popularity, especially among Crimean veterans. Still, until the end of the twentieth century, it was Nightingale's name and not Seacole's that became synonymous with medical care in the Crimea and very quickly afterward with nursing as a professional occupation. Now, however, over 150 years later, Mary Seacole's memory has been fully revived, this time by Jamaican and British nurses of color working in tandem with other allies. Beginning in 1954, the centenary of the Crimean War, Jamaican nurses reconsecrated Seacole's grave in Britain, paid for a refurbished headstone, and then renamed their headquarters in Kingston after her. Soon the Kingston Public Hospital and the University of the West Indies's Mona campus (Kingston) followed suit, dedicating a medical ward and a dormitory, respectively, in Seacole's honor.[4] At the same time, nurses of color in Britain have successfully championed Seacole for some three decades as a model of selfless dedication to the sick (she regularly attended to wounded British soldiers on the battlefield), as well as a reminder that the United Kingdom has habitually ignored the enormous contributions made by colonial subjects and their descendants at the metropole. Continuing on their mission to instantiate Seacole as a national hero, her supporters in Britain petitioned successfully for a coveted English Heritage blue plaque to be placed on her last known dwelling. Additionally, both to highlight the health needs of the United Kingdom's multicultural population and to demonstrate that nonwhite nurses and other health professionals have long been the cornerstone of health care for all Britons, a number of clinics and health centers now bear Seacole's name. Notably, a variety of awards in her honor are now bestowed each year to foster and celebrate the work of nursing. Finally, in 2016, after twelve years of fundraising, a ten-foot bronze statue of Seacole was installed on the grounds of the Guy's and St. Thomas' Hospital in London.[5]

The location of the statue is both fitting and highly controversial: fitting because St. Thomas' Hospital was the original location of Florence Nightingale's school of nursing, established in 1860 after her work in the Crimea, and controversial because the hospital also houses the Nightingale Museum. Indeed, the enduring persistence of Seacole supporters seems too strident to conservatives who think that "Black" Mary Seacole now threatens to displace "white" Florence Nightingale as a central female icon of the Victorian era. On the other hand, for pro-Seacole activists, the statue's location is a bittersweet response to the fact that, according to *Wonderful Adventures*, in 1854 Seacole was rejected because of her color by the committee recruiting nurses for Nightingale's Scutari hospital.[6] This historical reality has not been lost on generations of nurses of color in Britain, who have long served a critical role in the United Kingdom's National Health Service: advocacy for Seacole's memory, then, has also translated into a demand that their contributions in the present be fully recognized and honored. Inevitably, a similar demand has been taken up in the United States and Canada by Jamaican immigrant nurses, who also celebrate Seacole rather than Florence Nightingale as the foremother of nursing professionalism and dedication to patient care.[7]

Clearly, the recuperation of Mary Seacole in the present speaks to one of the many ways in which immigrant women from the Anglophone West Indies celebrate the real impact they have made in the hemisphere. Yet, though as a female Caribbean icon Seacole has been appropriately remade to serve the purposes of the present, her historical specificity as an early female West Indian global traveler on the margins of empire is still crucially important. Indeed, her *Wonderful Adventures of Mrs. Seacole in Many Lands* has much to teach us about how women of African descent under imperial rule negotiated highly restrictive social and political power structures that accorded them the lowest status. Without doubt, in her own historical time Mary Seacole proved herself to be the ultimate survivor. Though even she chalked up some of her successes to the plain good luck of being in the right place at the right time, her narrative attempt to assign meaning to her travels, business enterprises, and medical practice addressed geopolitical, social, and racial realities that were quite different from our own. Instead of coming to terms with these differences and their historical and literary implications, some of Seacole's advocates end up clumsily trying to iron out any fruitful contradictions in her story, while some of her detractors point to anything that could be described as *unsaintly* about her, to prove that she was an opportunist and impostor unworthy of comparison to Florence Nightingale. This chapter aims to explore Seacole in all her complexity as a mixed-race Jamaican; as a mid-nineteenth-century female African diasporic traveler of the Caribbean, Britain, and the so-called Near East; and as someone normally assigned to the lowest social rungs, who both embraced and subverted raced, gendered, and classed colonial regimes as necessary, to sustain herself as a woman of color operating on her own on the margins of empire.

Many a reader, past or present, has been drawn to *Wonderful Adventures* for the highly arresting autobiographical persona Seacole created to make her book an instant success.[8] Her tone is by turns genuinely funny, self-deprecating, teasing, empathetic, and confessional. At the same time, silences abound in *Wonderful Adventures*, making Seacole's text comparable to almost all autobiography, but especially early Black female autobiography, where narrators had to gauge their desire to be forthright with the white reading public's general assumption that the lives of ex-slaves and freeborn women alike were synonymous with immorality and degradation. In this vein, Seacole's text is in line with the work of her nineteenth-century Black Atlantic contemporaries Harriet Jacobs, Nancy Prince, Anne Hart Gilbert, Elizabeth Hart Thwaites, Maria Stewart, Jarena Lee, Julia Foote, and Zilpha Elaw, in that she veers away from the personal to focus squarely on the impact of her experiences, actions, or philosophy on the public good. Nevertheless, unlike her contemporaries, Seacole shows little overt interest in social uplift, mission, or domestic feminism.[9] At the same time, though her autobiography is careful to note a love of Jamaica and at one point celebrates the nobility of US runaway slaves, it never outwardly betrays any interest on her part in the economic and political struggles of her postslavery compatriots or, for that matter, in the economic deprivation that first drove her from home in the 1840s. Instead, Seacole seems always to be fostering an exclusively white, at times exclusively male, clientele for her successive hotel and eating establishments, while arguing the importance of her role as caretaker of British soldiers, whether as a purveyor of food supplies or as an experienced nurse who can cure a variety of tropical diseases. According to the narrative, this dual role is precisely what enabled her to become the needed surrogate "mother" to her European wounded and dying soldier "sons" so far away from home. And instead of any critique of England, Seacole presents an "enthusiastic acceptance of colonialism . . . in an empire that had systematically exploited and abused her native land and the majority of its inhabitants since the British conquered Jamaica in 1655."[10] Consequently, at first sight Seacole provides us little in the way of African diasporic networking or shared ideas, beyond the fact that a great deal of her considerable knowledge as a healer would have been derived from the medical practices generations of African slaves had brought with them via the Middle Passage.

Precisely because Seacole's *Wonderful Adventures* is an early Black woman's text that entirely exceeds the local, it raises several questions about race and gender in a nineteenth-century global setting shaped by both European and African diasporic patterns of migration and influence. For instance, what does *Wonderful Adventures* reveal about the complex intersection of race, class, and sexuality, as shaped by the historical conditions of gendered mobility experienced by Seacole, conditions that were shaped by the international reach (and often coconstituent nature) of European imperialism and African dispersal? Given that globalization and transnationalism have now become part of our theoretical vocabulary, how does Seacole's text challenge us to position the local in terms of gender, history, culture, race, and geography? How are race and labor figured in *Wonderful Adventures*, given that the text emerges out of a transatlantic shift from Black slavery to emancipation? Indeed, what are we to make of the fact that Seacole's construction of identity was a necessary product of a variety of intertwined global and regional power struggles over land, capital, and colonial control in the Americas, in Europe, and in the Near East?

In locating Seacole's strategy of self-presentation, Faith Smith interprets her embrace of the British as a manifestation of how Black West Indians generally "appropriated Englishness as a socially sanctioned means of becoming citizens." That is, Seacole comes to exemplify those colonial subjects who "utilized bourgeois British culture to read, write, and argue themselves into middle-class respectability" and "in so doing . . . reclaim an ideological terrain on which supposed 'truths' about them as people of African descent were propagated."[11] Just as crucial, though, is Simon Gikandi's thoughtful assertion that colonial women's texts such as *Wonderful Adventures* allow one "to read colonialism's culture in its contradictions and complicities, as a chiasmus in which the polarities that define domination and subordination shift with localities, genders, cultures, and even periods."[12] Indeed, the complexity of Seacole's narrative, especially its presentation of West Indians, Anglo-Americans, and Anglo-Europeans upon a worldwide, imperial stage, demands that we think beyond the one-to-one framing of Seacole as the emblematic, unitary Black colonial subject in the nineteenth century, juxtaposed against the equally emblematic, unitary English subject. Such framing elides the politics of mixed-race identity, nation, region, and transnational mobility, as well as the impact of class and gender ideologies on both Seacole and her British audience.[13]

For instance, in Panama and the Crimea, two primary areas of overseas activity for Seacole, we are confronted not merely with interchangeable localities on the imperial margin juxtaposed against a unified, stable metropolitan England. Rather, *Wonderful Adventures* depicts Central America as only recently liberated from Spanish control and battling with a growing Anglo-American encroachment signified by the construction of a trans-isthmus railroad. Backed by New York financiers, the railroad helped shift influence in the region from Europe to the United States. In the meantime, in the wake of British emancipation during the 1830s, railroad construction attracted Caribbean migrants in search of economic opportunity. These individuals found themselves in racial and cultural conflict with both Black and white Panamanians, with indigenous peoples of the area, and with white American prospectors (many of them proslavery) who crossed the isthmus en route to the gold fields of California. To make matters worse, given the regularity of malaria, yellow fever, and cholera epidemics, the battle for racial autonomy often gave way to the battle for human survival. If we consider the regional rather than merely the national affiliations encompassed by Seacole's narrative, then Panama marks the geographical and social intersection of Native American, Anglo-American, African, and Latin American nationalities—that is, the complex political life of the American side of the Black Atlantic, encompassing but also extending beyond the British Caribbean empire, including other forms of imperialism and local contests for autonomy.[14]

Half a world away, the Crimea was scarcely a more hospitable place, but it called into play a different kind of struggle, with different associations for Seacole and her British readers. Brought to the battlefield by Russia's invasion of Turkey, but also by an overblown sense of national pride, Britain lagged behind its ally France in the preparedness of its army for a foreign war. Because of mismanaged supplies and poor medical care, disease, starvation, and frostbite accounted for 80 percent of English casualties. Eventually, the war culminated in the fall of Lord Aberdeen's government and led to the questioning of a system of military governance that allowed men of wealth rather than merit to monopolize the officer corps. At the same time, with the emergence of Florence Nightingale as arguably the greatest celebrity of the conflict, the Crimean War challenged British assumptions about the role of women, both in the masculine sphere of war and on the colonial frontier.[15]

How do these locations and the social events they engender testify to the problems and consequences of displacement—in both a physical and a cultural sense—for Seacole and the Anglo-Europeans she served? Though the title, *Wonderful Adventures of Mrs. Seacole in Many Lands*, suggests a narration of tourist travel, the text presents a particular nineteenth-century international mobility governed by and in negotiation with existing social hierarchies, colonial structures of commerce, and imperial aggression.[16] A number of recent assessments of *Wonderful Adventures* pay close attention to the regional distribution of action within the text, as Seacole winds her way from Jamaica to Panama and then later to Britain, the Crimea, and back to Britain again. The varieties of physical and political displacement contextualizing Seacole's journeys point to the tenuous replication and sustenance of metropolitan norms at the margins in order to achieve colonial control, since in *Wonderful Adventures* the privileged status of particular race, class, national, and gender identifications shifts, according to the politics of location. Certainly, the United States would continue its involvement in Central America, and France and Britain would eventually defeat the Russians. However, as essentially uncontainable border regions of empire, Panama and the Crimea inadvertently represent sites of instability, where the assumptions of Anglo-American and British supremacy embody elements of tension, strain, and even failure.

Certainly, as a roaming, mixed-race female entrepreneur, Seacole confronted a variety of peoples and events in Panama and the Crimea. Yet, hers is a historically complex identity specific to the West Indies, an identity that contemporary critics continue to interrogate. Consistently drawn to frontier sites rendered almost uninhabitable by war, social upheaval, and pestilence, Seacole negotiated the politics of white crisis very deliberately, making use of the ideological fissures that inevitably came into being to achieve her own economic and social success. As Hilary McD. Beckles asserts, "Historical paradigms derived from slave society, such as 'white women consumed, Black women laboured and coloured women served,' need to be destabilized" to reveal the "diverse experiences of these women in terms of multiple encounters with complex systems of wealth and status accumulation rather than as direct expressions of hegemonic patriarchy."[17] Given the varied international terrains Seacole had to negotiate, the range of creative strategies she employed to gain both economic independence and moral currency (that is, everything from trading in European goods to trading the story of her patriotic service), and the vicissitudes of her financial position, her story exemplifies perfectly the kind of complex gendered economic experience to which Beckles refers.

For nineteenth-century British readers, the worldly and resourceful Seacole would have been inevitably measured against the stereotype of a closeted, chaste, middle-class white woman, in which case the colored West Indian hotel-keeper would have been found wanting among those who saw the need for policing the conduct of "other" females, Black or white. As has been reiterated time and again in almost every contemporary discussion of Seacole, her self-generated public image as "mother" serves to sentimentalize her economic opportunism, allowing her to craft an identity beyond that of Black female pariah. Yet, Seacole's choice of a maternal sobriquet also has important implications for the effects of globalization on racial stereotypes. In *Wonderful Adventures*, she certainly does not embrace the desexualized stereotype of American slavery's Black "Mammy." But neither does she claim the recuperative image of a Black, morally pure social activist (often structured through models of maternity) so often embraced by other nineteenth-century Black women autobiographers. Rather, Seacole deliberately takes on the role of a surrogate for British mothers, sisters, and wives who have been left at home, far from the foreign locations of conflict and colony. How do we interpret the cultural meaning behind an act of surrogacy where (ostensibly) Seacole claims to replace (when necessary) white women in a range of relations normally kept within the private space of the British family? At the same time, how does the meaning of her surrogacy change, depending on location? How does it change with her entry into various local economies as a lodging-house keeper and West Indian "doctress" catering to white men? How does it change considering the various class and national affiliations of those she serves?

The question of how Seacole's surrogacy would have been received specifically in the context of the Crimea is of particular importance, considering the presence of her unofficial rival, Florence Nightingale. Certainly, Nightingale would seem to be the most obvious figure against whom to set Seacole, since the former was imagined by nineteenth-century artists, poets, commentators, and biographers as "the English Sister of Charity, the self-denying caretaker—a mother, saint, or even a female Christ," without ego or ambition, inhabiting "a period-specific female role" that relegated to "the background any anomalies in her situation as a woman present at the scenes of war."[18] However, I would suggest that Seacole be placed against a broader pool of white women associated with the Crimean War, beyond just Nightingale or the Catholic nuns and carefully vetted laywomen in her nursing corps. British female participation in the war also included aristocratic officers' wives and working-class soldiers' wives. Though small in number, some of these women were present with Seacole at the battlefront. While all British women traveling to the Crimea were subject to dangerous diseases such as cholera and dysentery, those who chose to live at or very close to the front were, like Seacole, present for many of the war's major battles, literally venturing into no-man's-land in search of adventure or, more usefully, seeking to help the wounded and recover the dead. Male and female participants in the Crimean War may have been judged against rigid nineteenth-century Victorian race, class, and gender norms, but because of both the specific conditions of location and the shifts in public opinion generated by war, a variety of women's participation emerged that challenged traditional readings of white womanhood in important and unusual ways. The fluidity of this situation cannot be gleaned from simply reading Seacole against Nightingale. Rather, we need to think about how the global context of war and colonialism might have modified and transformed the classed and raced experiences of a variety of women overseas.[19]

The more general issue of shifting identities tied to race, class, gender, community, and location should especially condition any attempt to locate Seacole as both a West Indian and an African diasporic subject in the nineteenth century. Throughout *Wonderful Adventures*, Seacole asserts her specific racial identity as a colored Jamaican and a cultural citizen of Britain. In the first instance, she declares her membership in a particularly Caribbean mulatto population, which in the British West Indies encompassed a separate legal status. Indeed, such mixed-race groups traditionally negotiated a variety of relations with whites and full Blacks alike. But as Beckles has cautioned, colored West Indians "were [not] sufficiently homogenous to be discussed without reference to fundamental internal class and conceptual differences," a list which would, of course, have to include gender.[20] What possibilities for thinking about West Indian colored identity might emerge from a consideration of Seacole's femininity, her self-imposed exile from Jamaica, and her service to (mostly male) Europeans? Certainly, any interpretation of Seacole's "representativeness" as a nineteenth-century West Indian, or of her status as an early voice in the sounding of an African diasporic identity, must address her relational status as a colored woman entrepreneur within British Caribbean society to Blacks, to whites, and to "brown" people themselves. Though seemingly not the central concern of Seacole's self-presentation in *Wonderful Adventures*, this relational status leaves its distinct traces throughout her text, even in the unlikely setting of the barren Crimean Peninsula.

LOCATING MARY SEACOLE

Seacole may have been destitute by the time she published *Wonderful Adventures* in 1857, but as we have seen, because she nursed soldiers in the Crimea, she had already secured something of a celebrity status. Her appearances in bankruptcy court were avidly reported, for instance, and apart from the various well-meaning (if poorly run) fundraising events put on for her aid, she was the subject of lighthearted poems and stage musicals. On her behalf, brief but laudatory notices appeared in letters soldiers sent home, as well as in the *Illustrated London News*, *Punch*, the London *Times*, and published memoirs by officers, army surgeons, and noncombatants alike. At the same time, William H. Russell, the celebrated *Times* war correspondent whose scathing reports helped to raise public consciousness of the mismanagement of the war, wrote a glowing preface to *Wonderful Adventures*. In his memoir, the British army surgeon Douglas A. Reid affectionately recalled Seacole at Balaclava "with her stove and kettle, in any shelter she could find, brewing tea for all who wanted it."[21] Still, while these accounts bear witness to Seacole's extreme kindness to the sick and wounded and to her skills as a "sutler" or supplier of provisions to the army, one of the most extended accounts of Seacole's interaction with Europeans at the front, Alexis Soyer's 1857 *Culinary Campaign*, decidedly does not depict her actually nursing anyone.

As Nightingale's assistant in the reform of army hospital kitchens, the French chef Soyer describes his multiple encounters with Seacole as moments of comic relief mediating the surrounding tragedy of war. Noting the crowd of customers who hovered around Seacole's combination hotel and supply shop, Soyer describes Seacole as "a few shades darker than the white lily, . . . bawling out, in order to make herself heard above the noise," and exhibiting a somewhat tiresome habit of repeating the self-aggrandizing story of a single encounter with Nightingale: "This was about the twentieth time the old lady had told me the same tale."[22] On two separate visits to Seacole's Crimean hotel, Soyer describes a charming but mysterious black-haired, blue-eyed "Egyptian beauty" whom he identifies as Seacole's daughter Sally—mysterious because Sally never appears in *Wonderful Adventures*, and Seacole affirms early on in the narrative the death of her husband, who left her with no children. Indeed, it is her widowhood, as well as her presumed childlessness, that makes it possible for Seacole to claim her surrogacy as the symbolic "mother" to English soldiers far from home. By revealing (presumably) suppressed information, Soyer's account suggests the possibility of both Seacole's sexual misconduct (as a colored West Indian woman attending to the needs of white men, is she the mother of an illegitimate daughter?) and the presence of not one but two women of color available for male consumption. And certainly, whether he slyly comments on Sally's beauty as "the Dark, rather than the Fair Maid of the Eastern War" or kisses Seacole on her "deeply shaded forehead," declaring both that "it is very natural for a son to kiss his mother" and, somewhat disparagingly, that "you cannot say . . . upon this occasion, I have shown my love and taste for the fair sex," Soyer's humorous anecdotes are tinged with sexual innuendo.[23]

Whatever the truth behind Sally's origins, the flirtatious relationship between Seacole and Soyer as represented by the latter is not merely the product of unusual wartime conditions. It is, in fact, the trace of a locationally and historically specific West Indian tradition of relations between white men and colored women, now transplanted to the entirely different location of the Crimean War. In the West Indies, as Aleric Josephs has shown, "one of the main means towards economic independence for coloured women before and after slavery was the proprietorship of taverns, lodging-houses and houses of pleasure and ill-repute—sometimes separately, often in combination." These establishments "were more often than not derived from the bequests of former and/or deceased (white) lovers."[24] Given the sexual power dynamics of slavery, and the lower number of white women in the Caribbean (compared to higher numbers in the American South), a widely practiced and openly sanctioned system of white male–Black female miscegenation developed in the British West Indies. While the open practice of taking Black or colored "secondary wives" as part of the white male colonizer's acclimatization process further institutionalized the sexual exploitation of women of African descent fostered by slavery, it also made possible the creation of highly pragmatic relationships that gave these women a modicum of financial power. Thus, as historian Barbara Bush has observed, "this social mobility of both free coloured and slave women, created a minority group of leisured, well-off mulattos, some slave owners themselves, who were the forerunners of the coloured 'aristocracy' which dominates the social pyramid of modern Caribbean society."[25]

Perhaps the most famous of these colored female entrepreneurs was the late eighteenth century's Rachel Pringle-Polgreen of Barbados, who was immortalized by the illustrator and painter Thomas Rowlandson. Emblematic of a supposedly rampant Black female sexuality that pervaded so many white accounts of slavery, the image plays upon almost every possible stereotype of life in a tavern run by a mixed-race West Indian woman: the skimpily clad, light-skinned prostitute in the doorway of Pringle-Polgreen's establishment; the ogling white Creole as well as the white solider, both of whom are sexually enflamed by the prostitute's presence; the vulgarly posed matron herself serving as mistress of sexual revels, glaring shamelessly at the viewer. Indeed, Rowlandson's racist cartoon appears to capture and define Pringle-Polgreen in the over-determining white male colonial gaze, so that, as the largest figure in the illustration, she epitomizes the narrative of bodily excess Europeans imposed upon peoples of color in the Caribbean. However, if we read past these stereotypes, the story of Pringle-Polgreen, which may well be representative of many mixed-race women throughout the British West Indies, reveals her to have been an astute businesswoman who was determined to stand up to white male clients who attempted to exploit her.[26]

According to *Wonderful Adventures*, Seacole's mother was a lodging-house keeper in Kingston, as was Seacole's sister Louisa. While there is no evidence to suggest that the lodging houses run by Seacole and the women in her family doubled as brothels, their profession was, by association, tied to the kinds of enterprises made famous by women such as Pringle-Polgreen. According to Paulette A. Kerr, whether we regard these women as "victims" of white male sexual desire or "strategists" who made an impossible situation workable, we need to come to terms with the reality that they carved out a unique economic space for themselves by trafficking in goods (sexual or not) specifically for white male clients. Indeed, since colonial authorities granted tavern licenses to them more often than to their male counterparts, allowing them to establish a monopoly on the "comfort" trade, their specific economic activity quickly became institutionalized.[27] At the very least, their dominance as lodging-house keepers prompted Anthony Trollope to comment in his travel narrative that "there is a mystery about hotels in the British West Indies. They are always kept by fat middle-aged coloured ladies who have no husbands."[28] It is this linking of the economic and sexual identities of colored women with white male comfort that provides the frame for Soyer's "laudatory" reminiscence of Seacole in the Crimea.

Throughout *Wonderful Adventures*, Seacole embraces her identity as a colored West Indian female entrepreneur, despite the role's association with quasi-institutionalized miscegenation. Indeed, she is forthright about her origins as the daughter of a Jamaican mixed-race hotelkeeper and a Scottish army officer. About her mother, she said, "It was very natural that I should inherit her tastes."[29] Specifically commenting on the legacy of her mother as an Afro-Jamaican folk healer, Seacole stressed her inheritance of "a yearning for medical knowledge and practice" (56). And yet, the residual meanings of that phrase (that is, what *are* the "tastes" of Black women, mixed race or not, in the West Indian colonies?) would not have been lost on either Seacole or the nineteenth-century British readers who had witnessed Nightingale's attempts to purge nursing of its reputation for moral deficiency. The problem behind sending nurses to the Crimea "was the fact that [they] could not defend themselves against the sexual advances of the medical staff and patients."[30] But the alternate explanation was also true: that the "wrong" class of nurses might welcome or encourage sexual impropriety. When considering her as a nurse for British soldiers, the English interpreted Seacole's gendered West Indianness as highly problematic, and, not surprisingly, *Wonderful Adventures* describes the rejection of Seacole's application to join Nightingale's nursing corps. Indeed, despite her considerable reputation as a healer, Seacole is unrepresentable as a nurse even when imagined in a hospital, as a May 30, 1857, *Punch* illustration testifies. A visual allusion to Florence Nightingale as the Lady with the Lamp watching over her patients at Scutari, the illustration depicts a solemn but dusky-faced Seacole making the rounds at the bedsides of wounded soldiers. And rather than attending the ailing men, Seacole walks "through the wards of the hospital at Spring Hill, her arms laden with papers [in particular, copies of *Punch*], the contributions of kind officers to their sick men."[31] Given its mainstream audience, *Punch* offers a more sanitized version of Seacole than the racier image conveyed in Soyer's *Culinary Campaign*, but the resulting judgment of her as primarily a source of diversion underscores the assumption that real nursing could be associated with only the white Nightingale.

In light of this public framing, it is more than a little ironic that when Seacole finally writes her own claim to the title of "Crimean heroine," she sanctions a frontispiece to *Wonderful Adventures* (figure 1.2) that distinctly memorializes her profession not as a "doctress" but as a storekeeper catering primarily to a white male clientele. Surrounded by wine bottles, floor-to-ceiling boxes, and barrels containing (we are told in the narrative) everything from linen handkerchiefs to potted meats, and amid relaxing officers and male civilians, Seacole is shown offering refreshment to none other than Alexis Soyer. In contrast to the racist Rowlandson cartoon of Pringle-Polgreen, Seacole's frontispiece suggests no hint of sexual impropriety. Indeed, both Seacole and her clients are dwarfed in the illustration by the preponderance of material goods, affirming her investment in a wholesome and patriotic British (rather than a sexualized West Indian) capitalism. Yet at the same time, as the specifically West Indian colored female hotelkeeper, Seacole can evoke in the midst of war, disease, and

FIGURE 1.2. Frontispiece for *Wonderful Adventures of Mrs. Seacole in Many Lands*, showing Seacole entertaining British officers in the Crimea. (Schomburg Center for Research
in Black Culture, New York Public Library)

death a comforting nostalgia for a sanctioned set of colonial relations designed
to address the needs of white European men displaced from home.

Removed from the West Indies, this image of the colored female hotelkeeper
would have carried significant ideological weight for British readers looking
back to a frighteningly chaotic foreign conflict. In contrast to the Crimean disaster, the stability of English–West Indian relations embodied by Seacole's voluntary servitude reaffirms the British ability to "civilize" the imperial frontier.
Thus, Seacole's presence suggests not merely the availability of the comforts
of English clothing and foodstuffs but also the righteous force of Englishness.
In reality, of course, the illusory harmony depicted in the frontispiece belies
mixed-race women's historical status as both victims and agents working to
turn white male desire into financial gain at the same time that it enacts an
erasure of Jamaicans of African descent and the Jamaican-born white planter
class. And in a moment when Britain is recovering from war, the image works

to suppress the violent history of slavery and rebellion that would continue to mark life in the British West Indies long after emancipation. To uphold this illusion, *Wonderful Adventures* seems never to challenge the racial and social status quo demanded by British imperialism, and as a requirement for Seacole to appear "respectable," she is imagined with "no subjectivity outside the imperial infrastructure."[32]

When read against emerging nineteenth-century US and Anglophone Caribbean literary canons, the Anglophile nature of *Wonderful Adventures* appears disturbing only if we presume that the early literature of the Black diaspora must inevitably evince some form of group affiliation or experience, such as the Middle Passage, slavery, antislavery, or emancipation. While Seacole discusses slavery when she describes her life in Panama, as Evelyn Hawthorne notes, she was also "well aware of the British public's avid interest in literature about the Crimean war."[33] Therefore, Seacole's autobiography is composed with attention to the particular cultural registers encompassed by that tradition. Indeed, though it is an autobiography by a self-proclaimed West Indian woman, *Wonderful Adventures* falls dutifully in line with the many Crimean memoirs published by British soldiers and civilian eyewitnesses throughout the nineteenth and early twentieth centuries. Accounts such as Soyer's *Culinary Campaign*, Frances Duberly's *Journal Kept during the Russian War* (1855), Lady Alicia Blackwood's *A Narrative of Personal Experiences and Impressions during a Residence on the Bosphorus throughout the Crimean War* (1881), Timothy Gowing's *Voice from the Ranks: A Personal Narrative of the Crimean Campaign by a Sergeant of the Royal Fusiliers* (1892), and Douglas Arthur Reid's *Memories of the Crimean War, January 1855 to June 1856* (1911) focus exclusively on their authors' participation in the conflict and on what they witnessed firsthand as the basis for their claims to public attention. Doubling as travel narratives, these texts also express the relationship between the local and the global as binary experiences pitting a civilized English "homeland" against the alien, hostile Crimean battlefield crawling with foreigners "abroad." By rehearsing the horrors of the war at the same time that they memorialized the bravery of English soldiers serving overseas, such memoirs allowed British readers a multitude of vicarious experiences, whether they involved cringing at the devastation of the nation's army; soberly contemplating the burial of thousands of English soldiers on Turkish soil; revisiting notable sites and events, such as Nightingale's hospital at Scutari, the siege of Sebastopol, and the famous but futile Charge of the Light Brigade; or marveling at "exotic" Russians, "oriental" Jews, Turks, Greeks, and French Zouaves. Not surprisingly, such accounts were popular precisely because they enabled a national healing via an affirmation of the centrality and superiority of Englishness, despite the alarming mortality rate among British soldiers during the war.

But while *Wonderful Adventures* facilitates a British postwar agenda on the one hand, Seacole's presence *outside of* the West Indies raises the question of how stable these idealized images and their suggested colonial relations might actually be, so far from their location of origin. Clearly, *Wonderful Adventures* asserts the female freedom so often cited in traditional feminist discussions of women's travel writing, albeit from the point of view of a colored rather than a white female subject.[34] However, the tendency to appreciate Seacole as a pioneer of (nonwhite) female travel obscures the equally important issue of how her mobility impinges upon narratives of British national identity. If we think of Seacole's text as a prototype of early immigrant literature by nonwhite colonial subjects, then *Wonderful Adventures* poses a considerable challenge to the celebration of white English nationalism enacted by the literature of the Crimean War. According to Rosemary M. George, in the twentieth century nonwhite colonial migration "*unwrites* [first and third world] nation and national projects because it flagrantly displays a rejection of one national space for another more desirable location, albeit with some luggage carried over."[35] If we think about this concept in the space of Seacole's nineteenth-century migrations, then even as her journeys "worked [like those of other female colonial Others] to consolidate Britons as 'British,'" they also blurred the lines between "home and empire . . . as separate spheres."[36] And, while Seacole declares herself to be an Englishwoman, we are still left with the impact of her "luggage," to borrow George's metaphor—namely, her West Indianness defined as both the sexual associations made about the colored woman and her ability to travel and recreate "home" in any location.

Ironically, Seacole's language of domestic service to the British reverberates with a sense of white displacement. Consider, for instance, her declaration that "all who are familiar with the West Indies will acknowledge that Nature has been favorable to strangers in a few respects, and that one of these has been in instilling in the heart of the Creoles an affection for English people and an anxiety for their welfare, which shows itself warmest when they are sick and suffering" (108). While for a British audience this statement reassuringly equates postemancipation colored female self-determination with voluntary servitude, it also firmly fixes this same audience as constitutionally incompatible with their West Indian empire. When the same diseases in the West Indies reappear in the Crimea, the sickly English pale in comparison to Seacole and her ability to survive physical challenges the world over, whether she resides in Jamaica, Panama, the Crimea, or Britain. By implication, then, it is the West Indian colored woman Mary Seacole, rather than the imperial English, who is the sanctioned inhabitant of the lands beyond home shores.

Seacole's claim to the world is reflected in her autobiography's title, *Wonderful Adventures of Mrs. Seacole in Many Lands*, which is clearly at odds with the distinctly national framing of its fellow Crimean memoirs. *Wonderful Adventures* does not criticize the English government or the officers, but its displacement of England and the Crimea as the sole focus of attention and its inclusion of Panama centralize Seacole's experiences and successes not only as a world traveler but also as an African diasporic subject capable of negotiating space for herself outside of and beyond British control. Whereas Seacole seems to sublimate all other experiences in the wake of her sojourn in Turkey—the better to appeal to her metropolitan audience, so that "her experiences in [Panama] directly anticipate her experiences in the Crimea" by establishing her ability to deal with disease, death, and "chaotic social situations"—her use of Central America as an alternate destination also establishes other locations just as vital to her identity.[37] Thus, when she says, "I began to indulge that longing for travel which will never leave me while I have health and vigor," and "I was never weary of tracing upon an old map the route to England; and never followed with my gaze the stately ships homeward bound without a longing to be in them, and see the blue hills of Jamaica fade into the distance" (57), she collapses the desire to go to England with a more general desire to leave home, even if that means leaving the British Empire. If this is indeed the case, rather than reading the frontispiece to *Wonderful Adventures* as evidence of either Seacole's co-optation or (in its rejection of the overt sexuality associated with women such as Pringle-Polgreen) her completely transgressive and resistant subjectivity, we might choose to see it as a complex sign of both her profession and her refusal to define "home" in a particular "homeland or territory and a region." From this point of view, colored female West Indianness might be articulated as a decidedly unstraightforward process of adaptability negotiated at the intersection of white and Black colonial travel, and yet also beyond the conditions of variously raced, gendered, colonial Caribbean identities.

AT HOME IN PANAMA

The politics of adaptability surfaces very early in *Wonderful Adventures*, when Seacole first embarks for Panama. Although already well established as a widowed hotelkeeper in Jamaica, Seacole is frustratingly vague as to why she leaves Jamaica in 1850. She suggests that her move is prompted by a combination of duty (she wants to be of help to her storekeeping brother Edward, already in

Panama) and the desire for adventure ("I found some difficulty in checking my reviving disposition to roam" [62]). But, just as importantly, Seacole fails to mention that her journey to Panama coincided with a migration of Black workers trying to escape chronic unemployment in postemancipation Jamaica. With the 1846 lifting of trade protection for West Indian sugar as well as the importation of indentured laborers from India and China, Jamaican planters were loath to hire Jamaican free persons as agricultural workers, so many followed the call of labor recruiters for the American railroad in Panama.[38] Considered a vital regional center for trade and transportation, Panama also attracted many Jamaican small-business operators (such as Seacole and her brother) hoping to benefit from increasing commercial opportunities.

Ironically, though, instead of detailing any social connectedness even to people of Seacole's own class and caste, the text focuses on her similarity to the "alien" English whom she gently chides for being strangers to the region. For instance, en route to the city of Cruces, Seacole encourages comparisons between herself and an English lady traveling through dangerous territory, making note of her "delicate light blue dress, and white bonnet prettily trimmed, and an equally chaste shawl," in contrast to "the female companions of successful gold-diggers" who, once they assume men's clothing for the journey, are "in no hurry to resume the dress or obligations of their sex" (66, 72). In keeping with the conventions of nineteenth-century British women's travel narratives, Seacole's autobiography seems to affirm the incorruptibility of a distinctly European femininity, the implication being that if Englishwomen can persevere with little danger to themselves, then the superior power of British imperialism is not in question.[39] But even as Seacole presents herself as worthy of the English reader's cultural identification, she simultaneously eschews the Englishwoman's traditional role as "civilizer." Mid-nineteenth-century British missionary women justified their travel to "wild" territories by their necessity as helpmates, either to missionary husbands or—as in Seacole's case—to unmarried male family members. Also, British women travel writers expressed a "solidarity with people of other nations" that emerged from the "discourse of philanthropy which circulated through the nineteenth century and involved middle- and upper-class women."[40] According to Catherine Hall, these women linked their civilizing mission with imperial expansion, "seeing it as the duty of the Christian nations to colonize the 'heathen' nations, in order to convert them."[41] But since both Seacole and her brother are ultimately in Panama not to spread Christianity but purely and simply to make money, they inadvertently make visible the hemispheric strategies engaged in by colonial subjects trying to survive when their island home goes through an economic depression.[42] As two of many Jamaicans who migrated to an independent, anticolonial Panama for better economic opportunities, they would have been free to make and keep the fruits of their labor, since the British Empire had no legal claim to Central America.

Indeed, throughout the narrative, Seacole enacts a simulation of "English" civilization that serves to undermine any notion of the transformative power of Western cultural practices.[43] For instance, when she establishes an alcohol-free restaurant and lodging house, furnishing clients with poultry and eggs and even providing an in-house barber, her goal is not to promote temperance, a proper diet, or good hygiene but rather to attend to market demands. In a location where she competes with brothels and gaming houses as well as her brother's restaurant, chicken and eggs are the commodities surest to attract the highest-paying customers, while alcohol would in fact not be popular with the largely teetotaling Americans, who are more willing than others to pay extra for "a clean chin" (88). Also, though the Panamanian section of the narrative can be justified because it first reveals the kind of medical resourcefulness and charity she will display in the Crimea, Seacole is by far the antithesis of Nightingale's model of the ideal Crimean nurse, who neither encouraged morally compromising situations with men nor challenged the role of the male doctor. For instance, when the boat transporting her to the city of Gorgona is marooned on the Chagres River during a rainstorm, Seacole exhibits little distress about spending the night on the boat with crew members who "have a marked disregard of the prejudices of society with respect to clothing" (68). During a cholera epidemic, she is deeply touched by the sight of a "brown-faced orphan infant" (81); yet, upon the child's death, an unwomanly pragmatism replaces maternal grief, and she immediately launches into an autopsy. As the declared representative of traditional British values, Seacole moves interchangeably between the roles of mother and clinician, at once utilizing the Jamaican Creole medical practices she learned from her mother while also claiming as part of her medical arsenal the kind of objective scientific analysis generally associated with white male doctors.

Despite such ironic undermining of the British imperial values she seems at first to support, Seacole's lack of sympathy for Native Americans and Panamanians (whom she describes as lazy and exhibiting a "slavish despair" in the face of disease [78]) is disturbing. Curiously, only runaway slaves from the United States are exempt from Seacole's racism and ethnocentrism: Seacole is impressed that "the same negro who perhaps in Tennessee would have cowered . . . beneath an American's uplifted hand, . . . face[s] him boldly here, and by equal courage and superior physical strength cow[s] his old oppressors" (93).

Such solidarity with US-born Blacks is ironic, given the simultaneous historical presence of other ex-slave populations, such as Jamaican railroad workers and Black Panamanians. In the first place, though she speaks specifically about US-born Blacks, Seacole's focus on runaway slaves rather than Jamaican free persons suggests her understanding of the difference between traditional British abolitionist sentiment (which would have been on the side of the American slaves as victims) and growing racist attitudes in both England and the West Indies toward free Blacks, who were reviled for trying to define emancipation on their own terms.[44] If we read the American ex-slaves as a displaced reference to Seacole's compatriots (who, after all, have also "fled" to Panama to secure better opportunities), then Seacole's attention to the success and industry of US Blacks outside of slavery directly challenges the growing postemancipation English racism epitomized by Thomas Carlyle's infamous 1849 diatribe, "Occasional Discourse on the Nigger Question." Carlyle saw emancipation as allowing British West Indian ex-slaves to sit "yonder with their beautiful muzzles up to the ears in pumpkins, imbibing sweet pulp and juices . . . while the sugar-crops rot round them uncut, because labour cannot be hired, so cheap are the pumpkins."[45] According to Monica Schuler, such attacks on West Indian ex-slaves belied the move by planters to initiate "a racist antilabor campaign that deliberately and maliciously cultivated the myth of the lazy Quashie."[46] If we put Seacole's "embrace" of Englishness in this context, her celebration of the achievements of ex-slaves from the United States is a testament to the success of emancipation and thus a triple indictment of American, white West Indian, *and* British racism, despite the division she appears to draw between the United States and Britain and between the "real" victims of slavery and those free Blacks "abusing" their liberty by not submitting to West Indian planters.

Her celebration of American ex-slaves also allows Seacole to back a hemispheric anticolonialism that would have been severely condemned by Jamaican planters. Speaking more generally of the republic of New Granada (of which Panama was a part), Seacole suggests that the entire political scene was "influenced naturally by these freed slaves [from the United States], who bore themselves before their old masters bravely and like men," so that "the New Granada people were strongly prejudiced against [white] Americans" (100–101). According to Seacole, "when the American Railway Company took possession of Navy Bay, and christened it Aspinwall, after the name of their Chairman, the native authorities refused to recognize their right to name any portion of the Republic, and pertinaciously returned all letters directed to Aspinwall, with 'no such place known' marked upon them in the very spot for which they were intended" (101). Though the British had tried to establish a foothold in Panama, as Michael Conniff has shown, the Americans succeeded by 1846 in transforming Panama from "an isthmus of Jamaica into an isthmus of New York."[47] Seacole's attack on American imperialism is not tantamount to a desire that Britain replace the United States. Rather, she celebrates independent Latin America's commonality with the English ("It is one of the maxims of the New Granada constitution—as it is, I believe, of the English—that on a slave's touching its soil his chains fall from him" [101]), thereby flattering her white readers' support of abolition without necessarily supporting their imperialistic desires.

If my readings are indeed accurate, they would allow Seacole's narrative to fit comfortably within radical modern readings of transnational, diasporic solidarity between peoples of African descent in the Americas. In that sense, Seacole might be counted as a West Indian counterpart to mid-nineteenth-century American free Blacks such as Nancy Prince, Henry Highland Garnet, Martin R. Delany, James T. Holly, and J. Dennis Harris: all of these American Black activists were variously encouraged both by the abolition of slavery in the West Indies and by the idea of founding a Black homeland, and they either traveled directly to Haiti and Jamaica for that end or debated the possibilities of Black American immigration to the Caribbean and Central America.[48] But *Wonderful Adventures* is a text that never sits still, since it unmistakably complicates desires for consistent evidence of Black diasporic solidarity. Inasmuch as it appears to celebrate the possibilities of diasporic solidarity, it simultaneously demonstrates that the displacement of national in favor of racial affiliations does not necessarily preclude Black racism or announce the complete repudiation of power relations established under European colonialism. In Panama, all Black slaves would have been free by January 1, 1852; as newly enfranchised voters, Panamanian free persons were aggressively in support of liberal reform and might well have been the very people of African descent who defied the racial and national arrogance of white American travelers.[49] Ironically, Jamaican migrant workers faced great hostility at the hands of the Panamanians as well as other Afro-Latin Americans. Writer and scholar Olive Senior has speculated that these struggles were related to "linguistic, religious and cultural differences" between the English-speaking, Protestant Jamaicans and their Central American counterparts.[50] Thus, Seacole's silences about Latin American Blacks might well emerge out of particular traditions of intraracial and intraregional conflict. Still, in keeping with her more obvious celebration of Englishness, Seacole uses the complex politics of Panama as a foil to set off the resourcefulness that would make her an essential figure in the Crimea. To accept that persona, readers must also accept her iconoclasm, her celebration of Anglophone Blackness, and her veiled anti-imperialism. Fortunately for Seacole, her selective willingness to identify with social others can be translated, in the case of the Crimea, into her attentiveness to the British common soldier.

AT HOME IN THE CRIMEA

The Crimean section of *Wonderful Adventures* justifies the existence of the entire narrative, and Seacole's response to life with the British Army differs considerably from her response to Yankees and Central Americans in Panama. Throughout the autobiography, Seacole's strategy for gaining acceptance from her white audience emerges from her shrewd understanding of British public opinion in the aftermath of war. While the Crimean conflict initially pitted Britain and France against Russia after the latter's invasion of Turkey, the real motive for the war had less to do with protecting English shores than with Britain's competitive desire to exert influence in the Black Sea region. At the start of the conflict in 1854, British patriotism was high, but as the war dragged on and more British soldiers died as a result of poor medical care, starvation, and physical exposure, British public opinion shifted dramatically. Losses were so great that by December 1854 Nightingale and her nurses were allowed to go to Scutari to reform the care of the wounded, and by February of the following year, the British government resigned in the face of growing opposition. Increasingly, as war correspondents focused on the immense suffering of common soldiers, "battle lost its glorious aspect, support for the traditional military system collapsed, and the nation demanded its reform."[51] This cry for change extended as well to British attitudes about the army's officer corps, where commissions were purchased rather than earned, enabling the richest rather than the most talented men to achieve ranks of command.

The second half of *Wonderful Adventures* makes clear that Seacole's relocation to the Crimea as a sutler and lodging-house keeper rather than as a full-time nurse was wholly the fault of circumstances—and the racist judgment of the white women recruiting nurses on Nightingale's behalf—and not a personal desire to profit from the war. The start of the hostilities finds Seacole still in Central America, exhibiting the attitude of a thrill-seeking tourist rather than devoted camp follower: "no sooner had I heard of war somewhere, than I longed to witness it" (120). But she also draws on her audience's assumption of a special affinity between West Indian Creoles of color and their English masters, declaring as well "the delight . . . I [would] experience if I could be useful to my own 'sons,' suffering for a cause it was so glorious to fight and bleed for!" (122). With reports of the British Army's medical services and supply lines in crisis, the rejection of Seacole by Nightingale's associates puts the spotlight on bureaucratic incompetence, thereby justifying Seacole's resumption of commercial activities. When she opens "a mess-table and comfortable quarters for sick and convalescent officers" (127) in the Crimea, the move has to be applauded as a triumph over the army's grossly ineffectual supply system rather than as an attempt to capitalize on British suffering. Thus, Seacole can confidently frame her entrepreneurship as part of the larger humanitarian efforts enacted by the worried English public.

Though Seacole claims that the opening of a store and hotel was the only way she could afford to sustain herself in the Crimea, she uses the class politics of the war to ensure her continued economic success. For instance, while she treats common soldiers without a fee, she openly demands money from their officers; by this method, as well as by stocking goods that would attract those who were wealthy enough to pay for English food and clothing, she was able to subsidize her humanitarian efforts and even prosper. This policy of remuneration based on class allows the commercial side of her enterprise to be disassociated from war profiteering, functioning instead as a kind of necessary retribution within the troubled military establishment, where common soldiers increasingly bore the brunt of the conflict. Her actions ensured the affection of the rank and file but had a different effect on some upper-crust Crimean participants. In the single paragraph on Seacole in her *Narrative of Personal Experiences* (1881), Lady Alicia Blackwood comments that, while she appreciated greatly both Seacole's magnanimity toward the British wounded and her provision of "every variety of article, both edible and otherwise," she thought that Seacole charged prices that "were slightly usuriously added to on her behalf towards others."[52] The choice of the word *usuriously* to describe Seacole is telling, given the strong anti-Semitism that pervades Blackwood's text. Though she felt obliged to underscore Seacole's humanitarianism, Blackwood was still clearly irked some twenty-five years later by Seacole's determination to make aristocrats like herself pay for the pleasure of connecting with "home" via supplies from England. Thus, Seacole's successful exploitation of class politics so as to represent her commercialism as a patriotic act (in a sense, she merely redirected resources to needy fighting men) demonstrates how the Crimean War made visible particular conflicts hidden behind the facade of a united wartime Britain.

Blackwood's presence as a white lady also points to the range of women (beyond Nightingale) operating in the Crimea behind British lines. Despite the long shadow cast by Nightingale, we need to recognize that on or near the battlefield, Seacole was more often than not circulating alongside the wives of officers, chaplains, and common soldiers. Because of their husbands' wealth, the officers' wives were relatively well provided for and protected, but common soldiers' wives starved, froze, or succumbed to disease along with their husbands, or they found work as lady's maids, army cooks, and laundresses. Especially if they had only enough money to get to Scutari but not to the front, they struggled in dire poverty.[53] Therefore, when we think of Seacole's presentation of herself as a woman in the Crimea, we need to consider as well what limitations and possibilities emerged with the presence of such British white women located so far from an English home.

For one thing, Seacole was undoubtedly aware of the weight of comparison between herself and Nightingale. In a scene in *Wonderful Adventures* that recalls her rejection in London by the white aristocratic women screening applicants for the nursing corps, Seacole pays a visit to Scutari on her way to the front and finally achieves a polite but chilly meeting with Nightingale. The latter grants her accommodations for the night but is described rather flatly as "that English woman whose name shall never die" (136), suggesting that as a travel writer, Seacole merely goes through the motions of paying homage to the chief celebrity of the war.[54] Ironically, the chapter ends with Seacole spending much more narrative energy on the kindness of the white laundress whose bed she shares in the basement of Nightingale's hospital—that is, the very type of useful female participant (like Seacole herself) who would have been eclipsed by the public mythology already growing around Nightingale. Ironically, once Seacole establishes herself close to the conflict, many of the walking wounded flock to her Crimean store in lieu of going to Nightingale's hospital. To justify this apparent competition with Scutari, Seacole declares, "In the first place, the men . . . had a very serious objection to going into hospital for any but urgent reasons, . . . and in the second place, they could and did get at my store sick-comforts and nourishing food, which the heads of the medical staff would sometimes find it difficult to procure" (166). Here, Seacole's display of adaptability to any environment and her ability to deal with any disease make her the rival of both Nightingale and the white English military doctors. Not surprisingly, she uses the narrative to demonstrate her skills as a nurse, a demonstration that can come only with a reconnection to the Englishman's body. Suggesting that there was some approbation about her attending too closely to the wounded, she recounts how, without waiting for a doctor's approval, she adjusted soldiers' bandages as they waited for transportation to the hospital. In addition, she fills an entire chapter titled "My Work in the Crimea" with reprinted letters and notes from soldiers and officers, who testify to her effective medicines and her ability to cure, among other things, cholera, dysentery, and jaundice. According to Seacole, these documents prove "the position I held in the camp as doctress, nurse, and 'mother'" (166).

Seacole's redefinition of her role from hotelkeeper and sutler to "doctress, nurse, and 'mother'" might be read as the ultimate triumph over the stereotype of the mixed-race hotelkeeper welcoming male attention that emerges in Soyer's *Culinary Campaign* or, for that matter, Rowlandson's eighteenth-century racist cartoon of Rachel Pringle-Polgreen. In contrast, Seacole deliberately evokes colored West Indian female sexuality as a part of her representational arsenal in order to take advantage of reframed social interactions now that both she and the British are so far from familiar settings. For example, when she depicts the ideal paying customer of her Crimean British hotel as "the poor officer lying ill and weary in his crazy hut [who] often finds his greatest troubles in the want of those little delicacies with which a weak stomach must be humoured into retaining nourishment" (167), she deliberately draws on the well-known public image of the West Indian hostess. As the white traveler Trelawny Wentworth put it, speaking for other Englishmen away from home, "your necessities need anticipating, your appetite requires stimulants and coaxing and there is that instinctive eloquence in the female voice and especially in the fine drawn wheedling of a mulatto hostess."[55] Though throughout the narrative Seacole persists in representing herself as sexually unattractive with "a well-filled-out portly frame" (131), the supposed compatibility of colored women and white men is enmeshed in Seacole's language of self-promotion when, referring to white women, she claims, "I never found women so quick to understand me as the men" (135). As evidenced by the numerous testimonials in *Wonderful Adventures* that celebrate her ability to cure the sick, Seacole marshals the approval of the very white soldiers whom Nightingale and her nurses have vowed to serve, and thus she deauthorizes white women as her judges. Ironically, by playing on the traditional rivalry between white and colored women for the attention of white men, Seacole underscores the malleability of racial stereotypes emerging out of Caribbean colonies once they are displaced to new locations.

At times, Seacole pushes the potential sexualization of her colored female identity to the limit. Note, for example, her suggestion of herself as a potential replacement for white women: "More than one officer have I startled by appearing before him, and telling him abruptly that he must have a mother, wife or sister at home whom he missed, and that he must therefore be glad of some woman to take their place" (183). Equally problematic is her stint as a "lady's maid" to off-duty soldiers cross-dressing for amateur theatricals. Lending out her own clothes and turning her kitchen into a dressing room, Seacole recounts how "the ladies of the company of the 1st Royals were taught to manage their petticoats with becoming grace, and neither to show their awkward booted ankles, nor trip themselves up over their trains. . . . Although I laced them in until they grew blue in the face, their waists were a disgrace to the sex; while— crinoline being unknown then—my struggles to give them becoming *embonpoint* may be imagined" (216). Despite its comedy, the scene's suggestion of Seacole disrobing white men and attempting to reshape their "female" bodies testifies to a particular kind of familiarity between the West Indian colored female hotelkeeper and her male customers that would never have been considered appropriate for Nightingale's nurses. Such self-representation indicates a risky strategy of innuendo and disavowal that Seacole performs throughout the narrative, despite her claim to the title *Mother Seacole*. Consequently, I would argue that, rather than wholly embracing the stereotype of West Indian colored female sexuality, Seacole merely employs some of its representational grammar. The result is a more ambiguous, less restrictive identity for Seacole, one that skirts the stereotype of West Indian prostitute, yet also revises the sexless and equally restrictive stereotype of both "mother" and Black "mammy."

That Seacole could have maintained her audience's confidence in the face of such self-representation might seem hard to believe—that is, unless we recognize that this persona as the West Indian colored hostess is further contextualized against the working-class soldiers' wives who, like her, were located "at the bottom of the social pile, disadvantaged both by sex and class, a sharp contrast to the public role created for Florence Nightingale," but who, as we shall see, nevertheless achieved a certain amount of respect and compassion from some of their compatriots.[56] Again, Lady Blackwood's memoir provides a good example of the gendered and classed tensions of war in the Crimea, which Seacole used to her advantage in *Wonderful Adventures*. Volunteering her services at the military hospital in Scutari, Blackwood found herself charged by Nightingale with the care of impoverished soldiers' wives who had taken up residence in the dirty, overcrowded basement of the hospital building—the very basement, in fact, where Seacole was welcomed by the friendly white hospital laundress. Rather than recognizing that the destitution of these women was the result of an official policy of abandonment by British Army administrators, Blackwood ascribed their dirt and "vice" to their working-class origins. In an effort to "solve" the problem of the Scutari basement (and in an ironic parallel to Seacole), Blackwood opened up her own impromptu store, selling the soldiers' wives cloth, tea, and other personal and household goods. Although she drew on supplies that had been donated by the English public in packages specifically labeled "free gifts for the women," Blackwood justified her commercial enterprise by arguing that it would "encourage industrious habits" among the wives, since they would have to "earn what they spent—as well as retain the value of what they purchased."[57] Of course, Blackwood failed to see the irony of her own "usurious" treatment of the women and indeed failed to consider by what means they might, in fact, earn money honestly, since they were far from home in a war-torn foreign country. Yet, despite Blackwood's attempt to manage lower-class white female morality, the British public's charity in donating free supplies suggests that precisely because of their devotion to their husbands and their willingness to undergo hardship, the wives themselves were slowly earning the respect of the British public. I would argue that Seacole's unique self-image as a new kind of Crimean "heroine" is based on an appropriation and redemption of the class position of the soldiers' wives within her larger attempt to gain acceptance with a British middle-class readership.

This point becomes clearer if we compare Seacole to the officer's wife Frances Duberly, whose 1855 *Journal Kept during the Russian War* gained a wide circulation when it was published before the war was over and would surely have been known to Seacole. At first nicknamed Jubilee by some of the soldiers, Duberly traveled to the Crimea with her horses and actively cultivated male admirers among the Duke of Wellington's staff. Precisely for these reasons, Lieutenant Temple Goodman regarded her as a parasite: "[Mrs. Duberly] is known in the camp by the name of Vulture, from the pleasure she seemed to take in riding over fields of battle. I think her feelings (if she has any) cannot be very fine, and she is certainly more fit to follow a camp than to live in an English drawing room."[58] This comparison of Duberly to a camp follower suggests the dual contempt with which some members of the upper class regarded both soldiers' wives and ladies who asserted their independence beyond the domestic sphere. For her part, in letters to England, Duberly claimed that, as "the only woman"—that is, lady—at the front, she qualified for the newly struck Crimean medal.[59] But when news of her campaign for the medal reached yet another officer, Colonel Edward Hodge, he commented that Mrs. Rogers, the hardworking cook and laundress of his regiment, "deserves it [the medal] ten times more than half the men who will get it."[60] Coming from a war veteran, Hodge's praise of Mrs. Rogers challenges both Duberly's refusal to acknowledge the presence and immense contribution of lower-class women at the front and Goodman's (and Blackwood's) attack on so-called camp followers, since he argues for judging a woman's capacity for virtue and heroism not on her willingness for adventure or her class origins, but on her dedication to caring for the troops.

Undoubtedly, Seacole would have witnessed the tensions around class and gender that inevitably emerged as relationships between upper and lower classes were tested and remade by English displacement to the Crimea. As a result, in *Wonderful Adventures* Seacole proves her respectability not by trying to appropriate the title of "lady" traveler/tourist signified by Mrs. Duberly, but by highlighting her role as a deeply engaged participant, in the vein of the lower-class Mrs. Rogers. In what might almost be a calculated analogue to Duberly, who was so fond of riding that the war photographer Roger Fenton took a widely circulated battlefront photograph of her perched atop her favorite horse, Bob, Seacole offers readers a rival definition of virtuous womanhood as decidedly working class *and* colored: "Reader, if you were lying, with parched lips and fading appetite, thousands of miles from mother, wife or sister . . . and thinking regretfully of that English home where nothing that could minister to your great needs would be left untried—don't you think that you would welcome the familiar figure of the stout lady whose bony horse has pulled up at the door of your hut[?]" (167). This image of the dark-skinned Mrs. Seacole and her broken-down animal, bearing refreshments through the British army camp, is no less incongruous than the blond, stylish Mrs. Duberly dressed in voluminous riding skirts astride a gleaming stallion, posing for a photographer, and detached from all things military except for the figure of her nearby officer-husband. Despite her race, Seacole's self-presentation is more in keeping with the vast majority of Crimean photographs taken by Fenton, who had been commissioned by Prince Albert to record war scenes for an anxious public at home. A number of these revealed soldiers' wives, in particular Mrs. Rogers herself (figure 1.3), with rolled sleeves and pots in hand, surrounded by soldiers and busily attending to chores in camp.[61] In this context, Seacole's gentle suggestion that she was similar to a soldier's "mother, wife, [or] sister" takes on new meaning and seems less far-fetched, given the class politics within which *Wonderful Adventures* places her.

Another scene in *Wonderful Adventures* parallels and upstages a landmark event in Duberly's life—namely, the latter's narrow escape from Russian guns just before the infamous Charge of the Light Brigade. Consider Seacole's account of dodging bullets while venturing out to attend to soldiers wounded on the battlefield during the attack on the Redan, an important Russian fortification: "Upon these occasions those around would cry out, 'Lie down, mother, lie down!' and with very undignified and unladylike haste I had to embrace the earth, and remain there until the same voices would laughingly assure me that the danger was over. . . . Several times in my wanderings on that eventful day . . . I was ordered back, but each time my bag of bandages and comforts for the wounded proved my passport" (195). Again, Seacole's presence might at first seem just as incongruous during the battle for the Redan as Duberly's is moments before the Russian artillery annihilated the Light Brigade. How-

FIGURE 1.3. Mrs. Rogers with the Fourth Dragoons in the Crimea, 1855. (Library of Congress, Prints and Photographs Division, Fenton Crimean War Photographs)

ever, soldiers' wives routinely combed the battlefield to aid wounded husbands or recover the corpses of friends and loved ones. Seacole's strategy of self-presentation clearly balances the role of adventuress that Duberly signifies with the role of humble but devoted "wife," in order to justify her self-placement on the field of battle as not just an act of daring but a selfless effort of compassion for those hardest hit by the conflict. While some modern readers have tried to rehabilitate Duberly's reputation as a true heroine, and though she and Seacole were equally attracted by the excitement of battle, Seacole seemed to be more carefully attuned to the ways in which class and gender contradictions might be manipulated to reframe her iconoclastic behavior in a manner that could be translated into British patriotism. In her determination to cultivate male friendships and defy all possible Victorian conventions, Duberly is no less radical than Seacole. However, despite the advantages of class and color, she is finally a problematic figure in the public eye, because her rebellion founders on the very conventions of womanhood she sets out to defy. Because of Seacole's skill at presenting herself as the battlefield guardian angel of the British soldier, she emerges from the war with a full pension supplied by the Seacole Fund, while on her return to England, Duberly finds herself snubbed by Queen Victoria.

Within its frame, *Wonderful Adventures* reveals the intersection of "diaspora" and "colonialism" and therefore the intersection of different but related histories of displacement for a variety of populations. Seacole's text also exemplifies the ways in which intertwined categories of identity (both real and imagined) are highly contingent upon the politics of location and mobility. As I have tried to demonstrate by comparing Seacole with British women in the Crimea such as Mrs. Duberly and Mrs. Rogers, race, gender, sexuality, and class operate together in different modalities and along a wide spectrum of possibilities, once subjects are displaced by national politics and imperial expansion. Events such as the Crimean War did not change the age-old, diametrically opposed stereotypes of lascivious Black womanhood and chaste white womanhood, but *Wonderful Adventures* demonstrates the way radical locational reframing might create unusual and unexpected moments of refiguration for women normally restricted by the social norms of their places of origin. Also, in its literary identity as a woman's travel narrative, *Wonderful Adventures* is instructive for its complication of travel by a woman, especially one of mixed race in the age of nineteenth-century American slavery. Indeed, the radical nature of *Wonderful Adventures* resides not in Seacole's repeated migrations from place to place, but rather in her unique ability to successfully negotiate the costs, limits, and possibilities of the multiple communities she encounters.

FAITH SMITH'S SUGGESTION THAT "there is no predictable relationship between the utilization of Englishness by individuals or groups and their understanding of themselves in terms of their communities" applies to the nineteenth-century West Indians who laid claim to Englishness; and it applies, of course, to Mary Seacole, since her public embrace of Englishness is emphasized in *Wonderful Adventures* to the point of making invisible the fact that she maintained close connections to her family in Jamaica, remembering a number of relatives in her will.[62] In fact, as an alternate "text" to *Wonderful Adventures*, Seacole's will gestures ironically to all the unspoken ties to Jamaica that are deliberately pushed out of the frame of the narrative. The enforcement of silences in nineteenth-century texts by women of African descent has long been recognized as an important strategy for creating privacy in the lives of women who were denied the protection of domesticity. While Seacole is no exception in this regard, from the individuals mentioned in the will, we can move outward by recognizing that in Panama, she would have been surrounded by other economic migrants from Jamaica beyond just her brother, a detail that would have distracted her white audience from her role in the Crimea. To appeal to her audience, then, Seacole leaves hidden the variety of communities outside of the Crimea to which she belongs and the circuits of Caribbean economic migration in which she participated.

Narrating the moment in England when she tries to join Florence Nightingale's nursing corps, Seacole focuses solely on her rejection by the female aristocrats making the selection. That event, argues Seacole, is what prompts her to finance her own sojourn near the Crimean battlefield. According to Jessica Damian, one of the many opportunities provided by *Wonderful Adventures* is how and what it reveals "about the ways in which gendered socioeconomic capital was acquired and circulated within transnational contexts," especially in the postemancipation British West Indies. Also, both Damian and Jane Robinson bring attention to Seacole's trips to London well before her Panamanian adventure (for example, in the 1820s). Additionally, while in Panama she invests in a mining project, while also selling goods to a much broader set of customers beyond the Americans and other adventurers who frequent her establishment.[63] This kind of enterprise would not have been unusual, since independent women of color had to find ways of earning a living and attending to dependents. Therefore, Seacole's necessary embrace of the Atlantic World's commercial opportunities meant that travel was, in fact, a constant in her life: for her travel and commerce never made her rich but did allow her to support herself. It is all the more ironic, then, that her stated profession as a hotelkeeper gives the impression that she was a fixture in Jamaica's hospitality industry, such that at the beginning of her narrative, her white male customers exercise the privilege of international travel. However, Seacole's transatlantic mobility allowed her to participate in commercial networks not just between colonies and the metropole, but also between and among communities of color beyond the shadow of the Union Jack.

This idea of nineteenth-century free Black women using travel around the Atlantic Basin to connect to multiple economic opportunities is one thing. As Seacole's travel narrative demonstrates, one had to understand and learn to function along crosscutting imperial routes, because failure would have resulted in complete destitution. Chapter 2 takes us back to these very issues, this time from the point of view of Nancy Gardner Prince, a freeborn American traveler and missionary. A contemporary of Seacole, Prince was likewise a widow who seized her independence by way of transoceanic travel. In an interesting parallel, Prince published her *Life and Travels of Mrs. Nancy Prince* (1850, 1853) around the time of the Crimean conflict, and as with Seacole, her book was meant to generate income, proving that for these women, opportunities afforded by travel rarely led to real wealth. For Prince, travel could be a means of escape from dire poverty, but it could also be a reminder of a homelessness that nagged at Black Americans who utterly rejected the racial oppressiveness of the United States.

2. Home and Belonging for Nancy Prince

If *Wonderful Adventures of Mrs. Seacole in Many Lands* emerged from the context of West Indian mixed-race female travel within the transatlantic British Empire, the *Narrative of the Life and Travels of Mrs. Nancy Prince*, published in 1850, revised in 1853, and then reprinted in 1856, similarly sheds light on the complex world of African American women who participated in transatlantic travel, in this case in the service of foreign mission. Parallel to and intertwined with the Atlantic slave trade was the circulation of colonial armies, merchants, and in-animate trade goods, enabling some possible spaces for agency among African diasporic subjects. Agency did not mean freedom from financial stress, especially for Black women living and traveling on their own. Still, as transatlantic networks of evangelical Christianity emerged in the late eighteenth century and continued into the nineteenth, the need for missionaries unafraid of hard work and traveling to the ends of the earth created opportunities for working-class people, Black and white. My interest in Nancy Prince (1799–1857?), a free but initially impoverished Black New Englander, arises from the ways in which her self-authorization as a missionary and abolitionist through travel writing overlapped with larger American and Anglophone West Indian struggles for economic survival. Though Prince and Seacole never met, they crossed paths in a general way: as Seacole and many of her compatriots left economically depressed Jamaica in 1840s for Central America in hopes of economic opportunity, Prince sojourned in the same period in Jamaica's Saint Anne's Bay. Her goals were twofold: she had a great desire to minister to recently freed ex-slaves, and she wanted to assess the island as a possible homeland for free Blacks socially and economically crushed by racism in the United States. But long before she could accomplish any of this, she had to attend to her own family's grinding poverty and the dearth of opportunities open to her as a woman. Ironically, both Prince and Seacole justify their travels by pointing to their usefulness to larger communities. According to *Wonderful Adventures*, Seacole's raison d'être was to sustain and care for the British military (and, through this institution, white Britons themselves). In Prince's *Life and Travels*, however, her service is entirely on behalf of Black Atlantic populations.

Little is known of Prince beyond what she chose to reveal in her deceptively simple *Life and Travels*. Prince began life in 1799 in Newburyport, Massachusetts, a multicultural, mixed-race seafaring community made up of colonial whites, to be sure, but also Native Americans, Africans, and colony-born people of African descent. Though little is known of her father, Prince acknowledged that she was the granddaughter of a Native American woman and an African ex-slave who was a veteran of the American Revolution. When her biological father died, her mother married an African ex-slave and sailor. Acute poverty plagued her family, leaving Prince and her sister no choice but to go into domestic service, while a brother entered the merchant marine. This period of soul-crushing domestic labor finally came to an end in 1824 when Prince married a Black sailor and traveler named Nero Prince (figure 2.1). Employed at the court of the Russian czar, Prince's new husband relocated her to Saint Petersburg, where she remained for almost a decade. Giving the Russian winters as the excuse, in *Life and Travels* Prince recounted returning alone to the United States in 1833. Some years later she undertook two missionary journeys to postemancipation Jamaica, one in 1840 and then in 1842.

Whether in Russia or Jamaica, Prince undoubtedly encountered conditions that enabled particular forms of agency that would not have existed in the United States. These new conditions emboldened her to demand that her opinions be taken seriously, that she receive fair treatment from whites, and that she be given an opportunity to earn a living wage. But these expectations were fulfilled unevenly, in part because of racism and in part because, unlike Mary Seacole, Prince sometimes had difficulty adapting to the new and unfamiliar, even when she was among other people of African descent. As would have been the case with any traveler, Prince's experiences abroad were shaped not only by cultural difference (both in Russia and in a hemispheric context) but also by geographic and material conditions. In Russia, Nancy Prince seems to have enjoyed an unprecedented shift in social status, running her own business as a seamstress, letting out rooms in her home to students, and working for both

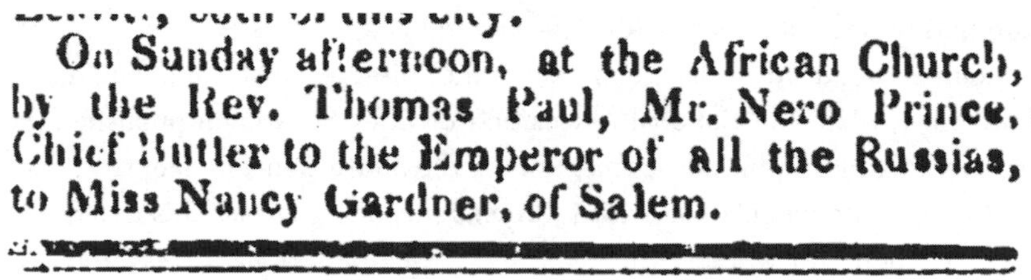

On Sunday afternoon, at the African Church, by the Rev. Thomas Paul, Mr. Nero Prince, Chief Butler to the Emperor of all the Russias, to Miss Nancy Gardner, of Salem.

FIGURE 2.1. Marriage announcement for Nancy Gardiner and Nero Prince in the *Boston Daily Advertiser*, February 21, 1824.

religious and social reform among Saint Petersburg's Protestants. However, according to her narrative, problems seemed to ensue once she returned home to the United States in 1833. By 1840 she had learned of Nero Prince's death in Russia, and in the capacity of respected widowhood she decided to investigate the British colony of Jamaica, in the wake of British West Indian emancipation. She hoped to gather information for African Americans at home about the possibility of emigration to the postslavery British islands and to help lift Jamaican ex-slaves—especially women and children—toward domesticity and a religiously ordered life in freedom.

Her second trip to Jamaica was cut short due to ill-health, yet despite this and other setbacks, upon her return to the United States she was very active in abolitionist circles. Indeed, though she omits any mention of it in *Life and Travels*, there exists an independent story about her passed down to the late nineteenth century by the National Association of Colored Women, that in 1847, after returning from Jamaica for the last time, she single-handedly attacked a slave catcher who had entered a home in Smith Court (a cul-de-sac that was a haven for runaway slaves, since the local residents were all Black). Physically hauling him out of a house, she then led a group of irate Black women and children who chased him out of the area for good.[1] If the story is true, Prince was a reformer who eschewed a life of female forbearance and religious piety, opting instead for a fierce antislavery activism. Her dedication to abolition was also evident at the Fifth National Women's Rights Convention in Philadelphia in 1854, where she protested the mistreatment of slave women.[2] Beyond these public activities, the years after 1847 seemed to have been particularly hard, and Prince apparently never regained the level of prosperity she had achieved as a businesswoman during her time in Russia. Indeed, both her travel narrative and her autobiography might be considered not only as texts that mark her engagement in African American emigration debates and international abolition but also as attempts to earn extra money. After the December 2, 1859, issue of the *Liberator* announced her death at the age of sixty, Prince disappeared from public record until 1894, when the National Association of Colored Women published the recuperative biographical essay mentioning the Smith Court incident.

As represented in *Life and Travels*, Prince's successive quests for social fulfillment as a domestic worker, wife, reformer, self-employed seamstress, and missionary referenced the political ebb and flow of a Black female authority often unevenly and precariously constructed in a variety of political and geographical locations, where disease and natural disasters shaped everyday life, and in relation to networks of male and female and Black and white social power. Along the way, Prince achieved a trajectory beyond her initial life in service and thus redefined her public image through an unending set of negotiations that involved her alternately challenging and embracing specific race, class, and gender norms, conditions of mobility, and patterns of religious authority emerging within and (if we include Russia) outside of the so-called Black Atlantic. Consequently, Prince's story demonstrates how different locations reframed each component part of her identity and how each reframing affected her relations with the communities she encountered. Nevertheless, her manner of textual self-presentation—in both the 1850 and 1853 versions of her travel narrative and in her 1841 stand-alone description of Jamaica titled *The West Indies: Being a Description of the Islands, Progress of Christianity, Education, and Liberty among the Colored Population Generally*—reveals a determination to define her roles within the perimeter of her own desires, even at the risk of alienating herself from those among whom she resided. These tensions emerged through her writing which, rather than providing a textual space to resolve and meditate on issues, reinforced this alienation and the resulting need for total self-reliance.

Clearly, Nancy Prince's shaping of a complex public identity within the confines of wifehood, a female reform tradition, travel, and missionary work challenges us to think deliberately about the gendered history of Black diasporic activism and intellectual engagement among nineteenth-century African Americans.[3] On the face of it, *Life and Travels* addresses Prince's classed and raced subject position as an American-born free Black woman searching for a place to fulfill her potential as a missionary and reformer. However, part and parcel of Prince's struggle to find a (proto)national space that validates her projected self-representation is her active participation in mid-nineteenth-century Black American debates about emigration as the only real solution to racial self-determination. From the early 1830s until the Civil War, free Blacks in the North held a series of conventions in Pennsylvania, Ohio, and New York to address not only the abolition of slavery but also the prospect of emigration.

By the 1830s, the largely white-run American Colonization Society (ACS) had already established Liberia as an official African "home" for Black Americans. However, the fact that Prince published *The West Indies* in 1841, years before *Life and Travels*, proves that she saw herself as a credible voice within the emigration debate and thought that her observations were objective enough to be valuable to fellow American Blacks who, like her, imagined that the key to survival might be to leave the United States altogether. In this sense, her trajectory from New England to Russia and then to Jamaica makes her unique among free antebellum Black Americans, the vast majority of whom lacked both the money and the circumstances for emigration or simply for independent travel.

Though Prince's narrative has a solipsistic quality about it, the existence of *The West Indies* and its later revival in the pages of *Life and Travels* put Prince in dialogue with men such as Henry Highland Garnet, the ex-slave turned minister who at one point in his career advocated strongly for emigration, whether to the Caribbean, Central America, Canada, or West Africa; the pro-emigration minister Alexander Crummell, who later moved to Liberia; the Jamaican-born John Russwurm, who toward the end of his life worked for the ACS and relocated to Liberia; and Martin R. Delany, the early Black Nationalist and sometime emigrationist who sought a destination beyond Liberia. Each of these men worked at some point to extend their political activism through overseas travel, using their experiences in Britain, the Anglophone West Indies, and West Africa as evidence of and object lessons in the particular strategies they urged their Black audiences back home to adopt. Written for related purposes and to some of the same audiences, Nancy Prince's travel texts can also be placed alongside Zilpha Elaw's *Memoirs of the Life, Religious Experience, and Ministerial Travels and Labours of Mrs. Zilpha Elaw, an American Female of Colour* (1846), Mary Ann Shadd Cary's *A Plea for Emigration; or, Notes of Canada West* (1852), and the speeches of Maria W. Stewart, all of which put forth important visions of how African Americans might project themselves into the world, not simply for their own salvation but for the benefit of other African diasporic communities.[4] These individuals did not necessarily agree with one another, but they did take it upon themselves to travel and report on potential homelands. Indeed, Mary Ann Shadd Cary published *A Plea for Emigration* after moving to and living in British Ontario: in what is essentially a handbook for those who wanted to move to Canada, Cary urged her readers to turn away from West Africa for the more healthful (or at least more familiar) climate of Canada, where they would avoid deadly tropical diseases such as malaria.

Additionally, because of her focus on the Caribbean, it is tempting to see Prince's 1856 reprinting of *Life and Travels* in conversation with an attempt by the freeborn Episcopal minister James Theodore Holly to persuade his fellow African Americans to abandon the United States for independent Haiti. In 1854, Holly had been a delegate at the National Emigration Convention of Colored People held in Cleveland. The following year, he lectured on the advantages of moving to Haiti "before a Literary Society of Colored Young Men" in New Haven, Connecticut, making the same case again before audiences in "Ohio, Michigan, and Canada West [i.e., Ontario] during the summer of 1856."[5] To guarantee an even wider circulation for his views on Haiti as a Black American destination, Holly published the lecture in 1857 under the provocative title *A Vindication of the Capacity of the Negro Race for Self-Government, and Civilized Progress, As Demonstrated by Historical Events of the Haytian Revolution; and the Subsequent Acts of That People since Their National Independence*. Whether or not Prince had an opinion about Haiti, in theory her final reprinting of *Life and Travels* in 1856 would have allowed for the dissemination of her opinions about West Indian immigration at the same time as both the Cleveland convention and Holly's lectures in New England and the Midwest. Given that Prince's travel writing enabled her to articulate her evolving identity as a missionary, domestic reformer, and abolitionist, her struggle to articulate "home" testifies not only to the gendered nature of early Black emigration debates but also to the role of women in early Black Nationalism.

We must also keep in mind the ways in which Prince's *Life and Travels* merges with *The West Indies* to reference simultaneously three subgenres: an autobiographical account of her life in the United States, a travel narrative describing first Russia and then Jamaica, and finally, a missionary report on Anglophone ex-slaves in the British Caribbean. Thus, if we go back to the earlier question of how we might read the cultural products of a transatlantic Black diaspora, we can use the occasion of *Life and Travels* to consider Prince's relationship to genres of travel writing that are particularly white, male, and middle class; genres that have been identified as foundational to paradigms of imperialist domination; and genres that traditionally inscribe separation rather than identification between the writing subject and the "other" individuals encountered.[6] Though Prince is no Mungo Park or Richard Burton, how much, if at all, do the features of traditionally male narrative forms leave their trace in *Life and Travels*?

In her work on women travelers, Karen Lawrence suggests that in the nineteenth century, "travel *writing* has provided discursive space for women, who sometimes left home to write home, discovering new aesthetic as well as social possibilities." Lawrence argues that the genre "creates a permeable membrane between home and the foreign, [between] domestic confinement and freedom on the road."[7] As Prince's *Life and Travels* demonstrates, however, "freedom on the road" was not achievable for working Black women who often had little choice but to be away from home, in quite the same way Lawrence assumes it was achievable for white, decidedly middle-class women. Indeed, Prince's autobiography poses instructive challenges to this liberated reading of the female travel writer, since as an autobiography, travel narrative, and missionary report, *Life and Travels* articulates less a sense of uncomplicated female freedom for Prince than a series of unresolved tensions between individual desire and duty to community, between woman as private domestic subject and woman as public reformer, and between the textual image of a Black female missionary supervising Black Jamaican "wards" and a Black American "sister" finally coming "home" to her Jamaican siblings.

As specifically a nineteenth-century Black woman's text, *Life and Travels* engages with "home" not through direct protests against slavery or Black disenfranchisement, but rather through a claim to the status of overseas missionary, a role which enables Prince ultimately to challenge the authority of white counterparts in Jamaica. And yet, what is subversive in one context might not necessarily carry the same disruptive effectiveness in another.[8] It should go without saying that as a Black woman, Prince had to articulate for herself a domesticity forged through a necessary and painful understanding of the raced and classed discourses of power—especially since in the white imagination, African Americans embodied the Other to be "civilized." Yet, Amy Kaplan reminds us that allied with but generally occluded by the "domestic" has always been the "foreign"; that is, nineteenth-century American domesticity traditionally relied upon "a sense of at-homeness, in contrast to an external world perceived as alien and threatening."[9] Prince's deliberate seeking out of a Black Jamaican community speaks to the ways in which her brand of Black female domesticity challenged any binary between "domestic" and "foreign" with the context of diaspora. However, the text never relinquishes a longing for (and therefore rootedness in) "a sense of at-homeness" within US borders and the need to create a Black community—even in Jamaica—based on moral and religious ideals that emerge out of Prince's first, American context. Therefore, while Prince might have seen her reform activities on behalf of Jamaican women and children as championing the rights of ex-slaves over the authority of their British colonial masters, her role as female missionary inculcated the structure of a US-based Black domestic authority that necessarily enforced and sustained a discourse of difference between her and the ex-slaves, a difference that ironically is also reinforced and enacted through her use of subgenres (the missionary and travel narratives) that function as the discursive pillars of western imperialism. Consequently, keeping in mind Kaplan's point, we need to ask how women's own brand of domesticity—white and Black—was deeply intertwined with the rhetoric of nation and empire, at the very moment of an apparent rejection of these concepts.

Importantly, in folding the contents of *The West Indies* into the 1850 and 1853 versions of *Life and Travels*, Prince deliberately reframes Jamaica from a potential site of Black American "home" to one stop on a larger journey from the United States to Russia and then back to the United States. Indeed, the 1853 version of *Life and Travel* does not advocate for Jamaica as a destination after all, suggesting that Prince finally settled on life in the United States. However, the match was as fraught on her return as it had been when she first left US shores for Russia. At the very least, *Life and Travels*, Prince's apparent abandonment of emigration to Jamaica, and her female vision of and responsibility to Black community articulated in the context of transnational mobility require us to think deeply about the relationship of Black subjectivities one to another in the Black Atlantic. How are we to read the balance between the racial unity and cultural difference that structures Black diaspora community? At the very moment that a figure such as Nancy Prince challenged and transformed genres designed to erase her as a Black female subject, should we assume that her struggle for individual visibility within forms of Eurocentric writing would alternately make visible all other Black subject positions within the intersections of histories produced out of New World slavery? In addition, how are we to theorize Prince's dual positioning as a member of the global African diaspora and a figure deeply intertwined with the regional politics of the Black Atlantic?[10] These questions arise from the fact that fully one-third of Prince's *Life and Travels* recounts her nine and a half years in czarist Russia, which was neither involved in the Atlantic slave trade nor connected to the geographic boundary of the Atlantic Ocean. I argue that Prince's engagement with Black Atlantic cultures in the United States and Jamaica is enabled in part by her experiences in Russia, suggesting that "the dialogue of power and resistance, of refusal and recognition, with and against" the presence and idea of a heterogeneous Europe "is almost as complex as the dialogue with" the African diaspora.[11]

NANCY PRINCE AND THE DISLOCATION OF HOME

With its heavily religious overtones and its distressing accounts of poverty and family strife, Nancy Prince's *Life and Travels* is hardly a militant Black separatist statement. However, what Prince shared most profoundly with a number of her Black American contemporaries was a deeply conflicted relationship with the United States as a viable homeland. Whereas David Walker deliberately locates his radical and hard-hitting *Walker's Appeal, in Four Articles; Together with a Preamble, to the Coloured Citizens of the World* (1829) within the larger public debates about slavery, citizenship, and revolutionary discourse, Prince seemingly embraces a more conventional "female" context, choosing to detail personal family issues as a way of commenting on larger struggles. Thus, at the start of the autobiography, the expected genealogical recitation of her childhood family circle centralizes displacement, oppression, and loss but also a resistance against enslavement or confinement of any kind. Prince's story thus encompasses a Native American grandmother who endured servitude under both the British and the Americans; the African grandfather Tobias Wharton, who fought for his freedom at Bunker Hill; and her African stepfather Money Vose, who escaped from a slave ship to enjoy freedom as a merchant seaman, until he was pressed into the British Navy during the War of 1812, finally dying "oppressed, in the English dominions."[12] Prince's matter-of-fact recall of family brings into powerful focus Black and Native American displacement in the "New World" and underscores her understanding of the contradiction of being deemed "free" in a pro-slavery nation. [13] Faced with limited economic opportunities, the death of their stepfather, and the growing mental instability of their mother, Prince, her older sister Silvia, and their brother George eventually join the flow of Black job seekers heading for Boston, their search for employment put into painfully ironic relief by the "migrations" of Prince's youngest siblings to neighboring households.[14] With her accounts of desperate journeys on foot and in open coaches during freezing weather to rescue Silvia from a Boston brothel and deal with a dissatisfied brother who runs away from caretakers, Prince describes a directionless, peripatetic existence that has little or no impact on either her family's prosperity or her personal well-being. In these years, her religious conversion and eventual baptism in 1816 by the Reverend Thomas Paul Sr. stand out as Prince's only moments of solace, though she eventually finds that even her newfound adherence to Christian faith will be challenged by employers who work her almost to death. According to Prince, "after seven years of anxiety and toil, I made up my mind to leave my country" (15), and she abruptly marries the older Nero Prince, a Black American sometime sailor and servant at the Russian court of Alexander I.

As with all things personal, *Life and Travels* offers no details about the courtship of Nancy Gardiner and Nero Prince, beyond the that Nero had been born in Marlborough, Massachusetts, and had made his first trip to Russia in 1810, leaving from Gloucester.[15] It was presumably on a return trip to the United States that, no doubt circulating in what was a small Black community of Gloucester seafarers and their families, Nero Prince met Nancy while visiting her mother's house. Since, according to his wife, Nero had already moved from a sailor's life to that of a servant to Alexander I by the time of their marriage in 1824, his visits to the United States were probably few and far between, suggesting that the couple could not have spent much time together before marriage. Still, whatever the conditions of their acquaintance, Prince emphasizes in the narrative that marriage allows an immediate shift in status from struggling servant girl to European traveler, and accordingly the narrative transitions into what appears to be the traditional "manners and customs" account of life in a foreign capital. Importantly, though she never speaks directly or in any detail about her financial circumstances, her new role as traveler involves a class ascent. Unlike Mary Seacole, whose travels take on a boom-and-bust quality as she makes and then loses money time and again, Prince gives the impression that her new-found overseas mobility takes her on an upward trajectory. (In contrast, once she returns to the United States, though she does not need to revert to domestic service, she certainly has to work for a living as a seamstress.)

While one might argue that Prince's marriage rescues her from American poverty, and that travel at the behest of her new husband enables her to experience refuge in Russia, she is absolutely insistent on establishing her agency in the face of dire circumstances. In both the 1850 and 1853 versions of the narrative, the declaration that "I made up my mind to leave my country" establishes her marriage as an act of individual social and economic survival. Curiously, in the 1853 version she changes the phrase "this country" to read "*my* country" (14; italics added). This change to a personal pronoun in the second version acknowledged an equivocal national identification but also some anxiety inherent in the decision to abandon native place, since the decision was tantamount to abandoning her family. Ironically, her departure from New England seems to support traditional scholarly assertions made about white male travelers throughout the eighteenth and nineteenth centuries. According to Dennis Porter, journey narratives traditionally associated with figures such as Boswell, Byron, and Stendhal "are entangled in the themes of 'the family romance,' foreground the questions of desire and transgression, point to the conflict between the pursuit of pleasure and the path of duty, or waver between sentiments of triumph and guilt."[16] But as a Black woman's narrative, Prince's *Life and Travels* challenges us to come to terms with the different meanings of *home* and *departure* that have resonated in Black-authored texts which traditionally come under the label *travel writing*. Prince's decision to escape through marriage and migration signified an active recognition of the conditions of Black American poverty that brings into vivid relief the kinds of social crises that would drive others (and Prince herself) to contemplate and encourage Black emigration. As a woman's narrative, Prince's autobiography literalizes the effects of poverty and disenfranchisement through dysfunctional family relations, so that the rejection of American citizenship is expressed through the rejection of family. She thus provides a measure of how even those African Americans born and living in freedom in the antebellum North might have experienced national affiliation in the nineteenth century as personal and communal crises.

In keeping with the idea of antebellum free Black families in crisis, Prince previously recounted how, under the abuse of their African stepfather Money Vose, she and her sister Silvia vowed as children "when [we] were large enough we would go away" (8). However, Prince's ultimate goal was not the condemnation of Black patriarchy, but rather an understanding of the constraints and legacies of that patriarchy in the context of slavery. Missing from the 1850 narrative, but substantially amplified in the 1853 version, are vivifying details that suggest Prince's unshakable relationship to and understanding of her own history as the descendant of kidnapped Africans—and therefore displaced Black New World subjects reinventing themselves in partial response to the Middle Passage.[17] In the first paragraph of the 1853 *Life and Travels*, Prince narrates an oft-rehearsed family story about Vose's midnight escape with a companion from a slave ship moored in a New England harbor. The story centers not on the Middle Passage itself, but rather on the final self-willed escape from the ship that has just taken him through that horror: "I have heard my [step]father describe the beautiful moon-light night when they two launched their bodies into the deep, for liberty" (2). Prince's narration of and reverence for this moment signified her embrace of a familial tradition of agency and escape from enslavement that resolved the domestic tensions enforced by Vose's mistreatment of his adoptive American family: within the narrative celebration of escape, Vose took a heroic place in her imagination as the African father offering his children a legacy of self-determination. Additionally, his example ties the children back to their grandfather Tobias Wharton, also an African, who fought in the American Revolution to achieve his freedom. Eventually Prince's brother George embraced sea life, first as a way of supporting the family but later, when his mother married a mercenary third husband, as a refuge from domestic strife. Thus, while her economic survival necessitated departure from the site of her nativity, Prince articulated familial connectedness via the enactment of successful escape.

And yet, if her grandfather Wharton, stepfather Vose, and brother George each achieved a tenuous freedom in the Americas through the male occupations of soldiering and maritime life, what does it mean that as a Black woman,

Prince had to "escape" to Europe, as the wife of a sailor no less, rather than as an entirely unfettered agent? Also, what does Europe as a site of refuge signify in a Black woman's narrative that draws heavily on resistance traditions emanating directly from the African diasporic experience in the Americas? Historians such as W. Jeffrey Bolster have demonstrated that Black men could achieve relative economic and personal independence via a life at sea, and that for early nineteenth-century Blacks as a whole, "maritime rhythms" were thus "entwined in the family life, community structure and the sense of self."[18] Unable to become a sailor herself, Prince married one to take advantage of the full range of mobility denied to her as a woman. And yet, her decision to reject her country also suggests that, despite the economic hardships suffered by all American Blacks in the nineteenth century, the particular site of the United States could not sustain a viable Black female existence, even as it might—potentially—enable a Black male existence in the world of maritime seafaring.

That Prince's escape is undoubtedly an achievement of physical emancipation is signaled by the fact that the narrative itself shifts after the marriage from a story of personal hardship to one of events and wonders in a foreign country. The shift to travel narrative also signals a deepening of Prince's religious rhetoric and transference of agency from her efforts to those of Divine Providence. In apocalyptic language that characterizes much of the autobiography, Prince describes the devastation of a cholera epidemic that carries off 9,255 Russians. Likening the plague to the retribution God visited upon the Egyptians in the Old Testament, Prince clearly underscores her miraculous salvation as one of the Chosen. She achieves a similar effect when she describes her narrow escape from a pit during an earthquake and flood in Saint Petersburg, after having made her way "through a long yard, over the bodies of men and beasts" (21). These stories of desolation in the lives of others shift the focus away from Prince's earlier fixation on her own physical sufferings as a young domestic servant, whose health was broken by long treks in freezing weather to arrange for her siblings' welfare or by cruel overwork in the households of insensitive employers. In contrast, the Russian stories mark Prince's achievement of a new status. Such a narrative strategy bolsters William Stowe's argument that both white and Black American travelers sought "to recast themselves as the kind of narrators, protagonists, and travelers they most wanted to be. Like spiritual autobiographies and saints' lives, travel chronicles attest to certain non-ordinary events, reformulate them to match approved cultural patterns, and depict their protagonists as ideal incarnations of respectable models."[19]

Indeed, Prince specifically formulates a "culturally accredited" voice based on a new role as a respected maternal figure.[20] Though she and her husband have no children, she embraces the role of public mother, taking in young student boarders to constitute a "family" and then rescuing them during a flood, an act of bravery that secures her claims to maternal authority. Eventually she goes into business as a manufacturer of infant clothing, crossing paths with the Russian empress, who becomes a patron and customer. Prince also performs missionary work among the Saint Petersburg Protestants and aids in the establishment of an orphanage in the city. As Prince emerges as both the successful provider and domestic figure that neither she nor her mother nor her sister was allowed to be in the United States, her achievements confirm that the wasted domestic desire of her past can come to fruition only beyond the circumscribed circle of Black American life.[21] Importantly, Prince now offers herself as the distinctly Black, nonaristocratic refiguration of true female domestic morality. For instance, she faults the Russians for being too eager to "pay [the empress] homage, and kiss the hands of that lump of clay" (29). In contrast, as the wife of a court servant, Prince constructs herself as an equally devout but more approachable—and therefore more appropriate—maternal figure. This particular strategy of self-presentation also suggests a decidedly Americanized rejection of monarchy, betraying Prince's ideological ties to a distinctly US home, specifically through the language of domesticity. However, there is a double irony in the fact that as a Black woman, Prince can embody an American ideal of democratic true womanhood only at the moment of self-imposed exile, reinforcing the notion that the revolutionary "America" she represents in Russia paradoxically may have engendered her ideal of womanhood but ultimately cannot sustain it.

In his study of American tourist travel, James Buzard suggests that an idealized Europe functions in many travel narratives as the repository of "culture" and emotional meaning, thereby rendering the United States, the site of the American tourist's original "home," as a place of loss: "Physical departure from one's busily modernizing society could take on the ideological appeal of a temporary, revivifying departure from compromised social existence. Invested with pent-up psychic energy, that which lay across any appreciable boundary (Atlantic, Channel, Alps) could be shaped into a vessel for deferred wishes."[22] As a free Black woman, Prince's "compromised social existence" in the United States translated into severe economic and social hardship, and therefore she is not entirely comparable to the elite white tourists to whom Buzard refers. However, as exemplified by her claim to a female respectability denied her in the United States, Prince presents Russia as a site of displaced engagement with the social conditions of her native land. Only in Russia can her true value be acknowledged. On coming to court, for instance, she is received by the czar and his empress with politeness and respect and is showered with gifts, since the Russians bear "no prejudice against color" (17–18). Ironically, in a text that eventually describes the author's attempt to embrace a non-American Black community, such implicit comparisons between Russia and the United States in fact centralize rather than decenter the United States as a site of denied ambition. This remains especially true because, with its intense class and ethnic divisions and its political upheavals, Russia never fully functions as the alternate site of equality and social justice that Prince seeks.[23]

Whatever her final feelings about Russia, Prince states in the narrative that by 1833 she was ready to return to the United States, pleading the severity of the Russian winter. (The plan was for Nero Prince to follow his wife back to America, but he seems to have died soon after her departure.) When she next turns to accounting for her life in Boston, Prince describes herself as determined to reengage with her homeland on different terms. Still, her successful transformation in Russia raised the question of whether this new persona forged outside of the conditions of her youth can be sustained in the United States. According to Buzard, "[Tourist] travel, like culture, offers an imaginative freedom not as a rule available in modern social life; it encourages the fashioning of special identities, good for the duration of the journey and afterwards—identities privately and intensely possessed, which are congruent with that freedom. And though self-designated 'travelers' may tell themselves that they are *truly* the people they become while on tour, the tour, like culture, fosters this belief inside well-marked boundaries; one must always return home, go back to work, resume the identity by which one is recognized among relatives, co-workers, employers."[24] But for Prince, a return to her slaveholding, racially divided American world means a return to degradation. Thus, the "escape" she achieves in Europe—or, more appropriately, achieves in the retelling of her transformative journey within *Life and Travels*—involves much higher stakes than those faced by middle-class white travelers who traditionally exemplify the name *tourist* in nineteenth-century Europe.

The Russian section of the autobiography focuses most strenuously on Prince's self-fashioning as a public icon of domestic respectability, suppressing personal details (for instance, the nature of her marriage, her childlessness, and her mysterious decision to return to the United States). Such representation links Prince's screening of her private life to similar strategies of self-protection in narratives by other Black women such as Harriet Jacobs, Jarena Lee, and Harriet Wilson. There is a similar lack of detail about her return and her engagement with Black life in Boston. Thus, it is just as important to consider the ways in which the strategy of screening restricts both the audience's access to Prince's private feelings about her American homecoming and any possible refiguration of herself as anything less than the referent for Black female domestic authority. Indeed, Prince speaks mysteriously about her means of self-sustenance, revealing only that "I passed my time in different occupations" (47), thereby sidestepping the material conditions of her life. Instead, she focuses almost exclusively upon her leadership of and work with committees for abolition, the amelioration of Black community life, and child welfare. Consider, for instance, Prince's description of herself upon her American return as instantaneously involved in reform activities. Taking charge as a community leader, she recounts, "I called a meeting of the people and laid before them my plan" for an orphanage (46). In this sense, then, she fashions a narrative that projects as real and sustainable the "special identity"—that of a socially committed, but ultimately solitary, female reformer—that Buzard suggests is possible only "on tour." Emerging at the very moment of her public engagement in charity work, this solitariness signifies a kind of protective disconnection from an American society that hitherto has been the source of emotional pain and familiar disintegration for Prince.

Not surprisingly, the echoes of familial suffering and social dislocation work themselves into the narrative, such as when Prince reports hearing of the deaths of her mother, her sister Silvia, and her former minister, Thomas Paul and of the turmoil in Paul's First African Baptist Church: "The old church and society was in much confusion; I attempted to worship with them but it was in vain" (46). At the same time, her efforts on behalf of the orphanage are thwarted by poor funding and an eventual petering out of support: "I gave three months of my time. A board was formed of seven females, with a committee of twelve gentlemen of standing, to superintend. At the end of three months the committee was dispensed with, and for want of funds our society soon fell through" (46–47). Up until 1840, Prince does take pleasure in being involved in the American Antislavery Society (AAS)—"until a contention broke out among themselves" (47), which leads to a split in the AAS and the subsequent formation of the alternate American and Foreign Antislavery Society (AFAS). Prince's narrative response to the political turmoil among antislavery activists—turmoil that bitterly divides Black as well as white abolitionist communities—is simply to reject both sides. In so doing, she submerges her disappointment in an apocalyptic rhetoric that, as in the Russian section, removes her from contamination by the hypocrisy of her local surroundings: "Possibly I may not see so clearly as some, for the weight of prejudice has again oppressed me, and were it not for the promises of God, one's heart would fail. . . . This power did God give man, that thus far should he go and no farther; but man has disobeyed his Maker, and become vain in his imagination, and their foolish hearts are darkened. . . . The sins of my beloved country are not hid from his notice; his all seeing eye sees and knows the secrets of all hearts" (47–48). This story of her growing alienation from the First African Baptist Church, as well as from interracial abolitionist organizations, makes manifest Prince's sense of American dislocation, such that her repatriation in either Black or white American communities is impossible, even though (according to the narrative) she seems able to assert a new persona as a Black woman reformer. National alienation, then, has been not rewritten but simply removed from the familial context to a more public area of activity. Not surprisingly, in 1840, the year of the abolitionist schism, Prince sets out for a new site to articulate her idealized self-conception, this time as a missionary to newly freed slaves in Jamaica.

Though the text demands that readers move swiftly from Russia to Jamaica, with barely two pages on her life in Boston from 1833 to 1840, some attempt to recover and interpret the silences in the narrative on this moment of failed American communities, Black and white, might help in understanding how Prince's sense of dislocation is tied to her own troubled negotiation of the female authority forged in Russia, but now displaced ironically to the land of her birth. In discussing the failure of the orphanage, Prince chooses not to mention her membership in the interracial Boston Female Anti-Slavery Society (BFASS), with which she collaborated in founding the Samaritan Asylum for African American Children. We ought not to be surprised by Prince's disconnection from the interracial BFASS since, able to neither transcend deep race and class divisions among its membership nor negotiate conflicts about its ultimate goals, the organization fell apart in 1840 "amid confusion, acrimony, and a bitterness that lasted for decades."[25] Prince's declaration in Life and Travels that "I do not approve of women societies; they destroy the world's convention; the American women have too many of them" (51) evidences a clear response to the traumatic fall of the BFASS and is thus a resounding rejection of female community, or at least the idea of interracial female cooperation. At the very least, her charge that they "destroy the world's convention" suggests her ambivalence toward women's activism in general as potentially unseemly or immoral. This is a curious statement, given that Prince works to sustain her European-forged identity as a Black activist and public "mother," and it might speak to the way her ambivalence about women's roles in public now surfaces outside of the particular conditions of Russia, in the different, broader context of US women's activism that included antislavery, temperance, religion, and suffrage.

What Prince also fails to mention in Life and Travels is the other roles in which she circulated among Blacks in Boston before her trip to Jamaica. Though the narrative is unclear about how she supports herself before she departs for the Caribbean, a notice that appeared on October 17, 1843, in the *Liberator* advertised her abilities in "dress and cloak-making, pantaloon-making [and] boys clothes," so one can assume that when in need, she fell back on her skills as a seamstress. Another advertisement in the March 8, 1839, *Liberator* announced a lecture "to be delivered by Mrs. Nancy Prince on the manners and customs of Russia," with an admission price of twelve and a half cents, suggesting that Prince was clearly working (understandably, since she was a self-supporting widow) to derive material benefit from her experience as a world traveler. Frances Foster has suggested that the preface to Prince's revised 1853 narrative explicitly decried any desire for notoriety, demonstrating that Prince "was very careful to establish herself as a respectable woman" who "eschewed publicity."[26] Yet, the fact that the autobiography recorded her reform activities but not a public lecture she delivered on her travels to Russia, complete with an exhibition of drawings depicting Russian cities, suggests not so much that Prince avoided publicity but that she was judicious in what kind of public image she sought to create. Prince's willingness to speak in public bears comparison to three of her contemporaries, the women preachers Jarena Lee and Julia Foote and the political speaker Maria W. Stewart. Lee and Foote earned the ire of the Black religious patriarchy, while Stewart's militant call for Black political empowerment made her unpopular with some Boston Blacks. However, Prince's lectures on Russia took place in Jehiel C. Beman's African Methodist Episcopal Zion Church, and since Beman would later lead the primary opposition against Foote, Prince's public appearance seemed to have been sanctioned by male community leaders.[27] One could speculate, then, that Prince herself might have experienced her return to African American community life not simply as a return to economic struggle, but also as a constant negotiation of her role as an independent-minded female activist, among a Black patriarchy that placed restrictions upon Black women's agency. Since in *Life and Travels* Prince seems to suggest that there is a greater freedom for Black female self-making abroad, it is not surprising that, after brief but disturbing references to disunity and alienation, she quickly moves to her sojourn in Jamaica.

Prince's stubborn commitment to the superiority of her own judgment compares in many respects to a similar belief in personal righteousness expressed by Black itinerant women preachers such as Lee, Foote, Stewart, and later Amanda Berry Smith, all of whom defied male figures of authority and institutional structures in the belief that their resistance to social control was an expression of God's will. Foote and Smith served as overseas foreign missionaries, convinced that their calling was global. All of these women published personal narratives outlining their spiritual growth, experiences, and travel. According to Claire Midgley, even within the male-dominant mission movement in Britain, there was an increasing interest in similar autobiographical texts by Christian white women who felt compelled not so much to preach as to serve and assist in foreign missions, alone if necessary, and even, in some cases, to die trying.[28] In light of this fact, one could argue that the works of Prince, Lee, Foote, Stewart, and Smith belong to a particular transatlantic tradition of religious autobiography among women whose sense of divine empowerment exceeded the traditional restraints of social norms.

PRINCE, MISSIONARY WORK, AND JAMAICA
AS A POTENTIAL HOME

In discussing her account of Jamaica, modern commentators generally focus on how Prince's representations subvert European ethnographic travel narratives that highlight the alien Other by rigorously refusing to distance or silence West Indian ex-slaves.[29] Yet, the Jamaican section is important not only for its use, revision, or appropriation of conventions of the nineteenth-century ethnographic narrative but also because it represents a narrative struggle for the extension of Prince's complex self-transformation that began in European exile. Her travel writings are clearly also an engagement with antebellum Black anxieties about home, social status, migration, and freedom. Indeed, once she incorporates *The West Indies* into the plot of *Life and Travels*, Jamaica rapidly becomes the site of compromise: neither the North American world where Prince suffers indignities as a member of the underclass nor the European world where she rehearses a displaced dialogue with the United States, Jamaica functions as an idealized New World community where the public persona Prince constructed for herself in Russia might in theory thrive within the boundaries of the Black Atlantic.[30] For those free Blacks who considered migration to the West Indies, Central America, Canada, or West Africa, this desire to thrive in every sense in a non-US Black community was a constant, even for those who could not afford the costs of relocating.

Prince's reform work in Jamaica offers her the chance to bypass both the narrow local politics of American abolitionists and potential Black anxieties about women's public roles, thereby allowing her to place herself within the context of an international antislavery campaign bringing together Britons and Americans. Despite her documented involvement within the US abolitionist movement, Prince's narrative never articulates an aggressive pro-abolitionist stance. Instead, her dedication to abolition finds its expression through a personal desire to "aid, in some small degree, to raise up and encourage the emancipated inhabitants, and teach the young children to read and work, to fear God, and put their trust in the Savior" (50). Though quite modest, her prose echoes the exuberant tones of the ex-slave turned minister Henry Highland Garnet, who declared at an American celebration of West Indian emancipation: "It is the distant voices of the freeborn souls have brought me hither—it is the shouts of the islanders of the sea, that come careening upon every wave that rolls westward. . . . And if these blessings are not *immediately* ours, they are *remotely*. The light which the present epoch of English history shall display among 'ocean's golden isles,' shall reflect over all the dark places of the earth—the dungeons of cruelty—the prison houses of despair, and the tombs of buried rights, shall be illuminated by it."[31] In projecting West Indian emancipation as a hemispheric wave of the future, Garnet speaks in palpable terms about a possibility that many Black Americans had already abandoned. It may well be, then, that such sentiments also motivated Prince to travel to Jamaica in 1841, to see and experience life in the absence of chattel slavery. Probably for the same reasons, postemancipation Jamaica proved to be attractive to many other Black Americans, including Garnet himself, who lived there as a missionary from 1852 until ill-health required his return to the United States; the ex-slave abolitionist and minster Samuel Ringgold Ward, who lived there from 1855 until his death ten years later; and Frank J. Webb, the freeborn author of the 1857 abolitionist novel *The Garies and Their Friends*, who was the island's postmaster from 1858 until 1869. In choosing Jamaica as a destination, therefore, Prince was one of a number of reformers who, temporarily or not, had decided to experience "the blessings" of emancipation firsthand, even if it meant abandoning the United States.[32]

As a stand-alone work, *The West Indies* also locates Prince in the category of transatlantic Black abolitionists in dialogue with distinguished white British counterparts such as James Armstrong Thome and Joseph Horace Kimball, who in 1838 published *Emancipation in the West Indies: A Six Month's Tour in Antigua, Barbadoes, and Jamaica, in the Year 1837*; Joseph Sturge and Thomas Harvey, who published *The West Indies in 1837; Being a Journal of a Visit to Antigua, Montserrat, Dominica, St. Lucia, Barbadoes and Jamaica* in the same year; and the Baptist minister James Phillippo, who published *Jamaica: Its Past and Present State* in 1843. Produced in the wake of British emancipation, such narratives provided eyewitness accounts of the truth about Black freedom, so as to discredit "those Americans who had anticipated chaos and economic ruin as the end result of emancipation" as well as to bear witness to atrocities perpetrated by ex-slaveholders.[33] Thome, Kimball, Sturge, Harvey, and Phillippo were variously authorized by their affiliation with British abolitionist and missionary organizations and as white *men* who were already well known not only in metropolitan Britain but also among reformers in the United States. Prince, of course, had neither their name recognition nor their institutional connections, yet she still claimed the right to participate in shaping the public verdict regarding the outcome of British West Indian abolition. Therefore, her texts place her squarely in the middle of an interracial, transatlantic reform discourse, even as they link her to US Blacks struggling for their own survival. This latter connection creates a sense of urgency for Prince, since her role is not as observer, but rather as one of the dispossessed.

Just as British abolitionist investigators do in their texts, in her autobiographical text Prince makes the rounds of Jamaica's jails, churches, schools, and local markets, offering her eyewitness testimony and reporting on her conversations with British clergymen, ex-slaves, colored Jamaicans, and the local American consul. She supplements her narrative with reports on West Indian flora, fauna, and climate. Here she borrows directly from Richard Brooks's *London General Gazetteer*, a popular reference work dating back to 1762 that went through numerous reprintings into the nineteenth century and was available on either side of the Atlantic. By distilling information available in the *General Gazetteer*, Prince maintains the circulation of basic scientific and geographical information, contextualized against her own strong views of what progress had been made since emancipation, to would-be African American emigrants who might still lack knowledge about the Caribbean. Clearly, despite Prince's eventual rejection of American community, in form and content the Jamaican portion of the narrative indexes her connectedness to the free Blacks in the United States. Therefore, *Life and Travels* forestalls the loss of her traveler's identity, buttressing it instead through her role as social and religious investigator for and eyewitness to still-evolving Anglophone Caribbean emancipation.

Yet, while Prince's decision to go to the West Indies set into motion another self-transforming journey, by the time she first published her *Life and Travels* in 1850, Jamaica had ultimately failed as a neutral site, precisely because the island's location at the intersection of Euro-American slavery and abolition enforced social and cultural conditions that could not be left behind in Boston. This failure occurred on two fronts, the first of which was personal. According to the narrative, Prince was recruited for missionary work in Jamaica by white American Congregational missionary David Ingraham. Ingraham had traveled to Jamaica for health reasons in 1837, and during trips back to the United States he had generated great interest among would-be missionaries. Although the Anglophone West Indies already had a strong network of British-based missionary organizations, most prominently the British Baptists, in 1839 five Congregationalist ministers from Oberlin College, accompanied by their wives, set up a series of missions in Jamaica, all of which were supposed to be entirely self-sustaining. Located primarily in the hills above Kingston, these were the missions Prince set out to join in 1840.[34] It is worth asking in what capacity Ingraham and his colleagues imagined Prince would serve among the Congregationalists. For American missionaries, the issue of whether single white women should be allowed to serve abroad was still unresolved. In 1816 the US-based Board of Foreign Missions approved the widowed Mrs. Charlotte H. White's application to serve as a missionary in Burma, but she would have been expected to work in conjunction with her fellow white American male missionaries and their families. According to R. Pierce Beaver, "the first single woman, not a widow, sent overseas" was the ex-slave Betsy Stockton, who accompanied a white missionary family to Hawaii in 1823, in the capacity of domestic servant. In her earlier employment as a maid to the president of Princeton University, Stockton had been allowed the use of her employer's library, and by the time she arrived in Hawaii, she was allowed to set up her own school. But when the missionary's wife fell ill, Stockton had to return to the United States, suggesting that her role as domestic servant superseded her role as missionary teacher.[35]

We do not know whether Ingraham saw Prince's recruitment as a means of securing "domestic" help for his brothers and sisters struggling in the field. By 1840, the American Congregational missionaries in Jamaica were reduced to slender resources, existing in "distressing circumstances" and no doubt reaching out for whatever help might have been procured for them.[36] As the historian Gale L. Kenny reports, Prince did spend some time employed as a teacher under the British Baptist minister Thomas Abbott, in his Saint Ann's Bay Church. However, when she attempted to correct the theological misunderstandings of her ex-slave charges, their complaints prompted Abbott to fire her.[37] Certainly among the white Baptist missionaries, then, Prince was not a respected figure. Did the American Congregationalists from Oberlin regard her as occupying a lowly state like that of Betsy Stockton in Hawaii? If so, then her claim to the stable middle-class persona achieved in Russia would have been severely undermined. Might Jamaica have become simply another site of displaced struggle between Prince and US conditions of disenfranchisement?[38] Regardless of what actually happened, within and through her narration of Jamaican experiences, Prince clings to the imagined power of a transformative Black diasporic community and makes no reference to her status relative to the island's white American or British missionaries. Rather, she consistently represents herself as a free agent on the island, unfettered by organizations and associations, mixing without restraint within her Black community.

In contrast to the Russian portion of her narrative, Prince bypasses the "customs and manners" descriptions that might have rendered the Jamaicans racial and cultural aliens and instead launches an attack on what she sees as a corrupt British Baptist missionary system, with its selling of Bibles at inflated prices, its issuing of membership tickets to enable the efficient collection of the ex-slaves' hard-earned cash and its establishment of a church resembling "a play house [rather] than a place of worship" (51). As the self-appointed spokesperson for the downtrodden ex-slaves, Prince's own judgments appear to be validated by the Black free persons themselves, who dubbed the British missionaries "macroon hunters" (53) after the popular name for Jamaican coinage of the lowest denomination. In defiance of both the British public and Americans at home, who were skeptical of emancipation, Prince bears witness to the industry of Black freeholders in local marketplaces, citing their desire "to possess property" and their ability "to take care of themselves" (54). And, as in both Russia and the United States, Prince's maternal concern for the welfare of destitute girls and children—referencing so poignantly her early family history—becomes part and parcel of her campaign of moral intervention. The apparently uncomplicated community relations that were repeatedly unachievable in Boston appear to be made manifest in Jamaica, specifically in the easy relationship Prince describes between herself and ex-slaves drawn together by a common experience of racial discrimination and by a mutual recognition of the need for Black self-determination in the face of white oppression.

It is precisely in this role as domestic guardian that Prince chooses both to resist white attempts to make her a subordinate and to articulate her solidarity with the ex-slaves. For instance, in one incident that occurs immediately upon her arrival in Jamaica, Prince describes her disembarkation in Saint Ann's Bay: "My intention had been to go directly to Kingston, but the people urged me to stay with them, and I thought it my duty to comply" (50). This is indeed the moment when Prince crosses paths with the British Baptist missionary Thomas Abbott, who hires her as a teacher while also arranging lodgings for her with a Jamaican ex-slave class leader. According to the practice of British missionaries, the class leader would have been a convert from the ex-slave population. However, after spending time with this woman, Prince is appalled by her unorthodox interpretation of Christianity. Equally indignant at the Jamaican woman's authority over her sister from America and irate at a threat of dismissal "unless I would yield obedience to this class-leader," Prince confronts Abbott: "I told the minister that I did not come there to be guided by a poor foolish woman. He then told me that I had spoken something about the necessity of moral conduct in church members. I told him I had, and in my opinion, I was sorry to see it so much neglected. He replied . . . that he hoped I would not express myself so except to him; they have the gospel, he continued, and it let them into the church" (51).

The ironic tensions of this moment emerge on several levels. Certainly Prince's anger serves as an indictment of Abbott for neglecting to educate the ex-slaves as to the requirements of Christianity. In her view, the class leader's ignorance reflects the inadequacy of the British Baptist mission and therefore the necessity of her presence as the Black American better able to address the needs of the ex-slaves. But in order for Prince to reinforce her image as the real moral authority on the island, no matter her racial or class status, her assertion of superiority absolutely has to extend over the class leader as well. While Prince achieves here in *Life and Travels* a strategic act of narrative figuration that reverses racialized power relations between herself and Abbott, how are we to assess Prince's equally necessary erasure of the Jamaican class leader as a reinterpreter of European missionary teachings? As historians Mary Turner and Philip Curtin have argued, Jamaican ex-slave converts within British missionary institutions ably negotiated their own power plays with the missionaries, and according to Curtin, they brought certain Christian practices in line with already existing African-derived religious beliefs.[39] As illustrated by this scene, Prince undoubtedly witnesses such complex negotiations but clearly misreads them as signs of a growing waywardness among the ex-slaves. But in so doing, she denies Black Jamaicans religious agency even as she battles with white Baptists she regards as corrupt. Though always conscious of the need for racial alliance with the ex-slaves, and of her own relative lack of education, Prince nevertheless appears at these moments of misinterpretation to resemble, through her own problematic negotiation of authority, the white missionaries she sets out to oppose.

There is further irony in that the Jamaican class leader's desire for authority mirrors Prince's own desire for autonomy and recognition, both in Boston and now in the presence of the British missionary Abbott. Prince implies that the white missionaries are, by birth and race, outsiders to the ex-slave community. Yet, though she shares a racial alliance with them, her identity as freeborn and American also renders her an outsider to the Black Jamaicans, a situation that bears unsettling similarities to Prince's inability to reintegrate within Boston's communities after her time in Russia. Her challenge to white male authority, then, unexpectedly complicates Prince's self-framing as a Black woman reformer, because of the power exerted by the politics of location. Yet despite such encounters, Prince never wavers in her desire to provide both education for Jamaican Blacks and relief for destitute women and children. On July 20, 1841, she returns to the United States to raise funds for a Jamaican school (figure 2.2), and less than a year later, in April 1842, she comes back to the island with money obtained from donations as well as from her savings. However, widespread civil unrest almost upends her plans. Prince then identifies her greatest enemies as "these people that I had hoped to serve"—presumably the white American Congregationalist missionaries. She describes them as "much taken up with the things I had brought[;] they thought I had money, and I was continually surrounded; the thought of color was no where exhibited, much notice was taken of me. I was invited to breakfast in one place, and to dine in another, &c. A society was organized, made up of men and women of authority" (64). She is especially enraged when the American missionaries seek her approval for a constitution, the fourth article of which reads, "As we have designed to take care of our sister, *we the undersigned will take charge of all she has brought*" (65). A few sentences later, Prince relates that she gave goods to one missionary, the Reverend J. S. O. Beadslee: "I also gave to others, where they were needed, which receipts and letters I have in my possession. Notwithstanding all this, they made another attempt to rob me" (66).

Struggling since their arrival in 1839 to support themselves on contributions from the equally impoverished local population, the American missionaries would have been in dire financial straits by 1842. (Indeed, the support of a foreign mission to Jamaica was considered to be an unusually expensive affair.)[40] Additionally, the American missionaries had arrived at a moment when the transition from enslaved to free labor saw freed people anxious to farm their own humble plots, rather than continuing to work for their old masters. At the same time, these old masters were unwilling to pay wages to men and women whose labor they had previously taken for granted. Though slave labor on sugar plantations had been supplemented by a small number of indentured workers from India and China before 1834, the supply of such workers increased tenfold after emancipation. But much to the detriment to the ex-slaves who had left the plantations, this emigration increase coincided with a series of droughts, which wrecked possibilities for many small famers. Given that their old plantation jobs had been taken over by imported contract workers, ex-slaves struggled for their economic survival. To make matters worse, the British dropped their protections for West Indian sugar, thereby ensuring widespread economic depression in their Caribbean colonies. By 1840, many Jamaicans of African descent had no choice but to move to Panama to work on an American-sponsored railroad project. Not surprisingly, then, those ex-slaves who were left behind

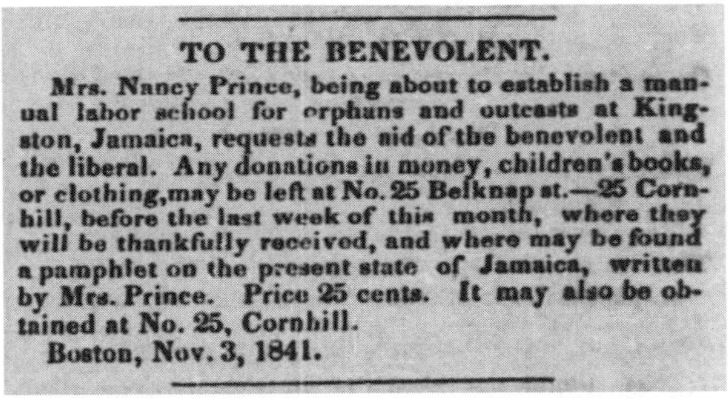
TO THE BENEVOLENT.

Mrs. Nancy Prince, being about to establish a manual labor school for orphans and outcasts at Kingston, Jamaica, requests the aid of the benevolent and the liberal. Any donations in money, children's books, or clothing, may be left at No. 25 Belknap st.—25 Cornhill, before the last week of this month, where they will be thankfully received, and where may be found a pamphlet on the present state of Jamaica, written by Mrs. Prince. Price 25 cents. It may also be obtained at No. 25, Cornhill.

Boston, Nov. 3, 1841.

FIGURE 2.2. Nancy Prince's fundraising appeal in the *Liberator*, November 3, 1841, in support of the Jamaican school for ex-slaves. The appeal continued for at least two more years.

had very little to spare for the sustenance of American Oberlin missionaries. Under these circumstances, the latter's eagerness to take possession of Nancy Prince's resources was, if not entirely excusable, at least understandable. Yet their response clearly heightened Prince's complex struggle to locate sites of community that did not manifest the class and racial hierarchy she so desperately wanted to leave behind. In this particular instance, Prince stood as a Black woman paradoxically empowered by her economic resources, voicing moral outrage at the selfishness of a white missionary class that, even in destitution, attempted to enforce old patterns of racial subjugation. In this sense, Prince's lament about being betrayed by "these people that I had hoped to serve" suggests a definition of "service" that establishes her absolute equality with the white missionaries. At the same time, however, the incident highlights the political conditions of transnational social involvement that had to be resolved before Prince could achieve her goal to be the ideal of the Black social reformer.

Prince's sense of confusion and disappointment only increases when, in these very sections describing her falling out with the white American missionaries, she intersperses equally disheartening evaluations of the Black Jamaicans themselves. Though she remains staunchly supportive of West Indian emancipation, she narrates abuses perpetrated upon the ex-slaves by the privileged mulatto children of former slaveholders. Even as her narrative subdivides the Black population in order to locate, based on color and class, the real community for her labors, she comments (at the same time that she condemns the white missionaries) that the "people are full of deceit and lies, this is the fruits of slavery, it makes master and slaves knaves" (65). Last but not least, she condemns the ignorance of yet another female ex-slave class leader: "This poor deluded creature was a class leader in the Baptist Church, and such is the condition of most of the people: they seem blinded to every thing but money. They are great for trade, and are united in their determination for procuring property, of which they have amassed a vast amount" (66).

In addressing her return to Jamaica, Prince's *Life and Travels* fails as a coherent text—indeed, her accounting of betrayals and disheartening encounters revolves more around her discouragement with the general scene on her return than with the particular guilt of either the missionaries or the ex-slaves. The resulting confusion suggests unresolvable conflicts between the intricate local politics of color, class, religion, and culture that structures Jamaican postemancipation society and Prince's need to find a Black community that enables the survival of her transformed identity as a Black woman reformer. What is painfully obvious is that the detachment Prince cultivated in Russia has now given way completely in the face of her palpable disappointment at the failed search for community, either among an emergent free Black population or among white Christian philanthropists. No wonder, then, that in her 1841 *The West Indies*, Prince takes pains to record the words of the American consul in Kingston: "[It is] a folly for the Americans to come to the Island to better their condition; he said they came to him everyday praying him to send them home. He likewise mentioned to me the great mortality amongst the emigrants." Her last words in the 1841 pamphlet condemn the idea of Black American migration to Jamaica: "The colored people of these United States are induced to remove to Jamaica, in consequence of the flattering offers made to them, to induce them to emigrate. Since my return they have been inquisitive to learn from me something respecting the place, and the people I have been among. For these inquiries, I have written this book, that they may have the advantage of what information I have collected, and knowing the truth, they may no longer be deceived."[41]

Expanding on her visit to Jamaica in *Life and Travels*, Prince reinforces her negative comments on Black American immigration to the island. No doubt this view gains further support in the context of her disillusioning experience during her second visit, providing evidence of the difficulties of life for Black Americans in Jamaica. Ironically, Prince concludes the narrative of her disastrous second voyage with the prayer that "with her liberty secured to her, may she [Jamaica] now rise in prosperity, morality, and religion, and become a happy people, whose God is the Lord" (67). However, even at the end she still harps on the corruption of the British Baptists, whose Black "communicants are so ignorant of the ordinance, that they join the church merely to have a decent burial" (76). It is significant, then, that in the autobiography Prince ends her discussion of Jamaica by reversing her narrative stance toward the island and its Black inhabitants to one that is detached, impersonal, and at times even tending toward a condemning bitterness, as if to signal a final, demoralizing recognition of her failed hopes. The narrative itself ends soon after, with Prince's harrowing journey back to the half-slave, half-free United States and her negotiation of economic uncertainty as a free Black woman.[42]

Despite the keen sense of emotional disappointment and betrayal from American missionaries and Jamaican ex-slaves alike, Prince records one endearing memory in her *Life and Travels* that provides both herself and her readers with a curious image of successful diaspora community that belies the reality of intraracial strife and allows for the ideal of resistant Black agency. At the same time she despairingly and angrily relates the negative encounters of the second voyage, Prince mentions the 1841 return of Maroons who had been deported to Sierra Leone in 1795 for their defiance of British authorities. Undoubtedly aware of their origins as fierce and independent descendants of slave rebels, Prince comments, "They had not forgot the injuries they had received from the hands of man, nor the mercies of God to them, nor his judgments to their enemies. Their numbers were few, but their power was great; they say the island, of right, belongs to them" (63). Prince might well have been aware of their return to Jamaica before she left the island in 1841 to raise money for her school. However, she mentions their arrival out of temporal sequence, during the account of her failed second trip in 1842. The effect suggests a salvaging of her Jamaican expedition through the vision of at least one Black Atlantic population functioning on the island with a venerable history of colonial resistance, unity, and racial heroism. As diasporic citizens with close ties to Africa who paradoxically achieve a return to their New World place of origin, the Maroons evoke Prince's own transatlantic struggle for acculturation and political identity, a struggle beginning with her displaced African forebears in Massachusetts and her fascination with and reverence for Money Vose's act of self-determination in the face of slavery. The Maroons, of course, maintained ties to an African past, and they immortalized themselves in the imagination of both Blacks and whites by terrorizing European slaveholders in other parts of the Caribbean (especially Jamaica) and in Central and South America. Thus, they are attractive to Prince precisely because they have become figures of heroic exile, apparently able to survive in mobility. Since she declares the Maroons to be the "true" Jamaicans (unlike the now-opportunistic ex-slaves of Prince's *Life and Travels*), their presence inspires her to rewrite Jamaica as potentially still the place of a transcendent Black determination. Consequently, the history figured in their romantic story (versus the current situation of postemancipation Jamaica) provides the imaginative basis of a diasporic connection that suggests the possibilities of overcoming intracultural Black difference and entangle-ments in national frames of antagonism.

After Prince leaves Jamaica, she recounts a horrifying stopover in New Or-leans, where she not only witnesses firsthand the hardships of American slaves but is herself almost sold into slavery. Once in Boston, things are barely bet-ter: "The first twenty months after my arrival in the city, notwithstanding my often infirmities, I labored with much success, until I hired with and from those with whom I mostly sympathized, and shared in common the disadvantages and stigma that is heaped upon us, in this our professed Christian land. But my lot was like the man that went down from Jerusalem, and fell among thieves, which stripped him of his raiment, and wounding him, departed, leaving him half dead. What I did not lose, when cast away, has been taken from my room where I hired" (86). In a sense, then, while one of the last lines of the auto-biography declares rather mournfully that in the United States "we have no continuing city nor abiding place" (87), the idea of the Maroons at least pro-vides the comfort of a utopian site of diasporic resistance, of the procurement—finally—of a Black home.

JAMAICA FAREWELL

This would, of course, be precisely the time when contemporary critics might be tempted to read the Maroons in Prince's text as the "model of cultural self-determination and recreation of local place for Blacks in the New World," when one could argue that, in spite of intraracial difference, the power of Black dia-sporic consciousness enables Prince a moment of relief in what, for the most part, has been a story of disconnection and dislocation.[43] In the words of Paul Gilroy, this moment of relief might gesture toward "the emergence of quali-tatively new desires, social relations, and modes of association within the ra-cial community of interpretation and resistance *and* between the group and its erst-while oppressors."[44] And yet, both for Prince's historical moment and for our own contemporary narratives about Black diaspora, the example of the Maroons speaks as much for the problematic politics of what historian Mavis Campbell has termed a history of resistance, collaboration, and betrayal as it does for cultural resistance in the New World.[45]

However much they were rightfully hailed for their heroic struggles against European slavery, the Maroons were infamous at other moments for their col-laboration with Europeans, all in an attempt to secure their own "local place." Indeed, throughout their early history in Jamaica, Maroon groups had signed treaties with the British and, according to Richard Price, "bought, sold and owned substantial numbers of slaves, hunted new runaways for a price, . . . gain[ed] the hatred of much of the slave population, and in many respects may have deserved their common post-treaty nickname, 'the King's Negroes.'"[46] Even their exile in Sierra Leone was a complicated affair since, once they were in Africa, the British employed them "as a military force to subdue" other rebellious New World ex-slaves who had been transported from Nova Scotia.[47] It is understandable that in Prince's reading, the Maroons must be romanticized, because she was probably unaware that they signified an alternate history of accommodation and compromise. But while one can appreciate the solace the image provided her, as modern readers we need to think about this encounter between Prince and the Maroons not merely as proof of the uselessness of nationalism as a model of interaction, or as a sign of the transcendent power of imagined Black diasporic unity. Rather, we need to think about such a moment of diaspora "consciousness" as the confluence of desires, anxieties, (mis)rememberings, rewriting, and even representational violations that make such consciousness "possible" or imaginable. My point here is not to attack Prince for her failures of memory, knowledge, or analysis but to demand from contemporary readers a greater awareness of *all* the hidden histories, conflicts, and consequences of a potential racial utopia. Prince's narrative must unwittingly enact an erasure of history, and (almost) of a community of Black people, to create the "imagined community" denied to her in the United States, and indeed denied to her in Jamaica by the very real contingencies of the local.

Nancy Prince undoubtedly felt keenly and protested vigorously against racism. However, just as was the case with her Black contemporaries, this life of protest was contingent upon her own submersion and final investment in a flawed American cultural citizenship, a citizenship constructed and buttressed by the desire for, and complicated denial of, diasporic identity. Thus, Prince's *Life and Travels* is significant not because it is an example of diasporic transcendence, but because it is one of many nineteenth-century narratives that display moments of rupture, moments rife with troubling discontinuities. Ironically, in her efforts to abide in and contribute to the postslavery world of the British West Indies, Prince is overconfident in her objective ability to "read" the ex-slaves, their socioeconomic condition, and their cultural motivations. As noted by Amber Foster, the result is a pejorative attitude toward her racial brothers and sisters in Jamaica that ultimately defines her position as almost alien, relative to a Black community in which she had invested so much hope.[48] Indeed, her return to the United States at the conclusion of *Life and Travels* strikes a grim note, though her subsequent revision and reprinting until 1855 of the text suggest her larger commitment to self-sustenance, as well as full political engagement on the ongoing question of emigration among many Black communities in the United States.

Despite its ending, this is fundamentally not a narrative about "failure," but rather one that dramatizes Prince's negotiation of complex racial and class possibilities that have opened up because of her ability to finance her own travel and so remain relatively independent. Prince encounters in Jamaica an ex-slave population dealing with the colonial conditions of emancipation, *as well as* the paternalism of different British and American missionary groups vying for converts. As an American, she can identify to a certain extent with the ex-slaves, but the colonial West Indies is simply not another version of the United States, and as the text taken from her 1841 *The West Indies* demonstrates, she continues to look on with the eyes of a sojourner, not a resident. Additionally, as a self-declared Black female missionary, Nancy Prince is at once working in conjunction with and in resistance to male-dominated religious structure on the island. She has a sense of racial commonality with the ex-slaves, but that commonality is, if not fully mediated, then at least refracted through the power structures that enable mission work in the first place. Whether she struggles with the British Baptists or the Oberlin missionaries, Prince relies—as they do—on the assumption that her charges must live up to her standards. The difference she makes is in her focus on the instruction of women and girls, a point of view which must have almost certainly reminded her of her early days of familial poverty and her struggles with first an insane mother and then a fallen sister. In many ways, then, even as her experience as a Black American woman creates points of commonality with the ex-slaves, transatlantic abolition, empire, and Christian evangelism necessarily impinge upon and help shape the experience of this commonality.

In fact, with the exception of Mary Seacole, for the figures in *Moving Home*, Christian mission becomes the important site of diasporic encounter. Indeed, Prince's heroic Maroons, recently returned from Sierra Leone, function as one link in the transoceanic chain between West Africa as the eastern edge of the Black Atlantic and New World locations such as Jamaica. The Maroons may have been deported to the British colony of Sierra Leone as punishment, but once there they become settler-colonialists as part of the African diaspora being reshaped by indigenous responses to a related pattern of British imperial expansion, British abolition, and British Christian mission. In Sierra Leone they share space with indigenous populations, with Blacks from Britain and Nova Scotia, and with a group of displaced African ex-slaves whose emancipation tells an entirely different story from those to be found in the West Indies and the United States. If in her *Life and Travels* Prince explored her role as the Black American traveler struggling to engage across class, culture, politics, and geography with Jamaicans, the West African convert Samuel Ajayi Crowther faced a different challenge—that of reframing the meaning of his identity from the category of former slave to that of a Christian Yoruba missionary and colonial Sierra Leone citizen. Indeed, both Crowther's biography and his travels allow us to explore what it meant to be a Christian convert and simultaneously a missionary.

As the next chapter reveals, Crowther's life as a native African traveler and missionary was deeply intertwined with the expansion of the London-based Church Missionary Society throughout West Africa. As a member of this large and powerful organization, he was relieved of anxieties related to financing his travels. Also, unlike the texts of Prince and Seacole, Crowther's travel narrative was sponsored by the society, the evangelical arm of the Church of England. Crowther was therefore expected to surrender any independent opinions in support of larger missionary goals. Additionally, his audience was decidedly white and not necessarily in support of African autonomy. What strategies did he employ, then, both to enable his own voice and to invest personal meaning in travel writing designed to bolster an institutional cause?

3. The Repatriation of Samuel Ajayi Crowther

Between 1807 and 1863, as they were about to begin the dreaded transatlantic voyage to the Americas, over fifty thousand African captives saw their vessels fired upon by the British Navy, then made to reverse sail, and finally forced to discharge every soul, slave or free, at Freetown, Sierra Leone. Hungry, dirty, and undoubtedly traumatized in mind and body, these slaves must have been bewildered at their first sight of the fledgling colonial capital. Not long after, they must have become grimly resigned when they found themselves again herded by men with whips into a European dwelling, this one dubbed "the King's Yard" by their new captors.[1] (Ironically, by 1818 the gate leading into "the King's Yard" would bear a plaque reading "Royal Hospital and Asylum for Africans Rescued from Slavery by British Valour and Philanthropy."[2]) Supplied with food, water, and rudimentary medical care, these so-called recaptives might have had to wait for days, weeks, and even months until the resident Court of Mixed Commission could be convened to decide whether the Africans had been illegally seized for transport via slave ships to the Americas. Each time the court found in favor of a group of incarcerated Africans, the Royal Navy seamen who had made their interception received their share of the prize money, while the "liberated Africans" were sent off to join others of their number scattered among settlements controlled by the Church Missionary Society (CMS).[3] Plied as they were by white missionaries in an entirely alien setting and far removed from their original homelands, many of these traumatized ex-slaves converted to Christianity and otherwise attempted to integrate themselves into the British colonial society of Sierra Leone. Not surprisingly, many remained haunted by the reality of their unwished-for exile, a situation magnified by the differences in language, culture, and history among them and between them and the indigenous ethnic groups who had lived in Sierra Leone long before the British arrived. And newly arrived ex-slaves were in a class by themselves when compared to the Jamaican Maroons, Afro-Britons, and Nova Scotian Blacks who made up the rest of the colony's settler population.[4]

Each arriving group of ex-slaves went through the same experience, settling afterward in Christian-run villages provided by the CMS.[5] Each village was staffed with its own Protestant missionary, who exposed the former slaves to the English language, the mysteries of Christianity, and new patterns of morality governing marriage and rules of conduct for men and women. Though everyone was offered the chance to learn to read and write, former slave men were encouraged to train as farmers or artisans, while women were steered toward the predictable European gender role of housewifery, all in the belief that former slaves would "yield like wax to any impression."[6] This was far from true, since many members of ethnic groups with sufficient numbers (such as the Yoruba) maintained their native languages as well as particular gendered indigenous practices, despite the integration of European cultural elements.

Eventually, in 1839, small groups of these "liberated" Africans set into motion a new dispersal, this time in a voluntary attempt to "return" to their places of origin, beginning first with visits to infamous slave-trading ports such as Badagry, Whydah, and Lagos and then moving increasingly deeper into the Nigerian hinterland.[7] Whereas in Sierra Leone they had been recognized as a distinct outsider class, on arriving at Niger Delta port cities, they heard themselves referred to by local people as the *Saro*, a term derived from the elision of the words *Sierra Leonean*. Ironically assigned an outsider status that seemed to challenge their claim to a preslavery identity, the Saro found integration within some urban centers problematic, in part because residents thought the migrants were simply too much like Europeans.[8] To add further complications, these Saro welcomed the protection of the British, especially the presence of CMS missionaries, who had provided them shelter in Sierra Leone. This seeming embrace of British expansion and British values would ironically create the needed foothold for the European colonial conquest that would be completed by the end of the nineteenth century. And yet, inasmuch as these former slaves were the direct agents of empire, their Christianized, English-speaking children and grandchildren were in the forefront of early West African nationalist movements. Thus, the Saro are often credited as being protonationalists and among the early founders of modern Nigeria.

Familiar enough to Africanists, the nineteenth-century Saro migration is rarely, if ever, considered by scholars of African American studies, even though it fits the general definition of diaspora subjectivity: "to see oneself in diaspora is to imagine oneself outside a territory, part of a population exiled from a homeland."[9] Certainly, since the Atlantic slave trade's dislocation of millions of Africans from one continental land mass to another exemplifies this definition in stark and dramatic ways, the formation and expression of African diasporic identity would logically seem to take shape in the Americas. Scholars have noted the powerful influence of African "retentions" on Black American art, language, religion, folk culture, and music; however, they argue, beyond these cultural imprints, Africa as knowable homeland has by necessity been replaced by the myth of Mother Africa, the symbol of shared origins and shared inspiration, "the great aporia which lies at the centre of our cultural identity and gives it . . . meaning."[10] Whether as a spiritual rallying cry or as a collective of post–World War II nations rising out of colonialism, when Africa does achieve scholarly attention in African American studies, it is usually in tracing the lineaments of twentieth-century Pan-Africanist thought and activism.[11]

And yet, events such as the Saro migration have prompted many Africanists, including the anthropologist J. Lorand Matory, to ask why diasporas are studied as if time has stopped in the homeland. Indeed, as Charles Piot, another Africanist and anthropologist, has argued, what new perspective might be gained if we saw the continent not as the "provider of raw materials" (namely, "bodies and cultural templates/origins"), but "as itself diasporic"? Recognizing the Middle Passage as coeval with enforced migrations on a similar, if not larger, scale on the continent, Piot recalls that in the late eighteenth and early nineteenth centuries, countless individuals were "captured and displaced to other centralized polities within Africa itself," a trajectory exemplified by the early nineteenth-century "liberated" African experience.[12] According to Richard Roberts, another anthropologist working on Africa, we cannot regard the patterns and effects of dispersal in both the New World and Africa as identical, simply because of their "functional similarities." However, any attempt to bring Africa into clearer, coeval focus requires us to "confront the fiction of *the* diaspora as a coherent unit of analysis" and instead pay more attention to the nature and relationships among a multiplicity of African diasporas.[13] In light of these arguments, far from being an incident properly concerning only scholars of colonial Africa, the Saro migration speaks to the intertwined nature of the Atlantic slave trade and the internal African slave trade, while also underscoring alternate experiences of dispersal and exile not encompassed by the Middle Passage. Thus, attention to the Saro migration not only "return[s] Africa to the diaspora" but also offers an additional model for thinking about African diasporic travel in the nineteenth century, with respect to early "return" migration schemes and the meanings such schemes accrued.[14] Again, it is impossible to think about diasporic travel in this period without taking into account the differences made by gendered experience, by intraracial complexities, by location, and, of course, by imperial expansion.

In general, those who study the phenomenon of dispersal have focused on contemporary manifestations, where modern diasporic subjects evoke return only in an idealized sense.[15] In the context of African American studies, enduring cultural transformation born of initial dispersal is almost always applied to the twentieth- and twenty-first-century African diaspora in the Americas, where return has largely been an imaginative gesture. This is not surprising, since literal attempts to recross the Atlantic for the purposes of finding "home" were part of an earlier pattern of diasporic thought and often ended in failure. If we look outside the Anglophone Americas, however, in these early periods, African-born ex-slaves from Brazil and Cuba were able to "return" to Sierra Leone and to principal cities on the Nigerian coast and integrate themselves within areas that were rapidly being colonized by Europeans.[16] Meanwhile, small groups of West Indians were recruited by European missionaries (for example, the CMS and a Lutheran mission in Switzerland) to establish a Christian community on the coast of what is now Ghana.[17] As with the Saro, then, these transatlantic migrants to West Africa were moving "home" to the land of their ancestors or indeed their birth, even as they were moving from one colonial space (the West Indies) to another, where both the cultural practices of the colonizer and the local structures of European control mirrored what they had left behind in the Americas. In the United States context, emigration projects ranged from Paul Cuffee's attempt to transport New England Blacks to Sierra Leone in the early 1800s, to Black American participation in the founding of Liberia by the American Colonization Society in the early nineteenth century, to the rise of Marcus Garvey's 1920s Universal Negro Improvement Association and his unfulfilled promise to move Black migrants to Liberia on steamers owned by association members. Short-lived or unachieved, such projects failed to attract large numbers of migrants, since most Blacks were focused on securing their rights as American citizens. For those who attempted an African migration, the search for "home" quickly devolved into a real-life confrontation with peoples who had supposedly alien cultures, customs, and languages. In addition, the climate, foods, and ecosystems were unfamiliar, and, above all, there were deadly diseases. In the case of nineteenth-century Liberia, large numbers of American settlers were simply devastated upon arrival, having contracted malaria or some other tropical fever while they were still waiting to disembark, causing them to quite literally die upon arrival. On the other hand, those Americo-Liberians who did survive were determined to impose upon local peoples—sometimes through violence—the principles of Western "civilization," all in the name of racial progress.[18]

Yet, while they may have had dubious success in West Africa, especially in the United States and the Anglophone Caribbean these repatriation efforts were extremely important for several reasons. First, though it was always seen as controversial by most US Blacks, emigration to Africa offered a highly visible example of self-determination in the face of racism and disenfranchisement. Second, as in the case of the founding of Liberia and the Garvey movement, emigration was politically galvanizing for a variety of New World Black communities, thereby creating the classic "network among [exiled] compatriots" usually imagined to be a central feature of diasporic identity formation. Third, despite the almost total disenfranchisement of US Blacks up until the middle of the twentieth century, the organizational requirements for supporting (or opposing) repatriation movements enabled new forms of activism among Black men and women.[19] Certainly, toward the end of the nineteenth century, the topic of repatriation was routinely referenced in early African American novels and periodical literature, having become a staple feature in discussions of racial destiny and national identity.[20] Thus, early repatriation movements certainly had profound cultural effects in North America itself, even if not reflected in actual emigrant numbers.[21]

Though the return migration of the Saro intersected with a number of Black migrations from the Americas, the southeastern dispersal of Sierra Leone's so-called liberated Africans offers a very different example of diasporic repatriation and its consequences. Unlike North American or West Indian Blacks, the Saro were not aliens to the topography and climate of West Africa. Also, many had retained or were at least familiar with the languages and cultural frameworks of their preslavery lives. A few were even successfully reunited with lost friends and relatives. Still, given the inevitable changes wrought by prolonged exile and acculturation in Sierra Leone, we cannot presume that Saro migrants were simply reeled homeward to the Niger Valley by an unbreakable cultural lifeline. Rather, complex intraracial, interethnic experiences of affiliation and disaffiliation undoubtedly figured into their experience of repatriation. This would have been occasioned initially by the fact that in many parts of Africa, to quote Charles Piot again, "every village . . . was touched, and most remade, by their encounter with slave raiders and expanding kingdoms."[22] Though the Saro encompassed a Yoruba majority, their numbers included other ethnicities, including the Hausa, Nupe, and Egba. Before captivity, they had practiced indigenous forms of religion or had been converts to Islam.[23] As an initially destitute and displaced population in Sierra Leone, they were expected to abide by European notions of literacy, religion, and dress, not only by the British but also by the immigrants of African descent from Britain, Canada, and the West Indies. Thus, as nineteenth-century West Africans, they were a culturally heterogeneous group in a region of other culturally heterogeneous groups. Many of these ex-slaves had been displaced from community to community as prisoners of war, slaves, and refugees—even as slave traders themselves. Still, despite barriers of language and culture, and whatever their occupations before enslavement, by 1839 evolving local conditions had enabled a number of ex-slaves and their descendants to become merchants. Additionally, as they became Christianized they served as cultural brokers between Europeans and local peoples.[24] Nor did these ties to Sierra Leone diminish when members of this community set off for what is now modern Nigeria. Even though some migrants calculated that the move to Nigeria would afford greater financial opportunities, they left behind neither Sierra Leone nor the European influences they had absorbed.

In addition to the challenge of working out their relationship with other Africans, beyond Sierra Leone the Saro—that is, the Sierra Leone migrants—crossed paths with Cuban and Brazilian Blacks who had settled in urban areas in the Niger Valley. This New World group relocated from the Caribbean and South America at different points throughout the nineteenth century. Indeed, among the earliest wave of Brazilian ex-slave migrants to Nigeria were some who had been born in or were closely identified with the Yoruba, and they vied with the Saro for economic opportunities in the places where they settled. As Matory has argued, these migrants from the Americas worked in concert with the Saro in commercial centers such as Lagos to create what is ironically known today as "traditional" Yoruba culture:

> What came to be classified as Yorùbá tradition fed on cultural precedents in the hinterland of Lagos, but its overall name, shape, contents, standards of membership, meaning, means of transmission, and relative prestige would have been radically different—if they had come into existence at all—were it not for the intervention of a set of diasporic financial, professional, and ideological interests that converged on the West African coast. Returnees [from Sierra Leone and the Americas] converged on Lagos during the nineteenth century and not only composed a novel African ethnic identity, but through a literate and politicized struggle, guaranteed that it would be respected in a unique way by generations of students of Africa and its diaspora.[25]

Consequently, as Matory points out, the impetus for early Nigerian nationalism arose as a result of broadly diasporic influences, influences which both shaped and were shaped by the Saro themselves. Because of the received myths held by many of African descent about African cultural "authenticity," these nineteenth-century forms of African hybridity are not always taken into account, such that primarily Black subjects from the Americas have come to be associated with the cultural hybridity of diaspora.

Still, even as Africanists have begun to argue persuasively that "the boundaries of 'African history'" must "include the history of Africans in the Diaspora" as well as the history of diaspora within Africa, a problem persists in the treatment of nineteenth-century return as primarily a discursive phenomenon shaping the formation and expression of Black identities of dispersal in the Americas.[26] Separate from their literal act of migration, mission-educated individuals among the Saro migrants to Nigeria would also have utilized particular rhetorical strategies to create and recreate continuously not only themselves and their histories but also their interpretation of the social and historical worlds in which they circulated. As the Saro made their mark on the cultural landscape of West Africa, such self-creations would have been necessary for migrants to articulate and resolve the confusion and discomfort inherent in their search for home. But how do we identify the kinds of texts Saro migrants employed to grapple with the meaning of their return? As Karin Barber reminds us, once they learned European forms of literacy, colonial Africans across the continent produced letters and diaries, as well as local newspaper columns and essays on religion, gender roles, art and music criticism, fiction, and even gossip—and the Saro were no different.[27] Much of this writing emerged as individual Saro related their trials and tribulations to sympathetic missionaries and colonial officials or as they went about their business as merchants, teachers, and catechists attached to various European missionary societies. Also, once they began to constitute a new economic and cultural class in West Africa, many individuals felt the need to publicly articulate an emerging personal and community identity. Generally seen as the seeds of a modern West African literary tradition, their texts have been crucial to historians working on nineteenth-century Sierra Leone, West African politics, the internal slave trade, and European colonialism.[28] If we accept the notion that nineteenth-century West Africa was as much a site of diaspora as the Americas, how would Saro writers have articulated both their unique African hybridity and their conditions of mobility, using genres originally designed to create and maintain decidedly European perspectives? How might gender have influenced not only day-to-day perspectives among the migrant authors but also their literary construction of persona, their narrative strategies, their choice of form, and their conceptualization of an audience? Since gender is both a marker of social identity and a widely utilized trope for the articulation of political relationships within same-sex groups, between and among classes, races, and ethnicities, and between national and regional entities, how would the language of gender have informed the representation of intra and interracial relationships created by the act of return and any written commentary on it? At the same time, how would the language of gender have affected the way in which inevitably nostalgic concepts of return, home, and memory were figured rhetorically in Saro texts?

Unquestionably, the most textually prolific Saro of this period—and certainly the most famous—was Samuel Ajayi Crowther (1808?–1891), a former slave who, after being taken to Sierra Leone by the Royal Navy, had a long and distinguished career with the CMS, eventually becoming the Anglican bishop of West Africa (figure 3.1). Born in a Yoruba village to a family of weavers, Ajayi was a teenager in 1821 when he experienced the breakup of his family and the complete destruction of his village by Fulani Muslims, who had come to kidnap slaves. Once in captivity, Crowther circulated from master to master until he was loaded onto a Portuguese ship bound for Brazil. After the Royal Navy intercepted his ship and landed everyone on board at Freetown, Crowther underwent his own "King's Yard" experience, until missionaries assigned him the trade of carpentry and attached him to the household of the Reverend James Wright, a former slave and Wesleyan convert who had risen in the missionary ranks. (The two seemed to have been a poor fit, and Crowther was later reassigned to an Anglican household.[29]) For the most part, after conversion he was educated by the CMS, and as was the case with so many of his peers, he was placed at the bottom of the mission hierarchy in the role of catechist and interpreter. Things changed when he proved indispensable on the ill-fated 1841 British Niger expedition, when almost two-thirds of the white members died from tropical fever. Always obedient both to his superiors and to the goals of the expedition, Crowther ministered to dying sailors, negotiated patiently with local Africans for wood and other supplies, and scrupulously recorded his impressions of the people he met and their attitudes toward slavery and the possibility of establishing a CMS mission at some point in the future. Impressed by his intelligence, religiosity, and skills as a mediator, the CMS supported Crowther's ordination as an Anglican minister in 1843. At the same time, his widespread fame as both a mission success story and an extremely articulate advocate for abolition occasioned a private audience with Queen Victoria, Prince Albert, and Lord Palmerston in 1851.

FIGURE 3.1. Bishop Samuel Ajayi Crowther in 1890, just a year before his death. (National Portrait Gallery, UK)

Some nineteen years later, Crowther rose to become the first Black bishop of West Africa, and in that capacity he worked hard to establish and nurture an independent, indigenous African church, even if at times this meant being in opposition to CMS officials in London. Still, throughout a career that spanned over sixty years, Crowther continued to represent the interests of the CMS on exploratory expeditions into the West African interior. In conjunction with his work as missionary and explorer, he achieved a reputation as one of the leading nineteenth-century scholars of African languages. In 1880, his contributions as an explorer earned him a gold watch and a lecture invitation from the Royal Geographical Society. As the epitome of the cultural broker, Crowther appeared to be the perfect crosser of boundaries. Indeed, the religious studies scholar

Lamin Sanneh has called Crowther "the ideal 'new man,'" one "deeply enough grounded in the old Africa to discern what its authentic values were and yet sufficiently molded by the new forces to be a credible and effective guide."[30]

Though Crowther never expressed a personal desire to leave Sierra Leone in search of his old homeland, as a CMS missionary he was a key figure in the expansion of Christianity throughout the Niger Valley. And, of course, this expansion was occasioned in part by the migration of the Saro and their vigorous encouragement of Christian mission. By the 1850s, Crowther and his family had moved from Sierra Leone to the Niger Valley in an effort to provide religious support to Saro migrants. As a result, Crowther was both a missionary and a Saro "returnee": while the lay migrants worked to make money and expand trading networks, Crowther worked to build new congregations and recruit more Africans for a native pastorate. He also used the opportunity to report on and promote abolition of the internal African slave trade and, of course, effect the Christian conversion of local peoples. Ironically, his religious duties required Crowther to revisit the locales where he himself had endured slavery. Indeed, he was among the few Saro who reunited with lost family members, in his case his mother and a number of siblings. Despite these reconnections, as with his fellow Saro, Crowther had no interest in submerging himself in preslavery religious frameworks. Rather, he hoped to transform indigenous "heathens" with Christianity and European notions of literacy, to supplant traditional clothing with Western dresses and suits, and to replace inland slave trading with the production and sale of agricultural raw materials such as cotton and palm oil—in other words, the "three Cs" (Christianity, civilization, and commerce). Clearly, as with the first Saro who described ambitious plans to reshape what they referred to in an 1839 petition to Queen Victoria as "our Land," Crowther set out for a Niger Valley world which he and other ex-slaves from Sierra Leone were determined to reinvent.[31] Not surprisingly, then, virtually all of Crowther's letters, journals, and narratives, as well as his work as a translator, were shaped by his experiences as a former slave, as a missionary participant in and a witness to the Saro migration, and as a highly influential figure in the new cultural and political world that was inevitably cocreated by slavery, repatriation, colonialism, and internecine conflict among unconverted West African ethnic groups.

In light of such a remarkable life, how do we integrate a gendered analysis of Crowther as both writer and African diasporic subject? The role of missionary was a male category and required rigidly prescribed forms of letter writing, journal keeping, and, in the context of expeditions, ethnographic travel writing. Certainly, first as wives and daughters and then later in the nineteenth century as wage-earning teachers, European women were allowed to operate as missionaries in the field, and therefore some of them maintained individual correspondence with the CMS Parent Committee. However, they are sparsely represented in the nineteenth-century portion of the archive, their letters and narratives often embedded within the papers of male relatives or mission superiors, further underscoring the close association between missionary writing and the construction of a range of masculine subjectivities under colonialism. Mary Louise Pratt and others have convincingly argued that as the nineteenth century wore on, Anglo-European expedition narratives were crucial ingredients in constructing an imperial masculinity by enforcing a contrast between the "effeminate" native and the manly explorer. At the same time, since the language of gender helps to articulate difference in a variety of social contexts, such a narrative form encouraged white writers and their readers to envision imperial conquest via the representation of a dangerously chaotic and fecund African landscape, requiring the order and discipline of colonialism in the form of the plow, the rule of (European) law, and the establishment of European-style trade.[32] What forms of African diasporic masculinity would such literary conditions have enabled or foreclosed for Crowther, who in the mission field took on what seemed, at least, to be roles equal to those of his European colleagues? What would it have meant for Crowther to create meaning for his "return" journey, within a textual framework specifically designed to articulate white male arrival in West Africa?

These issues become even more complicated when we remember that, in addition to the white men in whose company he traveled and the indigenous Africans he encountered, Crowther would have come across Black men from Britain and the Americas, some of whom were missionary agents from other Christian denominations vying for influence in the region. Recent methodologies for gender analysis provided by Africanists Andrea Cornwall, Nancy Lindisfarne, Lisa Lindsay, and Stephan Miescher collectively suggest that in colonial contexts, African men who stood at the intersection of social and cultural change would have been presented with a range of heterogeneous African and European masculine models, both Christian and non-Christian, within their immediate social world.[33] Depending on the politics of cultural context and change, these models might themselves have been flexible and open-ended. In light of this formulation, Crowther's self-construction both within the texts he contributed to the CMS archive and within the tradition of the expedition narrative would have occurred against a mosaic of Black and white, indigenous, European, and Black American models of masculinity. Since their various roles as soldiers, prisoners, traders, peasants, chiefs, religious leaders, adventurers, settlers, colonial officials, and missionaries guaranteed that Africans, Black Americans, and white Europeans would interact on various levels, we should think in terms of permeable and heterogeneous West African and European cultures in transition, cultures continually being reshaped by the demands of religious change, political upheaval, the Atlantic and internal African slave trades, and European colonialism. We might then augment the concept of multiple masculinities by recognizing how the models Crowther would have encountered come to be in cross-cultural dialogue in the first place, and how that dialogue reveals the exigencies of dispersal and return.

CROWTHER AND SARO HYBRIDITY

Though Sierra Leone's liberated Africans never crossed the Atlantic Ocean, their lives were still transformed by the dramatic rupture of enslavement. Even before they were sold into slavery and herded onto ships, many lived through a major political crisis that had reverberated throughout the region starting at the end of eighteenth and continuing into the nineteenth century. Until the early 1800s, a variety of West African ethnicities were subject to the administration of the centuries-old Yoruba Kingdom of Oyo. In 1789, with the death of the *Alafin*, a central figure in the Kingdom of Oyo's administration, the bitter rivalries for leadership among senior chiefs led to civil war and thereby the creation of countless refugees and prisoners of war, many of whom ended up as slaves— either circulating in the mainland slave trade or headed for the slave ships of the Atlantic coast. One of the provisions of Britain's abolition of the transatlantic slave trade was the stationing of Royal Navy vessels along the northwestern coast of Africa, with orders to intercept all vessels deemed to be slavers. As the primary British port on the West African seacoast, Freetown became the disembarkation point for the ex-slaves. Faced with the arrival of hundreds of ex-slaves a year, the British worked with missionary societies to streamline what they all assumed to be a necessary "Europeanization" to transform the newly liberated into a civilizing force for Africa.

Despite the missionaries' assumption that they were helpless victims of slavery, African ex-slaves refused to be patronized, even as some West Indians, Black Nova Scotians, and Afro-British settler groups looked down on them as barbarians. Modern-day historians have lauded the unique hybridity of what has been called Sierra Leone's *krio* identity, a term used to describe the rich and presumably harmonious mélange of cultures that evolved after the establishment of the colony at the end of the eighteenth century.[34] However, by the early 1800s, the hierarchical social structure within Sierra Leone had sufficiently overdetermined relationships among multiple African diasporic communities such that differences in skin color, education, Anglicization, and personal history created substantial rifts, even though among the non-African settlers, migrants had been motivated by the same goals of repatriation. Founded in 1788, Sierra Leone first served as a so-called province of freedom for four hundred or so of Britain's "Black poor," who were considered to have a better chance of advancement in their ancestral home. Then, in 1792, an even larger contingent of Black loyalists who had fought for the British during the American Revolution arrived from Nova Scotia. Unable to return to what was now the United States but unwilling to live in Canada, they had opted to make a new start in Africa. These two communities routinely squabbled with white colonial officials, with each other, and with indigenous peoples such as the Susu, the Temne, and the Mendi. Indeed, the colonists were in a state of open rebellion when, in 1800, over five hundred Jamaican Maroons arrived—relatives of the Maroon descendants Nancy Prince encountered in 1840s Jamaica. As Christopher Fyfe reports, having been lately deported from Jamaica for rebellion, "the Maroons were in good health and spirits," and when recruited by the colony's administrators to help restore peace among the settlers, they were "delighted at the suggestion they stretch their legs in familiar warlike pursuits."[35] Also from the West Indies, a small community of middle-class, often light-skinned and sometimes well-educated Blacks completed this settler portrait. The West Indians had been officially recruited by the British to serve as mid-level officials and clerks, since tropical diseases generally kept the colony's white population low.[36] Thus, the liberated Africans would have experienced Sierra Leone as a loosely coalescing but heterogeneous set of exiled African diasporic communities produced and set into motion by Britain's continuing efforts to create a stable and unified American empire. Without question, there were cultural and political differences among overlapping African diasporic communities, all of which were articulated through the grammar of a hierarchy-bound British colonial system of management.

Ironically, even the Saro's 1839 plan for migration "home" to the Niger Valley had a West Indian connection. In the British Caribbean, 1839 coincided with the end of apprenticeship. No longer bound to their previous owners, two Hausa ex-slaves from Trinidad passed through Freetown en route to the Niger Delta port city of Badagry. So it was in 1839 that three Sierra Leone ex-slaves purchased a ship and set out with sixty-seven passengers on an initial trading voyage, also to Badagry, to scout out possibilities. On their return to Freetown, these "Saro" merchants brought news of tremendous local encouragement and unlimited trade opportunities. The phenomenon of an internal African reverse migration in tandem with the arrival of African ex-slaves from the West Indies speaks mightily to the ways in which many of the Saro, only lately rescued from slavery, reimagined themselves as agents within the larger cultural as well as economic space of the Black Atlantic, reminding us of the multiple worlds of experience created by multiple African diasporas. In this context, we might well ask how terms of identification such as *African* and *West Indian*, as well as *Nupe*, *Hausa*, and *Yoruba*, spoke to different aspects of cultural heterogeneity, rather than to a false opposition between "pure" origins and a cultural hybridity born in the hold of a slave ship.

Viewed as "liberated" slaves in Sierra Leone, they soon recreated themselves as the Saro, by the very act of agentive migration. Additionally, they were identified by Nigerian populations to which they had formerly belonged and by their experiences abroad. As one would expect, these population shifts created numerous possibilities for cultural innovation, but also a variety of alliances and disidentifications. For instance, in contrast to the Saro, Brazilian ex-slave migrants were commonly referred to as the "Amaro," or "those who have been away from home." "Through time," reports historian Jean Kopytoff, the moniker *Saro* "acquired . . . other connotations, some derogatory, as, for example 'mingy,' or 'stingy.'"[37] Adding yet more texture to this pattern, Femi J. Kolapo has recently suggested that such rejections in large urban areas were not to be found within smaller rural communities. Rather, "the minute, daily, local, and short-run" encounters between these locals and Christian Saro migrants sometimes evidenced "a radical variation to the general pattern of conflict." Thus, depending on the local histories of stability or flux, many returnees— even culturally chauvinistic Saro migrants determined to convert their heathen compatriots—were accepted "within preexisting sociological and political frameworks. These were constructs already in use to integrate the different diasporic immigrants or settler groups (with their distinct cultural, religious, and political experiences) [especially] into young settlements."[38] Depending on where they chose to go, then, the Saro might have had a range of experiences that would have affected their "return."

As a "liberated" African, Crowther chose the missionary path instead of pursuing a trade or becoming a merchant. Once CMS officials witnessed his great intelligence and considerable linguistic skills, he was immediately maintained at the expense of the society in its Christian Institution near Freetown (later Fourah Bay College). This blossoming association with the CMS opened up an entirely different community for Crowther, one that was egalitarian under God, with no regard (at least in theory) for color or conditions of birth. Not surprisingly, Crowther married within the liberated African community, eventually dividing his time between his religious studies and raising a large family with his wife Susan. Still, though he was ever devoted to mission work and CMS authority, we should not assume that Crowther had simply discarded the cultural frames that many Yoruba ex-slaves in the colony managed to preserve. He was still fluent in his native language, and as his later translations of Yoruba proverbs demonstrate, he maintained a lifelong interest in Yoruba oral culture. Also, while he was committed to the Christian conversion of Africans, he understood that he had to approach African Muslims with respect, since Islam was well established regionally.[39] This sense of cultural flexibility emerged in other areas, as well. For instance, though he encouraged Christian marriage, Crowther was less distressed by polygamy than were some of his white colleagues. Also, in 1859, the CMS learned what was to them the surprising fact that his wife, Susan, regularly engaged in trading. Since such practices were forbidden among CMS missionaries, she was required to stop her activities. However, as reported by historian T. E. Yates, in an 1861 letter Crowther "assured [the CMS] that Mrs. Crowther had never kept a store, had agreed not to sell cotton or palm oil for profit, but did not 'hypocritically bind herself not to sell at all.'"[40] Traditionally, one of the ways in which West African women accrued assets while maintaining and consolidating their social agency was through the trade of agricultural and household goods. This practice did not stop once female slaves from the Niger Valley were set free in Sierra Leone. As a liberated African herself, Susan Crowther seemed not to have been conflicted about integrating this form of West African gendered activity into her life as the wife of an Anglican missionary. We can assume, then, that Crowther tolerated her activities and that if the CMS had not discovered her additional source of income, she would have gone on, literally, with business as usual. Though Susan Crowther is largely an invisible figure in discussions of her famous husband, this example demonstrates the ways in which Crowther and his family recognized and engaged with a range of indigenous West African cultural norms. At the same time, amid the group tensions in Sierra Leone by the late 1830s, Crowther was ever supportive of a Christian education for ex-slaves.

GENDER, GENRE, AND THE NARRATION OF DIASPORIC IDENTITY

The first time Crowther traveled from Freetown to the Niger Valley was as a member of the ill-fated 1841 Niger expedition. Chosen because of his talents as an interpreter and general student of African languages, his job was to assist the Reverend J. F. Schön, a German native who had joined the British CMS and now served as the chief CMS representative on the expedition. The expedition had been conceived by missionaries, reformers, and British government officials for roughly two reasons: as a way to impress upon Africans the virtues of abolition and as an opportunity to map the upper reaches of the Niger as a prelude to creating European trade routes. Halfway into the journey upriver, the expedition ended in disaster when over 40 percent of its white participants died of malaria. Despite this loss of life, the posthumous journal of the expedition leader was published, alongside the travel narratives of Schön and Crowther, together with latter's 1837 slave narrative. The notes upon which these texts were based had to be scribbled in between attempts to nurse the sick and comfort the dying—and, according to all reports, the dying went on for days on end. Nevertheless, the published narratives by Schön and Crowther outlined the extent of "heathenism" along the river, the suffering of African slaves in the internal trade, and, most important, the largely positive reception of local Africans to the idea of Christianity. Though Schön was the lead CMS spokesman, the compassionate yet clear-eyed and detail-oriented narrative produced by Crowther made an especially strong impact on his readers. It no doubt helped his image greatly that both the expedition narrative and the slave narrative revealed him to be a fiercely intelligent yet humble and unassuming African catechist with whom the British could feel comfortable. This fact, coupled with his universally acknowledged role as an effective negotiator and interpreter, made him instantly famous in Britain among missionary supporters once they read the narratives. Taking advantage of his growing popularity, the CMS vigorously promoted Crowther as the ultimate example of what could be achieved in "savage" Africa, and for all intents and purposes, his became a household name among the society's lay membership at the metropole. Given such public celebration of his talents, it was inevitable that Crowther would be allowed to take holy orders in 1843 and that his presence would be required on future expeditions to the Niger Valley. In 1846, he accompanied two white colleagues to Abeokuta, a large and influential town recently founded by refugees of the civil wars of Oyo, to establish the first successful CMS mission outside of Sierra Leone. Once the Abeokuta mission was put in place, it was followed slowly but steadily by the establishment of others, due in part to the increasing role Crowther came to play as an African representative of the CMS, a role that he self-consciously fostered and in which he sincerely believed.

While the 1841 expedition inaugurated Crowther's journeys of "return," his work as a CMS missionary also put him in the path of another agentive migration, that of the white missionary dispersal effected by the CMS's goals for West Africa. These white missionary men brought their own notions of masculinity, but their goal was not so much to impart these notions to their African subordinates as to shore up their own racial authority as Europeans in West Africa.

Crowther's affiliation with the Saro, with the CMS, and with indigenous groups with whom he made contact during his travels demanded that he create a masculine identity for himself within and against other identities—including, in the case of the CMS missionaries, identities that were dependent, in part, upon missionary writing. The second half of this chapter will be devoted to a detailed discussion of what challenges were posed for Crowther by missionary writing, and then to a careful examination of Crowther's self-presentation in his 1841 Niger expedition journal. The journal itself is a wonderfully hybrid document, functioning at once as a travel narrative and, because it was commissioned by the CMS, as a missionary journal.

Though Crowther authored countless letters and reports throughout his time with the CMS, I focus here primarily on the early period of his authorship, as it was expressed specifically in the 1841 Niger expedition narrative. Crowther's ethnographic eye is much keener in the later narratives, which is why his texts have proven very useful for modern readers who wish to understand the nature and dynamics of precolonial life in Nigeria. However, the 1841 narrative marks Crowther's first attempt to write an extensive document for a white metropolitan audience, thereby calling into being that confident and engaging voice the scholar Jacob Ajayi has found so impressive. Indeed, the 1841 narrative offers a unique perspective on how Crowther originally set about deploying a European genre to articulate an evolving, mobile African masculinity in the midst of representing his first gestural "return" to an "original homeland."

In his consideration of how native agents of the CMS might have inhabited missionary genres, J. D. Y. Peel has argued persuasively that the mandatory journals kept by African clergy should be seen as "narrative representations of life," fully plotted, with the African-born missionary especially and necessarily present within the scene, rather than as an omniscient, disembodied observer.[41] According to Peel, African missionaries such as Crowther "were both insiders and outsiders to the society they were writing about [and] they show an intense awareness of the narrative implications of [Christian] mission."[42] Rather than seeing such genres as an imposition, Peel writes, native missionaries fully integrated them into their daily lives, as part of an ongoing process of cultural accommodation. According to Peel, "Narrative empowers because it enables its possessor to integrate his memories, experiences, and aspirations in a schema of long-term action. The more potent narratives have the capacity to incorporate other agents, so that they become accessories to the authors of the narratives. To the extent that (for whatever reason) narrative cannot be achieved, agency or self-motivated action—the hinge between the past of memory and the future of aspiration—becomes impossible." In arguing that missionary writing by Africans functioned discursively to envision and enact at least a narrative resolution of their experiences, Peel implies that, rather than being an "alien" genre which had to be "appropriated" and subverted, the journal format proved to be a malleable form. Consequently, for liberated Africans who became agents of the CMS, the journal could thus function as a means of resolving the disjuncture created by exile and return through the very process of narrative. At the same time, Peel reminds us, African Christians "were even more saturated with Biblical language and imagery than the Europeans," so that the infusion of religious language within these journals would not have been burdensome.[43]

Still, despite their real investment in and facility with the missionary journal, the resulting textual appropriation by native missionaries must be understood in terms of the ways missionary writing in general was constructed by the CMS Parent Committee in London. Within the mission field, all CMS missionaries, whether they were African or European, were required to communicate directly with the Parent Committee on a regular basis via letters and journals. Generally, letters reported on a wide range of events or needs in the life of a mission. For example, the author might describe the behaviors, illness, or death of European colleagues, ask questions about staffing, report on the state of supplies at the mission station, or ask permission to marry or to return to Europe due to ill-health. In contrast, mission journals were expected to describe day-to-day life, including encounters with heathens and converts alike, relations with migrants and colonial officials, and even the slightest ethnographic observation that might help with African conversion. On a quarterly basis, missionaries were expected to forward their journals to London, to give the Parent Committee a sense of how work in the field had progressed (or not) over time. Not surprisingly, there were moments when the dividing line blurred between the genre of the letter and the genre of the journal.

As with all such organizations, the CMS devoted itself to establishing a transnational reach: thus, it makes sense that a dissonance existed at times, simply because of the vast distances between the mission field and the CMS leadership in London. To ameliorate such effects, the society enforced strict rules about *how* missionaries should actually write. As Judith Irvine has observed, "Missionary journals were not a genre in which authors freely expressed individual ideas and feelings. . . . They were subject to the rulings of the Parent Committee and other parties in the organizational hierarchy, as to appropriate topics, tone (spiritual) and style."[44] Such rigid requirements helped the CMS Parent Committee enforce unity of both purpose and point of view, since London relied heavily on missionaries to be the society's ears and eyes in the field. Letters and journals also provided the CMS with raw data that could be excerpted and even reworded for propagandist use in lay publications. As Anna Johnson has demonstrated in her study of nineteenth-century British missionary writing for the London Missionary Society, parent committees deliberately manipulated accounts from the field "to inculcate public support for missionary endeavors; to ensure an ongoing supply of donated funds from individuals, institutions and governments; to cultivate a community of like-minded British citizens who would stand up for missionary interests . . . ; and to encourage a community of potential recruits."[45] Because they also received copies of lay religious publications, both African and European missionaries were fully aware of how their materials could be used and so might well have deliberately provided highly "quotable" chunks of writing.

Thinking back to Peel's discussion of how African CMS agents used their texts, one might ask how native missionaries engaged with the broader politics of gendered identity within a highly mediated form of writing that still needed to be personally meaningful to them, while also satisfying a white British audience. The dynamics of this balancing act are exemplified in one of the most referenced extracts from Crowther's early journals: the description of his reunion with his mother, Afala. Composed in the late summer of 1846, the entry was reprinted the following year in the *Church Missionary Gleaner* as evidence of how well things were progressing with the establishment of the Abeokuta mission. When British Christians at home opened their spring 1847 issue of the *Gleaner*, they would have seen:

Aug. 21, 1846—The text for this day, in the Christian Almanack, is, *Thou art the helper of the fatherless*. I have never felt the force of this text more than I did this day, as I have to relate that my mother, from whom I was torn away about five and twenty years ago, came with my brother in quest of me. When she saw me, she trembled. She could not believe her own eyes. We grasped one another, looking at each other with silence and great astonishment: big tears rolled down her emaciated cheeks. A great number of people soon came together. She trembled as she held me by the hand, and called me by familiar names by which I well remembered I used to be called by my grandmother, who has since died in slavery. We could not say much; but sat still, and cast now and then an affectionate look at one another—a look which violence and oppression have long checked—an affection which had nearly been extinguished by the long space of twenty-five years. My two sisters, who were captured with us, are both with my mother, who takes care of them and her grandchildren in a small town not far from hence, called Abàkà. Thus unsought for—when all search for me had failed—God has brought us together again, and turned our sorrow into joy.[46]

This description has the power to move past and present audiences because Crowther momentarily steps outside of his adult identity as an Anglican priest to articulate every slave child's deepest longing: not just for a reunion with his mother, but also for her active quest to *redeem* him. At the same time, along with the joy of reclamation, Crowther intimates the trauma of violent captivity and enslavement, of cultural and spiritual violation, of loneliness for family—that is, those private, unspeakable memories that by necessity exclude his white readers. However, since the redemption of Crowther's family is understood as an extension of God's will, his journal extract proves Peel's point that the style of African missionary journals plotted a narrative of providential progress that made sense of what at first seemed to be the irrevocability of slavery's dispersal.[47] Thus, not only Crowther but also his "heathen" family members are blessed and protected by God's will.

Yet, given the religious and the secular connotations of redemption as an idea, this evocation of deep personal loss and recovery also sets the stage for a more earthly rescue of the son by his mother, since it is she who has come "in quest" of him. By granting agency to Afala, Crowther negates his own agency and the institutional context of his "return" to Nigeria as a CMS missionary carrying out the society's directives. Return then becomes refigured as rescue, with the Saro desire to find "home" both answered and subsumed under the more powerful desire of those first left behind. As if to illustrate this unbreakable link, Afala and Ajayi recognize each other as mother and child via his memory of childhood and her handed-down language, despite her son's cultural transformation into Samuel Crowther, the urbane, European-style clergyman. For nineteenth-century readers familiar with both Crowther's life story and the geographical location of Abeokuta, the emotional weight of the description would have been heightened by the fact that the city was located barely fifty miles south of Crowther's birthplace. Ironically, what the published journal extract does not make clear is that it was Crowther who had discovered that his mother was living in the area, and that it was he who had first sent word to her. At the same time, since Afala and the adult children who remained with her were essentially displaced refugees, Crowther's narrative undercuts the reality that, in a sense, they were all exiles working to create a new home. Not surprisingly, "return" has to be figurative, despite the literal, public drama of reunion between mother and son. Crowther uses his narrative to articulate what could be, a move that looks forward to Afala's own baptism two years later as Hannah, the mother of the Biblical Samuel. According to Peel, "as Afala bore Ajayi in the flesh," now Samuel would look forward to being "reaffiliated . . . with Hannah in spirit. . . . Crowther's reconnection with his past, in the person of his mother, through the medium of a narrative that grounded his own religious commitment . . . served to relaunch him on his life's career."[48] Both the extract and this reading illustrate how Crowther uses narrative effectively to imbue the initial business of mission (to establish a Christian outpost in the refugee city of Abeokuta) with a highly personal interpretation of familial "return."

In the rest of this published version of Crowther's journal, we see that Crowther has integrated his account of reunion in ways that confirm the authority of his white readers. Treating them first to a detailed, matter-of-fact account of where enslavement had taken his mother and sisters and how much they had to pay to redeem themselves, Crowther ends with what seems to be a relinquishing of the agency he had first granted to Afala. But neither does Crowther invoke the power of Providence:

> Could the friends of the Africans witness the happy meeting of those who have by their means been restored to the bosom of those from whom they were violently taken away, it would, I am sure, rejoice their hearts that their labour has not been in vain, nor their money spent for nought. Could they hear this moment how many thanks are given to them by African parents, whose minds have been cheered in their declining years by the return of their children, from Sierra Leone, they would thank God and take courage to go on in their work, which God is singularly blessing, and the effect of which is seen and felt in the interior of this country.[49]

Mission stations around the globe were directly financed by the contributions of the society's British lay membership, so Crowther attributes to them the status of God's redeeming agents. Those whom he advises to "take courage to go on in their work" undoubtedly include the European agents in the field. As Crowther and his audience understood all too well, European men who traveled with their wives to the African continent had to confront the alarmingly high death rate among whites, relative to the alarmingly low rate of conversion among native Africans. From this perspective, Crowther reaches out to his white audience with an awareness of their financial sacrifices and their anxieties that foreign missionary service often entailed a white migration from which there was frequently no return.

As a complex rhetorical strategy used by the native missionary to fulfill a variety of audience demands, Crowther's closing statements replace the tragedy of African dispersal through slavery (as well as the Saro initiative to return to the Niger Valley, with the English in tow) with concern for the tragedy of white exile and sacrifice. While the public understanding of the white missionary dead included women and children, Crowther's characterization resonates with Victorian notions of "muscular Christianity." As Norman Vance explains, muscular Christianity was less about "muscularity" than about "a combative Christianity involving urgent ethical and spiritual imperatives." Though men and women participated equally in the support and maintenance of overseas missions, "the manly work of social improvement" meant that "manliness and Christianity were strictly bound up with each other."[50] Crowther's evocation of African male passivity thus encourages and validates a white male intervention that Crowther implies is powerful enough to transform the face of West Africa. What was, in essence, a white response to an act of liberated African reconstitution of community in Abeokuta is refigured now as the central force behind return. Thus, far from being simply a literal act of mobility or a nostalgic desire, diasporic repatriation functions here as a trope for a complex interracial pattern of agency in the context of colonialism.[51] Such moments demonstrate Crowther's twofold use of narrative, first to mediate and resolve the politics of his own displacement, and second to provide CMS supporters at home with a tangible sense of their empowerment as philanthropists. The latter established beyond question both Crowther's selflessness and his negotiation of white agency.

Virtually all scholarly discussions of the above extract rely on the version published in the 1847 *Church Missionary Gleaner*. When we compare the published version to the original entry in Crowther's own handwriting, we see deleted text marked in the editor's pencil. On the face of it, the edited version reads more clearly and preserves the drama of reunion. However, a crucial difference between the two versions revolves around a small but important paragraph that was deliberately omitted from the *Gleaner*'s version:

> My father had five wives, two died, three are now living. Of his children five are now living besides myself, the seventh was stolen away a few years ago and has not yet been found. My father died before I left this country. The preservation of my father's family from being sold into foreign slavery is one of the singular cases of escape here and there to be met with in the country. Some families have been swept away altogether when half of others have been carried off.[52]

For nineteenth-century British readers, the power generated by Crowther's description of meeting his mother rests in part on the abolitionist's familiar evocation of maternal devotion, a virtue that allowed British men and women to achieve a sentimental rather than literal identification with African ex-slaves via the figurative language of domesticity. At the same time, the *Gleaner's* version of what Crowther calls his "fatherlessness" seems to remove the problem of African masculinity from the white abolitionist tableau. Indeed, it is the absence of his father that allows the sense of familial helplessness and vulnerability evoked in Crowther's closing remarks in the *Gleaner* to be so effective. In the excised passage, Crowther evokes not only the memory of his dead father but Yoruba patrilineage, which was traditionally buttressed by the "heathenish" practice of polygamy. Consequently, this deleted passage gives new meaning to Crowther's opening quotation from Psalm 10:14, "Thou art the helper of the fatherless." Instead of being merely a reference to God's protection of bereft widows and orphans, the quotation suggests that God's response to Crowther's plight is to restore that protection given by a father to his family—in this case, through the restoration of Crowther's mother and siblings. If fatherlessness in the biblical sense implies not just material dispossession but also the loss of home and familial belonging, then the "singular [case] of escape" exemplified by his family's fate allows for the possibility of reconstituting that home.

The deleted manuscript passage also resonates with a moment in Crowther's 1837 slave narrative (the one included with the published 1841 Niger journals), where he vividly recalls his final memory of his father in the act of protecting family members: "The last view I had of my father was when he came from the fight, to give us the signal to flee. . . . Hence I never saw him more—Here I must take thy leave, unhappy, comfortless father!—I learned, some time afterward, that he was killed in another battle."[53] Here Crowther's family portrait shifts from the stock abolitionist image of the slave mother and child (who are then ultimately "saved" by white philanthropy) to one that represents Yoruba manhood as providentially sustained and sustaining. Given that, in his father's absence, the returning Crowther would undoubtedly unite the scattered family members and effect their conversion, the implication in the extract is that as his father's descendant, the son emerges on the other side of slavery as the new, agentive patriarch. And since Crowther the son has now mastered Christian practices, he is in essence a dramatically hybrid extension of a moral, courageous, preslavery Yoruba masculinity. If, as Peel suggests, the earlier passage about Afala helps Crowther reconnect to his past via his mother, this ignored moment in the original handwritten entry (which was deliberately included by Crowther as part of the submission to the Parent Committee) creates a more balanced reconnection to both his father and mother as well as to his father's other families via his polygamous relationships.

As the manuscript version of the 1846 journal entry suggests, Crowther envisioned for himself a mobile, male identity created through diasporic experience, ideally one transformed through Christian conversion but still closely related to his preslavery roots. This hybrid masculinity is the production of his negotiation of the models of manhood presented by white CMS missionaries—models which, rather than representing a stable set of values, were just as contingent upon evolving contexts created by dispersal. Indeed, such models were shaped in part by both transnational mission policy in the nineteenth century and the specific social conditions brought into being by the Saro diaspora.

Throughout the nineteenth century, despite a consistent public front on the part of the CMS that emphasized a harmonious interracial brotherhood among European and African missionaries, white male CMS agents were constantly threatened by the presence of their African counterparts. For instance, when in 1862 word reached the Reverends Henry Townsend, David Hinderer, and C. A. Gollmer (the white missionaries who had accompanied Crowther to Abeokuta twenty years earlier) that Crowther was to be named bishop, they strenuously petitioned the CMS Parent Committee against the appointment, specifically on the grounds of race. As Hinderer put it in an 1864 letter to the society's General Secretary Henry Venn, "Not that I should have the slightest objection to Bishop Crowther being over myself and the congregation which God may give me. . . . But . . . because God gives us influence as Europeans among them [our authority] is very desirable and necessary to us, but if they hear a Black man is our master, they will question our respectability."[54] Rather than dismissing Hinderer's comments as garden-variety racism on the colonial frontier, I suggest that they touch on the challenges faced by white male CMS agents within the class-conscious, anglicized context of the society.

For one thing, the average white male missionary who served the British CMS in Africa was not necessarily English or middle class. With a white missionary death rate from 25 to 65 percent, a posting in West Africa was an emotionally wrenching experience that sorely tested the faith and, just as importantly, the institutional loyalty of the average white CMS agent. In the first half of the nineteenth century, the CMS seemed to have little success recruiting from among either the middle or the industrial classes in Britain. However, as sociologist Jon Miller suggests, this may not have posed a problem. In his study of the Lutheran mission headquartered in Basel, Switzerland, Miller argues that strong institutional control was required if missionary organizations were to establish functioning and effective outposts in the field. Miller contends that, like the Basel Missionary Society, the CMS deliberately tried to select men who exhibited humility and a lack of personal ambition, which very often turned out to be rural men from modest circumstances.[55] Thus, in the first half of the nineteenth century, of the small number of recruits the CMS did obtain from Britain, many had been valets, sons of farmers, glove makers, carpenters, and small-trades men: that is to say, men who were not agitators for social reform at home.

To supplement this group, the society went overseas to none other than the Lutherans of Basel, since their seminary specialized in producing male missionaries with the desired class origins and temperament.[56] The resulting social structure within the missionary organization mirrored an idealized world of class hierarchy, since Parent Committee members were drawn from among the educated and wealthy professional and mercantile classes, in stark contrast to the lower-class missionary men who were to be sent into the field. As the Anglican Bishop Edward Steere commented toward the end of the nineteenth century, "It has been the custom far too much to think of missionaries as an inferior set of men, sent out, paid and governed by a superior set of men formed into a committee in London. Of course then you must have examiners and secretaries and an office to see that the inferior men are not too inferior; and you must have a set of cheap colleges in which the inferior men may get an inferior education and you must provide an inferior sort of ordination which will not enable them to compete in England with the superior men."[57] Thus, the CMS and other organizations deliberately cultivated a specific category of white masculinity that would be ill-suited to producing radical change either at home or abroad. At the same time, the supplementation of CMS missionary personnel with Basel seminarians resulted in missionary communities in Sierra Leone and Nigeria that included both English and German speakers, both displaced from their European homes. As a result, while English-speaking missionaries had a hard enough time contending with language differences between themselves and Africans, the Basel recruits had the added problem of moving from German to English as they attempted to master the languages of their potential converts.

Despite cultural and linguistic barriers, their posting to unknown and dangerous surroundings, and the fact that they were handpicked essentially for their institutional obedience, both the British and the Basel recruits were alive to the opportunities they might accrue by cultivating their usefulness to the CMS. Though their training was inferior to that of Protestant ministers in Britain, white male agents of the CMS were guaranteed a steady salary, medical care, a pension, a basic education beyond mere literacy, the opportunity to meet and marry socially superior women within their Christian communities, and, if they had children, schooling for their offspring.[58] At the same time, once they were among what they regarded to be a "heathen" population, their racial identity as white men could be effectively consolidated, since they assumed themselves to be the sole agents of civilization. The one catch, of course, was that all these benefits were achievable only if they agreed to be stationed overseas in foreign locations where the CMS had the greatest need, but where deadly tropical diseased also reigned.

In the end, even with the graduates of the Basel seminary, the CMS could not send missionaries to West Africa at a rate to surpass those dying in the field. From as early as the 1820s, then, the Parent Committee took the pragmatic step of training African male converts to run their own native churches as the only remedy for the situation. Theoretically, all the benefits of employment as a white male missionary were then potentially available to Christianized West Africans men, provided they could prove their fitness. The problem with this notion of an interracial fraternity through mission, however, was the dissonance that existed between the largely middle- and upper-class male leadership of the CMS and the "inferior" whites who served in the field. Thus, when in 1864 Gollmer, Hinderer, and Townsend (the first two being Basel graduates, the third formerly a rural English schoolmaster) opposed Crowther's appointment as bishop, their racism evinced a deep-seated anxiety that the emergence of native missionaries would undermine the social status that they, as so-called muscular Christians, had risked their lives for in the first place. Indeed, such animosities only increased with time, so that by 1880, Bishop Crowther was ousted by younger white missionaries who, armed with improved methods for preventing and treating tropical diseases, were actually surviving foreign postings and so could claim their authority over ordained West African ministers.

Long before he became bishop, Crowther was well acquainted with the gendered politics of status that shaped the lives of white CMS missionary men in the field, particularly from his time as a pupil at the CMS's Christian Institution at Fourah Bay. As a student in the 1820s, Crowther had been allowed to go to Britain for several months for education; soon after, the CMS offered him another such invitation, but the headmaster of the institution, the Reverend Charles Haensel (himself a Basel graduate), strongly disapproved of extending such offers to African boys. From Haensel's point of view, Crowther would return to Sierra Leone "a conceited fop, with wants unknown to those brought up in the Colony as to dress, food, and residence and dissatisfied as long as he is not put on an equality with the Europeans" (emphasis added). Additionally, argued Haensel, when such a youth was ready for marriage, he would then be dissatisfied with the selection of native women in Sierra Leone, a point which touched on the missionary's broader anxiety over interracial relationships, whether legal or illicit, between whites and Africans.[59] Or perhaps the question was really about who would determine and shape this intimacy: if left to his own devices, Haensel had a plan to mold his protégé into the perfect native assistant, since "he is learning my ways exactly" and then when Crowther was "allowed to marry . . . his wife would prove an additional help . . . in the domestic concerns" of the CMS mission school.[60] On the one hand, the mobility of the Saro as presented in Crowther's 1846 journal entry was seen as the point of opportunity for the agency of white British Christians to spread the gospel among the "heathens." On the other hand, as Haensel's comments suggest, mobile African men as unfettered agents, many with their own dreams of advancement, were a threat to the social order precisely because of the possibility that they could be remade in the image of the white missionary.[61] Such fear of a power reversal reveals the highly contingent nature of lower middle- and working-class white male missionary status.[62]

This sense of anxiety provides an interesting context for reading Crowther's narrative strategies in his account of the 1841 Niger expedition, especially given the discursive power of the genre to enable the social construction of white masculinity. His presence on the expedition constituted his first journey "back" to Nigeria. The narrative it generated was the first major piece of writing (other than his earlier slave narrative) that Crowther completed under the auspices of the CMS. While he had an idea of the professional benefits that would accrue to him from writing the narrative, I would argue, following Peel's notion, that this text becomes a vehicle for Crowther to imagine himself reconnected to the places and peoples from which he had been kidnapped.

It might be helpful to think more generally about the notion of exploration as the immediate context of Crowther's narrative production. In his discussion of the cultural politics of European explorations in nineteenth-century Africa, Johannes Fabian coined the term "mobile colonies" to indicate that these journeys were "never simply 'travel.'" Rather, an expedition "was never outside an existing, if constantly changing, context of local and international political power."[63] Public anxiety in Britain about the dangers faced by white members of the 1841 expedition rendered almost invisible the nonwhite sailors from Britain, the West Indies, and West Africa who made up the crew. Focus on whites also drew attention away from the small group of Black settlers leaving Sierra Leone and Liberia (again, some from Africa, some from the Caribbean, and some from the United States and Britain) who accompanied the expedition. Indeed, among the native agents of the CMS under Schön's supervision, there were a few ex-slave interpreters, in addition to Crowther, who doubled as servants.[64]

As with all travel narratives of the period, Crowther's journal dutifully describes the landscape, the peoples who inhabit the riverbanks, their customs and manners, and so on. This reflected the society's desire to find a suitable location for a mission station, among friendly Africans but also close to trade and transportation routes. In terms of the persona generated by the narrative, Crowther represents himself as the picture of humility, simply recording details and following orders. More often than not, he reproduces the appropriate vision of the future possibilities of British commerce expected of him. For example, he writes at the mouth of the Niger, "The coast, as far as I went, was low and swampy; which is very much against this highly-interesting part of it, as here ought to be a sea-port, where goods from England might be landed, as well for shipping off the produce from the Niger."[65] And when he makes contact with native Africans, he presents himself as the perfect intermediary for the white explorers and missionaries. Before one such group of locals, he reports:

> I commenced my message—That the Queen of the Country called Great Britain has sent the King of the ship to all the Chiefs of Africa, to make treaties with them to give up war and the slave-trade—to encourage all their people to the cultivation of the soil—and to mind all that the White People say to them; as they wish to teach them many things, and particularly the Book which God gives, which will make all men happy. I added, likewise, that there are many Nufi, Haussa, and Yaruba people in the White-man's country, who have been liberated from the Portuguese and Spanish slave-ships; that they are now living like White Men. (315)

Clearly, the journal does not appear to challenge the European philanthropic fantasies of Africa as a fertile field waiting to be cultivated. Rather, Crowther presents the British and Christianized Africans like himself working in unison in support of white philanthropy and "civilization."

Throughout the text, Crowther is deeply respectful of his white superiors and is saddened by the loss of life on board, presenting the late Captain Allen as a heroic Christian martyr from the first day of the voyage. However, after the necessary genuflections, he provides at least as much attention to the other formerly enslaved African interpreters who, like himself, had been selected to model Black civilization for the locals. Crowther does not contradict white accounts of the obi (ruler) of Aboh as a fickle, corpulent leader, comically attired in dirty, mismatched European clothes and adorned with jewelry made of coral beads, brass trinkets, and leopards' teeth. Yet, in light of the potential of Africans for industry and the Niger River for the establishment of ports, the obi represents the "old" Africa in need of discipline, his odd collection of European commodities a sign of his uneducated—though nonetheless very present— valuation of white civilization. In their respective journals, both Crowther and Schön note the obi's request that the expedition leave behind one of its interpreters—the formerly enslaved African Simon Jonas—but Schön is the one fearful of Jonas "falling into sin," suggesting that once he is removed from white company, the veneer of civilization provided by his conversion to Christianity would wear away (134).

But the obi's selection of Jonas reveals a greater comfort with African than white Christians, and indeed, like Simon Jonas, Crowther himself spends long periods inland, visiting local communities, noting language differences, and gathering information about politics, with little harm to his faith and character. In effect, according to Crowther's narrative, the formerly enslaved Africans seem to perform the real tasks of the expedition, while the whites slowly become incapacitated by malaria. Indeed, Crowther repeatedly narrates the presence and interventions of himself and other African catechists as God-directed. During a voyage that would be memorialized in the minds of the British public as a journey of white death, Crowther notes early in the journal his own providential rescue when a heavy piece of equipment loosened from its moorings narrowly misses his head. Later, he reports, "The Captain's clerk, who has been raving [from fever] for some days, threw himself overboard from a port-hole in the Captain's cabin. Providentially he was caught by a Black sailor, who immediately flew overboard in pursuit of him" (332). Thus, we see early on that Crowther engages in a struggle to represent West Africa as belonging firmly to the "returning" "Saro" or Sierra Leone ex-slaves heading to Nigeria.

While Crowther's journal articulates significant differences in perspective under the guise of the transparent native reporter, his imagined reentry into Nigeria is deeply intertwined with white male anxieties about basic survival. For instance, consider the accounts of the expedition's time at the British outpost of Cape Coast Castle in Ghana. The official expedition journal drawn from the late Captain Allen's writing notes the grave of Victorian poet Letitia Elizabeth Landon, or L.E.L., as she was known to her public. Landon left London under a cloud of scandal to marry the castle's governor, George Maclean, in 1838. In his review of the Niger expedition narrative, Charles Dickens (like many white travelers, armchair or otherwise) memorialized Landon's death as the tragic collision of all that was civilized and good in England with the savagery of Africa.[66] Crowther himself notes such white anxieties when he reports that as the

British neared the mouth of the Niger, "some [white sailors] could not help remarking, that they were going to their graves" (274). This rendering of English death in the body of Landon (she was, after all, the symbolic figure of white social and cultural refinement), coupled with the incongruity of her presence in Africa, goes a long way toward enhancing the heroism of the white explorers who pay homage to her, while also emphasizing Africa as dangerous and alien, so that conquest becomes all the more dramatic and empowering. Since the dead Landon becomes the foil for white manhood and Englishness, she can be more easily resurrected, the scandal clouding the final years of her life falling away before the larger threat of African barbarity.

As with the official Niger expedition narrative published by the British government, Crowther marks the obligatory graveyard visit at the castle, but with a major difference:

> While [the ship's surgeon] Dr. Marshall was taking a sketch of the monument of Mrs. M'Lean . . . he requested me to copy for him, from another monument, the following Inscription:—

> Sacred to the Memory
> Of the
> Rev. Philip Quaque
> Native of This Country,
> Who Having Been Sent to England
> For Education,
> Received Holy Orders 1765,
> And Was Here Employed Upwards of Fifty Years,
> As Missionary
> From the Incorporated Society for the Propagation of the Gospel in Foreign Parts,
> And as Chaplain to this Factory.
> He Died 17th October 1816,
> Aged 75 Years. (265)[67]

In the letter appended to the CMS journals, Crowther comments that "who the individual [Quaque] was, I know not," which might well have been true (350). However, those white readers equipped with the history of Christian missions to Africa might have known Quaque's history. He was an African from a locality neighboring the castle, who at the end of the eighteenth century had been selected by the Society for the Propagation of the Gospel for missionary training in England. Upon his return to West Africa with a white wife in tow, Quaque became the chaplain of Cape Coast Castle. By the time of his appointment, he had thoroughly lost his native language and had little, if any, success converting his fellow natives. Indeed, he was, for the most part, an outcast from his former community and was often ridiculed and ignored by white officials of the castle.[68] In that sense, then, the example of Quaque might well be a cautionary tale for British readers about the effectiveness of native clergy, once they were left to their own devices. As Quaque's case proved, the one asset that an African clergyman might have over his white counterpart in his attempt to gain converts—a natural and abiding fluency in his own native language—was certainly not to be relied upon. But Crowther's apparently naive reading of Quaque as a success ("What attracted my attention was, that he was a Native of that place—sent to England for education—received Holy Orders—and was employed in his own country upward of *fifty years!*") transforms the dead African minister into a figure of affirmation for returning African catechists such as Crowther, at the very moment when the white male encounter with Letitia Landon's grave signifies white displacement and death.[69] In this sense, the superimposition of a story of African male success over that of white vulnerability (Landon) implies that the border-crossing hero is not the white explorer, but his liberated African interpreter.

Given that the failed expedition was noteworthy to the British public for the horrific loss of white lives, the strategy of representing Black slavery or suffering, of representing the emotional weight of Black return, would have misfired in Crowther's narrative. However, it is precisely on this question of linguistic ownership that Crowther chooses to reintegrate the liberated African's experience. Again, at Cape Coast Castle, Crowther visits the church of the Reverend John Birch Freeman, the English-born, mixed-race Wesleyan missionary who preaches to a local congregation with the help of a native interpreter. After the minister selects his text from the Bible and delivers his sermon, the interpreter supposedly renders the ideas verbatim in Fante, but Crowther notes that "frequently, the Interpreter occupied more time than the Minister. . . . How much of the meaning is lost . . . I know by experience; unless the Interpreter is a well-known qualified person, as I have every reason to believe the one at this place is" (266–67). Crowther's matter-of-fact observation implies that it is the native interpreter who is in control, and he underscores here his own observations as a bilingual African Christian, fluent in English and his native Yoruba, that European missionaries often fail to reach their African audiences: "The attention of a great part of the Congregation was pleasing; while others appeared to have been brought there merely from curiosity" (267). For Crowther, the only remedy is for missionaries such as Freeman to learn the local languages, "a tedious and difficult work, as it takes years to bring it to perfection" (268)—or for the

British to relinquish the work of mission to bilingual Africans themselves, who are already native speakers. As Crowther uses the *Journal* to document his extensive work as a linguist during the expedition, his own candidacy might well be implied. Since the role of the linguist was at times combined with the role of explorer, Crowther's suggestion, for all its courtesy, implies some competition with the traditional white male leadership of African exploration. [70]

Significant, too, is Crowther's comment: "How much of the meaning is lost . . . I know by experience." Here he refers to his own postslavery memory in Sierra Leone, as a young Yoruba-speaking ex-slave in a CMS-supervised village, experiencing the disorientation (and possibly boredom) of listening to a Christian service in English. Crowther's memory of his first experience in a Christian church is far removed from the experience of the Fante in that the congregation had not been kidnapped and sold into slavery. However, the narrative reduces the cultural distance between Crowther and Africans he encounters after leaving Sierra Leone, thereby gesturing to a common experience *as Africans* of a confusing moment of first contact with whites. This moment also points to an equally ironic separation of Crowther from the white missionaries, even though he is himself engaged by them. Thus, we are left not so much with a transcendent, unproblematic reconnection to Africa or a triumphant subversion of the white explorer's narrative as with a more subtle, at times blatantly resistant and at others troubling, negotiation of inevitable differences that inhered within the context of "return."

The challenge of reconnection is also figured in the very person of Freeman, who in 1841 was the most famous Wesleyan Methodist missionary on the coast. Indeed, had he been given enough support by the Wesleyan Parent Committee, he—rather than the Anglican CMS—would have established the first Christian organization in Abeokuta. Given his central importance to West African mission history, it is significant that Freeman was born in Britain to a working-class white mother and a freed African father. Ironically, his own travel narrative, *Journals of Various Visits to the Kingdoms of Ashanti, Aku, and Dahomi, in Western Africa*, appeared in serialized form in the *Wesleyan Missionary Notices* between 1840 and 1843, making him famous in both Britain and West Africa. As the chaplain of Cape Coast Castle, Freeman was, like Crowther, the spiritual descendant of Philip Quaque.[71] There were, of course, other Black men from Britain, the West Indies, and the United States who served as missionaries to Africa under the banner of European (and later American) missionary organizations, including the Reverend Edward Jones, a freeborn South Carolinian and the first African American to attend Amherst College, who had been in Sierra Leone since 1831 and who took over the running of the Christian Institution the year

Crowther set out on the expedition.[72] Therefore, in distinguishing between European missionary newcomers and native Africans, Crowther both embraces and rejects African diasporic missionary fraternities that operated along the same circuits as white mission fraternities, articulating his own sense of identity in relation to the intraracial difference inherent within the convergence of peoples of African descent on the west coast of Africa.

THE STORY OF CROWTHER and the Saro encompasses a range of involuntary and agentive nineteenth-century travel patterns that linked those whom David Northrup has aptly named "Atlantic Africans" with Black subjects in the Americas.[73] Involuntary migration was the by-product of enslavement. For the emancipated, migration translated into the search for employment, for trade opportunities, and for political independence. The Saro, the British colonial authorities, and the CMS recognized that the desire for and the literal act of repatriation unlocked a range of new possibilities, both political and social. For everyone concerned, repatriation also enabled particular rhetorical forms specific to the precolonial conditions on the ground in Sierra Leone and Nigeria. The purposes and deployment of those forms were site specific: despite its ubiquity in the Americas and among the Saro, "return" by necessity meant different things to different communities in different places. As the example of ex-slaves such as Crowther suggests, physical "return" was achievable and even desirable, not to recover what had been taken away, but to articulate inevitably new and shifting identities. The removal from Sierra Leone to Nigeria had little to do with retrieval of land, family, or ways of being and almost everything to do with creating, dismantling, and negotiating new and existing power structures and cultural frames. There is, of course, much irony that Crowther's "return" to Nigeria was initially figured through a British exploration of "unknown territory," except that Crowther necessarily filtered everything through new eyes and within a historically contingent and at times semipermeable missionary power structure. His dedication to Christian mission was as unshakable as his Christian faith, so he embraced the goals of the CMS as his own, especially when it came to creating a native pastorate. In this sense, repatriation came to be framed within and achieved through mission. Therefore, Crowther—as well as Philip Quaque, for that matter—has something in common with generations of Black Americans, from the eighteenth century onward: the linking of African repatriation to the evangelical impulse.

Part travel text, missionary journal, autobiography, and ethnography, Crowther's 1841 Niger Expedition journal incorporated not only historical and sociological data but also a sense of what we (anachronistically) call diaspora as both a spatial and a cultural phenomenon created in the shadow of empire. My reading of Crowther's journal is not to mine his text for historical details about Christian mission or ethnography or even to argue that his intent was to deceive his white readers or rebel against his white superiors—or, worse, that he was somehow clairvoyant and was hinting at his future advancement in the CMS hierarchy. Rather, my approach has been to listen for resonances and moments of dissonance in his text, because such reverberations would have been the inevitable result of a piece of writing created under the weight of multiple expectations and audiences. In this sense, Crowther's journal is very much an *institutional* document, literally commissioned by the CMS for the benefit of Christian readers. In this sense, his text was a personal narrative designed to enhance his image (like Mary Seacole's) or to excite a unity of feeling and action toward the redemption of other people of African descent (like the writings of Nancy Prince). Additionally, as an institutional document, his journal was never meant to serve the function of an official expedition narrative—the white military survivors of the expedition took care of that aspect of the record keeping themselves. Even as Crowther wrote of what he *saw* and *heard*—that is, as he was responsible for putting on display the "new" scenes and peoples encountered on the voyage—he was himself a specimen of sorts, equally on display to white CMS administrators and agents, as well as the British public. In other words, the success of his text rested not only on what he wrote but also on his ability to prove through his text that he was not merely the so-called barbaric African with a veneer of civilization. This figuration would have been entirely different in the case of the white explorer-author, for whom an expedition narrative would have confirmed intellectual superiority, valor, heroism, and international fame.

The next chapter continues with the theme of nineteenth-century travel in the form of African repatriation, this time from the point of view of the freeborn explorers Martin R. Delany (the United States) and Robert Campbell (Jamaica). Both men wrote from a sense of duty under the exigency of finding some site of refuge, where Blacks from the Americas could find relief from poverty, racism, disenfranchisement, and violence. Both men wrote with the hope of convincing Black readers to join them in going "back" to Africa to start anew, while also requesting help from US and British audiences in enabling that refuge. Delany and Campbell activated an imperial gaze of sorts, confirming that any repurposing of travel writing comes with its own baggage. Their story also expands on the notion of locational specificity. Because Delany was an American, while Campbell straddled the United States and the West Indies, the question of what constituted *Black* and *American* becomes central.

4. Martin R. Delany and Robert Campbell in West Africa

Though they were enslaved in Britain's thirteen colonies, many kidnapped Africans and their American children still hoped for repatriation across the Atlantic. And especially when talk of "liberty or death" grew among the white colonists, slaves continually pressed the glaring irony of their own literal need for emancipation. For example, in the winter of 1773, the slave "Felix" submitted to Boston authorities an abolitionist petition that offered a stark contrast between the colonists' personal investment in North America and the slaves' abject dispossession: "We have no Property. We have no Wives. No Children. We have no City. No Country."[1] For "Felix," freedom was not merely the absence of enslavement. Rather, he understood the need to belong *somewhere* in order to articulate that freedom in the bosom of family and community. This question of belonging arose yet again a few months later in a joint petition by the slaves Peter Bestes, Sambo Freeman, Felix Holbrook, and Chester Joie. Without any expectation that free Blacks might live and prosper in the same society that had enslaved them, they informed Boston's colonial government that they would seek all "peaceable and lawful attempts to gain our freedom," so as to return to West Africa: "We are willing to submit to such regulations and laws, as may be made relative to us, until we leave the province, which we determine to do as soon as we can from our joint labours procure money to transport ourselves to some part of the coast of Africa, where we propose a settlement."[2] Though very few Africans and Creole Blacks would achieve this ambition, in 1776 two Rhode Island slaves named John Quamine and Bristol Yamma used the proceeds of a winning lottery ticket to purchase their freedom, declaring their intent to sail as Christian missionaries for what is today the Ghanaian city of Anomabo on the African Gold Coast. Quamine, in particular, sought a long-awaited reunion with the wealthy father who had originally handed him over to a white man "for an education among the English." But before they could arrange a transatlantic voyage, both men became engulfed in the American Revolution, never to be heard from again.[3] Finally, in 1811, Paul Cuffee (1759–1817), a freeborn mixed-race merchant and sea captain from Westport, Massachusetts, sailed one of his own ships to Sierra Leone to investigate possibilities for Black American emigration. Encouraged by what he saw, Cuffee returned to the United States, and in 1815 he successfully landed thirty-eight Black passengers at Freetown. He died two years later before he could relocate a second emigrant group, thereby ending an all-too-brief period of Black autonomy over African repatriation. Instead, the newly founded and white-run American Colonization Society (ACS) would dominate African repatriation from the time of Cuffee's death into the early twentieth century.

Behind the society was a coalition of white abolitionists who argued that Blacks would never find equal status, even if slavery were abolished, and pro-slavery advocates who feared the growth of a free Black population in the South. Both groups saw West Africa as the target destination, and after securing a $100,000 contribution from Congress, in 1821 the ACS sent out its first shipload of free Black emigrants on the *Elizabeth*. After a two-year sojourn in Sierra Leone and great loss of life to tropical fevers, the settlers finally landed on the coast just south of the British colony, establishing what would become in 1847 the Republic of Liberia, the second Black nation after Haiti.[4] Yet despite what appeared to be success, the majority of free Blacks in the United States deeply distrusted the society, in part because reports from disillusioned settlers contradicted the organization's propaganda. Indeed, there was the great difficulty of establishing subsistence farming in Liberia's rocky soil; the appallingly high mortality rate due to malaria, yellow fever, and other ailments; and the supplies the ACS provided settlers that were insufficient to last until the harvest of their first crops.[5] Repeatedly, settlers complained about the shortage of basic building necessities such as iron nails and metal wire. Though they sought to stretch their rations by bartering with indigenous populations for extra food, settlers often lacked the alcohol and tobacco so highly prized by those with whom they hoped to trade. Some transplanted Blacks abandoned altogether any hope of earning a living by legitimate means and, in a stunning role reversal, embraced slave trading. As for those emigrants who sought to "civilize" and convert local Kru, Mandingo, Grebo, Vai, Gola, Kissi, Mende, Bassa, Mano,

Gio, Krahn, Dey, Gbandi, Belleh, and Kpelle peoples, the result was inevitable disputes and eventually open warfare.[6] Not surprisingly, anti-emigration Blacks seized upon the violence between settlers and the indigenous populations to declare Liberia's absolute unsuitability, casting the ACS as a white organization that cared little for the settlers' lives and collective welfare. Caught between stories of extraordinary hardship in Liberia, on the one hand, and the unyielding nature of American white supremacy on the other, many Blacks still clung to the hope of migration, albeit to some alternate destination. But while some considered Mexico, the British West Indies, or Canada, the question of West Africa lingered, to be officially engaged yet again in 1858 by Martin Robison Delany, the Black Philadelphia physician, radical abolitionist, journalist, race philosopher, and early Black Nationalist.

Determined to establish an autonomous Black settlement in West Africa as far away from Liberia as he could manage, Delany began a series of practical steps toward securing land in what is now Nigeria.[7] First, at the 1858 Negro Convention on emigration in Chatham, Ontario, Delany proposed a three-year exploration of the territory north of Lagos, which missionaries and explorers had been calling Yorubaland. Enthralled by reports of friendly native inhabitants and expanses of uncultivated land, Delany saw the region as ideal for the settlement of educated, enterprising Blacks anxious for self-determination. Regarding his as a high purpose for the benefit of the race, Delany named himself chief commissioner of the proposed expedition, enumerating would-be companions including "Robert Douglass, Esq. Artist, and Professor Robert Campbell, Naturalist, both of Philadelphia, Pennsylvania, one of the United States of America to be Assistant Commissioners." Delany also included on his list "Amos Aray, Surgeon; and James W. Purnell, Secretary and Commercial Reporter, both of Kent County, Canada West." True, he had made the briefest of inquiries among these men and, in the case of Campbell, he had bypassed altogether formal contact. Regardless, declaring this team to be a "Scientific Corps," Delany proposed at the convention "a Topographical, Geological and Geographic Examination of the Valley of the River Niger, in Africa, and an inquiry into the state and condition of the people of that Valley, and other parts of Africa, together with such other scientific inquiries as may by them be deemed expedient, for the purposes of science and for general information."[8] Convention attendees had come to discuss emigration destinations in the Americas, and though they gave Delany's proposal an appreciative nod, they steadfastly refused his request for funding. Undaunted, Delany merely scaled back the expedition from three years to nine months, then set about pressing his commissioners into fundraising.

FIGURE 4.1. Martin R. Delany as a major in the 54th Massachusetts Colored Infantry Regiment, 1865. (Schomburg Center for Research in Black Culture, New York Public Library)

In the end, only the Jamaican teacher Robert Campbell responded in the affirmative, and by 1859 the two men departed from New York—Delany heading straight to Liberia and Campbell taking a detour to London. After reuniting in or around Lagos, they set out for Abeokuta, where they negotiated with the local Egba to obtain land.[9] Once they gained space for a settlement, both men departed to Britain for extensive speaking tours to raise funds. Ironically, despite his hard work and enthusiasm for African repatriation, Delany never made it back to Nigeria. With few American supporters for his project and the United States heading into civil war, Delany turned his efforts toward the recruitment of free Black men to join the 54th Massachusetts Colored Infantry Regiment (figure 4.1). After a brief return to the United States, Campbell settled in Lagos permanently in 1863. Despite their very different paths, in 1861 Delany and Campbell managed to publish individual exploration narratives covering their African journey: Delany's *Report of the Niger Valley Exploring Party*, "a Topographical, Geological and Geographic Examination of the Valley of the River Niger," and Campbell's *A Pilgrimage to My Motherland*, covering "the state and condition of the people of that Valley," in particular the Egba of southern Nigeria.

Today, most students of nineteenth-century African America acknowledge the existence of Delany's *Report* as a part of his larger body of work but turn their attention to his more philosophical articulations of an early Black Nationalism. This traditional emphasis places Delany within a genealogy of radical Black thought carried into the twentieth century by Marcus Garvey, Malcolm X, the Black Panthers, and other advocates for Black power and self-determination. This deliberate turning away from Delany's only encounter with West Africa finds legitimacy in the fact that, during and after Reconstruction, he spent his life agitating for full Black citizenship in the United States. Meanwhile, those few scholars who have paid attention to Campbell note his West Indian origins and his relocation to Lagos but set off his time in the United States as nothing more than a brief stop along an otherwise British nineteenth-century imperial trajectory.[10] Nonetheless, the intersection, however brief, of Campbell's path with that of Delany provides an example of how early Black West Indians and African Americans might have shared and shaped each other's visions of Africa as home.

For one thing, they would not have interpreted West Africa from the same perspective, raising questions about the different connotations of *American* and *West Indian* as cultural categories in this period. Despite having spent time in the United States, the light-skinned Jamaican Robert Campbell would have carried with him an understanding of class and color politics shaped by British imperialism, even as he recognized the common oppressions and experiences he shared with Black Americans. How did Campbell's bitter experiences in the United States compare to and contrast with his equally bitter, but differently modulated, negotiation of Black, white, and colored status in Jamaica? Initially, Campbell attempted to return to Abeokuta, to make good on the concessions provided by the treaty with the Egba. However, under pressure from the British, the Egba backed away from the original agreement. Campbell then had no choice but to settle in Lagos, which had just been annexed by the British. As it had done in Sierra Leone, Britain put in place a small cadre of educated West Indians and Christianized West Africans to help run the new colony. In many ways, then, Campbell "returned" not so much to "Mother Africa" as to an all-too-familiar British colonial stratification, with the few whites in the colony at the top, followed by a tiny group of Christianized and, in a few cases, highly educated elite comprising immigrants from the British West Indies, Sierra Leone, and even Brazil. There was also a plethora of antislavery, white-run American and British missionary societies, including the Church Missionary Society and the Methodist Missionary Society, both of which included Afro–West Indians, Afro-Britons, African Americans, and Christianized Africans among a smattering of key white European agents on the ground. On the bottom rung of the social ladder were local African converts apprenticed to their Western-educated compatriots. True, there were great differences between colonial Jamaica and colonial Lagos, but Campbell's negotiation of life in his new African home would have been among a specifically immigrant diasporic population, united as much by their desire to "develop" Africa as by their experience of British colonialism.

RACE, GENDER, AND EXPLORATION

Beyond Liberia, a handful of nineteenth-century Black American men and women went abroad to investigate new possibilities for establishing home, not just for themselves but also for their larger communities. These travelers usually returned to the United States with "ocular proof," gathered by way of a personal account of what they saw at some new destination. This was the case with Nancy Prince (Jamaica); Mary Ann Shadd Cary (Ontario in British Canada); Prince Saunders, Thomas Paul, and James T. Holly (Haiti); and James Monroe Whitfield (Central America). Many of these Black travelers published letters and narratives, while also delivering public lectures that covered, to varying degrees, the customs and manners of local inhabitants; practical details about soil, agricultural conditions, and climate; the prospects for woodcutting and the rearing of livestock; and existing local governments that might either aid or impede the growth of a free Black community. The useful information they disseminated helped educate their audience while also binding them to that audience, thereby solidifying the basis of their public authority, regardless of their gender. Though one was American and the other Jamaican, as Black men Delany and Campbell were similarly in search of "ocular proof" regarding the prospects for settlement in the Niger Valley. They engaged in the same project of community education for the purpose of resistance. However, by employing a genre—that is, the exploration narrative—which during and after the European Enlightenment was focused on observation for the purpose of producing empirical "science" about peoples and places beyond Europe, Delany and Campbell were claiming for themselves a form of knowledge production traditionally employed by whites in both the United States and Europe when they argued for the inferiority of darker-skinned populations. What was at stake for Campbell and Delany in appropriating this genre as they worked to elevate themselves as Black men via the representational mechanisms enabled by exploration—an activity that, according to Mary Louise Pratt, Adriana Craciun, and Janice Cavell, routinely celebrated white male heroism?[11]

The ambitious migration project envisioned by Delany and Campbell went hand in hand with their display and celebration of a Black male agency that prized competency, practicality, mental dexterity, physical bravery, education, and, in particular, a presumed innate racial affinity with Africans that whites could never attain. Also, in adopting the stance of explorers, Delany and Campbell deliberately sought to make themselves legible to American and British whites engaged in both abolition and the expansion of Christian mission on the African continent. In so doing, they highlighted on a world stage the talents and self-determination of civilized and educated men of African descent in the age of slavery. Both men understood Africa not just as a future home but also as the basis of their intellectual and moral authority in the eyes of the world. From this perspective, to borrow the words of literary historian Robert Levine, the *Official Report of the Niger Valley Exploring Party* and *A Pilgrimage to My Motherland* were unquestionably "nineteenth-century 'narratives of masculinity'" that "inevitably became narratives of personhood" for Delany and Campbell.[12] If I take Levine's meaning correctly, then, in the nineteenth century Black men could and did claim for themselves various aspects of white Victorian gender norms, regardless of whether whites saw them as deserving of consideration *as* men. Additionally, as has often been argued of Martin Delany, Frederick Douglass, William Wells Brown, Henry Highland Garnet, and James Forten, to name but a few leaders, ambitious and capable nineteenth-century Black men imagined themselves as "representatives" of their race. In other words, they saw themselves as men of integrity, piety, propriety, chivalry, bravery, and intellectual achievement—all qualities that white supremacists argued Blacks were constitutionally unable to embody.

According to Mary Louise Pratt, though the heroic act of exploring "unknown" lands had traditionally been the province of white aristocrats and military officers, as time went by the conventional exploration narrative evinced a flexibility that enabled a range of possibilities, such that men of humbler station might cast themselves in the role of heroes. Indeed, even the idea of "hero" became more flexible. According to Pratt, in Mungo Park's 1799 *Travels in the Interior Districts of Africa*, the Scottish explorer positioned himself as a self-effacing traveler who not only related what he had seen with his own eyes but also described firsthand the personal horrors he experienced at the hands of Africans. Park's heroism emerged not through any form of aggression, but through his own stunning perseverance.[13] Later in the nineteenth century, David Livingstone, a member of the London Missionary Society and the author of *Missionary Travels and Researches in South Africa* (1857), among other texts, presented himself as the survivor of the wild animal attacks and deadly diseases of central Africa, showing a willingness to sacrifice himself in the name of Christian mission. According to Adriana Craciun, by Livingstone's time white explorers had become "consumer product[s] of the early tourism and travel industries developing in the nineteenth century age of empire," a point exemplified by the rise of Welshman and American Civil War veteran turned *New York Herald* journalist Henry Morton Stanley. (Stanley's claim to international fame rested on his 1872 *How I Found Livingstone: Travels, Adventures, and Discoveries in Central Africa*.)[14] By the second half of the nineteenth century, white narratives about the African continent constituted what writer and explorer Winwood Reade termed "African literature." As Felix Driver reminds us, in 1873 Reade even created a map of the continent celebrating previous explorers. Published in his *African Sketchbook*, Reade's otherwise blank map of the African continent superimposed the names of white explorers on all topography that had been verified by observation.[15]

A cartographic memorial to his forebears, Reade's map imagined no room for the actual inhabitants of Africa, their experiences, or their version of events. Additionally, says Driver, all explorers, including Reade, would have "relied heavily on the assistance of European missionaries, traders and officials, as well as many unnamed African servants and porters. But few of the latter received much of Reade's attention, in literal contrast to his collection of books, 'brought out not as furniture, but as friends.'"[16] As Adriana Craciun has observed, eighteenth-century explorers usually acknowledged a great variety of sources, including native informants, Arab scholars, and mapmakers at home. According to Craciun, the knowledge of all of these individuals came together in the production of what were essentially multidisciplinary works covering climate science, botany, zoology, linguistics, and ethnography. But from the Enlightenment onward, these crucial human contributors were subordinated to the ideal of the singular white hero who increasingly came to embody the role of multidisciplinary scientific expert. Thus, the Victorian white male hero signified not just bravery and physical toughness but also (at least on paper) an extraordinary, even all-powerful intellect that could marshal together broad bodies of knowledge at the drop of a hat.[17] And yet, as Craciun urges, rather than accepting this hero as a solidified role with a fixed set of characteristics, we must still press the question "What is an explorer?" That is, we must theorize rigorously the rise of that hero as a historically contingent, ongoing process of self-making. Craciun aligns with Mary Louise Pratt in suggesting that the very model of white explorer-hero celebrated and romanticized by the late nineteenth and early twentieth century might have been somewhat more pliable and more adaptable in the first half of the nineteenth century. If so, then we have to consider to whom and for what reasons this category of manhood might have been available.

No doubt Delany and Campbell gravitated toward the exploration narrative because the genre had a long-standing transatlantic pedagogical function. They used the genre to support their authority as Black male leaders of an entire migration movement that might redeem both Blacks of the New World from second-class citizenship and African peoples from their "heathen" ways. Consequently, the projection of Black male authority went hand in hand with the production of an idealized Black homeland, and vice versa. Additionally, in investigating the feasibility of a settlement, Delany and Campbell simultaneously followed a set of well-rehearsed rules for the collection and evaluation of scientific information. As Pratt and others have long argued, the exploration narrative functioned as a key technology of empire, as successive white male explorers collected crucial data on everything from edible flora to little-known mountain passes to arid plains, watering holes, river valleys, climatic anomalies, and newly discovered animals, conveying their observations not only in print but through lecture tours and widely disseminated maps and illustrations. Ironically, Delany and Campbell also collected valuable firsthand cultural and linguistic information about indigenous populations—that is, all the key information one might need to establish a colonial beachhead. Though their goals were not identical to those of white explorers, once they had completed their tour of Nigeria, Delany and Campbell engaged in the same type of publicity-making speaking tours as their white counterparts. When they arrived in London, Campbell was invited by the Royal Geographical Society to publish a paper summing up his observations, while Delany was asked to deliver a presentation at a membership meeting of the society. Their respective exploration narratives were also read and commented upon by British reformers such as Henry Venn and by perhaps the most prolific white explorer of the Victorian age, Sir Richard Francis Burton.

In the end, even though Delany never returned to West Africa and Campbell ended up as a member of the colonial elite in British Lagos, did their exploration narratives contribute to the larger white and Western masculine project for the consumption of Africa? For one thing, their experience in Nigeria as racialized subjects would have been different from that of a white explorer, since they discovered a world where whites were not only very scarce but also seemingly powerless to command.[18] In Nigeria, everyone had Black skin, whether they were rulers, soldiers, traders, farmers, blacksmiths, fishermen, or weavers. Indeed, West Africans and not Europeans controlled every community, every manufacturing center, and every military body. Perhaps for the first time in their lives, then, both men would have been surrounded by an emotionally invigorating display of unadulterated Black power. Evidence of this alternate sensibility surfaced in the treaty Delany and Campbell negotiated "with the native authorities of" Abeokuta, an important inland city founded by refugees of internecine warfare. Both men reproduced this treaty in their narratives. According to "Article First" of the treaty, "the King and Chiefs on their part agree to grant and assign unto the said Commissioners [Delany and Campbell], on behalf of the African race in America, the right and privilege of settling in common with the Egba people, on any part of the territory belonging to not otherwise occupied." In exchange for land, settlers were expected "to bring with them . . . intelligence, education, a knowledge of the arts and sciences, agriculture, and other mechanical and industrial occupations, which they shall put into immediate operation by improving the lands and in other useful vocations."[19] Though the document promoted the so-called civilizing mission, establishing American Blacks as the projected engine of progress, it also paid homage to the fact that nothing could go forward without the full agreement and cooperation of the Egba. This condition alone elevated the treaty as an anticolonial document.

Perhaps not coincidentally, the story of the treaty in each narrative contrasted sharply with the American Colonization Society's story of first contact with local West Africans of what eventually became the colony of Liberia. The society's own pamphlets reported that when the settlers finally made it to the Liberian coast in 1821, the white ACS agent Eli Ayres, along with Lieutenant Robert Stockton from the US warship *Alligator*, went on shore to negotiate with the Bassa chieftain, "King Peter," for land that later become Cape Mesurado. According to the ACS's official story, surrounded by "savage beasts with muskets" and "native barbarians . . . gaping with wonder," Ayres and Stockton felt things deteriorating once the Bassa realized that an American settlement would disrupt their lucrative share of the Atlantic slave trade. Faced with escalating indigenous hostility, Stockton drew one of his "pistols [and] pointed it at the head of the king, while raising his other hand to heaven [in an appeal for] protection." Instantly "King Peter flinched before the calm courage of the white man"; miraculously, all were suddenly "awed and subdued . . . while their chiefs began to listen with respect to advances and proposals now made to them."[20] Supporters of the ACS at home understood these events as the triumph of white civilization over African barbarism, but from that moment on, Liberia's early history would be marked by armed resistance from the Bassa, Dey, Krahn, Mandingo, Grebo, Gola, Mano, Kru, and Mende peoples. Such was the case in 1822, when a coalition force organized by the Bassa, Dey, and Gola twice attacked that initial ACS settlement at Cape Mesurado. This violence was still in evidence some twenty years later when, in an 1840 letter to his former Virginia master, James Hartwell Cocke, Peyton Skipwith related how he and a particularly vengeful party of settlers unleashed a vicious attack upon an indigenous village. The battle left many Africans dead, including a chief. As the remaining villagers fled, they attempted to bury their deceased leader, but the Black American settlers dug up and then mutilated the corpse. According to Skipwith, the leader's "head was taken from his body and . . . made an ornament in the Hands of . . . Governor Buchanan." At an earlier point in the same letter, Skipwith muses, "it is something strange to think that those people of africa are calld our ancestors[. I]n my present thinking, if we have any ancestors they could not have been liked these hostile tribes in this part of africa for you may try and distell that principle and belief in them and do all you can for them and they still will be your enemy."[21] By the time Liberia gained independence from the ACS in 1847, such attitudes were widespread among many of Skipwith's fellow settlers. Ten years later, at the same time Delany put forward his ambitious exploration project in Chatham, ever-present tensions between settlers and indigenous peoples boiled over when Liberia's tiny sister republic, Maryland-in-Africa, completely succumbed to a joint Grebo and Kru rebellion. Unable to protect itself, Maryland-in-Africa turned to Liberia for aid, eventually agreeing to a protective annexation and then complete absorption.[22]

In sharp contrast to the deadly struggles facing settlers in Liberia and Maryland-in-Africa, the treaty signed by Delany and Campbell with the *alake* (king) of Abeokuta affirmed the mutual benefits that were to accrue from the arrival of American settlers. According to the fourth article, "The laws of the Egba people shall be strictly respected by the settlers; and, in all matters in which both parties are concerned, equal numbers of commissioners, mutually agreed upon, shall be appointed, who shall have power to settle such matters" (OR, 78). That Delany and Campbell made a point of stressing these particulars signaled their commitment to an alternate repatriation plan where Africans were willing hosts, where settlers and Africans would find common ground, and where mutual respect would triumph over violence. With such a landmark agreement in hand, there still remained what proved to be insurmountable challenges: recruiting immigrants, securing funding for transatlantic passage and the construction of farms and other means of self-sustenance, and, finally, contending with Britain's attempts to outmaneuver any non-African trade competitors in Lagos and its hinterland. Still, at least on paper, this imagined moment when Africans would welcome "back" the descendants of the first slaves became a literal and figurative process whereby Delany and Campbell might considerably alter the identity of male explorer, because of their experiences as African diasporic subjects.

In what follows I offer separate analyses of the exploration narratives by Delany and Campbell, with particular emphasis on how each appropriated and redefined for himself the category of *explorer* in relation to a shared belief that indigenous West Africans were racial brothers and sisters and that the African continent was their logical birthright. Both men clearly drew on different aspects of the white male explorer-hero stereotype, and therefore each employed particular narrative conventions to characterize their relationship to the landscape, to West African manners and customs, and to the internecine warfare they encountered on their tour of Nigeria. Of particular importance was each man's understanding of himself as simultaneously a national, racial, and—in the particular case of the Jamaican Campbell—imperial subject. Notably, Delany and Campbell appear to have divided up the larger task of writing about their journey. Delany's narrative focused on practical scientific questions of climate, soil, the nature and treatment of disease, agriculture, and native flora and fauna. On the other hand, Campbell addressed almost exclusively the traditional "customs and manners" discussions, expounding on the character, physique, clothing, family, dwellings, daily life, and political structures of the Yoruba and the Egba. This bifurcation of the larger narrative purpose necessarily shaped not only the significance of what each had to say but also their respective self-presentation to transatlantic audiences.

One goal in this chapter is to tease out the ways in which Martin Delany and Robert Campbell worked to shape the transatlantic discussion of West Africa's future and, by extension, what they imagined as the fate of the African. Indeed, through their collaboration and within their respective narratives, Delany and Campbell extended and elevated forms of Black male agency within an interracial transatlantic abolitionist context. At the same time, as abolitionists and pro-emigrationists, Delany and Campbell attempted to map out the practical means by which Nigeria might enable a group of self-sustaining free Black migrants to carry out their own plans for working with local Africans. Both men felt that only Blacks (specifically those who were morally upright and educated) had the right to go into West Africa and proselytize, that only Blacks could be sensitive to African needs, and that only Blacks had a real interest in creating a strong and unified Black nation that would eventually take its place among the world's great civilizations.

Seven years before he visited Nigeria, Delany envisioned "A Project for an Expedition of Adventure, to the Eastern Coast of Africa." Framed within his larger treatise *The Condition, Elevation, Emigration and Destiny of the Colored People of the United States* (1852), this prospectus likely served as the genesis for the eight-man scientific expedition Delany would propose at the 1858 emigration convention in Chatham. However, in 1852, his emphasis lay with East rather than West Africa—perhaps to avoid having anything to do with Liberia, perhaps to get as far away from the United States as possible, or perhaps both. According to the prospectus, eight men were to set out "on an expedition to the EASTERN COAST OF AFRICA, to make researches for a suitable location on that section of the coast, for the settlement of colored adventurers from the United States and elsewhere. Their mission should be to all such places as might meet the approbation of the peoples of South America, Mexico and the West Indies, &c."[23] Delany continues:

> The Creator has indisputably adapted us for the "denizen of *every soil*," all that is left for us to do, is to *make* ourselves "*lords* of terrestrial creation." The land is ours—there it lies with inexhaustible resources; let us go and possess it. In Eastern Africa must rise up a nation to whom all the world must pay commercial tribute.
>
> We must MAKE an ISSUE, CREATE an EVENT, and ESTABLISH a NATIONAL POSITION for OURSELVES; and never may expect to be respected as men and women, until we have undertaken, some fearless, bold, and adventurous deeds of daring—contending against **every odds**—regardless of every consequence.[24]

In Delany's concept of this Black nation, neither indigenous East Africans nor the Indian Ocean slave trade are in evidence, creating the illusion of blank, unoccupied land open and accessible to Black American settlers, enabling them to become giants of global commerce rather than the objects of trade under slavery. In proclaiming African American rights to apparently unclaimed land, Delany tapped into both diasporic fantasies of African "return" and the idea of ex-slaves and the freeborn as the inheritors of the earth, with East Africa presenting "the greatest facilities for an immense trade with China, Japan,

Siam, Hindoostan, in short all of the East Indies—of any other country in the world." For Delany, successful Black nationhood would be expressed through regional financial power, at the level of Dutch, British, French, and Portuguese commercial interests in southern Africa and Southeast Asia during the rise of early European colonization.[25] In this moment, Delany most resembled white American and European imperialists, as they too envisioned an "Africa" without Africans. His ideas also adhered to the traditional nineteenth-century imagining of nation building: "the claims of no people, according to established policy and usage, are respected by any nation until they are established in a national capacity"—a "capacity," he argued, that must arise out of a Black (and presumably male) desire for "adventure," which we might interpret as trials and tests of bravery, ingenuity, and adaptability.[26] In Britain and France, white male explorers also employed the idea of adventure to confirm their superiority. In Delany's prospectus for a Black East African empire, he envisioned a way not only to prove Black male equality with white men but also to demonstrate to his Black audience that they had the capacity for greatness. There was indeed more at stake in the pursuit of adventure than just successful global commerce.

In the opening pages of his *Official Report of the Niger Valley Exploring Party*, Delany makes clear just how unrelenting attacks could be on the character and capability of any free Black man who dreamed of such great feats. In his preface to the narrative, Delany recounts that in 1854, the Pittsburgh *Daily Morning Post* railed against attendees of the Colored Convention held in Cleveland on the topic of "national emigration." The *Post* reported in a derisive tone that under Delany's guidance, a special committee had drawn up "a plan for Emigration to countries where [Black Americans] can enjoy political liberty, and form nations 'free and independent'" (OR, 34). Taking a pro-ACS stance, the *Post*'s editorial essentially blasted any relocation site in the Americas, including the West Indies, Central America, and parts of South America. According to the *Post*:

> If Dr. D[elany] drafted this report, it certainly does him much credit for learning and ability; and cannot fail to establish for him a reputation for vigor and brilliancy of imagination never yet surpassed. It is a vast concept of impossible truth. The Committee seem to have entirely overlooked the strength of the "powers on earth" that would oppose the Africanization of half the Western Hemisphere.
>
> We have no motive in noticing this gorgeous dream of "the Committee," except to show its fallacy—its impracticability, in fact, its absurdity. No sensible man, whatever his color, should be for a moment deceived by such impracticable theories.

On the African coast already exists a thriving and prosperous Republic [of Liberia]. It is the native home of the African race; and there he can enjoy the dignity of manhood, the rights of citizenship, and all the advantages of civilization and freedom. (OR, 35)

By including these attempts by the white press to condemn Black American self-determination, Delany reminded his readers of the contempt with which, even in the North, their independent activism was regarded. Yet both Delany and his keenest readers knew that regardless of the *Post's* attempt to declare the Americas off-limits, antislavery Britain had already set aside land in Ontario to accommodate runaways and free Black people who wanted to live on truly free soil.[27] Delany himself, along with free African American families such as the Shadds of Delaware, had relocated by 1858 to Chatham and Buxton, two small towns just across the US border from Detroit. Additionally, the Cleveland convention committee's plan for migration to alternate territories in the hemisphere made sense, given that some Black Americans had already migrated to Haiti and to the British West Indies. Upon gaining independence from Spain, the former colonies Mexico, Nicaragua, and Colombia had abolished slavery, making these new nations equally suitable as destinations. With these possibilities available, the goals of the Cleveland convention would not have seemed a "gorgeous dream" to its Black audience. Thus, Delany's use of the newspaper excerpt at once confirmed white refusal to believe in the ability of African Americans and underlined his faith that Black efforts were already yielding fruit. For the rest of the *Official Report*, then, descriptions of West African flora and fauna represented a body of information independently verified by a member of the audience's own community and, in particular, someone who understood the migrant experience personally. In this, Delany operated as part of a broader pool of Black community leaders working to expand options for all Black Americans.

Britt Rusert has stressed Delany's keen interest in nineteenth-century science, enumerating him as one of several early African Americans who left "a vibrant and artful archive of Black engagements with natural science, engagements that built evidence against regimes of scientific racism, but also sought to mobilize forms of popular science with no particular connection to the science of race . . . in the production of an expansive imaginary of and for emancipation."[28] Indeed, if we think of Delany's profession as a medical doctor, his publications such as *Principia of Ethnology: The Origin of Races and Color* (1879), his fascination with astronomy as noted by Rusert, his keen interest in comparative anatomy, and the multiple roles he embraced as geographer, botanist, climatologist, and ethnographer on his Nigerian expedition, it is clear that the entire enterprise would have been a test of all his intellectual faculties, not to mention his physical stamina. Therefore, Delany would have seen himself articulating an expanded model of Black masculinity that was certainly physically hardy but also erudite, inquisitive, and intellectually ambidextrous—that is, more than qualified to achieve full dominion over all "terrestrial creation." Certainly, in section VIII of the *Official Report* Delany places himself within the growing pantheon of white explorers of the African continent, in particular the two feted Scotsmen Hugh Clapperton (1788–1827) and David Livingstone (1813–73). Delany cites not only Clapperton's *Journal of a Second Expedition into the Interior of Africa, from the Bight of Benin to Soccatoo* (published posthumously in 1829) and Livingstone's *Missionary Travels and Researches in South Africa* (1857) but also the American Baptist missionary Thomas Jefferson Bowen's *Central Africa: Adventures and Missionary Labors* (1857).[29] Though he counts himself among their company, as a Black man with an African grandfather whom family legend reported to have been christened Shango after the Yoruba *orisha* or demigod of thunder, Delany implied a proprietary claim over West African territory rooted in racial identity.

Although some readers imagined Nigeria as a disease-ridden land overtaken with rank vegetation and warlike "savages," Delany reveals instead a tame near-paradise, stocked with all the necessities to enable settler success: "The whole face of the country extending through the Aku region or Yoruba, as it is laid down on the large missionary map of Africa, is most beautifully diversified with plains, hills, dales, mountains, and valleys, interlined with numerous streams, some of which are merely temporary or great drains; whilst the greater part are perennial, and more or less irrigating the whole year, supplying well the numerous stocks of cattle and horses with which this country is so well everywhere provided. The climate is most delightful" (OR, 70). Ironically, in keeping with many of the white narratives he evokes, Delany addresses the landscape and its properties (i.e., soil depth, mineral content, forestland) first, before moving on to its human inhabitants, in particular the local craftspeople who run the "blacksmiths' shops" and "iron smelting works," producing iron, brass, copper, and zinc (OR, 71). Decisively rejecting the stereotype of indolence often ascribed to Africans by white explorers, Delany underscores the Nigerians' self-determination and productivity, nicely bringing them in line with the kind of African Americans he hoped to attract to his yet-to-be-established settlement. Yet another subversion of the white explorer's gaze is evident in Delany's vivid rhetorical flourish of unfurling the "missionary map of Africa" (OR, 70). Bending over the map, side by side with his Black reader as it were, in lieu of impenetrable jungles and miasmatic swamps Delany conjures up a bird's-eye view of rolling hills and dales—hardly the vision of the "White Man's Grave" that haunted the British imagination regarding the west coast of Africa. Likewise, his delineation of a manageable West African world differs considerably from reports of Liberia, with its stifling heat and humidity, thick forests, stony soil, and hostile ethnic groups. Indeed, "civilized" by African industry and local commerce, Delany's Nigeria beckons rather than repels.

Still, we must assess Delany's co-optation by the very practice of exploration and its unavoidable cultivation of an imperial worldview. That Delany sees Nigerians in need of Christianity and "civilization" is a given. At the same time, simply by employing and reproducing the analytical technology available to him at the time—namely, the missionary map and the narratives of Clapperton, Livingstone, and company—Delany (and perhaps that Black reader by his side) comes dangerously close to sounding like an Anglo-European. Ironically, the very quality that made a "missionary map" especially comforting to the white Western viewers was its tendency to simply erase from sight anything that would complicate the civilization of the heathen and the expansion of an empire of Christ. As Ruth Kark has argued, maps commissioned specifically by missionary associations projected a set of assumptions about local inhabitants that (not surprisingly) did not reflect the views of Africans on the ground. Some maps, for example, highlighted various towns and villages not for their importance to local inhabitants but for their direct usefulness to European missionary plans. So, according to Kark, if an important market city had a strong Muslim presence that would prohibit Christian proselytizing, that city might either be de-emphasized or altogether erased from the map, in favor of smaller towns and villages deemed more hospitable to the creation of a mission station.[30] In terms of his daily negotiation of nineteenth-century Anglo-European masculine ideals, Delany prided himself on his ability not merely to handle but to *own* this technology. Ironically, though, as with most whites from the Americas and Europe, he used the missionary map in the way it was meant to be used—for the invention of the specific version of West Africa he needed to find. Indeed, Delany's commitment to his singularity of vision was that he failed to mention that he and Campbell left Nigeria at the start of the Ibadan-Ijaye War (1861–62). Rather, with his opening scene of gentle hills and meadows, Delany invites his Black American audience to experience their potential homeland through his eyes, making clear that his goal is not the enslavement and exploitation of the indigenous peoples of Nigeria but rather the empowerment of the Black settler. And as the representative of this settler, throughout his text Delany acts as the keeper and mediator of specific knowledge for the benefit of his people, doling out, when necessary, basic facts about West African plants, crops, and domesticated animals, all of which miraculously appear to be perfect counterparts to the plants, crops, and domesticated animals of the American Northeast. In Delany's assessment, every risk, from impenetrable vegetation to devastating heat to nonarable land, could be contained, in part because the technology he was using (e.g., the map, narratives by other explorers) was simply not designed for truth telling. As a Black American explorer, then, does Delany merely replicate the same attitudes and blind spots within traditional exploration literature?

In the same way, Delany tries to minimize malaria, but his *Official Report* still evinces a flutter of anxiety on the topic. By cross-referencing Delany's narrative with Campbell's *Pilgrimage*, we discover that Delany did indeed contract malaria and that he was plagued with recurring illness throughout the expedition. Notably, Delany first sets foot on African soil in Liberia, having taken a merchant ship owned and operated by Americo-Liberians on their way from New York to Monrovia. As with almost all ACS migrants, he likely contracted malaria or a similar "acclimatizing fever" from a mosquito bite received aboard ship in the harbor or soon after disembarking. After recovering somewhat, Delany proceeded from Liberia to Lagos, apparently without incident, and then to Abeokuta. Recalling their travels together, Campbell reported frequent stops to allow Delany to rest, indicating that the latter continued to struggle with fever. Instead of focusing on his own illness, however, Delany depersonalizes the experience of fever so as to introduce his readers to what he suggests is the real underlying condition—namely, fear of change:

> The first . . . impressions of the coast of Africa are always inspiring, producing the most pleasant emotions. These pleasing sensations continue for several days . . . until they gradually merge into feelings of almost intense excitement. . . .

> [After the onset of] febrile attacks, . . . nausea, chills, or violent headache [the patient experiences] *"a feeling of regret that you left your native country for a strange one; an almost frantic desire to see friends and nativity; a despondency and loss of the hope of ever seeing those you love at home again.*

> These feelings must be resisted, and *regarded as a mere morbid affection of the mind* at the time. . . .

> It is generally while laboring under this last-described symptom, that persons send from Africa such despairing accounts of their disappointments and sufferings, with horrible feelings of dread from the worst to come.

When an entire recovery takes place, the love of the country is most ardent and abiding. (OR, 64)

In his discussion of African fever, Delany did not so much eliminate the possibility of death as reframe it in the more familiar context of what nineteenth-century Western medicine regarded as *nostalgia*, or homesickness. According to the prevailing medical view, nostalgia was a disease of the mind that exhibited a range of symptoms, including fever, hallucinations, loss of appetite, extreme lethargy, dizziness, despondency, and a general wasting away where the patient essentially loses the will to live. By making this statement, Delany reminded his reader that he was a physician by training and, in his expert opinion, there was little difference between the symptoms of a tropical fever such as malaria and the condition called nostalgia. This collapsing of one disease with another suggested that one's recovery from tropical fever had everything to do with the will and desire to transfer allegiance from the United States to the ancestral homeland of Africa.

In fact, malaria, dengue fever, and yellow fever killed one out of every three foreign visitors to the West African coast, prompting the Black American newspaper editor Mary Ann Shadd Cary to declare in 1852 that Africa was "teeming . . . with the breath of pestilence, a burning sun and fearful maladies," all of which led unmistakably to "moral and physical death."[31] In 1855, Delany himself described Liberia, sight unseen, as "the tide-swamp of the coast of Guinea, . . . a national Potter's Field, into which the carcass of every emigrant . . . would most assuredly moulder in death."[32] In the midst of his own struggles with tropical fever, Delany must have feared his own death, provoking an understandable terror at the prospect of expiring thousands of miles away from his family and friends in Chatham. Having survived this ordeal, Delany theorized African homecoming as a mental struggle (evidenced by external symptoms) that, once overcome, enabled a figurative rebirth in the ancestral homeland. Let us be mindful here of David Anderson's useful suggestion that we have to understand the concept of "home" for those nineteenth-century patients afflicted with nostalgia. According to Anderson, "Home is, and means, so much more than any particular place; home is a conglomeration of memories and senses, it is the knowledge and familiarity of locale; home articulates belonging and our feelings toward its setting and surroundings proffers comfort and assurance."[33] In his description of the disease process, Delany theorized that tropical fever and nostalgia were one and the same and that would-be settlers already had within their grasp the means to survive—namely, the ability to let go of a "particular place" (America) in favor of intangible "memories and senses"

(Blackness as African ancestry). As for the centrality of "knowledge and familiarity of locale," Delany's expedition proved the value of existing exploration literature and mapmaking for giving potential settlers everything they might need.

Also implied here is Delany's careful distinction between what he imagined to be a Black settler's experience of fever and that of the white explorer. In almost all white-authored African exploration narratives, loss of life to tropical fever looms large, underscoring a traditional association of fever with the untamed nature of a "savage" land. The occasion of white death in these narratives—and particularly the recounting of the deaths of previous European explorers in a particular location—justified the notion that Africa had to be civilized so as to bring nature under proper human control. Yet regardless of real or imagined conquest, at least until there was a better understanding of what caused these diseases (and that came toward the end of the nineteenth century), Europe remained the site of white belonging. By conflating nostalgia with tropical fever, Delany's *Official Report* picked up where white narratives of African exploration left off—namely, through his insistence that survival of malaria or yellow fever confirmed an emotional knowledge of African belonging. Thus, if white explorers such as Park or Livingstone became heroes because they braved the backwardness and disease of the African continent, Black Americans could become heroes when they embraced in body and mind the disease process as reaffiliation. Looking back to Delany's 1852 "Project for an Expedition" and what appeared at first to be a somewhat naive call to "adventure," we might well ask if the acute physical and mental suffering brought on by fever symbolized in the *Official Report* the character-defining tests of self-control and endurance required for the success of Delany's great African enterprise.

Ironically, given Delany's 1855 condemnation of Liberia as a proverbial, swamp-ridden potter's field swallowing up the corpses of ACS settlers, his refiguration of tropical fever also suggested something of a shift in his presentation of the Black nation. According to the *Official Report*, Delany came down with fever in Monrovia, where he was cared for by the same Americo-Liberians he had previously maligned. Thus his actual recovery (and therefore his reconnection to Africa) took place in Liberia. Though Delany never relinquished his dislike for the ACS, he used the narrative as a means to make peace with individual Americo-Liberian settlers. As a narrative necessarily composed in retrospect, the *Official Report* therefore promoted cooperation rather than conflict between Delany and his Liberian hosts. Ironically, it was Americo-Liberians themselves who ushered him into West Africa: after all, he had booked his passage "on a ship christened *The Mendi*, in tribute to the Sierra Leonean slave rebels of the *Amistad*, owned and operated by three Americo-Liberians."[34] His description of disembarkation also boded well: "Saturday, July 10.—I landed on the beach at Grand Cape Mount, Robertsport, in company of Messrs. the Hon. John D. Johnson, Joseph Turpin, Dr. Dunbar [the owners of the ship], and Ellis A. Potter, amid the joyous acclamations of the numerous natives who stood along the beautiful shore, and a number of Liberians, among whom was Reverend Samuel Williams, who gave us a hearty reception. Here we passed through the town (over the side of the hill), returning to the vessel after night" (OR, 47). The easy hospitality lavished on Delany by Americo-Liberians belied the complex emotions that must have been at play on both sides in the actual moment, since his hosts were all well aware of Delany's published and personal views. However, Delany's representation of his reception suggests an unusual unity of purpose:

> At Grand Bassa I held a Council with some of the most eminent Liberians, among whom were several members of the National legislature—the venerable Judge Hanson in the chair. Several able speeches were made—the objects of my mission and policy approved; and I shall never forget the profound sensation produced at that ever-memorable Council, and one of the most happy hours of my life. When the honored judge and sage, sanctioning my adventure, declared that, rather than it should fail, he would join it himself, and with emotion rose to his feet; the effect was inexpressible, each person being as motionless as a statue. (OR, 58)

By referring to these dignitaries as a "noble band of brothers" (OR, 60), Delany implies that his reception in Monrovia was already on its way to being a familial homecoming.

Yet even in metaphorical terms, familial connections could not overcome other problems that, for Delany, made Liberia unlivable. Though Americo-Liberians provided him with lodging and nursed him back to health, and though his tone had softened considerably, Delany still employed Liberia as the negative foil to Nigeria: "The native fever which is common to all parts of Africa, in Liberia while . . . not necessarily fatal (and in by far the greater percentage of cases in the hands of an intelligent, skillful physician, quite manageable), is generally much worse in its character there than in the Yoruba country, where I have been. The symptoms appear to be much more aggravated and the patient to suffer more intensely" (OR, 65). Had Americo-Liberians truly relinquished their connection to the United States? Indeed, Delany directly faulted Americo-Liberians for creating the conditions where tropical fevers might flourish. According to the *Official Report*, because the inhabitants of Monrovia had neither cleared "rank" vegetation from the land nor drained the surrounding mangrove swamps, their inaction enabled a fever-carrying miasma to range over settler homesteads, resulting in acute illness and death. Indeed, Delany blamed "the [more extreme] character of the disease" in Liberia on the gluttony of Americo-Liberians who, he claimed, were fond of "improper food and drink" (OR, 65). Thus, reports from Liberia of intense suffering brought on by fever suggested (according to Delany) a widespread moral deficiency among the Black nation's settler-citizens. Add to this the apparently shortsighted and lazy indigenous populations who, "unlike those of the Yoruba . . . cultivate nothing but rice, [cassava], and yams . . . in small patches," and Liberia would most likely remain a stalled national project (OR, 66). In peevishly criticizing Americo-Liberians for their lack of "public buildings of note" (OR, 59), Delany described Monrovia and the surrounding territory in ways that showcased his apparently more sensible ideas for clearing innumerable acres of land and building paved roads, piers, and grand buildings to demonstrate Black civic and commercial ambition. Given that the resources to achieve such projects were abundantly available (for example, large quantities of stone), Delany underscored once again a failure of will among Americo-Liberians. Consequently, the stage is set in the first half of the *Official Report* to confirm and promote Nigeria as the true site of Black nationhood. At the same time, Delany set himself up as the more knowledgeable Black American expatriate, since he presumed to know more than the Americo-Liberians about managing land to secure general public health and the effective use of natural resources.

Not surprisingly, in the remainder of the *Official Report* Nigeria turned out to be everything Liberia was not. In contrast to Liberia's lazy indigenous farmers, the Yoruba raised peas "such as are raised for horse and cattle feed in Canada and other parts of America" (OR, 73). According to Delany, "there is little difference between [local yams] and potatoes," and he argued that "beets, parsnips, and carrots . . . could be successfully raised, if desired" (OR, 74). Just as he conflated tropical fever with nostalgia, Delany seemed to collapse Nigeria with North America, such that hogs, horses, and game birds were virtually the same as American species—so much so that people moving into the Niger Valley would feel as though they had never left the United States. Importantly, in contrast to the ongoing conflicts between Americo-Liberians and indigenous Africans that continued to plague Liberia, Delany described his welcome by the king of Ilorin: "Many, very many were the thanks given me that day by these, my native kinsmen and women" (OR, 76). While his first encounter with Americo-Liberians was cordial enough, Delany described how the king of Ilorin opened his arms to both him and Campbell, because "we were 'his people'"; this was "a privilege which he never allowed 'a strange white man,' who was never permitted to look upon his royal black face publically" (OR, 80). Here

Delany conjured up a native African acceptance of diasporic Blacks that completely revised the traditional white narratives of settler colonialism, ironically exemplified in Liberia.

Delany's dealings with local Yoruba and their cousins the Egba generated both pride and paternalism: pride for the industriousness and systems of government adopted by the communities he encountered, and paternalism because he saw these same Africans as needing improvement. Note, for example, his interaction with the Yoruba trader and political power broker Efunporoye Osuntinubu Osumosa, known more simply as Madame Tinubu. According to Delany, "She had promised to place the entire management of her extensive business in my hands, as much advantage was taken of her by foreigners" (OR, 79). Though of humble origin, Madame Tinubu had nevertheless taken advantage of the custom that a woman, regardless of her marital status, had the right to own property and run businesses, keeping the money she made for herself and her children. Known as both a shrewd negotiator and a formidable foe, the twice-widowed Tinubu accumulated great wealth and military power in her heyday, due in part to the fact that at different points she not only controlled much of the region's extremely valuable palm oil trade but also traded in slaves. Though by the time Delany encountered her in Abeokuta the British had successfully diminished her influence, it was highly unlikely that she was an easy and naive target for unscrupulous foreigners.[35] In order to cast Madame Tinubu as the naive Victorian female, Delany had to present her as ready to yield power to men—ready for the civilizing influences only Black American settlers could bring. Indeed, his encounter with Tinubu proved the need for settlers, justifying Delany's argument that "*a new element*" had to be introduced into Nigeria— namely, immigrants "possessing all the attainments, socially and politically, morally and religiously, adequate to so important an end" as the advancement of Africa (OR, 110). In the final pages of the *Official Report*, Delany proclaimed the slogan "*Africa for the African race, and black men to rule them,*" which, while it pronounced a theme that would later guide modern-day Black Nationalists, appeared equally blind to the pitfalls of Black American arrogance that so plagued Liberia (OR, 121). Regardless, Delany's *Official Report* proved both his superior knowledge of Nigeria and his capacity to lead a new settlement.

But did the two—that is, his display of scientific knowledge and his practical assessment for founding a settlement—actually go together in the narrative? There is no question that Delany's preparation for this expedition was intense. He was well read, given the body of information available at the time, and he had obviously obtained whatever maps had been available, perhaps having no idea that they were flawed. Why, then, did he minimize or ignore altogether the specific dangers settlers would probably face? Like white explorers, Delany projected his own fantasies upon the landscape, though certainly not in quite the way exemplified by Winwood Reade and his map of "African literature," for example. Delany sought mastery over what Reade called African literature in order to use it for the benefit of Black Americans, without being disrespectful to the authority of the Egba. However, even after undergoing what must have been considerable suffering with malaria, Delany was simply determined to represent Nigeria as the antithesis of Liberia, regardless of the realities.

COLONIAL DISPERSAL IN ROBERT CAMPBELL'S
A PILGRIMAGE TO MY MOTHERLAND

Martin Delany and Robert Campbell may have agreed ahead of time to cover specific aspects of their expedition so as not to produce duplicate discussions of the same material. Delany's *Official Report* largely addressed the physical landscape, disease, agriculture, and climate. Campbell, on the other hand, focused close attention on the ethnic groups he encountered, providing the traditional "manners and customs" descriptions, while dramatizing repeatedly what appeared to be carefully nurtured personal affiliations with a range of Nigerians, some among the ruling class but others just ordinary people he met along his journey. Indeed, to the same extent to which Delany absented himself as a participant in his narrative, Campbell deliberately wrote himself into the action at every opportunity. From this perspective, *A Pilgrimage to My Motherland* reads like a series of picaresque vignettes, as Campbell makes his way from one community to the next, acknowledging the men hired to travel with him (including, at different times, a guide, a cook, and a boy who seemed to have acted as a valet or general servant). In the narrative, Campbell seems everywhere present alongside Africans as they go about their daily activities at home, at the market, during festivals, or, on occasion, during interethnic warfare between neighboring towns. Take, for example, his description of the Egba authorities of Abeokuta, the city near which he and Delany intended to create their settlement. Here Campbell describes a particularly favorable encounter with Okukenu, the city's Egba alake: "My reception with the King was very cordial. I explained to him the object of my visit to his country, which he was pleased to hear. He observed that for people coming with such a purpose [i.e., from the United States to found a settlement], and for missionaries, he had great 'sympathy,' and would afford every encouragement; but some of the people (emigrants from the Brazils, Cuba, and Sierra Leone) who were coming into his dominion, especially traders, gave him much trouble" (P, 170). The new arrivals from Brazil, Cuba, and Sierra Leone were Christianized former slaves who had moved to Nigeria to advance their commercial interests. Based on the alake's support for Campbell's mission, readers were to assume that an African American contingent of settlers would be more respectful of indigenous authority and thus more to the alake's liking. Schooling his readers in the importance of showing deference to their future Egba hosts, Campbell recalls his subsequent audiences with "the principal chiefs, to explain the object of my visit and to make to each a small present. Though humble, these presents were well received and in every instance a return present of cola nuts . . . or of cowries was given" (P, 171). Throughout his narrative, Campbell rehearses such examples to emphasize the extent to which, whether or not they were "heathens," indigenous authorities had to be respected.

Campbell's stance here resonated with his very personal title *A Pilgrimage to My Motherland*, since this was not merely a journey for the production of useful knowledge but a realignment of loyalties, from the fraught contexts of Jamaica and Philadelphia to racial acceptance in the African homeland. To this end, Campbell built on his favorable portrait of the Egba by undermining traditional racist assumptions in both Britain and the United States that Africans favored white skin:

> The white man who supposes himself respected in Africa, merely because he is white, is grievously mistaken. . . . One of the chiefs . . . Atambala, was with us one day when a young [white] missionary entered, and passed him with only a casual nod of the head. As soon as he was seated the haughty old chief arose and said, in his own tongue: "Young man, whenever any of my people, even the aged, approaches me, he prostrates himself with his face to the ground. I do not expect the same from . . . civilized men, . . . nevertheless remember always that I shall demand all the respect due to a chief. " (P, 172)

In having Atambala speak for himself, Campbell imbued the latter with agency, dignity, and a deep understanding of traditional authority, while suggesting that, for all their "civilization," white missionaries were both ignorant of and arrogant toward local customs. Additionally, the white missionary's discourteousness only threw into sharper relief Campbell's assiduous attempts to respect and honor Egba leaders. Both Campbell and Delany had already noted the presence of CMS agents such as the Reverend Henry Townsend, apparently "an intimate acquaintance" of the alake Okukenu, since the latter allowed Townsend to sit "on an end of his mat" (P, 171). Campbell earlier introduced readers to acting consul Lieutenant Edward Francis Lodder, whose presence served as a reminder that the British were on site eagerly representing their own agenda—namely, to take advantage of the lucrative trade in palm oil and other agricultural products. However, until the British achieved any final takeover, Atambala's rebuke of the missionary proved the limits of Egba tolerance toward visitors. This incident with Atambala and the badly behaved missionary must also have had an effect on Campbell himself. In Jamaica, and especially in the United States, men of African descent—whatever their color—risked life and limb if they resisted white demands. What must it have been like for Campbell to see an African man in authority, exuding the dignity and presence to lecture a young white man on his bad behavior? The role reversal must surely have been stunning.

To top off these observations, Campbell pointed to the consequences accruing to his own light complexion: "The natives generally at first regarded me as a white man, until I informed them of my connection with the Negro. This announcement always gained me a warmer reception" (P, 171). As both Campbell and Delany would learn, non-Christianized locals categorized non-Africans as "white men" regardless of their skin color, by virtue of their Western clothing, language, and manners, suggesting that the Egba relied on proof of cultural affinity rather than merely falling for appearance or cultural performance. Campbell's negotiation of his skin color in West Africa underscored a sharp contrast to the importance given to mixed-race identity in the British West Indies, where Campbell would have had access to some privilege. In West Africa, however, Campbell highlighted an environment where treating others with respect mattered more than the reputed superiority associated with whiteness in the rest of the Atlantic World. This reversal contradicted the experiences of Campbell's own readers, Black and white, while also stressing the suitability of life in Abeokuta as an antidote to New World racism.

In contrast to Martin Delany, who came to Nigeria only after he was strong enough to leave Liberia, Campbell arrived via packet ship from Liverpool to Lagos, having begun his journey in England on a fundraising mission for the Niger Valley expedition. The traditional route of packet steamers took Campbell to ports that either were already controlled by Britain (for example, Cape Coast Castle, Accra, and Freetown) or had a substantial British presence (Lagos).[36] Though unmentioned in the narrative, the steamer's scheduled stops in British colonial territory might have enabled Campbell to make the acquaintance of members of a tiny British West Indian community that had sprung up among the colonial civil servants. (His fellow passengers would also have included West Indians and Christianized Africans.) As Nemata Blyden has shown, at different points these nepotistic Trinidadian and Jamaican immigrants saw themselves as being above indigenous Africans, above ex-slave converts, and above ex-slave immigrants from Cuba and Brazil. Indeed, as Blyden asserts, their sense of West Indian difference was reinvented and consolidated by and through their active participation in British colonial policy in West Africa.[37] Additionally, there was a contingent of West Indian traders, professionals, and merchants in British-controlled ports, such that Campbell would have encountered fellow Anglophone West Indians—if not in great numbers, then certainly as people of some status. It is significant, however, that Campbell refuses to mention any encounters with British West Indians. Instead, in seeking out the Egba and later the Yoruba (who also welcomed him), Campbell rejects literally and symbolically the world created by his white father, for what he hopes will be a full embrace of people on his mother's side.

Campbell's attitude toward local Africans bears comparison to ways in which the latter were often figured in narratives by white explorers, who included indigenous peoples when such revelations served particular narrative purposes. For example, in a famous 1857 lecture delivered at Cambridge's Town Hall, the Scottish missionary David Livingstone described his interaction with various members of the baKwena people, in what is now the modern state of Botswana. Livingstone focused special attention on the chief Sechele because the latter decided, at the missionary's urging, to convert to Christianity. Because of his status as a chief, Sechele was crucial to Livingstone's plan for mass conversion, since he mistakenly assumed that the baKwena were mutely obedient to their leader and would follow his example without protest. As it turned out, Sechele's Christian conversion caused discontent among both his household and his subjects, such that the baKwena chief became Livingstone's *only* convert during the latter's time in southern Africa. Given this failure, Livingstone's portraits of the intractable baKwena transformed them into a convenient foil against which to project his superiority as a white Christian man. For example, during a particularly bad drought, the baKwena justified to Livingstone their belief in a variety of rituals to bring rain:

> I endeavoured to persuade them that no mortal could control the rain, and their argument was, "We know very well that God makes the rain; we pray to him by means of medicines. You use medicines to give to a sick man, and sometimes he dies: you don't give up your medicine, because one man dies; and when any one is cured by it, you take the credit. So, the only thing we can do is to offer our medicines, which, by continued application, may be successful." The only way to eradicate such absurdities from the minds of these poor people is to give them the Gospel.[38]

If in this instance Livingstone makes the baKwena visible so as to provide an appropriate example of why the "civilizing mission" has to be accomplished in Africa, at other points he renders them invisible so as not to interrupt his rumination on the parts of the Kalahari Desert closest to the Zambezi River and its floodplain, and specifically the number of life-sustaining but largely hidden resources that any future European expedition would need in order to survive:

> In the Kalahari desert there is not a single flowing stream, and the only water there is found in deep wells; but at certain periods of the year water-melons are found in abundance, upon the fluid of which oxen and men have subsisted for days, obviating thereby the necessity for canning water. Animals are also plentiful; and though they took care to keep out of bow-shot, I found that with my gun I could kill as many as were wanted. In my journey beyond the desert, I met with many antelopes of a kind before unknown to naturalists, besides elephants, buffaloes, zebras, &c.[39]

The image here is of Livingstone unveiling a deceptively arid panorama to his European reader, pointing out the existence of hidden sources of water and food that would sustain a large caravan. Of course, the source of all this knowledge was none other than the local population upon whom Livingston would have relied for guidance. Only local indigenous people would have known about the changing availability of food resources tied to the water level at different points in the year. Additionally, Livingstone would have been accompanied by indigenous hunters engaged in their own pursuit of game, allowing him to make the comparison between hunting by "bow-shot" and hunting by rifle. In his narrative, then, the indigenous inhabitants appear and disappear as needed to make Livingston solely responsible for his "discoveries."

In striking contrast, Campbell uses his narrative to stage chronologically a slowly emerging familiarity with the Nigerian landscape, akin to a slowly developing awareness of and interaction with local peoples around him. Unlike Livingstone's self-staged command of the landscape, Campbell at first represents himself as the utterly naive and even terrified outsider. Just after his disembarkation at Lagos, but before he begins the overland journey to Aboekuta, Campbell accompanies Mr. Williams, an indigenous convert who served as translator to the acting British consul Lieutenant Lodder, to see Williams's farm. Once at the desired rural location, Campbell leaves his host engaged in some planting to wander off in pursuit of a bird he hopes to shoot and stuff as a curious specimen. After gaining his prize, Campbell suddenly realizes he is lost. Stumbling along "for more than two hours" (P, 165), he finally stops to assess his lack of progress: "I . . . found myself in the midst of an almost impenetrable jungle, the shrubbery and vines so thickly interlacing, that it was with the greatest difficulty that I could break through: the ground too was swampy, and I sometimes sunk nearly to my knees. By this time my friends were as busy seeking me. I never felt more joyful than when I heard their voice in response to my own. From hunger, fatigue, heat of the sun and excitement, I returned home about 2 P.M., with severe headache and fever" (P, 165). Here, Campbell fully acknowledges his otherness as a stranger, and he relies happily on Williams and his associates for transportation home. Indeed, Campbell's sense of alienation takes on a psychosomatic quality, incapacitating him with the symptoms of malaria, suggesting an interesting parallel with Delany's description of similar symptoms in his *Official Report*. By naming Williams as his savior, Campbell pays homage to yet another African guide and host, something that would have been almost unthinkable in a white-authored expedition narrative. The sense, too, of Williams and Campbell as savior and sufferer calling to each other turns the tables on the usual projection of white savior and indigenous heathen. Not surprisingly, after the passage of many weeks during which he traveled from city to city, Campbell presents himself as having acquired a new level of comfort with his surroundings. For example, when a recurring bout of fever incapacitated Martin Delany at the side of the road, Campbell "rode on as fast as possible to find a place at which we could sojourn for the night, and fortunately found a small farm village about four miles further on" (P, 217). Though Campbell also suffers from recurrences of this "acclimitizing fever," for the most part he uses Delany's apparently more frequent lapses in health as a foil for his ability to withstand the new environment, to the point where he capably negotiates the countryside on his own. Whether he had been informed of the location of the village by a local African or not, Campbell turned himself into Delany's savior, just as Williams had saved him.

Still, while Campbell used his narrative to upend colonial racial politics created through imperialism, and though he paid homage to the dignity of both the Egba and the Yoruba, he also sought to establish his own authority at the expense of non-Christian Africans. One could argue that he had not been allowed to express his social identity as a Black man in either Jamaica or the United States, but once in the Niger Valley for the purpose of his expedition, he claimed the ability to inhabit social roles hitherto denied him. This shift had a consequential effect on his narrative voice. Late in the text, Campbell crosses the Ogun River, unexpectedly ending up in the middle of a no-man's-land where hostile parties, including Muslims from the cities Ijaye, Oyo, and Awaye, battled each other, taking prisoners of war. Repeatedly, Campbell falls back on his status as a "civilized" stranger to cross from one enemy's territory into another, all the while pretending not to understand the inquiries made to him by patrolling war bands. Finally, as he prepares to leave Awaye, "a woman with her son and daughter besought me to permit them to go under our protection" (P, 230). Campbell graciously receives them. But no sooner have they set out on the road than they are met with "two hundred Ibadan soldiers." The soldiers demand a gift as the price for allowing Campbell and his party to leave unharmed; however, their idea of a "gift" turns out to be the woman and her two children. Campbell immediately rejects their command: "I told them it was impossible for me to leave these people, they had placed themselves under my protection, therefore I could not permit them to be taken away, except with myself also; that they could take my horse, my watch, my money, all I had in short; but I would not permit them to take these people" (P, 231). Eventually, even the soldiers' commanding officer has "almost a tear in his eye," declaring, "'Oto, oto, oyibo, molo! 'Enough, enough, white man, go on'" (P, 231).

Campbell knew full well that the woman and her children would have become slaves, so he struck a blow for abolition and Christianized Black manhood with his roadside defiance. Ironically, the commander's description of him as a "white man" resonates in the narrative, since Campbell could not (indeed, perhaps desired not to) leave behind his New World identity as a "civilized" person of African descent. At the same time, Campbell's heroic gesture toward the woman and her children engages the title of his narrative: as a first-time Victorian visitor to his "motherland," he becomes the Black father figure who *should* protect enslaved African women from capture and eventual transportation in the transatlantic slave trade. In this sense, only in West Africa can Campbell become the Black patriarch that his own white father—and white men of his father's class in Jamaica—could never be. Interestingly, while Campbell saved the woman and her children, the Ibadan military leader's sentimental tears mimicked the emotions commonly favored by mid-nineteenth-century transatlantic abolitionists who routinely drew upon scenes of Black mothers and children cruelly separated by slavery, so as to move even the most skeptical Anglo-European heart. As depicted in the narrative, the Ibadan commander responded in correct sentimental fashion by (almost) crying. In fact, crying was exactly the empathetic response required, suggesting that even the most hardened African warrior was capable of fine feelings of sympathy, and therefore of Christian conversion.

This scene hardly suggests equality between Campbell and the commander, and when he does build close relationships with native Africans, Campbell turns to the native convert (think here of Williams, the translator and farmer). In this case, he looks to the brothers Samuel Crowther Jr. and Josiah Crowther, sons of none other than the former slave turned Anglican bishop Samuel Ajayi Crowther. Native missionaries had already moved to Abeokuta by the time Delany and Campbell arrived, but Campbell's positive relationship with the Crowthers turns not only on the experience of shared racial oppression but also on their common experience as British colonial subjects. Samuel Jr. and Josiah were educated in Britain, the former as a doctor and the latter as an industrialist. Though Campbell did not have the advantage of a foreign education, in their formative years the Crowther brothers and Campbell would have lived along similar rhythms of English colonial life, sharing something of a common vocabulary with respect to education and Christian upbringing. His origins halfway around the world in another British colonial setting—in addition to his identity as the son of a Scotsman and a woman of African descent, his initial profession as a printer, and his later work as a schoolmaster—identified him as a member of the colonial elite. Consequently, though the locations and populations were different, Campbell and the Crowther brothers would have recognized each other across the expanse of empire. (These moments of recognition no doubt reminded all three of the overbearing nature of the British, so as to refigure new alliances of resistance among them once Campbell moved to Lagos. Still, Campbell must have viewed Nigeria as relatively "free" from white control compared to Jamaica.)

Campbell's affinity with the Crowthers shows itself during a meeting in a local village square between the brothers and local healers. The description betrays an entanglement of African diasporic connection (between Campbell and the Crowthers) even as it reveals the shadow of elitism toward the "heathens" in the village:

> In the afternoon the regulars appeared, clothed in their most costly garments, and well provided with orishas or charms attached to all parts of their persons and dress. In the mean time Mr. Crowther had also prepared to receive them. A table was placed in the middle of the room, and on it a dish in which were a few drops of sulphuric acid, so placed that a slight motion of the table would cause it to flow into a mixture of chlorate of potassa and white sugar. A [cuckoo] clock was also in the room . . . and this was arranged so as to coo while [the local people] were present. . . . Presently the bird came out, and to their astonishment cooed twelve times, and suddenly from the midst of this dish burst forth flame and a terrible explosion. The scene that followed was indescribable: one fellow rushed through the window . . . ; another in his consternation, overturning chairs [and] tables . . . took refuge in the bed-room, under the bed, from

which he was with difficulty afterward removed. It need not be added that they gave no more trouble, and the practice [local healers] sought to break up was only the more increased by their pains. (P, 178–79)

The comical triumph of Western science over African superstition affirms Campbell's desired affiliation (as the narrator and traveler) with the forward-looking, Western-trained Samuel Crowther Jr., at the expense of the locals who are imagined to be so ignorant they have to be tricked into accepting the authority of Western medicine. His decision to include this, of all stories, is noteworthy when we consider that after leaving the West Indies for lack of opportunity, Campbell temporarily ended up in Philadelphia as a science instructor. While he had the full support of the white Quakers who hired him to teach in their school for Black youth, Campbell faced ample racism in his attempt to take classes at the University of Pennsylvania toward improving himself as an educator.

Campbell's affiliation with the Crowther brothers is also important because their acceptance of him affirmed his place within this new world of African opportunity, even as he embraced and respected the traditional authority of non-Christians such as the Egba alake in Abeokuta. This sense of uneasy bonding in the narrative is underscored every time Campbell notes being called a white man by an African. While he hastens to point out that, regardless of their race, all foreign Westerners are regarded as white by the Yoruba and the Egba, Campbell also mentions the vast disparity in skin color between himself and the darker-hued Martin Delany. Repeatedly in the narrative, Campbell describes himself as continually forced to declare his racial credentials, since "Africans are not as keen in the recognition of their descendants, as are the Americans of the same class of person" (P, 178). Again, as members of an elite colonial class enabled in part by British colonialism, the Crowthers emerged as the acceptable model of the kinds of diasporic authentication Campbell hoped to achieve: "Let any disinterested person visiting Abbeokuta, place himself in a position to notice the manner in which such a person, for instance as the Reverend Samuel Crowther, or even his son of the same name, each a pure Negro, is treated, and he would soon perceive the profound respect with which Africans treat those of their own race worthy of it. The white man who supposes himself respected in Africa, merely because he is white, is grievously mistaken" (P, 172). Campbell's use of the Crowther brothers to explain his concept of "worth" was based not on skin color—as distinguished from race—but on their (and his) ability to serve as cultural mediators between non-Christian Africans and Anglo-Europeans.

Although Crowther's account of the 1841 Niger Valley expedition provided an opportunity to reflect on the landscape and populations tied to his preslavery childhood, the fact remained that he was obliged to the Church Missionary Society and to editors willing to reshape his observations to fit institutional purposes. In contrast, Delany and Campbell had neither institutional sponsors nor ready-made white audiences awaiting the publication of their respective narratives. They had financed the expedition themselves, and once they left West Africa, they set out on separate speaking tours to publicize their cause of African repatriation. With the help of the London-based African Aid Society, Delany embarked upon a five-month speaking tour of Britain, covering material that would later form the basis of his *Official Report*. (In fact, his narrative was published in London in 1860 and in the United States a year later.) Though Delany's lectures did not yield the financial contributions he had hoped for, he had nothing to prove to white intellectuals. Validation even came from the Royal Geographical Society, which extended an invitation to Delany to present on his West African expedition at its next meeting. Across the Atlantic, on April 8, 1861, both Delany and Campbell spoke to the African Civilization Society (of which Delany was a founding member) in Brooklyn, New York. According to the meeting minutes, after Delany and Campbell spoke the membership resolved to send Henry Highland Garnet "with a select company to Yoruba, for the purpose of . . . effecting a settlement there."[40] Of course, any such project faced the same daunting task of fundraising, so nothing came of this idea. Later on, to mark the first anniversary of the African Civilization Society's creation, white abolitionist minister Dr. Joseph Parrish Thompson spoke at an organizational meeting about the promise of Nigeria, citing Delany and Campbell for being among those who had brought vital information about Africa to the public.[41]

For his part, Robert Campbell turned his attention not only to speaking engagements but also to his personal plans to relocate to West Africa. After leaving Nigeria, he wrote to the abolition-minded Manchester industrialist Thomas Clegg to purchase a cotton gin for use in West Africa and then made his way back as soon as possible. Especially because the British were involved in their own negotiations with groups such as the Egba and Yoruba, the repatriation plans of Delany and Campbell did not win approval from the government, or for that matter from the CMS. Still, Henry Venn addressed Campbell's *Pilgrimage* in a May 1861 review for the *Christian Observer*. In "West Africa; Viewed in Connection with Slavery, Christianity; and the Supply of Cotton," Venn reviewed several publications on the startling uptick in the illegal Atlantic slave trade, as well as the general unreceptiveness of many African "heathen" to Christianity. As a hopeful antidote he quoted from the overwhelmingly positive in-person observations laid out by Campbell in his *Pilgrimage*, and seemed pleased with Campbell's report of the good character and industrious habits of the peoples who lived in and around Abeokuta. In mentioning Westerners who had recently published findings on Nigeria, he referred to Campbell as "a highly-educated, intelligent gentleman."[42] Clearly Venn positioned Campbell alongside key CMS missionary investigators on the ground, including Henry Townsend and Samuel Ajayi Crowther. Such validation by the CMS secretary suggests that, despite his misgivings about the larger scheme, Venn deemed Campbell's contributions on par with those of white men and that he sought to honor both Black *and* white contributions to the dissemination of knowledge on West Africa.

Did this mean that Delany and Campbell had reached the apogee of the nineteenth-century white exploration tradition? The answer might lie in a response to both narratives penned by none other than the racist, anti-Semitic explorer Sir Richard Francis Burton. A proponent of polygenesis, Burton showed somewhat less contempt for Muslims and some ethnic groups in British India, but at the very bottom of his schema were Africans and anyone of African descent.[43] After Campbell and Delany published their respective narratives, Burton left his post as British consul on Fernando Pó (modern-day Bioko) for his own expedition, retracing many of the routes in Nigeria taken by the American Baptist Thomas Jefferson Bowen and later by Delany and Campbell. His expedition account, *Abeokuta and the Cameroon Mountains: An Exploration*, was published on his return to England in 1863.

Beyond sharing ethnographic and geographic information, Burton's two-volume work is pointedly aimed at attacking what he sees as the unscientific, sentimental, and missionary-minded accounts of the region by four writers: Sarah Tucker's *Abbeokuta: or, Sunrise within the Tropics* (1852), Bowen's *Central Africa* (1857), Mary Ann Serret Barber's *Oshielle: or, Village Life in the Yoruba Country* (1857), and Campbell's *A Pilgrimage to My Motherland*. Burton makes quick work of the first three texts, reserving his most scathing attacks for *A Pilgrimage to My Motherland* and for Campbell himself. (And, though Burton does not centrally address Delany's *Official Report*, the African American comes in for his own excoriation.) The features in *A Pilgrimage to My Motherland* that Campbell most relies upon to imagine his belonging to Nigeria are exactly the targets of Burton's contempt. Referring to the Jamaican derisively as "a 'cullud pussun,'" Burton mocks Campbell's description of Orange Cottage, the home of his friends the Crowthers, as well as the notion that the Crowthers are the promulgators of British civilization: "'Orange Cottage, the beautiful residence of the Brothers Crowther,' as the Pilgrim [Campbell] to his Grandmother's land is fain to call it. This edifice reminded me of a third-rate training stables in some ultra-Cockney part of England. . . . It is partially painted and wholly hideous, its ugliness being surpassed only by its pretentiousness."[44] Ridiculing the notion of "African return," Burton implies that the only forefathers to whom African Americans should pay homage are white ones. Then he charges Campbell with an "animosity" toward whites by repeating a rumor that while "at Lagos . . . on one occasion, when a European colony in Yoruba was spoken of, he [Campbell] swore with fury that 'no white man, if he could help it, should ever plant foot in Western Africa.'"[45] Not content with these attacks in the first volume of his narrative, Burton continues in both the text and footnotes of volume 2 to malign Delany and Campbell for their treaty with the Egba, assuming that they did not understand that according to custom, land in West Africa could not be owned and so could not be sold or given away. Clearly, Burton was angered by any attempt by a Black man to claim the role that he and his fellows had carved out for themselves. Regardless, it was very clear that he had read the narratives by Delany and Campbell in great detail.

Interestingly, Burton laid out his own imperialistic proposal for not one but *three* segregated settlements close to what is now Nigeria's eastern border with Cameroon: a sanatorium for whites recovering from tropical fevers on the cooler slopes of the Cameroon mountains; "a convict station," peopled with the most incorrigible offenders from Britain; and "a colony, selected from 45,000 negroes who, instead of loafing about Canada—a Canadian once told me that if anything could reconcile him to slavery it was the presence of these fugitives— might here do valuable work in lumber cutting, cacao growing, exporting the fiber and meal of the plantain, and expressing cocoa-nut and palm oil."[46] Burton's comments traced the familiar British habit of moving Black colonial populations, in this case from Canada, to create front-line settlements in West African territories it planned to annex. In terms of his actual journey, Burton ironically traveled almost the exact overland and river routes taken by Delany and Campbell, encountering some of the same individuals, including Williams, the native convert who rescued Campbell from the forest and who still served as a translator for English officials in Lagos. But where Campbell marveled at the dignity of ordinary West Africans, saw room for alliance, and praised native industry, Burton condemned one worthless group of Africans after another, be they the Kru men who manned his canoe or the hospitable local people who provided him food and shelter each night of his expedition.

IT IS UNCLEAR WHETHER Martin Delany read Burton's *Abeokuta and the Cama-roons Mountains*. More likely he was retooling to contend with a United States at war. Historians have assumed that Delany, faced with the urgency of recruit-ing for the 54th Massachusetts Colored Regiment and the possibility that the Union might actually defeat the slaveholding South, simply put aside his reloca-tion plans to Nigeria forever. Yet Delany's experiences in West Africa had be-come a lens through which to see new possibilities, albeit in the United States. While he was still lecturing in Britain in September 1860, one British news-paper reported Delany's descriptions of the commonalities shared by animals and fowl in tropical West Africa and the temperate regions of the United States and Britain. More importantly, his presentation linked the Africans he met to the Egyptians, thereby challenging the popular contemporary theory by the En-glishman George Gliddon that Egyptians were white. According to the report, Delany "then gave traits, illustrating the negro's self-respect, and his capacity for the participation of civilized life."[47] Once he returned to the United States and threw himself into war work, similar content showed up in his speeches during recruitment tours in northern states. This was the case in 1863, when the May 1 issue of William Lloyd Garrison's *Liberator* summarized one of Delany's Mas-sachusetts speeches. According to the abolitionist paper, Delany argued that "American schoolbooks inculcated, notwithstanding recent discoveries, very erroneous notions of [Nigeria] as sandy and barren, the soil unproductive, the air full of pestilence, the vegetation poisonous, the very animals unusually fe-rocious. All of this was more or less false. . . . He had travelled three thousand miles in the country and had seen it in all its phases of social and moral life."[48] Delany not only praised the systematic nature of "the African language" (pos-sibly Yoruba?), the *Liberator* reported, but also recited lines of "African" poetry in translation and "reminded his audience of the simple and beautiful extem-poraneous song which the negro woman sang over the poor Mungo Park, the traveller, when he sat sorrowing by her tent door, and to whom she supplied, in her womanly kindness, with milk."[49]

Surprisingly, he even defended polygamy as "an old and venerable institu-tion" with "a genuine Oriental origin. Solomon was the arch-polygamist of the world and the Africans who followed his example were no worse than he." Ac-cording to the news report, Delany went on to state that

> women were universally respected in Africa, and the men paid them chivalrous attention. They were not allowed to do any physical labor whatsoever except to draw water; and this they insisted upon as their pe-culiar right and privilege. This also was an Oriental custom of immemorial

usage; and was frequently alluded to in the Scriptures. . . . Chastity was sacred amongst them, and any one violating or insulting a woman was decapitated. . . .

An African house [owned by a wealthy man] often contained hundreds of women, who were called wives by courtesy. . . . These were daily occupied in spinning, basket-making, weaving cotton fabrics, &c., which they sold in the markets.[50]

As Robert Levine rightly argues, in this speech Delany "was implicitly pointing out the genealogical sources of the moral and social energy that he believed the Black troops would bring to the Union's war against slavery."[51] By referencing what he had seen and experienced in West Africa, Delany also sought to validate the origins of Black Americans and the lives of the Africans he had encountered in 1859–60.

Finally, a specific detail from the *Liberator*'s report stands out: to substantiate his authority as an explorer, during his speech Delany appeared in "a long dark-colored robe, with curious scrolls upon the neck as a collar. He said it was the wedding dress of a Chief, and the embroidery was insignia, and had a specific meaning well understood in African high circles. He wore it because he thought it becoming, and fitting the occasion."[52] Additionally, Delany "produced a grammar of the [Yoruba?] language, and made quotations from it."[53] Of course, the frontispiece image of Campbell's *Pilgrimage* (figure 4.2) has him dressed in what appears to be a very similar garment, though that version includes a turban. The donning of "African" clothing and, in Delany's case, the use of a written grammar confirming the "reduction" of an oral language to writing speak to a colonizing tradition enacted specifically by European orientalists— those European gentlemen (and some ladies) famously described by Edward Said who claimed to "know" the "oriental" subject, whether that subject was Turkish, Chinese, or South Asian. The most famous orientalist to combine linguistic skill and masquerade was again Richard Francis Burton, who in 1853 donned a series of "Arab" disguises so as to pass as a Muslim pilgrim making the Hajj—according to his *Personal Narrative of a Pilgrimage to Al-Madinah and Meccah*, he was able to pull off the ruse. Yet even Burton admitted that a number of Muslim pilgrims saw past his disguises but either did not feel compelled to tell their companions or stopped short of confronting him. In one of the best readings of Burton's masquerade, Parama Roy argues: "The easy transition [for a white man] between varied identities underwrites imperialism's avowal of faith in a stable and coherent colonial self that can resist the potential pollutions of this trafficking in native identity. If the colonial self is stable and unassailable,

FIGURE 4.2. Frontispiece portrait of Robert Campbell in *Pilgrimage to My Motherland*, 1861. (Hatcher Library, University of Michigan, Ann Arbor.)

then it should follow . . . that the native self is, like all blank or dark spots on the map, a void, an uninscribed and infinitely malleable space. Thus can the native be made over in the image of the colonizer."[54] According to Roy, the point of Burton's masquerade lies in his desire not to become the "inscrutable" oriental but to render the oriental meaningless as a subject, such that whiteness itself becomes the inscrutable or, as she says, the "unassailable" entity.

Delany and Campbell had no plans to invalidate or dishonor their Egba hosts and were not interested in deceiving anyone. Did their postexpedition costuming function as a symbolic reminder of what must have been an astonishing three months in Nigeria?

Nineteenth-century Nigeria had a strong Muslim presence, a fact clearly evident in Delany's speeches about West Africa and also reflected in both Campbell's choice of costume. Though Delany has very little to say about clothing in his *Official Report*, in *Pilgrimage* Campbell is obsessed with clothing. Consider, for instance, his meeting with Okukenu, the alake: "His body above the loins was nude: otherwise his attire consisted of a handsome velvet cap trimmed with gold, a costly necklace of coral, and a double strand of the same ornament about his loins, with a velvet cloth thrown gracefully about the rest of his person" (P, 170). Then there is the *adelu*, whom Campbell describes as "king of the Yoruba nation": "He was seated under an *acabi*, one of the turret-like arrangements already mentioned, surrounded by his wives, his head reclining on one, his feet resting on another; one fanned him, another wiped the perspiration from his face; one held an umbrella of many colors over his head, and another a small vessel carefully covered up, in which his majesty occasionally deposited his salivary secretions. . . . His dress consisted of a costly tobe and shocoto of the same pattern, both nicely embroidered, a cap of red silk-velvet, and Mohammedan sandals" (P, 215). Is Campbell confusedly processing here some of the cultural evidence of Islam in West Africa? While his descriptions suggest the power and magnificence of West African rulers, the recurring weight of such images of (potential) sexual indulgence, voluptuous clothing, and sluggishness owes much to the same European orientalist discourse promulgated by men such as Burton.

This image from Campbell's *Pilgrimage* also contrasts sharply with a curious moment in the narrative when Campbell most resembles not the returning African son but the European explorer. Repeatedly exasperated by the unreliability of his African porters, Campbell has solicited their cooperation by "lending each carrier a shirt, for so great is the respect entertained for the civilized, that even the assumption of the garb affords protection and the liberty of passing unmolested through a hostile country" (P, 213). Then, toward the end of the narrative, as he argues for the ease with which native Africans might be civilized, he observes that "as soon as any one of these people assumes the garb or other characteristics of civilization, [traditional African laws] cease to exercise jurisdiction over him" (P, 244). Throughout his narrative, Campbell maintains a near-obsession with African clothing and the need to distinguish the "civilized" from the noncivilized, based on who wears shirts and who does not. With "civilized" garb functioning in these stories as a talisman, a fetish object among the Africans, their eagerness to wear Western clothes ironically underscores their lack of civilization. With respect to the frontispiece, we observe a moment of reversal when Campbell sheds his Western clothes, pointing out on the most obvious levels a rebirth, a reinvention from a New World Black subject to a bona fide African. Yet how much does this transformation echo the tradition of masquerade regularly enacted for centuries by white men in colonial contexts?

The related masquerade of the exotic performed by Delany and Campbell made legible to European and American audiences—and especially to African Americans—not only the "scientific" information they had labored so hard to obtain in West Africa but also their claim to the region which was above that of white Europeans. From Campbell's point of view, the "new" African self he imagined in the frontispiece portrait of *Pilgrimage* symbolized the triumph of a "new" Africa over the "old" one, thereby fulfilling the fantasy of the son's return to the motherland. However, as both Campbell and his audience understood intuitively, this romanticized identity would itself collapse in West Africa, because were Campbell to wear such garments in Lagos, he would cease to be the civilized, superior brother. For his part, Delany's costume might have functioned not just as a prop but indeed as a reminder of his own remarkable journey, in the midst of the Civil War.

5.   *Sarah Forbes Bonetta and Travel as Social Capital*

As anthropologist Karin Barber has demonstrated, by the late nineteenth century, mission-educated Africans exhibited "a remarkably consistent and widespread efflorescence" of writing in the form of private letters and diaries, produced by elite and nonelite colonial subjects alike under British rule.[1] Barber argues that the nonelite population readily utilized letters and diaries to enable "new forms of self-examination . . . new styles of self-projection and self-dramatization," even though for a great many, lack of funds made continuing education at secondary school or university virtually impossible.[2] Given the traditional attention to "reading and writing by [Anglophone African] academic and political elites" of the colonial era, Barber advocates for closer attention to the "hidden histories" of everyday writing by the nonelite.[3] Though Barber is right in making this class distinction, some mid-nineteenth-century elite figures were not necessarily economically secure in the high social positions they occupied.

My focus once again will be on the Saro—that is, ex-slaves brought to Sierra Leone by the Royal Navy anti-slave-trading squadron starting in 1807, and who later migrated to Nigeria in the hope of expanding trade and "returning" to their places of birth. Over time, these Christianized ex-slaves generated enough real wealth to provide a better range of educational opportunities for their children. These men and women also produced a "hidden history," by way of letters, diaries, commentaries, and newspaper columns, that enabled the creation of a community identity. Especially for the wealthiest members of this colonial

FIGURE 5.1. Sarah Forbes Bonetta, photographed by Camille Silvy, 1862. (National Portrait Gallery, UK)

elite, overseas travel to Britain was crucial for consolidating their relationship with the white merchants who purchased their goods, for expanding social and professional networks in their region, and for proving they had leisure time to be tourists. In all, overseas travel, especially to the metropole, made evident the extent of their financial power in the British West African colonies that they were themselves helping to build. Indeed, in many parts of the British Empire, including Africa, life "at home" might have, in part, revolved around the scheduled arrival and departure times for packets, not just for commercial cargo but also for letters and loved ones on their way to or from Britain.

Sarah Forbes Bonetta (1843?–80) was a Christianized West African ex-slave who married into the Saro colonial elite in Lagos. Usually relegated to the footnotes of books or articles on colonial Nigeria, Bonetta came to public notice in the early 2000s because she had been the ward of Queen Victoria, starting in 1851. In 1862 she married James P. L. Davies of Lagos (figures 5.1 and 5.2),

FIGURE 5.2. James P. L. Davies, photographed by Camille Silvy, 1862 (National Portrait Gallery, UK)

a wealthy, self-made merchant in the palm oil business and a protonationalist from the early days of colonial rule.[4] As with almost all of the colonial elite in Lagos and Freetown, Sierra Leone—the two West African cities in which she spent substantial time—Bonetta made at least four round trips to Britain but never published a formal travel narrative. However, she generated informal writing that revealed a life shaped not simply her own travel but also by that of her husband, her children, and the overseas Church Missionary Society (CMS) network linking the metropole to West Africa. After marriage, Bonetta created at least one travel diary to memorialize an emotionally and physically difficult journey to Britain. Once on land and among friends she had left behind when she married, she used her diary to articulate the pleasures of rekindling and consolidating old friendships at the metropole. At the same time, she and her husband corresponded frequently when one of them was away from home, and both received letters from their oldest child, Victoria, who attended an English finishing school, complete with a class trip to the European continent so that she and her classmates could practice their French and German. In unpublished writing connected to her travels and that of her family members, Bonetta wrote sometimes solely for herself and at other times to loved ones. Her topics were often traditional, even seemingly mundane, domestic issues, including motherhood, shopping, seasickness, embroidery, religious devotion, and simply being quiet in the company of friends.

Bonetta's first "journey" was one of violent uprooting and exile: when she was five or six years old, slave traders murdered her family, destroyed her town, and imprisoned her in the residence of Dahomey's King Gezo, where she remained for two years. Then a serendipitous meeting in 1850 with Lieutenant Commander Frederick E. Forbes of the Royal Navy's anti-slave-trading squadron led to her being taken to Britain as the "slave" of Queen Victoria, who promptly freed her and made her a royal ward. From this point until 1862, when she married James Davies at the age of nineteen, Bonetta experienced postslavery life not as a series of journeys at her own behest but rather as a series of commands from Queen Victoria. The queen and members of her household staff—who no doubt meant well—made decisions about Bonetta's schooling (in Freetown), foster family (in Chatham, Kent), and marriage (in Lagos) that uprooted her from one *settled* situation after another, in the interest of turning her into the perfect, and perfectly "civilized," young African woman—proof that the "heathen" were yet redeemable.[5] After her marriage to Davies, Bonetta was able to exert more control over her comings and goings, and at this point her letters and diary provide a window into how the act of travel helped shape her self-perception and her classed identity as a member of the Lagos elite. Indeed, her travel writing helped define and reveal the deeply gendered expectations regarding her behavior on tour. Specifically, her writing reveals the ways in which she had internalized modes of social control so as to always generate a so-called good report of her conduct in public. Without any money of her own, as she traveled in adulthood from one location to another, Bonetta instead harnessed the social capital she accrued from "good reports" of her scrupulously dignified behavior, such that she created some room for agency, despite the dependency of being a royal ward and an elite colonial wife. By all appearances, Bonetta cultivated for herself an unimpeachable reputation as the quintessential Victorian-era surrogate daughter and wife, and as such she embraced the social and material advantages attending upper-crust metropolitan travel. Rather than being "merely" a tourist, however, Bonetta was both a colonial subject and an ex-slave, and her actions as a traveler were shaped by the demands of two very different audiences: Queen Victoria, on the one hand, and Davies and his Lagosian community on the other.

The particular meaning and consequence of Bonetta's individual journeys become clearer when framed by the larger context of Saro travel, starting around 1839 to Nigeria and then continuing through the latter half of the nineteenth century. Although by that time elite colonial figures across the British Empire traveled to the metropole for education, employment, and business, the decision by many mission-educated "Saro" to leave for Nigeria in hopes of pursuing lucrative trade opportunities troubled the CMS missionaries who had been put over them in Sierra Leone. In 1840 the CMS assistant general secretary, Dandeson Coates, was alarmed that no one seemed able to control the flow of Saro moving to southwest Nigeria ahead of Britain's official efforts to explore and map territories in the Niger Valley as part of the 1841 expedition: "It is requisite . . . that [Saro migration] should be carefully regulated and controlled. . . . If any considerable number should move before arrangements have been completed . . . disappointment if not something worse would ensue. . . . They should be most strongly dissuaded from moving rashly and prematurely and placed under a course of instruction and training which would fit them to move at the proper time."[6] Coates's description of the migration as chaotic and impulsive speaks to his fear that once mission-educated ex-slaves became their own actors, the dependency and obedience that the "civilizing mission" should have instilled would be eroded. Yet only the year before, in 1839, the abolitionist Thomas Fowell Buxton had praised independent overseas travel to Britain by prosperous ex-slaves and their children as clear evidence that British "civilization" was indeed making a difference in West Africa. According to Buxton, those ex-slaves "considerably advanced in wealth and civilization" eagerly provided "European educations for their children of their own accord, without advice or pecuniary aid from others, and moved thereto solely by a conviction of its intrinsic excellence."[7] Coates and Buxton were clearly at odds, since the opinions of the former represented the needs of some CMS officials for an obedient African flock. Saving the soul of a "heathen" should have no connection to making that convert equal in thought and action to the missionary. However, even if Coates had been able to stop the Saro migration to Nigeria, there was little to be done given the point made by Buxton about wealthy Christianized parents who chose to send their children to Britain.

Indeed, there was especially internal resistance, some subtle and some not, to any form of overseas travel by Sierra Leone ex-slaves and their children. This resistance stood at odds with the general secretary of the CMS, Henry Venn, who believed in educating male converts so they could sustain their own native pastorate, independent of whites. One outspoken critic of this goal was the missionary Henry Townsend. In an 1860 letter to Venn, Townsend was quite blunt: "I should not like to send a [West African] young man to England for whom I have any respect. . . . I don't think we should lead young men into temptation especially upon the weak side of their character even for the amount of knowledge they may obtain. . . . Every case sent has been a failure or something very like it."[8] The implication that their presumably simplistic nature put Africans catechists at risk of moral regression spoke to a race- and class-based anxiety on Townsend's part, which indexed his reliance on an institutional structure that gave meaningful authority to working- and lower-middle-class missionaries such as himself.[9] Europeans employed by a missionary organization would have taken a step up the class ladder in terms of having a steady salary, a pension, medical care, and a choice of possible spouses who believed that a married couple would best be able to model proper gender roles for the "heathen." If African catechists went to Britain and returned home as ordained ministers, what would then distinguish them from their white teachers? And certainly, this power dynamic especially threatened to fall apart when young, Christianized Africans returned from Britain with educations that might well surpass that of white missionaries.

Though missionaries criticized the converts' desire to travel by arguing that the latter would immediately lose the thin veneer of "civilization" that they had obtained, such criticism hinted at a degree of envy. Throughout the 1850s and 1860s, a stream of letters to Henry Venn from Julia Sass, the headmistress of Freetown's CMS Female Institution, complained bitterly about wealthy converts and their penchant for overseas travel. Instead of being obedient to white wishes, argued Sass, the entrepreneurially minded ex-slave converts of Freetown were "fast losing their simplicity," "seriously bent on gain and show," and entirely consumed with "their persons, their houses, clothes, tables and the getting of money." This embrace of Western values created a sense of entitlement that spread to the "young girls and young women," making the latter "proud, vain, . . . disobedient and ungrateful." These attitudes, said Sass, had caused them to reject her school's admittedly pedestrian curriculum (reading, writing, religion, sewing, and drawing) in favor of posh finishing schools in Britain. Sass also expressed alarm to Venn that "the people do not yet care for the education of their daughters" because "they . . . seem to think that if they send them, when sixteen years old to England that even if they know nothing before, they will in a year or so learn all necessary to make them ladies."[10] Ironically, after Venn did not sufficiently address her pleas for a white assistant, Sass found herself begging for permission to take two of her African pupils to Britain for teacher training. Clearly feeling threatened by her own proposal, Sass quickly assured Venn (and herself) that once her "two best girls" were in England "they [would be] quite under my control" since, after all, "I do not wish to make 'Ladies' of them, or to raise them above their positions."[11] Ironically, as a missionary, Sass was required to give up autonomous travel, since the CMS Parent Committee reserved the right to make all decisions related to posting, especially requests for leave. Consequently, Sass's petition to travel to Britain with her pupils was also a request for her to leave the mission field, even temporarily. Sass became depressed and overworked, and eventually, in poor health, she requested permission to return to Britain. Even in this difficult hour, however, she had to produce a medical certificate from an approved physician attesting to her poor health, in order for the CMS to pay for her passage home.

Clearly, mission-educated Africans did not need to go overseas to articulate their desire for self-determination, but wealthier members of the elite took advantage of these opportunities. One side effect of economic stratification was that overseas travel quickly began to structure the way Christianized Africans judged and rated each other. An 1883 editorial in the Lagos *Eagle* argued that while marriageable girls might gain "a good, sound, and solid foundation" at the local mission school, their education was "incomplete without their proceeding to a foreign civilized place, if only for a short time." The result would be a "land teeming with well-educated mothers," which would place Christianized West Africans "amongst the most beatific, and the undoubtedly blessed."[12] The implication was that only young women who had gone to overseas finishing school could have a transformative effect on the colonial population. Indeed, many a mission-educated African girl of marriageable age might have found herself publicly marked for her *lack* of foreign travel. This was the case in 1882 for Lagos residents Miss Paulina Davies (no relation to Bonetta's husband) and a Miss Garber, performers in a local Handel festival. The reviewer of the Lagos *Observer* gave their performances a backhanded compliment, suggesting that they played "intelligently and well *considering they have been no further than the beach*."[13] In contrast, the same reviewer heaped accolades upon female pianists from a previous concert, namely the "Misses Macauley, Thomas, and . . . Johnson . . . our young ladies lately [returned] from England."[14]

In both its pettiness and its racial defiance, this was the Lagos community context that gave shape and value to the journeys made by the adult Sarah

Forbes Bonetta. Nevertheless, her letters and diary point to the particular slippage between her use of informal writing to make travel meaningful for herself and the ways in which other people—including her husband—imagined her travel as meaningful to themselves. As Davies's wife, the expense of her travels to and from Britain served a social purpose, since the display of luxury both validated and broadcast to colonial officials and members of his elite community that Davies had great wealth and presumably the freedom to act on his own. But if Bonetta's travel consolidated her husband's desired public image, where and how do we locate Bonetta's agency in relation to this travel? The answer requires a teasing out of the specific interpersonal, interracial, and class-bound colonial relationships that enabled and shaped each of Bonetta's voyages. Her letters and diary entries reveal a highly self-conscious and ongoing process of self-making by someone who understood that she had to embody perfectly Victorian codes of conduct. She used her writing to examine the fears, ambitions, and frustrations arising from the social expectations she worked to fulfill. It is worth considering what avenues might have been foreclosed or enabled for Bonetta as a result of her understandable circumspection, as she moved back and forth between colony and metropole. Additionally, from the moment she set foot on English soil and was emancipated by Queen Victoria, she learned that her caretakers believed in the repatriation of former slaves and free Black people, whether they had been born in Africa or not, so that they could convert their "heathen" brothers and sisters to Christianity. In other words, Africans and people of African descent could sojourn in Britain, but "home" had to be somewhere else. Yet, despite the peripatetic nature of her postemancipation years, Bonetta developed close emotional ties to numerous families and individuals. Instead of abandoning these relationships because she had to relocate to Lagos, the adult Bonetta expressed her agency by way of a remarkably flexible understanding of "home," "belonging," and African "return" that pulled Lagos and Britain into the same emotional orbit, making obsolete the idea that her final destination was the African continent.

INVENTING SARAH FORBES BONETTA

For better or worse, the biography of Sarah Forbes Bonetta prior to her removal to Britain comes from a single source. In 1850, when Lieutenant Commander Frederick E. Forbes encountered the slave child who would become Sarah, she was one of a number of "gifts" he was to transport from Dahomey's King Gezo to Queen Victoria. Forbes's original mission was to request that Gezo permanently set aside slave trading. The king scoffed at Forbes's message, since the trade generated enormous revenue. Appalled by Gezo's rebuff, especially his mocking the abolition-minded Queen Victoria by sending her a slave, Forbes took his revenge in *Dahomey and the Dahomans* (1851), published on his return home with the royal "gifts." Not surprisingly, Forbes used his two slim volumes to condemn Gezo as an unredeemable and bloodthirsty "heathen," while also pointing out the commercial possibilities if and when Dahomey's territory fell into productive British hands. Only at the very end of volume 2 does Forbes mention the now-emancipated African child, the one great accomplishment of his expedition. Forbes's description of Bonetta is worth quoting in its entirety:

> I have only to add a few particulars about my extraordinary present, "the African child." In a former portion of these journals I have mentioned the Okeadon war; one of the captives of this dreadful slave hunt was this interesting girl. It is usual to reserve the best born for the high behests of royalty, and the immolation on the tombs of the deceased nobility. For one of these ends she had been detained at court for two years; proving, by her not having been sold to the slave-dealers, that she was of a good family.
>
> So extraordinary a present would have been at least a burden, had I not the conviction that, in consideration of the nature of the service I had performed, the government would consider her as the property of the Crown. To refuse would have been to have signed her death-warrant; which, probably, would have been carried into execution forthwith.
>
> Immediately on arriving [in England] I applied through the Secretary of the Admiralty, and received for answer that Her Majesty was graciously pleased to arrange for the education and subsequent fate of the child. God grant that she may be taught to consider that her duty leads her to rescue those who have not had the advantages of education from the mysterious ways of their ancestors!
>
> Of her own story she had only a confused idea. Her parents were decapitated [during the Okeadon war]; her brothers and sisters, she knows not what their fate might have been. For her age, supposed to be eight years, she is a perfect genius; she now speaks English well, and has a great talent for music. She has won the affections, with but few exceptions, of all who have known her, by her docile and amiable conduct, which nothing can exceed. She is far in advance of any white child of her age, in aptness of learning, and strength of mind and affection; and with her, being an excellent specimen of the negro race, might be tested the capability of the intellect of the black: it being generally and erroneously supposed that after a certain age the intellect becomes impaired, and the

pursuit of knowledge impossible—that though the negro child may be clever, the adult will be dull and stupid. Her head is considered so excellent a phrenological specimen, and illustrating such high intellect, that Mr. Pistrucci, the medallist of the mint, has undertaken to make a bust of her, intending to present a cast to the author. Her mind has received a moral and religious impression, and she was baptized, according to the rites of the Protestant church, Sarah Forbes Bonetta.[15]

Undoubtedly Forbes's conclusions about Bonetta's origins were drawn from available knowledge and from his own experience as an officer in the Royal Navy's anti-slave-trading squadron. However, it was perhaps because Bonetta was destined for Queen Victoria's court that Forbes was inclined to use the phrases "best born" and "of a good family," since abolitionist lore often touted the irony of African royals whose status failed to protect them from the Atlantic slave trade. Regardless, Forbes's description quickly became synonymous with the belief that in Africa she had indeed been captive royalty, a belief apparently supported by Gezo's choice of her in the first place. Regardless of what the truth might be, from here onward Bonetta the child must have come to realize that her task was to prove the success of the so-called civilizing mission, lest she embarrass her gracious benefactor. Indeed, given that Bonetta must have been in Britain for only a few months, Forbes was already projecting her future "return" to West Africa once she realized "her duty [to] rescue those [Africans] who have not had the advantages of education." This rhetorical use of the ex-slave to both justify and enable the mission in Africa made clear that though she was not a Christian, she was still an alien figure out of place in Britain—homeless, in other words, until and unless she and others like her were willing to recreate a Christian country in Africa. This argument was also in line with Forbes's goals as a naval officer in the anti-slave-trading squadron; that is, intercepted slaves were not taken to Britain but were "returned" to "Africa," which usually meant the unfamiliar British colony of Sierra Leone.

Before leaving West Africa, Forbes arranged for Bonetta's baptism. *Sarah* was a common enough female name but, following the widespread missionary practice of assigning the name of a white philanthropist to a "heathen" convert, Forbes felt justified in inserting his own name, so that figuratively he stood as the surrogate father who made Bonetta's Christian rebirth possible.[16] Going further, Forbes completed the ritual by adding the name of his warship, the HMS *Bonetta*. Joan Anim-Addo has correctly pointed to the supreme irony in Forbes's assignment of this final name, since it mirrors the "tradition established during slavery when ship captains assumed the practice of [assigning] whimsical names [to] Africans."[17] Yet this coincidence is startling for an additional reason: as an African child traumatized by violent enslavement, Bonetta's unarticulated, unrecovered pre-emancipation story is presumed to be a silence, a blank canvas, suitable for being inscribed to honor Forbes, as well as his squadron. Called into being by the 1807 British law against the slave trade, the Royal Navy's anti-slave-trading squadron had by the mid-nineteenth century failed to make a dent in the Atlantic slave trade. As a result, some members of the British public regarded the squadron as a waste of money.[18] A year before going to Dahomey, Forbes addressed this point of view in *Six Months' Service in the African Blockade* (1849), drawing on multiple examples of squadron captains in action not only intercepting slave ships but going inland to negotiate an end to the kidnapping of slaves from the interior, in very much the same vein as his original mission to Dahomey. To demonstrate success, Forbes also spent a great deal of his book celebrating the intercepted slaves, who were now Christians and were freed in Sierra Leone. By adding his warship to Bonetta's list of names, Forbes also made her emblematic of the squadron's success.

The question of Bonetta's unarticulated life before slavery is important, because not all slaves "recaptured" by the squadron were similarly unable to remember. According to James Davies's biographer Adeyemo Elebute, when she reached young adulthood Bonetta began signing her name as *Ina*, which Elebute explains is the Victorian spelling of the Yoruba name *Aina*, used to refer to a child "born with its umbilical cord twisted round its neck."[19] Was the name *Ina/ Aina* part of Bonetta's partial recollection of life with her original Egbado family? Many ex-slaves who had been Christianized undoubtedly looked forward to baptism; the ritual might indeed have been a symbolic move forward into a future of Christian freedom. Baptism might also be the moment to pay homage to what had been left behind. When young Samuel Ajayi Crowther was captured by Fulani raiders, he witnessed the murder of his father. While Crowther deliberately chose at his baptism the name of an early nineteenth-century London vicar, just as deliberately he added his original Yoruba name *Ajayi*, to honor his past. Did Bonetta's adoption of *Ina* spring from a similar desire to memorialize and honor what little she could remember of her original life? Might this have been an attempt on her part to finally assert her own agency against that of Forbes?

DISTANCE AND DISOBEDIENCE

As her decision to sign herself *Ina* suggests, as Bonetta grew older she developed a mind of her own, which from the point of view of Queen Victoria would have made her potentially harder to control. According to palace correspondence, by January 1851, just months after Bonetta's arrival in Britain, the queen was already inquiring about the Female Institution in Freetown.[20] However, such a distance posed a threat to the very notion of "control," even though Bonetta would be supervised directly by Julia Sass. Still, the queen's keeper of the privy purse, Sir Charles Beaumont Phipps, working with Henry Venn, left nothing to chance. Venn, meanwhile, had made it his personal business to track Bonetta's progress, or lack thereof, in Freetown. As evidenced by surviving notes and correspondence, those in charge of Bonetta's welfare were mindful of every detail, creating exacting lists (complete with specific prices) of the number of bonnets, ribbons, petticoats, pairs of stockings, soap bars, buttons, spools of cotton thread, and sewing needles regularly sent to the Female Institution for her use.[21] Though once she arrived Bonetta was placed under the supervision of Julia Sass, a telling incident proves the extent to which Bonetta's travel away from "handlers" in Britain generated anxiety. At the start of 1853, Phipps asked Venn about a receipt listing Bonetta's expenses from the autumn of the previous year. According to Phipps, the privy purse was being billed over three pounds for "a maple [picture] frame with glass" to hold an image of the queen. Assuring Phipps that "I can myself see no grounds for such an encroachment upon the liberality of Her Majesty," Venn in a flurry of correspondence immediately ordered Sass to launch an investigation as to whether "application [had] been made" for the frame, either by Bonetta "or [on her behalf by] any other party."[22] As soon as possible, Sass reported back that the inclusion of the maple frame had been a clerical error, and things would be easily resolved with an amended total. In a January 7, 1853, letter, Venn clearly interrogated Phipps about anything Sass might have told him not only about the frame but about any other items on the list.[23] Venn's inquiries about whether Bonetta might have asked for unauthorized items correspond to the skepticism earlier expressed by Henry Townsend and Sass that, if not closely watched, the young African convert abroad might evince signs of moral deterioration.

What is also ironic, however, is Venn's concern that there might be "any other party" involved—presumably another CMS employee. While the anxieties of Phipps, Venn, and Sass reflect the fundamental challenge of controlling African converts, according to sociologist Jon Miller, missionary societies were also concerned with the attenuation of authority over missionaries themselves and became more so the farther the mission field was from headquarters. As a result, missionary societies developed the procedure of "mutual watching," where at every level of the enterprise it was the duty of each person to surveil everyone else. In other words, missionaries were trained to be loyal to the organization, not to each other.[24] While this larger phenomenon had little to do with Bonetta in the long run, Venn's multiple questions speak to the ways in which surveillance was central to the disciplining of Bonetta, as it was for her missionary teachers. In a sense, then, through the meticulous reading and rereading of mundane details, Phipps, Venn, and Sass surveilled their charge. A few months later, Bonetta shows up in a letter from Sass to Venn on student misconduct at the Female Institution. The pupil "Susan Firth," Sass writes, "[is] my greatest trial, particularly as [she] occasioned the dismissal of two of my eldest Girls." Sass went on to say that "Susan's bad conduct would soon have effected materially the reputation of our institution." In the same letter, Sass reveals additional inquiries from Phipps, since "the Queen has expressed much satisfaction with [Sarah's] progress, who is now getting *tamed* a little, and gets on nicely with all she learns and will, I hope, prove worthy of all that is done for her. She is a dear little girl, *but requires at times a very firm hand*."[25] Clearly high-spirited, the young Bonetta seemed to have given Sass a hard time, but since she was Queen Victoria's ward, any serious complaints would have reflected not so much on Bonetta but on Venn, Sass, and the CMS Female Institution. In a sense, then, multiple reputations rested on whether Bonetta could be kept in line. It is no wonder that she developed a growing recognition that her behavior had consequences for others, that good behavior would garner her widespread approval, and that she could call upon that approbation when necessary as empowering social capital.

By 1862, when the queen granted James Davies permission to marry Bonetta, a letter from Phipps confirmed the extent to which she had become an abolitionist success story. Bonetta, he wrote, had been "most carefully educated," and "always by her excellent conduct fully justified and repaid the care that [had] been bestowed upon her."[26] To some extent, the compliment echoed Sass's opinion that Bonetta could be tamed to be what one needed her to be. While this was indeed the impression Bonetta left in the minds of those who thought they knew her, in fact she turned Davies down when he made his proposal in 1861. Among the complicated reasons for her refusal was that after the queen brought her back to Britain from the Female Institution in 1855, she became happily settled with the family of CMS missionary James Frederick Schön, who had retired from service in Freetown and met Bonetta when he was serving as the chaplain of the Melville Naval Hospital for Sailors and Mariners.[27] After Bonetta rejected Davies, the queen ordered her removed from "Mama" and "Papa" Schön and their brood of loving children, sending her instead to Brighton to be a companion to a Miss Welch and a Mrs. Simon.[28] In an impassioned letter to "Mama Schön," Bonetta declared, "I do not feel a particle of love for [James Davies] & never have done so." "There are others that I prefer," she wrote. "I have prayed & asked for guidance but it doesn't come, & the feelings of perfect *indifference* to him returns with greater force." Against her own views, Bonetta weighed the opinion of others: "I know that the generality of people would say [Davies] is *rich* & your marrying him would at once make you *independent*, and I say 'am I to barter my piece of mind for money?' No never."[29] As a partial window into Bonetta's internal struggles, this letter to Mrs. Schön reveals the great distance between her outward behavior and her internal anxieties over what she was expected to do. Acting on her own desires would result in banishment from those she loved. Eventually Bonetta buckled to the queen's pressure, and when Davies proposed a second time, she quietly accepted. Still, her rejection of the general notion that marriage to a wealthy husband would put her on a path to independence is worth keeping in mind. At the age of nineteen, she understood full well that after her life as a royal ward, real freedom would, in fact, never be hers. She also clearly understood that her thoughts had to be carefully separated from her actions.

ARRIVING IN LAGOS AND RETURNING TO ENGLAND

When Bonetta accompanied her new husband to his home in Lagos, she would have found a crowded, commercially vibrant city, the one-time governing seat of a small kingdom that had been a major hub for the Atlantic slave trade. As Kristin Mann describes it, after annexation by the British in 1861, Lagos remained "an international port" but now under colonial rule, with large volumes of overseas trade in palm oil, which abolitionists expected would take the place of Atlantic slave trading.[30] Separated from the Atlantic Ocean by a lagoon formed as a result of an east-to-west sandspit, Lagos saw the comings and goings of many indigenous populations—some of whom were Christians, some Muslims, and some followers of ethnic religious practices. Bonetta would have encountered small-time farmers, traders, artisans, and palm-oil producers selling their wares, some employing slaves to supply the manual labor required to collect and crush palm kernels, despite the official British ban on slavery. She would have been introduced to the few white colonial officials in town and to CMS and other missionaries attached to local congregations, including Baptists, Wesleyans, and Catholics—many of whom were members of the interdenominational London Missionary Society. Then there was King Dosunmu, surrounded by extended family members, various advisers, generals, and intermediaries. He had suffered the indignity of an early version of indirect rule, which James Davies had hoped to alleviate by helping the king in his negotiations with the British. Bonetta would also have met not only Saro families but also Afro-Brazilian and Afro-Cuban immigrants who traced their cultural roots to the Nigerian hinterland. There were also British West Indians such as Robert Campbell (see chapter 4) who had relocated to Lagos hoping for better opportunities. Some of these immigrants were highly educated and professionally successful, while others occupied a range of class positions. When Davies took her to their house, Bonetta would have been delighted to see that it faced the Anglican Saint Paul's (Breadfruit) Chapel, so named because breadfruit trees from Tahiti once grew nearby. Inside her new home she would have met Davies's widowed mother and the servants in attendance.

Of course, Bonetta's celebrity status as the queen's ward would have preceded her. By the time she arrived in Lagos, the Jamaican immigrant Robert Campbell had established the *Anglo-African*, the city's first Black-run English-language newspaper. After Bonetta gave birth to her first child, Victoria, in 1863, as the paper's editor Campbell treated his readers to a description of "the beautiful baptismal present our beloved Queen has made to the infant of Mrs. J. P. L. Davies of Lagos, a lady well known as having enjoyed the high honour of being a protégé of her majesty. . . . The cup and salver are both inscribed as follows: To Victoria Davies [From] Queen Victoria."[31] While the announcement of births, deaths, marriages, graduations, packet ship arrivals and departures, and the establishment of new businesses would have been covered in the *Anglo-African*, Bonetta's unique connection to Queen Victoria would have stood out, especially after the queen agreed to be godmother to her infant namesake. Bonetta's unusually high status also explains why she would have attracted Davies's attention even during her schoolgirl years at Julia Sass's Female Institution and why he pursued her, even after she rejected him. Here Kristin Mann's study of marriage among early Christianized Anglophone West Africans is extremely useful: "Elite wives could . . . establish homes where rising merchants, colonial servants or professionals would feel comfortable entertaining Europeans and other educated Africans. On these occasions men and women could establish and strengthen useful social ties. Then too, elite women could accompany their husbands to church, parties and Government House, where an educated, fashionably turned-out wife by a man's side served as a persistent reminder of his status."[32] In addition to filling all of these roles, Bonetta would have provided Davies with an opening to a range of philanthropists and senior missionary figures—and she was young enough to bear children. So, marriage to Bonetta might well have been a strategic maneuver to enhance and consolidate his social standing in the colony, among both local whites and his own class.

Regardless of how each spouse had calculated the pros and cons of their marriage, as husband and wife Davies and Bonetta came to share a loving union, with Bonetta settling into the expected role of pious and dutiful Victorian wife and Davies continuing to run his business while also challenging racist colonial officials and patronizing white missionaries. Though Davies doted on his wife, he took the traditional route of controlling finances, which made Bonetta entirely dependent upon him.[33] Certainly, Bonetta had a royal affiliation that almost always came to bear in the way she was treated by others. However, she also made sure of her own carefully studied behavior, knowing that as the queen's former ward and now the wife of a prominent member of the Christianized elite, she would still be under close observation. In almost every context with CMS missionaries, letters praising her behavior were dispatched to Henry Venn. Such was the case in 1865 when the Lagos missionary Adolphus Mann noted with pleasure her volunteer work with the "good [Christianized African] wives of inferior station" who made up his congregation—though not before belittling native catechists, whom he believed were working to usurp his position as minister. In the middle of these complains about arrogant male converts, Mann identifies Bonetta as the only African worthy of praise, even suggesting and then undercutting a desire for spending more time with her:

> Mrs. Mann will be happy to work in concert with Mrs. Davies. My own private opinion is that Mrs. D is far the best of the African ladies in my acquaintance. I should like more of her company for the work—but for mere pleasure as it has been sought for—we do not wish for nor do we seek it—and then there is the distance of our houses, the change of congregations and lastly the political bias, that dominates in Capt. Davies, [which] shows him an enemy in, and in Bishop Crowther and anyone who pays visits to B. Cr[owther] who is in an evil report at Abeokota, must be mindful that he is looked on with suspicion, that goes even to uncivilities.[34]

Mann's comments suggest that part of Bonetta's appeal is her seeming "un-Africanness." What's more, Mann's letter reveals the extremely delicate social situation in which Bonetta found herself after moving to Lagos. Schooled from her time at the Female Institution and later in Britain during visits to Queen Victoria, Bonetta had long ago taken the measure of white expectations of Africans and would have known exactly how to comport herself. (And she was probably well aware, too, that the working-class Mann and his wife were likely awed by her royal connections, which would have further confused their racist reflex to see her skin color as a mark of inferiority.) In taking her place on Lagos's interracial stage, Bonetta clearly had to tread delicately with white CMS agents, especially since her husband had become increasing unpopular due to his resistance to white racism.

By the early summer of 1867, Bonetta had lost Alice, her second child, and would still have been in mourning. Regardless, she set off with little Victoria to visit Britain, first and foremost to see her surrogate family the Schöns and then several other friends, saving the obligatory visit to Queen Victoria for later in the trip. Part of a travel diary composed during the journey to Britain has survived, covering July–September 1867. Additionally, a separate letter from Bonetta to Mrs. Schön places her at Windsor Castle on December 13.[35] After that date, it is difficult to pinpoint when she returned to Lagos. As with all diarists with no plans to publish their observations, Bonetta recorded only the places, events, and interactions that held meaning for her.[36] Consequently, in the diary she laments the burdens of caring for Victoria, whose health remained very poor throughout the ship's journey from Lagos to Liverpool. She mentions problems with her wardrobe, as well as shopping in London, sightseeing at the navy docks, and sharing tea with her friends. As travel writing, Bonetta's diary operated within an entirely different register from the published texts discussed in previous chapters. Rather, her diary emerged from and engaged with the culture of travel that shaped the lives and gendered identities of the Christian West African elite community to which she belonged. This community included Lagos while also exceeding it, and it directly shaped her understanding of herself as a wife and mother and ultimately her experience of the length and breadth between Lagos and London, not as a move outward from home and a return "back" but rather as an environment where "home" could be "here" and "there" simultaneously. This is not to say that Bonetta had no sense of belonging in Lagos. Nor am I suggesting that Lagos and Britain were identical sites of "home." Rather, instead of a transparent recording of what she saw and did, Bonetta's diary manifested the social and emotional rhythms of a self-defining mobility tying together both locations in the shaping of her larger life story.

In the era of steamships, the journey from Lagos to Liverpool was so routine that for colonial travelers it might well have become tedious. This would have been especially the case for Bonetta, who spent a good deal of time in her first-class cabin because of little Victoria's chronic ill-health. At the same time, there were rules of social etiquette to consider, as well as unwanted attention from those who knew of her social connections. In large part, Bonetta writes about the sea journey as merely the means to an end, her entries measuring out the time between ports of call, even as her short entries explore her role as wife and especially as mother to an ill child after having lost that child's sister. The following entry, for example, demonstrates the ways Bonetta turns inward to her own affairs and then outward to mark the progress of the ship:

Sunday July 7, [1867]

Off Accra; we came into port at 7 o'clock this morning. We are pretty well today. . . . I gave Vic some paregoric for her cough which is still rather troublesome. The Dr. has sent me a rhubarb powder for her at my request[;] she will be better I hope after that. We read the two last chapters of Job and sang some hymns[. We] are taking in cargo today so we had no [Sunday] service. Mr. Ussher came on board to go to Cape Coast[;] also Dr. Lee but he went on shore again.

The death of Alice just months earlier explains well enough Bonetta's concerns for Victoria's health, and she keeps vigil in much the same way she must have done at home during Alice's illness. Likewise, her observation of Sunday worship in the cabin maintains a comforting ritual that also ties mother and child back to their Lagos home. Indeed, the sickroom drama played out in Bonetta's cabin could just as easily have taken place on land, given how she occupies her time when not caring for Victoria:

[Tuesday,] July 9—at sea

Left Cape Coast about 6 yesterday morning, a little rain on deck, and came to cabin where we stayed all day. Vic's cough rather troublesome, gave her some rhubarb powder, she coughed a great deal but slept well, the powder [having] taken no effect. Did a little wool work.

[Wednesday,] July 10—off Cape Palmas

Arrived here about 3 o'clock noon, did not go on deck again the whole afternoon. The powder has yet taken no effect on Vic—shall give her a saline draught tomorrow.

[Thursday,] July 11—at sea

We are to reach Monrovia [Liberia] this night at 12 o'clock. Forgot to give Vic her draught till she had drunk her sago. She is not looking well and her appetite is bad. She needs a companion I fancy. Begins to cry at the least thing. It is rather trying work with her but I trust in [H]im who is the same yesterday, today and for ever.

In trying to be the ideal mother, Bonetta elevates Victoria's health above all else. But, as "home" is refigured in the stifling privacy of her first-class cabin and without the benefit of mother-in-law or hired servants, these entries also foreground Bonetta's enforced isolation. Not surprisingly, the mounting tension between Bonetta's maternal duties and her own desire to get out and move around (e.g., "did not go on deck again the whole afternoon") finally breaks loose but must be suppressed yet again by the rededication of her efforts to be dutiful. Bonetta's repetitive focus on her daughter suggests a highly conscious self-denial of pleasurable activities during the journey, such as interacting with passengers or simply taking in fresh air on deck. Indeed, her ironic prayer to "Him who is the same yesterday, today and for ever" suggests that life in the cabin represents stasis, even as the ship progresses in chronological time toward Liverpool. Though she and the other passengers are carried along in the ship, based on her diary's characterization of the voyage, for Bonetta the journey has yet to begin.

Given the cabin turned sickroom's nonprogressive time, Bonetta's matter-of-fact reportage of passenger names and points of embarkation and her recording of each passing port function as markers of time, of distance traveled. The entries about passengers have the same consistency as those about Victoria, as she mentions Mr. Mills (who is possibly from Lagos and headed to the Schöns' Palm Cottage and with whom she had intermittent contact on the ship), Mrs. and Mrs. W. R. Taylor (from Cape Coast), Mrs. Bell and her two young children (perhaps from Lagos), and Miss Duff and Mrs. Graham (from Madeira). By noting the ports of call (e.g., Accra, Cape Coast, Cape Palmas, Monrovia, Portuguese Tenerife, Madeira, and Gibraltar) Bonetta enumerates a string of satellite points linking a larger social and commercial network of communities that were under some form of European influence. This litany of personal names and places follows the tradition of similar lists that were commonplace in newspapers in Europe and the colonies. Bonetta's list-making impulse also enumerates achievements of a colonial class on the rise. Her mingling of names, regardless of racial identity, suggests she regards Christian African elite travelers as completely equal to Anglo-Europeans, thereby proving that skin color and place of origin posed no obstacle to acquiring wealth, education, and social prestige. On a personal level, Bonetta's list of names and places also demarks the categories of time aboard ship: the sickroom as opposed to the upper decks, where passengers come and go.

When Bonetta does leave her cabin, she disembarks briefly, with Victoria in tow, to fulfill an apparently prearranged errand at Freetown:

> July 13—at sea
>
> We hope to reach S. Leone at about 4:30. We are ready to go ashore, 5 o'clock. Wellington came off in a boat to meet me. . . . We came ashore and I walked to the house . . . met Bishop Beckles and his son on the way and learnt that Mrs. Beckles will go to England by this steamer. Messrs. Jarrat and Cole came to see me[;] asked me to take charge of their children. . . .

July 22—at sea

 Woke up before six this morning and attended to Vic who has been vomiting. She has worms I think, and will get her medicine when we arrive. . . . The two . . . under my care Mary Campbell and Cole [both from Sierra Leone] are rather lazy[; they] won't get up and out of the cabin, are always sick.

Bonetta's familiarity with Freetown and especially members of the CMS clergy would, of course, have dated back to 1851, when she attended the Female Institution. Here Bonetta returns as a celebrated and well-trusted matron with substantial personal connections in both West Africa and England. Who better to chaperone the girls Mary Campbell and Mary Cole, the latter traveling with Bonetta all the way to the Schöns' Palm Cottage? It was one thing to take her very young daughter to England but quite another to assume responsibility for the two Marys. However, despite her obvious impatience (and her underlying exhaustion), Bonetta willingly serves as the means by which all three girls can experience overseas travel and thereby prepare themselves, even at such a young age, for the elevated class positions they will occupy once they reach adulthood. In shaping the destinies of these three children, Bonetta takes on the role of the figurative mother of her class by reproducing, developing, and extending through them the kind of lifestyle that marked the Anglophone Christianized elite. Also, by serving as a kind of community mother or female traveling mentor to the two Marys, Bonetta essentially blurs the lines between inside and out, between "private" (her cabin) and "public" (the ship—and the coast—at large), thereby revealing not only that her woman's sphere is vital to the continued existence of all Christianized elite communities in the region but also that the claim on one in her position to an African "home" is not limited to a single location. Thus, rather than being in opposition to or at least outside of the world of the journey, Bonetta's mothering practices both describe and reinscribe coming-of-age rituals long familiar to those elite populations. Further, if we contextualize the journey by Bonetta, Victoria, and the two Marys with Bonetta's own maiden voyage to England in 1850 with the naval officer Frederick E. Forbes, which initiated *her* into a new, postslavery life, Bonetta's subsequent growth from child to woman and mother places the welfare of the next generation in her hands. Thus Forbes's well-meaning abolitionist paternalism—his imposition of his surname at Bonetta's baptism—has been long superseded by Bonetta's colonial self-determination to make her own world.

 As a routine event for those who could afford it, the journey to England was essentially not a move *out* of community, but rather a ritual of class consolidation that expanded community across space and time, including but also exceeding the Anglophone West African coast. From Bonetta's perspective as a wife and mother, however, this form of connectedness across elite communities could also be a source of unintended pain and deep sorrow. On July 23, after a deck-side Sunday service conducted by the ship's captain, Bonetta records that the three-month-old infant of a Mrs. Bell is dying: "I am sorry for her[;] it reminds me of my first great sorrow[,] little Alice. Mrs. B was crying about the child." Regardless of Mrs. Bell's race, which Bonetta does not specify, this meeting brings back Bonetta's own tragedy. Before the child expires, Mrs. Bell deepens their connection by asking Bonetta to serve as godmother. After the baptism ceremony, the baby—now christened little Louisa—dies during the night, and "she was admitted to the deep at 3 o'clock." As if to shield herself, Bonetta follows the news of the tragedy with a rapid reordering of priorities: "[Vic is] better in health[;] she and I have been sleeping this afternoon[;] we are in sight of . . . Tenerife but seven miles off yet. We cannot reach the port this night, so we shall go the first thing in the morning. I shall buy some . . . embroidery at Madeira and shall write to Lagos DV. I've been so sick these 3 days."[37] In an attempt to shift gears from baby Louisa's death, Bonetta maps out plans that for the first time have nothing to do with duties of family or class. Neither her acts of communal mothering nor her kindness toward Mrs. Bell might have alleviated her own personal suffering, so she deliberately ends her grief by considering the extremely quotidian activities of sightseeing and shopping. Having been ill herself, this move also suggests Bonetta finally indulging herself.

The ship stops next at Tenerife. Up till now, Bonetta's use of the collective *we* seems to include the entire ship and its passengers as the vessel has docked, increased speed, and so on. As the ship closes in on Tenerife, she begins to share a common excitement with the other passengers, since they are now leaving Africa for a truly "foreign," "exotic" island destination. Bonetta takes on the role of tourist, while also weighing the pros and cons of exercising her class privileges. Once the ship docks at Tenerife on July 24, Bonetta pits personal desire against wifely duty. Pressured to go on shore by the good-natured Mr. Mills, she refuses because "dearest Jim says I'm to land nowhere and it is the best arrangement too."[38] Here Bonetta not only chooses to honor Davies's demand for aloofness before the "common" attractions of the world; she also agrees with him—though her need to write down this last opinion suggests she has to convince herself that he is correct. Indeed, Bonetta weighs the possible delights of touristic exploration against duty to family, to husband, and to class demands, until she settles on the argument that Davies's prohibition "is the best arrangement too," as if she has been slowly convincing herself to follow her husband's strictures.

On July 25, a day before the ship docks in Madeira's capital, Funchal, Bonetta writes, "I am persuaded to go on shore but am firm on this point that I shall do no such thing." However, when the ship finally arrives, her struggles resume:

July 26th 1867—off Madeira.

Came into port at 7a.m. The scenery is lovely, everyone is going on shore. Hawkers have overrun the ship already. I've asked the stewardess to get me some embroidery on shore and expended altogether £6. I am afraid this is rather extravagant . . . the articles are cheap [but] I don't think he'll mind.

A Portuguese possession, Madeira was a popular nineteenth-century tourist destination for the very rich and the very royal, in part because its dry climate was supposedly ideal for respiratory illnesses. Given the social status of many of its visitors, the island boasted elegant hotels as well as pleasant paths for walking and riding. Throughout her entries covering the journey from West Africa to England, Bonetta demonstrates her strong awareness that agentive travel merely in the service of oneself disrupts traditional routines and requirements of home. In this entry, however, we must assume she went on deck to see the scenery, the passengers going ashore, and the hawkers, suggesting the desire to sightsee. In the end, though, she stays obedient to Davies's wishes and balances her desire and her husband's dictates to her best advantage, by purchasing expensive embroidery. By presenting her obedience to Davies's demands as a weighing of options and then a final, personal decision, she confirms her agency, demonstrating the extent to which, as a Victorian-era paterfamilias, Davies still had to rely on his wife's sense of discretion. To some extent, then, despite the distribution of financial power and the gender roles to which Bonetta was expected to adhere, the marriage relies on her tacit collaboration. Bonetta's internal debate about getting off and exploring Madeira demonstrates that she is very much in touch with her desires for innocent fun and excitement. This self-knowledge leaves open the questions of how, why, and when Bonetta might have decided that her own wants should take precedence.

Once her ship departs Madeira, Bonetta's diary entries look forward to the next phase of her journey—docking at Liverpool—even as her gaze once again telescopes through the lens of her maternal responsibilities to Victoria: "Vic woke with an ear ache and fever, she did not leave her bed till after breakfast and then went to sleep and woke feeling better. I am afraid she will be a delicate child in England and I will devote myself to her God helping me."[39] Even with this statement of rededication, once the two are finally in England, Bonetta's dutiful tone gives way almost entirely to descriptions of fulfilling personal friendships forged before her marriage and delightful reunions with the Schöns, the white surrogate family of her teen years. To be sure, little Victoria and Bonetta's husband resurface in the second half of the diary, but compared to the descriptions of her stay at Palm Cottage, they are no longer the central feature of her entries. Bonetta writes from the cottage several days after docking at Liverpool: "I did not go to church [on Sunday, August 4]. Shall go to London tomorrow shopping and sleep a night. Vic is covered in heat bumps[;] she went to a birthday party this evening. I am still feeling tired. Have written Lagos and S. Leone."[40] A week later, even with new concerns (errands, preparing her wardrobe and that of Victoria for upcoming outings, situating one of her Sierra Leone charges, and so on), Bonetta displays a more upbeat, refreshed attitude:

> August 13—Palm House
> Mrs. S. Eunice and I went to London on 8th and remained till Saturday shopping. . . . Went to Trinity Church Sunday morning and heard a good sermon by Mr. Willis[;] rather high church service and there is a pair of candle sticks and cross at the corner of the communion table. . . . I must write to my benefactress today to inform her of my arrival in England. I ought to have done so last week. Vic is a dear child and gets along with everyone.[41]

Despite her obligations to Queen Victoria, now that she has reached one of her primary destinations and has others to watch her young daughter, she finally indulges.

Indeed, there seemed to have been a pleasant informality at Palm Cottage that allowed Bonetta a freedom well beyond the limits required by either Queen Victoria or her husband, with his increasing worries about maintaining status in the racist atmosphere of Lagos. Instead, the visit to England enables a connection between the happiest moments in her past and the extraordinary good fortune in her present:

> August 14—Palm House
> Today is the anniversary of my wedding day and my dear husband's birthday, I feel there is much to be thankful for [a] kind husband and a dear little girl both God's gifts. May the remembrance of these things inspire my heart with greater love to him who is the giver of every good and perfect gift. I have dosed myself this morning and shall be better for it. I trust Vic is well and happy. I wrote 9 letters yesterday and must write 2 more today. Emily is coming home this evening and Annie, I must do

some plain work today. Robert has gone up to his job this day, I will be quite near Fred.

August 15—Palm House

This has been an exciting day, received a letter from my dear husband, and a draft, from Miss Thompson asking me to go for a few hours to see her mother and answered it. Wrote to Clara and Co on business. Received visit from Messrs. George and Lewis. Emily and Fanny returned from Bromley. Had a note from Mr. M. wrote 2 days ago about monograms. Yesterday received letters from Messrs Taylor and Cole. Practiced [the piano?] this morning and unstitched my dress partially preparatory to dyeing it. Sent the jewelry entrusted to my care to be mended. Rather a rainy day.[42]

If her first sentence celebrates her husband and child, Bonetta's palpable delight at the prospect of reuniting with the Schön sons and daughters Emily, Fanny, Robert, and Fred stands out equally, ahead of routine business matters. Here her diary articulates a link between Lagos and Palm Cottage, such that these become the most important points across a span of chronological time, from her childhood to her current status as a woman and wife. However, in *returning* to England, the adult Bonetta gives voice to emotions that collapse time and space. As such, Bonetta's understanding of "home," "belonging," and "return" rest not upon a specific physical location but upon the ineffable emotion generated by genuine bonds of affection tying Lagos to England.

Without the requirement of a particular script to rehearse, and without the necessity of protecting her reputation by cultivating aloofness, Bonetta enjoys an abundance of innocent pleasures with little Victoria:

August 19

Three days ago we spent the evening with the [?] and enjoyed it much. The next day we were invited to see the "Beacon" and the "Blanche" [?] launched in the dockyard. Afterwards we went to luncheon at the Thorntons where we had great fun but I caught a severe cold on my chest which prevented my going to church yesterday. I lost my voice nearly. I received an invite to go to the Forbes tomorrow and am going in spite of the cold with Vic till Saturday. The cold is better this morning and hope will keep so.[43]

Here, Bonetta's feeling of acceptance among her English friends allows her to revisit the pleasure she enjoyed in their company before Queen Victoria required her to marry Davies and move to Lagos. For example, both at Palm Cottage and on a visit to Lady Buxton (the widow of abolitionist Sir Thomas Fowell

Buxton) at Northrepps Cottage, Suffolk, Bonetta indulges in two of her favorite pastimes, playing the piano and singing. Though she seemed fond enough of Lady Buxton, Bonetta had yet to be introduced to the rest of the family, including her hostess's four sons. After meeting the latter over dinner, Bonetta joins with yet another new acquaintance to provide the evening's entertainment: "Very pleasant, some singing, Isabel Johnson and myself."[44] Here Bonetta takes pride in her considerable musical talents and is happy to show them off.

Bonetta's entry about the impromptu concert at the Buxton home resonates in telling ways with two letters she received from Davies in 1875 during her second visit to Britain, this time for the "lying-in" period before the birth of her last child, Stella. By this point, Davies had been charged with fraud (falsely, as it turned out), his business was suffering, and he felt hemmed in by enemies. He took a dim view of his wife's desire for what he imagined to be unbecoming social intercourse, and he set down even more stringent rules of conduct than before. In the first letter, dated November 10, 1875, he instructed, "You will not stand to sing with anyone," and a few lines later added, "You will not stand [and] sing with anybody in my lifetime in Lagos [for] the Amusement of the R[a]bble." Davies allowed that singing was fine in church, but not in a secular setting. Given his troubles and his concerns—which were probably valid—that his enemies might use his misfortune to bring him down, Davies understandably felt jealous of Bonetta's time away. However, his demands conflicted with her love of singing, which she enjoyed even when there were strangers in the audience. It is doubtful that she would have disobeyed her husband, given the difficulties now pressing upon him, as he once more attempted to anticipate her desires and then control them from afar.

The second letter, dated a few weeks later, is exceedingly anxious in tone, with several more prohibitions:

> November 28, 187[5]
>
> My dearest Sarah,
>
> I have this morning received your long and important letter of the 26th inst. The contents please me. I am so happy that after all you did not attend the party. [I] wish nothing or very little to be said of you. Many wish to see you out with everybody or to be very familiar with someone else than me so that the world may have to say this thing or that thing to you and the world will be against me. . . . Let me know the number of time[s] the friends called in my absence[;] keep a regular journal of it. [Other than?] my grief when you give me cause, of dissatisfaction I am in good spirit[s]. . . . And the sooner you give up dancing parties the bet-

ter[;] do not let our fame go out as good dancers. Good [men] or ladies do not praise anyone for dancing excepting the world. . . . Read this seriously and to yourself and say if all I say are not true. . . . I hope dearest that you [do] not go from [one room] to another in night gowns. Dress before you leave your room. . . . do attend to this[,] don't be girlish. now I say this because when I am at home you go to mother's room in [your] nightgown and she comes to yours . . . the same.[45]

Once more, the tone of Davies's letter is understandable, considering his public embarrassment, and in other letters to Bonetta and various trusted friends, he complains bitterly of being hounded at every corner by those who seek to destroy his hard-earned reputation. However, this letter hints at previous conversations when Bonetta did not follow his advice and instead did exactly what she wanted. His prohibitions against going out to dances also suggests that she enjoyed such activities and that he understood she was a popular figure at social events. His almost-panicked admonitions resonate to some extent with Henry Venn's 1852 letter to Julia Sass about whether Bonetta has asked for an indulgence. Here Davies struggles with the attenuation of his male authority because of the distance between Lagos and Britain; however, when Bonetta tours on her own, it is up to her to decide whether she will follow her husband's requirements, even though he has financed the journey.

James Davies had no interest in the approval of the British, and, not surprisingly, his assertiveness had won him enemies even before he went bankrupt in the 1870s. In 1861, before the British took over Lagos and made it a crown colony, Davies protested on behalf of King Dosunmu, the city's indigenous ruler, when contemptuous white negotiators pushed for harsh terms in the annexation agreement. Dosunmu finally signed the agreement after threats of violence, and in sympathy Davies drew up protest petitions for the eyes of Queen Victoria, on behalf of indigenous chiefs and citizens.[46] Once Lagos was controlled by the British, Davies harshly criticized the policies of a series of bigoted British colonial governors who raised taxes and tried to strip all Africans, Christianized or not, of their rights. (There was a brief moment of rapprochement in 1873, when the new governor, John Pope Hennessey, appointed Davies as the only African to the legislative council of West African settlements.)[47] In 1875, he wrote to Bonetta, "I do not at all associate with any of the Europeans[;] they are all afraid of me, specially Judge Mr. Marshall. I have had two or three matters before him and he was oblig[ed] to take my side[.] You know well that I do not go in for a fight for pleasure[;] I do so to maintain our rights."[48] While Davies was supportive of white missionaries, merchants, and government officials who treated him with respect and as an equal, he was contemptuous of those who attempted to patronize him.

For her part, Bonetta's reliable social networks in Britain may have given her the confidence to negotiate her way in a range of social contexts. However, in a particularly self-reflective diary entry, she admits that her social acceptability depended greatly on her ability to win approval: "I believe my besetting sin is love of praise and want of [Chris]tian charity in the best sense."[49] Was her desire for "praise" in fact part of her survival strategy as she moved through different communities? It is all the more telling, then, that she complains in the same entry about young Victoria's lack of interest in pleasing adults, even as she recognizes the unreasonable expectation that a toddler should behave like a much older child.

The positive affirmation of Bonetta's 1867 visit to Britain is finally threatened by none other than Queen Victoria and the royal family. After enjoying the late summer and autumn with friends, Bonetta finally pays a visit to the queen in mid-December. This side trip lasts for a few days, as Bonetta and Victoria stay with friends in the town of Windsor while they await one or more official invitations from the palace. In the middle of their stay, Bonetta offers an account of events in a letter to Mrs. Schön:

> We are well, but dear Victoria has a cough that she brought with her. We went to see the Queen on Monday & Vic was sent for again on Wednesday. She . . . returned with a beautiful doll. The conversation was all about Captain D[avies] & myself, so out of delicacy I was not asked to go up. They were all Charmed with the child, & the Queen gave her on Monday a dear gold locket with a brilliant on it & her likeness inside . . .
>
> Victoria has just had her photo done for the Queen—tis to be colored.
>
> You cannot think how affected they all were with her, & yesterday Prince Leopold took possession of her & the Queen gave her sweets. No one saw her with Her Majesty yesterday except the Prince and P[rince]sses.[50]

Bonetta is deeply moved by the fondness displayed by the British royal family; however, as she had shown in the case of Bonetta's initial rejection of Davies as a husband, Queen Victoria could be grossly insensitive and imperious when it came to her former ward's feelings. Specifically, as recounted in the letter, the queen saw nothing wrong in discussing Bonetta and her husband, such that the former was unwelcome to attend the visit with little Victoria. Nevertheless, Bonetta works on nurturing Victoria's socially valuable relationship with her godmother the queen and focuses on the child's success in gaining the royal family's approval. If in many ways Bonetta's 1867 journey to England reanimated moments of great personal happiness, as she recovered her past with the Schön family, it also demonstrated how much, as a presumably "white space," the metropole could be a site of personal humiliation. Therefore, Bonetta's personal investment in Lagos and England as dual sites of "home" has to be imagined and then qualified by degrees. Certainly, if an English home is provisional, a Lagosian home might not necessarily provide substantive refuge either, especially given that the Christianized elite continually found their desire for autonomy challenged by the British.

TAKING A STAND IN LAGOS

Though Bonetta's 1867 visit sheds some light on how she experienced the relationship between the England of her youth and the Lagos of her adulthood, we have little information on how well she interacted with her Lagosian counterparts during those early years. Certainly, though she was no longer supported by the queen, her royal affiliation sometimes enabled an elevated social access that would have been denied other Christianized West Africans. Her tools would have been not just the connection to the queen but also the dignified effects of her own carefully studied behavior, which had been honed during her years of interacting with the monarch and her intermediaries. Bonetta's investment in her Lagos community continued to increase through work for indigenous congregations in the city and her own church, Saint Paul's Chapel. Meanwhile, the simmering tensions between the Christianized elite and the white CMS missionaries only worsened, with one local church crisis after another. For example, in attempting to raise funds for a school attached to the Aroloya Church, a small group of CMS missionaries put on a concert that yielded a very modest sum. Having among their number much more accomplished, European-trained musicians and orators, the African elite's Lagos Philharmonic Club staged a more lavish and better-attended fundraiser, netting close to seventeen pounds (almost £1,300 today), which they dutifully sent in as a donation to the school. Feeling upstaged by their more talented (and well-heeled) African congregants, the white missionaries flatly refused the money. According to a letter by missionary spokesman J. A. Maser to Charles Foresythe, president of the Philharmonic Club, the rejection was based on allegations that "the recent entertainment [by the club] was of such a character as to give offense to good people." Maser further argued that this "offense" only promoted the "great prevalence of licentiousness which sadly hinders the prospects of families and churches in this place."[51] Knowing that the club would write to the

CMS Parent Committee to lodge a complaint, Maser defended the decision to reject the donation in separate correspondence to London, arguing that "our agents [among the Christianized Africans] are without the proper sense of looking to those who are placed over them for guidance. The principle of obedience to superiors . . . is unknown to them."[52] From Maser's perspective, the quarrel over the immorality of the concert touched on larger resentments, where white missionaries refused to acknowledge the right to independent action on the part of their elite congregants.

After almost five months of back-and-forth correspondence between Maser and Foresythe, the latter finally lost his temper in a September 29 letter to Maser, speaking plainly for the first time on the real cause of the dispute: "I cannot fathom your grounds for not having confidence in us as not to wish us to undertake to do anything by ourselves without dragging [in] the ministers. I ask do you intend us to be forever infants in this church? Are we not to learn to act for and by ourselves and so get used to mov[ing] in our social and religious spheres without that ever-leaning helplessness on pastoral guid[ance], too much of which has ever kept us since in a helpless state?"[53] Foresythe's indictment of the local CMS establishment also touches on the fact that from the early nineteenth century, under the direction of Henry Venn, the CMS had pledged support for a self-sustaining West African church equipped with its own native pastorate. Even then, however, as demonstrated by the comments of Henry Townsend and Julia Sass about why Africans should not be sent to Britain for advanced education, the white CMS agents in the field felt personally threatened by Venn's goal. Ironically, Venn gave up the reins of the CMS in 1872 and died the following year. With him went the early vision of African religious self-governance. In its stead, the new CMS general secretary, Henry Wright, pushed for increased white control, which, of course, validated white agents such as Maser, as well as Adolphus Mann, who had years earlier described as enemies James Davies, Samuel Crowther, and one of Crowther's sons. After Foresythe explicitly confronted Maser, the Philharmonic Club members made good on an earlier threat to found their own Association for Promoting Educational and Religious Interests in Lagos. Bonetta's husband, James Davies, was quickly elected president of the association, and its first meeting was held in their home.

There is no letter or diary entry available that reveals Bonetta's thoughts as she witnessed these months of disputes and the rising anger of her friends and neighbors as they were maligned by Maser and his fellow missionaries. Importantly, though, the struggle being played out in the correspondence between Foresythe and Maser was related to an earlier decision by the missionary finance committee, headed by Maser, to transfer the well-liked white minister Lancelot Nicholson of Saint Paul's Chapel to Sierra Leone permanently. As active congregants at Saint Paul's, Bonetta and Davies were as outraged and disappointed as their fellow worshippers that the local finance committee blatantly disregarded their firm preference for Reverend Nicholson rather than Adolphus Mann, his proposed replacement. While her husband and his male colleagues were involved in organizing the association, Bonetta placed herself squarely in the middle of the controversy over Nicholson, writing two private letters in the late summer of 1873. The first, dated August 7, bypassed Maser and his local authority and instead went directly to CMS assistant secretary Edward Hutchinson, the official in London with authority over the Yoruba Mission, which included Lagos. The second letter, dated August 14, went directly to the late Henry Venn's replacement, Henry Wright, also at CMS headquarters in London. Both letters argued that a reconsideration of Reverend Nicholson's transfer would signal the CMS's respect and support for Saint Paul's African congregation and were sent ahead of a petition being drawn up by the congregation in an attempt to sway the opinions of Wright and Hutchinson.

To Hutchinson, Bonetta wrote: "It is with great regret that we have learned that the [Lagos Finance] Com[mitt]ee of the Church Miss[ionary] Society has decided on sending the Rev. L. Nicholson to Sierra Leone instead of Lagos. . . . I have been requested to write and solicit that Mr. Nicholson's departure from England be delayed till the Society [in London] shall have received and considered the subject of the Petition." She assures Hutchinson that Nicholson's Lagos congregation will "relieve the Society of all charges in regard to [his] salary and expenses."[54] Bonetta's wording shifts responsibility for the letter from herself to other parties, implying that someone else realized that London should be alerted about unfolding events in the colony, since the petition would not be ready in time for immediate viewing. Perhaps unsure of how forceful she should be in the letter to Hutchinson, whom she has never met, Bonetta displays appropriate woman's modesty in hopes of appealing to his gentlemanly side. Also, by signing herself not as "Mrs. James P. L. Davies" but as "Mrs. Sarah Forbes Davies," Bonetta strategically distances herself from her husband, identifying herself instead as an individual representative of Nicholson's devoted flock (that is, "It is with great regret that *we* . . ."). While Bonetta and Hutchinson had never met, he would undoubtedly have heard of her and her connection to Queen Victoria, and she, in turn, undoubtedly counted on his knowledge, as well as her record of service (such as her work with the Manns). By naming herself as part of the collective "we," Bonetta was, in effect, lending her celebrity to (and therefore validating) the signers of the soon-to-be-completed petition and naming her goal and theirs as one and the same.

In her letter to CMS general secretary Wright, Bonetta's strategy is much bolder and more direct, drawing explicitly on her coveted membership in the same aristocratic social circles to which Wright himself belonged:

> It will surprise you to receive a letter from me, for I do not think you will remember me. Julia Tebbs is a dear friend of mine and she is your sister in law. . . . My object in writing to you is my wish to solicit your assistance and influence in getting Mr. Nicholson back to Lagos. I fear his removal will almost cause the breakup of the congregation of Breadfruit Church. . . . Knowing something of Mr. Nicholson's strong sense of duty in going wheresoever the Society send[s] him, I feel sure he will say nothing; but I cannot express to you what a *bitter* disappointment his removal is to every member of his congregation, besides nearly all the European merchants resident in Lagos. . . . The last time Mr. Nicholson went to England, I had to appeal many times to Mr. Venn, and now that he is gone from the midst of us to rest, and you have taken his place, I beg that you would have done the same for us as he would have done. . . .
>
> My husband Capt. Davies returned from England last week[;] he told me he went to Mission House once or twice, but I do not think he saw you, which we both regret.[55]

Before her marriage, Julia Tebbs was Julia Phipps, daughter of none other than Sir Charles Beaumont Phipps, Queen Victoria's keeper of the privy purse until 1866, who had controlled every aspect of Bonetta's life until her marriage to Davies. During her childhood visits to Windsor, Bonetta had been a guest of the Phipps family and would have been well known to Julia and her siblings. In pointing out her social kinship with Wright, Bonetta implies that she matters to people who matter to him. Hers is a tacit demand, then, that Wright treat her with the same respect he would give to a white member of his circle. Just in case their social connections are not sufficient, Bonetta presses on the new general secretary's loyalties to the late Henry Venn and Venn's well-known support for native Christian control of African churches. In not-so-subtle tones, Bonetta implicates Wright in knowing as well as she does that Venn always listened to her and always supported keeping the Reverend Nicholson in Lagos. Finally, at the end of her letter, Bonetta switches easily from her personal and institutional connections to Wright, Venn, and the CMS to her connection to the Saint Paul's congregation when she reminds Wright that Venn "would have done the same for *us*."[56]

After working to shrink the distance between herself and the most powerful official in the CMS hierarchy, Bonetta finally mentions her husband's earlier attempts in London to gain access to either Wright or his subordinate Hutchinson. Here her thinly veiled indictment of Wright rests on the common knowledge that Venn, who officiated at her wedding to Davies, had always made time to meet with her husband and indeed that Bonetta herself had been a regular guest in Venn's home since childhood and during her earlier trips to England. By not mentioning her husband's name in the letter to Hutchinson, Bonetta chose caution, undoubtedly because she knew local white missionaries such as Maser and Mann had sent negative reports about Davies to London. On the other hand, by bringing up Davies in her letter to Wright, Bonetta implies that the general secretary's prior knowledge of both her and her husband should supersede any negative rumors or outright charges by those who possess only a superficial knowledge of her husband's moral character. And though she chose not to mention it, she knew that Wright had heard that John Pope Hennessy, the colonial governor of Lagos at the time, had given Davies a position on the influential West African Affairs Committee, making him the first African to have a seat at the table. Still, determined to have her voice be independent of her husband, Bonetta signed herself once again "Mrs. S. F. Davies." After her appeals against the removal of Nicholson came the signed petition from the congregants, followed by letters from Foresythe and Davies directly to the CMS Parent Committee in London regarding the Lagos Philharmonic Club fundraising controversy, as well a September 1 letter of complaint by Davies about his treatment when he last visited the CMS London office. Clearly, Bonetta had worked alongside both her husband and the leading men of her congregation, who brought their own individual and group voices to bear on Wright.

Finally, the Lagosians received a compromise, halfhearted though it was. On October 30, Hutchinson wrote personally to Davies, apologizing for his reception in London and informing him that while the Parent Committee still saw fit to send Nicholson to Sierra Leone, "yet . . . there are various important matters needing [Nicholson's] occasional presence in Lagos and the Com[mittee] has hereby given him the opportunity of visiting Lagos." Presumably because Davies was president of the Association for Promoting Educational and Religious Matters in Lagos, Hutchinson offered polite but qualified support for "the new movement under Mr. Foresythe" and argued that "some are more ready to recognize the merit and work of the Africans, or more able to see and make allowances for their weaknesses than the [Lagos Finance] Committee."[57] Though it was only a partial victory, Bonetta's efforts in the enterprise undoubtedly earned her the respect of her fellow Christians in Lagos: clearly, she understood the value of being modest and quiet when necessary, but she could also be bold and strategic in particular situations. Though ultimately her efforts and those of her fellow Lagosians did not achieve all of their intended goals, Bonetta proved that she was not fearful of challenging white male missionary leadership in London, using the cultural capital she had accrued through her strong ties with high-ranking families and figures in Britain. In the incidents related to the Philharmonic Club and the transfer of the Reverend Nicholson, Bonetta took a stand that demonstrated where her true loyalties lay. While she was greatly at ease in the English world of the Schöns and Lady Buxton, if less so with Queen Victoria, the stance of her letters to Hutchinson and Wright articulates her considerable investment in Lagos. And while these letters are not travel writing per se, they function as connectors across space, enabling her the opportunity to project her own will across the miles.

A TIME OF DESPERATION

Bonetta's actions in the case of Reverend Nicholson's transfer demonstrate that the feistiness of the nineteen-year-old who tried to defy Queen Victoria was still present. However, there was ultimately nothing she could do to ameliorate her husband's financial distress. Where once Lagos had been a city of unparalleled commercial possibility, enabling men such as Davies to make their fortune, it had become a site of recrimination and shame. As Davies was struggling to find the means to keep their eldest child, Victoria, in her English boarding school, as well as to look after his wife and mother, in 1879 he was once more accused, this time of refusing to turn over assets from a repaid load to his creditors. The strain of this new persecution adversely affected Davies's health, and soon he was complaining of chest pains. The impact on Bonetta was worse: having long suffered from tuberculosis, she took an almost fatal turn at the end of that year. Both Davies and Bonetta shielded Victoria from the bankruptcy and her mother's deadly illness, a factor which made her letters home from boarding school all the more poignant. Having been introduced at the age of four to the world outside of Lagos by her mother, Victoria—now sixteen—sent excited letters home to West Africa describing a class trip to France and Germany, where she perfected her languages and after lessons attended costume balls, utterly unaware of the unpaid tuition bills being sent to her father. Though Davies tried everything to escape the inevitable, the charge that he had pocketed money which should have gone to his creditors led to a criminal trial in Accra. Perhaps because he was alarmed at Bonetta's deterioration, perhaps because he wanted to spare her the humiliation of the trial, or both, Davies persuaded his wife to travel with their youngest child, Stella, who was no more than three or four, and an Afro-Brazilian nanny to Madeira, the island which Bonetta had been tempted to explore during her 1867 journey to see the Schöns.

Given the seriousness of Bonetta's condition, the voyage to Madeira must have been excruciating. Upon arriving in the capital, Funchal, Bonetta, Stella, and the nanny settled into the Royal Edinburgh Hotel, run by the Scotsman William Reid, one of the most exclusive establishments on the island.[58] In an April 1880 letter informing Mrs. Schön that she "nearly died in Lagos of this last illness," Bonetta reported some improvement in her condition. Although she was cautioned against "walking far or even much driving," she still imagined what her stay on the island might be like if she were in better health: "There are beautiful mountains all around us & lovely flowers, such excursions one could make here climbing over the mountains to the other side." She remained socially engaged, reporting that "there are two or three nice family parties in this hotel staying[;] they are all very pleasant."[59] As usual, wherever she went, her connection to Queen Victoria followed: despite the damage done to her husband's reputation by his bankruptcy and its attendant humiliations, Bonetta attracted a range of visitors, including George Hayward, the British consul.

In May 1880 Bonetta wrote to her husband, "I am very anxious, and yesterday was to me a most miserable day thinking of all [your] worry and trouble." By this time she was unable to sleep, and swallowing food and liquids had become extremely painful. To make matters worse, Bonetta was overcome with childcare concerns: "Stella is well but getting wild[;] everyone plays with her, she begins to get spoilt and I have often to punish her." The nanny, she declared, was "too dumpy and stupid [to?] take the trouble to amuse the child or teach her obedience . . . I am getting tired of holding and punishing the child. . . . [N]ow that I am getting rid of my cold she will be more with me." There was also the inevitable discussion about financial resources. Trying to save her husband some money, she had bargained with her hotelier for cheaper rooms: on the one hand, she reported that "they have made a reduction for us," while on the other she was confident that she would be able to secure a "larger room which I can go into in two days time. I do not think they will charge much more as during the summer time [rooms] are cheaper."[60] While Davies's money had previously allowed Bonetta to travel wherever and whenever she desired, by this point his bankruptcy had forced her to negotiate for a room. Over the intervening months, her health sharply deteriorated. Meanwhile, with Davies fighting for his good name before a hostile English judge in Accra, there was no more cash or credit, leaving Bonetta unable to pay for room and board for herself, her child, and their servant, or for her medical care. Rather than turning her out, her hoteliers allowed her to keep her rooms; they fed Stella and the nanny and paid out of pocket for her medical care until she died in August. A few days after her death, Davies won an acquittal from the colonial court in Accra, but Bonetta had already been interred in Funchal's only Protestant cemetery, at the expense of the Royal Edinburgh Hotel. The hotelkeepers also paid passage for Stella and her nanny to return as far as Freetown, Sierra Leone.

It must have been a sorrowful blow for Davies to be unable to help his dying wife in Madeira, forcing her to rely for comfort on complete strangers. What followed next merely added to his humiliation, as his late wife's effects were reduced from tokens of remembrance to objects of commercial exchange. Despite their kindness to the dying Bonetta, the owners of the Royal Edinburgh Hotel had never expected to provide for her free of charge. Indeed, they had written to Davies about Bonetta's bills, to no avail. Finally, they took the audacious step of confiscating Bonetta's jewelry case filled with expensive pieces from Queen Victoria. Since the hoteliers received no response from Davies, they contacted George Hayward, the British consul on Madeira, demanding reimbursement for the £91.17.4 credit that had been extended to Bonetta, in exchange for the jewelry. In his communications with Windsor Palace, Hayward suggested that "the value of [Mrs. Davies's jewelry] exceeds the amount of the . . . debt" owed to the hotel. Additionally, Hayward commented, "I had several conversations with Mrs. Davies during her stay here and was much impressed by her pleasing manner and the appreciation which she expressed of Her Majesty's benevolence to her."[61] (Of course, Hayward's praise of Bonetta echoed that of Julia Sass, Charles Phipps, and Adolphus Mann, suggesting that whatever people's opinions of James Davies, Bonetta's exemplary conduct had been her calling card.) Despite questions about whether Davies had sent any money to Madeira, in the end Queen Victoria paid Bonetta's debt to the hoteliers and took possession of the jewelry case.[62] The incident is an eerie reminder of the first redemption of Sarah Forbes Bonetta in 1850, when Queen Victoria set her free from slavery. After her death, the object of redemption was her jewelry.

Ironies abound here, not least of which is that a penniless nineteenth-century ex-slave turned tourist died at one of the most popular resort destinations of the era—a destination she was once loath to visit because her husband had cautioned her against rubbing shoulders with ordinary people. Ironic, too, was that Bonetta's death signaled the fragility of the autonomous touristic self she expressed in the 1867 travel diary. Though she once scoffed at the idea that marriage to a wealthy husband would make her independent, in fact that husband's bankruptcy made her even more dependent on the charity of others. How do we define *freedom* for Bonetta, then, when as an emancipated African woman, she depended upon those who felt bound to dictate her role as a young woman and a wife? Certainly, although Bonetta's travel to England was materially enabled by her husband's money and her connection to Queen Victoria granted her entry into British aristocratic circles, it was Bonetta's own social successes that kept her within them. Perhaps this was just enough to prompt the queen in the end to provide for her daughter, Victoria Davies.

FULL CIRCLE

In the years following Bonetta's death, James Davies cultivated as best he could his family's connection to the British royal family. For example, soon after his criminal vindication, he sent Queen Victoria summaries of the court proceedings, wrapped in black-edged stationary. At the death of the queen's youngest son, Prince Leopold, in 1884, Davies sent a note of condolence "as the representative of Her Majesty's most loyal subjects of Lagos," while also thanking the queen for her "noble acts" toward Bonetta and their children during his bankruptcy. He requested that Victoria Davies attend "the mournful funeral [of Prince Leopold] to represent Her Majesty's subjects on the coast of Africa."[63] Inevitably, with the death of Queen Victoria in 1901 and the retirements and deaths of individual palace staff who had been familiar with Bonetta and her family, the story of her connections began to fade. At some point in the early twentieth century, the adult Victoria (now Victoria Randle) seems to have initiated contact, presumably by letter, with the keeper of the privy purse under King Edward VII. A typed but undated memorandum in the Royal Archives suggests that Victoria's communication to the king's staff may initially have been confusing, since the document appears to be a hastily researched statement as to the identity of Sarah Forbes Bonetta:

> Mrs. Victoria Randle (nee Davies)
> She is the daughter of SALLY FORBES BONETTA who was as an infant found by Captain Forbes in a boat drifting on the West Coast of Africa, and whose parents had been killed in some inter-tribal fight.
> Captain Forbes picked her up and christened her after the name of the boat he then commanded, "The Sally Bonetta."
> On bringing her to England Queen Victoria took an interest in the child and educated her.[64]

Laughable for its inaccuracies, the memorandum nevertheless suggests a final devolution of Bonetta and her story into total myth, as is the case currently, since Walter Dean Myers's 1999 young readers' biography and almost every blog universally refer to her as "an African princess." Though the rest of the document correctly identifies "Mrs. Victoria Randle (nee) Davies" as god-daughter to the late queen, the misrepresentation of Bonetta as an infant lying in a drifting rowboat styles her as symbolically more powerless and abject than she was when Frederick Forbes received her in 1850. Once again, the name of Forbes's ship, the HMS *Bonetta*, fills the blankness represented by the fantastical African infant in her drifting boat. Bizarrely, the biblical story of baby Moses in the bulrushes comes to mind, suggesting that as with Moses, Bonetta was raised by foreign royalty believing herself to be a princess. In the Old Testament, Moses finally realizes his identity as an Israelite and returns to his people, suggesting that when Bonetta recognized her identity as an African, she "returned" to Lagos through her marriage to Davies. While it is impossible to know what the author of the memorandum was thinking, in fact Bonetta's life was not that of an impostor living in the land of strangers. Rather, for Bonetta the world of Lagos included the world of Britain, and not merely because Britain was the seat of colonial power. At a September 19, 1881, memorial service in Saint Paul's Chapel, where she had been a congregant, native CMS minister Henry Johnson eulogized her as "a bright ornament" in the lives of all who knew her.[65] Yet Bonetta was more than a mere ornament. As an ex-slave, royal ward, and finally elite Christianized African wife, she lived an extraordinary life of privilege, suggesting the achievements attainable by her community, itself descended from former slaves migrating to Nigeria from Sierra Leone. Rather than a blank canvas, Bonetta proved the power of agentive migration and travel among West Africans exercising their own self-determination. Though full control over her own mobility was in the end provisional, Bonetta's life in travel speaks to the dramatic range of experiences free Africans and people of African descent were able to create for themselves in the nineteenth-century Atlantic African diaspora.

Coda

What did "moving home" really mean to the culturally diverse writers explored in the preceding chapters? The most obvious answer is that this group of formerly enslaved and freeborn men and women used their travel writing to shape complex public identities for themselves, in the context of slavery and abolition and at a moment when national belonging, though much desired, was still a dream. While the individual writers Mary Seacole, Nancy Prince, Samuel A. Crowther, Martin Delany, Robert Campbell, and Sarah Forbes Bonetta addressed related goals (including uplift, racial self-determination, Christian mission, and abolition) that tied them to a range of transatlantic Black and African communities, they were hardly united by their origin stories or their cultural histories. Indeed, the coherent selves they imagined through their writing were severely challenged in everyday life, leaving each of them still waiting, as Harriet Jacobs was in 1861, for a hearth of their own. But while "home" in the fashionable nineteenth-century sense would have meant a physical domicile, family, strict gender roles, and an imagined division between public and private, for these writers "home" had to include communities far beyond the locations that defined the proscriptions of their age.

As independent Black female entrepreneurs, Mary Seacole and Nancy Prince continued to live precarious lives. Settling in England, Seacole was "rescued" only after Queen Victoria granted her a modest stipend. After her Jamaican sojourn, Prince made her presence felt at American women's suffrage conferences, in letters she wrote to the *Liberator*, and in a legendary anecdote where she headed a group of angry Blacks in Boston's Smith Court to run a slave catcher out of the neighborhood. Though both women ended their respective travels and settled in specific locations, a sense of their instability and their refusal to be ignored in the larger story of colonial and community relations emerges from archival silences. In contrast, as an African American male thinker and reformer, Martin R. Delany has had a different fate: due to the careful work of countless scholars in African American studies, his place as the father of Black Nationalism has been secured and (most of) his writing recalled and revived on a regular basis. However, Delany was ever restless after he departed from Lagos. In Britain he was highly esteemed by the abolitionist crowd. By 1863 he was back in the United States recruiting Black soldiers for the Union's cause, and by 1865 he accepted the appointment to major in the 54th Massachusetts Colored Infantry Regiment. During Reconstruction he fought hard for Black equality, but his dreams of citizenship had unraveled by the time of his death in 1888, with the rise of segregation, white supremacy, anti-Black violence, and Black voter suppression.

Certainly, it is possible to make similar arguments about "home" denied to Robert Campbell, Samuel Ajayi Crowther, and Sarah Forbes Bonetta. However, as "returnees" within the larger project of African homecoming, Campbell, Crowther, and Bonetta faced an entirely different set of challenges—moving back to "familiar" ground (quite literally, in the case of Crowther) but as entirely creolized individuals, as a result of both colonialism and the transatlantic slave trade. Campbell fulfilled his dream of moving back to the ancestral homeland of his Black Jamaican mother—where, according to R. J. M. Blackett, he became a thorn in the side of British officials—while also joining forces with elite West African Christians in Lagos to assert their rights and class privilege in the face of European racism. In many ways, "home" for Campbell may well have been that community fight, even as he struggled through a number of failed businesses to keep his family financially solvent.[1] For his part, Crowther literally returned to the land of his birth, even reuniting with his mother and some of his siblings. But while he was physically "home," he had to create "home" in the new role of a Christianized African ex-slave and later as an ordained minister. Though by the end of his life he was brushed aside by younger white leaders of the Church Missionary Society post–Henry Venn, he had contributed mightily to the growth of a native pastorate and to the same West African colonial elite with whom he had thrown in his lot.

But what of Sarah Forbes Bonetta? As a nineteenth-century African woman, Bonetta seems to be a socially precarious figure, especially in the context of the colonial archive. Scattered as they are in a range of other people's papers, her letters and diary require a determined excavation: indeed, there is still more to discover, a task I am happy to leave to future scholars. Hitherto almost always relegated to footnotes, or recognized in an extremely qualified way by aficionados of Queen Victoria, Bonetta seems overshadowed by her apparent lack of public achievement when compared to the likes of Seacole and Prince. Though she is claimed by Afro-Britons today to refute arguments that English identity has always been white, her personal struggle with belonging was constant. To feel truly "at home" requires considerable agency and recognized control of material resources, qualities affirmed (at least in theory) by national citizenship, depending on time, place, race, and gender. Bonetta exerted agency as often as possible, but her class-based obligations to both her husband and Queen Victoria were always at odds with this agency, even as her carefully tended relations enabled her a certain freedom to order the world according to her desires. As a colonial subject, she was technically a British citizen. However, as a Victorian-era colonial wife, she had to respond to the sometimes overbearing desires of her husband, James P. L. Davies, even as he worked daily to thwart the racism of British officials in Lagos. Also ironic is that she lived among Christianized West African women merchants who, though they too were Victorian wives, still wielded a certain amount of financial power because of their skill as traders.

Stepping back, we can easily imagine the connections between Seacole, Prince, Crowther, Delany, Campbell, and Bonetta, western-educated Atlantic Africans who negotiated internecine warfare and a growing European presence. This sense of commonality might easily lead us to assume a bona fide literary tradition in early diasporic writing, despite the fracturing of this potential canon along the lines of local goals, audiences, and cultural contexts. Yet the countless modulations of class, race, color, gender, ethnicity, cultural citizenship, and community allegiance in these works generate enough differences to trouble any neat list of shared features. Engaging locations as diverse as Jamaica, Panama, Lagos, the Crimean Peninsula, rural Canada, England, and the island of Madeira, whether as published books or diaries and letters, writing by these men and women brings into clear focus the ways in which Black Atlantic subjects were at times enmeshed in the making of European empire, even as some ultimately sought to bring an idealized Black American or creolized African community independence into existence. Many were also painfully aware that the social authority that might accrue to them in one location could easily be challenged or entirely diminished in another. Additionally, what "Blackness" or "Black" skin signified in the United States and British Jamaica had an entirely different set of meanings among the Egba, in Panama, or on the barren, wind-swept plains of the Crimean Peninsula. What has interested me throughout this project are these differences, even more than the commonalities.

Even as I have anchored *Moving Home* firmly in the nineteenth-century Atlantic world, my choice of texts underscores the ways in which Black travel exceeded the Atlantic world, as Black American and African travel has always done. For example, though Seacole and Prince were Black subjects from the Americas, the geographic range they covered (Central America, Turkey, and Russia) illuminates the need for what, in a different context, Yogita Goyal has called "new diasporas."[2] Seacole's positioning of herself with the British Army in the Crimea and Prince's memorialization of her role as maternal landlady in Saint Petersburg force us to think beyond the reverberations of the transatlantic slave trade to include non-Atlantic, non-European empire building as well as other world populations with differing histories and regimes of race, ethnicity, gender, and economic status. Often presented as an example of early Black Atlantic literature, and more specifically as an early form of the slave narrative, *The Interesting Narrative of the Life of Olaudah Equiano, or Gustavus Vassa, the African* (1789) has always posed something of a problem for literary scholars and historians. Beyond the slave trade and abolitionist discourse, what are we to do with Equiano's voluntary travels to the Arctic?[3] As with Delany's *Report of the Niger Valley Exploring Party*, this aspect of *The Interesting Narrative* represents Equiano's attempt to define his creolized African identity as encompassing the same curiosity and bravery traditionally assigned to white scientists and explorers of his day. But early "science" and "exploration" were fraught categories, tied as they were to emerging discourses of empire building and race science.[4] In such a context, what does *diasporic identity* come to mean in the nineteenth century, in the absence of communities of African descent?

In her 2015 *The Intimacies of Four Continents*, Lisa Lowe makes a cogent argument for exploring in more detail the early Atlantic World enabled by white settler colonialism, transatlantic slavery, and Chinese and Indian indenture. Lowe's project involves rereading the well-combed archives of the East India Company and the British Colonial Office to explore the ways in which the exploitation of laborers of color in the Americas enabled the seemingly inclusive liberalism ushered in by the European Enlightenment. Lowe's readings are greatly instructive and a valuable starting point, especially when she points out the subversive quality of social and sexual intimacies between and among colonial laborers, be they African, Indian, Chinese, or indigenous.[5] Precisely because, as Lowe confirms, colonial officials sought to police any interactions between subject populations, I am increasingly fascinated by early African

Americans who traveled beyond the Atlantic world and in spaces where Euro-American colonial designs were present but still unasserted.

A text that immediately comes to mind is Matthew Henson's *A Negro Explorer at the North Pole* (1912). In 1909, the African American Henson accompanied white American explorer Robert Peary on his Arctic expedition to find the North Pole, at the height of the early twentieth-century rush to claim the literal ends of the earth. Predictably, while Peary was celebrated as the hero of US polar exploration, Henson fell into obscurity, dying in 1955.[6] Today, Henson's rediscovery and promotion by Black educators as a crucial example of African American contributions to science speak to one of the key goals of African American studies: to make visible the absolute centrality of Black Americans in the creation and continuance of the United States. Yet his story should also provoke a range of questions not so easily answered by the modern politics of uplift. With Henson we must once more deconstruct the category of Arctic *explorer*. While Equiano offers his readers only a brief glimpse of his time in the Arctic, after their 1909 expedition both Henson and Peary suggest in their respective accounts that Henson was better able to communicate with the Inuit men and women upon whom they depended for survival. Both men would go on to impregnate Inuit women.[7]

Early in *A Negro Explorer*, Henson comments, "I have been to all intents an Esquimo, with Esquimos for companions, speaking their language, dressing in the same kind of clothes, living in the same kind of dens, eating the same food, enjoying their pleasures, and frequently sharing their griefs. I have come to love these people. . . . They are my friends and they regard me as theirs."[8] In addition, his two appendixes to *A Negro Explorer* provide both an ethnographic description of the Inuit and a list of 218 Inuit men and women who directly aided the expedition.[9] These appendixes should give modern readers pause. On the one hand, in listing those who kept the expedition alive, Henson intentionally honors the contributions and sacrifices of the Inuit women as well as Inuit men. No doubt he fully understood that Peary and his white companions—not to mention white readers—would have looked down on these indigenous people in much the same way they looked down on Black Americans. In creating this list, Henson defied the traditional exploration narrative form as it had evolved by the first decade of the twentieth century. However, Henson's other appendix, "Notes on the Esquimos," provides racist "facts" about the Inuit that represent at best an attempt at benevolent paternalism. My point here is not to condemn Henson because he lacked a twenty-first-century sensibility. Rather, I am fascinated by the tension in Henson's account between his determination to make the Inuit visible as the backbone of Peary's entire expedition and his deployment of scientific racism to mark his status as not only a cultural broker but also the cultural superior of those he hoped to honor. A full analysis of this tension would take the current discussion of Matthew Henson beyond hagiography by teasing out the inevitable contradictions inherent in exploration as a colonizing practice, even if that explorer is Black.[10]

In his recent work on African American travel writing, Gary Totten reminds us that Henson had to contend with Peary's obsessive attempts to micromanage and with virulent Jim Crow racism that followed him all the way to the Arctic, in the form of Peary's intense jealousy. Both Henson's struggles as a Black American and his awareness of his readers shaped the ways he assigned meaning to his experiences in the Arctic. In this sense, A Negro Explorer reverberates with the aftermath of slavery and the turn-of-the-century nadir in American race relations. However, rather than reading Henson's claim to the appellation *explorer* as exclusively a sign of his demand for equality with the white Peary, we must also think of how he negotiated the cultural and racial power dynamics that undergirded his relationship with the Inuit. In *Wonderful Adventures*, Mary Seacole rubbed shoulders with Greeks, Turks, and a range of Eastern European and Mediterranean populations, but she deliberately omitted any mention of them, since they did not serve a narrative purpose. On the other hand, since she had different practical concerns, Nancy Prince took pains to highlight aspects of Russia and the Russians that were unfamiliar to American readers, so as to cultivate her authority as a knowing traveler and lecturer in Boston. As with Prince, Henson's Black American identity was shaped in A Negro Explorer by the meanings he assigned to those he encountered—in his case, the Inuit—and especially to statements and silences around his sexual intimacy with at least one Inuit woman. Though the Inuit descendants of Henson and Peary hold their American ancestors in esteem today, Henson's relationship with the expedition's indigenous guides and seamstresses requires more research.[11]

As another way of exploring the intersection of mobile Black subjects with other populations of color, let me conclude with some thoughts on a recent archive brought to light by Caribbean studies scholar Verene A. Shepherd in 2002 under the title *Maharani's Misery: Narratives of a Passage from India to the Caribbean*. Essentially a set of depositions collected in 1885 by colonial authorities in British Guyana, the first-person testimonies in *Maharani's Misery* recount the death of a young Indian woman whose name Shepherd uses in the book's title. An indentured agricultural worker bound for the Anglophone Caribbean, Maharani began her voyage from Calcutta months before the depositions were taken, on the HMS *Allenshaw*. According to the testimony of the ship's white officers, the racially mixed crew, and the indentured passengers, one night while the ship was still in the Indian Ocean, Maharani went on deck in search of the water closet and was raped by one or more of the crew. As a result of the rape, Maharani developed peritonitis; on her deathbed, fevered and in great pain, she still managed to describe her assailants to two women passengers. According to her confidants, at least one rapist was the Black sailor Robert Ipson, who vehemently denied the charge. As Shepherd points out in her masterful introduction, since Maharani died long before the *Allenshaw* even entered the Atlantic Ocean, her voice was essentially absent from the proceedings, even as her words were relayed by the other women. As Shepherd reminds us, Maharani's confidants, as well as any number of female indentured workers, were regularly the target of sexual assault. The other depositions—all from men—were marked by competing accounts and even misdirection, depending on their rank, their race, and their places of origin. Consequently, though the crew testified to a man that the officers regularly took sexual advantage of the female workers, the officers made Robert Ipson their scapegoat. On the other hand, the few indentured male passengers who were interviewed implicated both officers and the multiracial crew as sexual predators on the ship. (For their part, members of the crew complained that it was unfair that the officers were allowed to take sexual advantage of the female passengers while common seamen were severely punished for the slightest attempt at fraternization.)

To keep the story from turning into an account of male class rivalry, Shepherd understandably takes control of the collected testimonies so as to refocus attention on the deceased Maharani. However, though not mentioned in her commentary, another male rivalry on the *Allenshaw* falls right in line with historical scholarship that represents the Black sailor as a figure of agency in the world of shipboard life. Indeed, the crew's testimonies identify the accused rapist Ipson as the leader of a multiracial mutiny in response to the captain's theft of the sailors' rations. Did the captain—who came to blows with the mutineers before the latter were thrown in the brig—condemn Ipson as the rapist, as a way of punishing him? Since the most credible account of Maharani's assault (from an indentured male passenger) describes her being seized by a group of sailors, including Ipson, and forced belowdecks to the crew's quarters, did the same white crew members who participated in the mutiny enforce the stereotype of the Black rapist by shifting all transgression onto one who had only recently championed their rights? Finally, did the other two Black sailors on the *Allenshaw* distance themselves from Ipson because they feared for their own safety among the officers and crew? These questions point to expressions of shipboard masculinity that turn on endlessly intersecting classed and raced allegiances, where the crew might at some points band together across race lines to fight against an oppressive white captain while at other times splinter along those lines, as each man sought to protect himself. One thing is clear: regardless of their stances, both the white officers and the multiracial crew expressed a deep hatred for the indentured passengers, male and female.

As a collective document, these testimonies bridge Caribbean, imperial, migration, and especially Black Atlantic history since, if we set aside Maharani's suffering for a moment, Ipson's bravery in fighting the captain would support traditional assessments of Black sailors as the embodiment of resistance to white authority at sea. As Michael A. Schoeppner has demonstrated, before the abolition of slavery in the United States, southerners were terrified of the arrival of free Black sailors to their ports, because they inevitably carried the "contagion" of liberty that would then infect slaves with whom they came into contact. Indeed, the category of Black seamen as a symbol of freedom appears in a range of antebellum Black Atlantic texts, including Equiano's 1789 *The Interesting Narrative*. The liminal space occupied by the Black seaman was so productive that a sailor's disguise enabled Frederick Douglass to escape from slavery in 1838 and Harriet Jacobs to leave her hiding place in 1841 to arrange for her children's passage to the North. Similarly, the eponymous American-born runaway slave of Martin Delany's serialized novel *Blake: or, The Huts of America* (1859–61) gained access to Black rebels in Cuba as a result of becoming a sailor after his escape.[12] As a historical actor, Ipson appears to represent this storied Black Atlantic heroism, potentially an easily romanticized Black male diasporic subject operating at the intersection of white male power on land and at sea.

Yet, the story of the *Allenshaw* reveals myriad power struggles among white officers, multiracial crews, and male and female immigrants that must have taken place on numerous transports between the British Caribbean and Calcutta. The inclusion of Indian Ocean subjects completely reorients the plain of human experience in the Black Atlantic, requiring new questions, new tools of analysis, and archival rereading.[13] Ipson's possible role in Maharani's rape does not negate the racist betrayal of his white comrades. Rather, his story and that of Matthew Henson challenge us to think more capaciously about the social and historical conditions under which these individuals lived, thereby accounting for all possibilities as we read the past, regardless of whether the conditions fit the outcomes we crave today. For me, Seacole, Prince, Crowther, Delany, Campbell, and Bonetta were not purely resistant heroes who always overcame. Extraordinary though they were, their feats of survival also exposed numerous prejudices, flaws, and ethnocentric misreadings. These are not problems to be downplayed; rather, they necessarily affirm the ultimate humanity of Black subjects.

INTRODUCTION

1. Pratt, *Imperial Eyes*. The habit of representing a landscape as either "blank," wild, and potentially tamable or strange and unique also appealed to white writers who sought to reimagine towns, the countryside, and populations of their own or similar nations, whether in Europe or in the United States. A Frenchman who became an American citizen, Hector St. John de Crèvecoeur left his readers in no doubt as to the focus of his *Letters from an American Farmer: Describing Certain Provincial Situations, Manners, and Customs, Not Generally Known; and Conveying Some Idea of the Late and Present Interior Circumstances of the British Colonies of North America* (1782). In 1791 Samuel Johnson described his perambulations in *A Journey to the Western Islands of Scotland* (1775), while James Fenimore Cooper turned his eye to Europeans' attitudes in *Notions of the Americans: Picked Up by a Travelling Bachelor* (1828). Meanwhile, Frederick Law Olmsted offered social commentary in his *The Cotton Kingdom: A Traveller's Observations on Cotton and Slavery in the American Slave States* (1861). Ironically, the trope of the alien Other was even applied to classed populations in a writer's homeland, as was the case in William Booth's *In Darkest England* (1890). In fact, the title of Booth's book coincided with that of Henry Morton Stanley's *In Darkest Africa*, published that same year. By collapsing "darkest Africa" with poverty-stricken Englanders, Booth championed the civilizing mission as the cure to all ills, and he employed the language of colonialism that was part and parcel of imperial travel writing to construct a particularly raced and classed sense of English identity. In this case, writing associated with the English traveler enabled a flexible worldview that buttressed a range of powerful interests behind late nineteenth-century British nation and empire building.

2. See especially Bassett, "Cartography"; Fabian, *Time*; Fabian, *Out of Our Minds*; Driver, *Geography Militant*.

3. Scholarship that does address Delany's *Official Report* in detail includes Blackett, "Martin R. Delany," as well as Blackett, *Beating against the Barriers*. Additionally, see J. T. Campbell, *Middle Passages*.

4. For a sampling of important work see Grewal, *Home*; Griffin and Fish, *Stranger*; Fish, *Black and White Women's Travel Narratives*; Totten, *African American Travel Narratives*.

5. Youngs, *Cambridge Introduction*, 3.

6. See, for example, Wong, *Neither Fugitive nor Free*. Scholarship that discusses the relationship between slave narratives and travel texts includes Murphy, "Olaudah Equiano"; Brawley, "Fugitive Nation"; Brawley, "Frederick Douglass' *My Bondage*"; Brusky, "Travels"; Chaney, "Traveling Harlem's Europe"; Kelleter, "Ethnic Self-Dramatization"; Lucasi, "William Wells Brown's *Narrative*"; Baraw, "William Wells Brown"; Bohls, *Slavery*. On the general topic of pre–Civil War travel in the United States by freeborn Black Americans, see Pryor, *Colored Travelers*.

7. See *Oxford English Dictionary*, s.v. "travel," accessed June 7, 2021, https://quod.lib. umich.edu/cgi/o/oed/oed-idx?type=entry&byte=507106248.

8. See Brusky, "Travels."

9. Craft and Craft, *Running a Thousand Miles*, 56–57.

10. For a specific focus on Ellen and her masquerade as an ailing white man, see Samuels, *Fantasies*.

11. Totten, *African American Travel Narratives*.

12. Harriet Jacobs, *Incidents*, 201.

13. See Samuel Richardson, *Pamela*, where the fifteen-year-old maid wins over her exploitative male employer by resisting his sexual entreaties until he finally realizes the value of her character and responds with marriage.

14. For useful discussions of nineteenth-century European white women and travel, see Blunt, *Travel*; Lawrence, *Penelope Voyages*; Russell, *Blessings*; Kelley, "Increasingly 'Imaginative Geographies'"; Dúnlaith Bird, *Travelling in Different Skins*; Loth, "Writing and Traveling."

15. For recent work on the slave Mary Prince and travel, see Bohls, *Slavery*; Simmons, "Beyond 'Authenticity.'"

16. Gordon-Reed, *Hemingses*, 239.

17. For a wonderful introduction to the narratives of Jarena Lee, Zilpha Elaw, and Julia Foote, see Andrews, *Sisters*; see also Smith, *Autobiography*.

18. For an excellent summary of the productive challenges posed by Africanists working on Black Atlantic cultures, see Mann, "Shifting Paradigms." In particular, Mann points out the goals of the Diaspora from the Nigerian Hinterland Project, whose organizers maintain that "persons born in Africa carried with them into slavery not only their cultures but also their history, and that if we understand the experience of slaves and the histories of the societies from which they came, then we will be able to trace these influences into the diaspora." Mann, "Shifting Paradigms," 5.

19. Proponents of this argument include Kopytoff, *Preface*; Matory, "English Professors"; Roberts, "Construction"; Piot, "Atlantic Aporias"; Joseph Harris, "Expanding the Scope"; Zeleza, "Rewriting the African Diaspora."

20. For a sampling of discussions treating Equiano's relationship to capitalism and imperialism, see Hinds, "Spirit"; Pudaloff, "No Change"; Field, "'Excepting Himself.'" The triangle trade is a metaphor that vividly exemplifies the continuous circuits of trade in bodies and goods that linked European imperial designs, the Atlantic slave trade, and the

extraction of resources from American colonies. By the time the Atlantic slave trade had reached its height in the early eighteenth century, vessels from Europe filled with metal pots and pans, woven cloth, beads, and European weapons instantiated the first leg of the proverbial triangle as they plied the African west coast, trading inanimate objects for slaves. The next leg of the triangle was articulated by the Middle Passage, westward from Africa to the Americas, where slaves were sold off at various colonial ports from South America to as far north as British Canada. As they traveled from port to port, slave ship crews gradually replaced human cargo with the fruits of empire, including cotton, tobacco, furs, sugar, spices, hardwoods, rice, and other raw materials. The return to Europe of slave ships now carrying these goods completed the third and final leg of the triangle.

21. For the traditional argument that Equiano is the father of the American slave narrative, see Baker, "Figuration."

22. Lovejoy, "Construction," 8. For a summary of Caretta's argument, see his "Does Equiano Still Matter?"

23. See Gilroy, *Black Atlantic.*

24. Berlin, "From Creole to African." For an updated extension of Berlin's argument, see Law and Mann, "West Africa."

25. See, for example, Northrup, "Becoming African"; Matory, "English Professors"; Piot, "Atlantic Aporias"; Zeleza, "Rewriting the African Diaspora."

26. Northrup, "Becoming African"; see, more generally, Northrup, *Africa's Discovery.*

27. See Matory, "English Professors."

28. For useful discussions of krio identity in Sierra Leone, see Spitzer, *Lives In Between,* and, more recently, Cole, *Krio.*

29. Pratt argues that "contact zones" are "social spaces where disparate cultures meet, clash, and grapple with each other, often in highly asymmetrical relations of domination and subordination—like colonialism, slavery, or their aftermaths as they are lived out across the globe today." Pratt, *Imperial Eyes,* 4.

30. The British outlawed slavery in the nation in 1772 with the Somerset case, the Atlantic slave trade in 1807, and slavery in Canada and its West Indian colonies in 1832. Many northern American states outlawed slavery soon after the end of the war for independence. By 1808 the United States ended its participation in the trade, though slavery in the South continued until Abraham Lincoln's executive order (the Emancipation Proclamation) in 1863. Congress finally ratified the Thirteenth Amendment in 1864, ending involuntary servitude permanently (unless you were a prisoner). The Haitian slaves had revolted and freed themselves in 1791, while revolutionaries in France ended slavery in the nation's other West Indian colonies in 1794.

After the Haitian Revolution, most of Spain's colonies in Central America and South America won their independence, whereupon they all abolished slavery by the 1830s. The importation of slaves to colonial Cuba ended officially in 1820, but lack of enforcement meant that kidnapped Africans were still being brought to the island until 1867. Likewise, Brazil still imported slaves, even though the trade was officially banned in 1831. Brazilian slavery did not come to an end until 1888.

31. The topic of African American responses to empire, especially though not exclusively in the context of diaspora, has generated a growing body of scholarship, including

Sanneh, *Abolitionists Abroad*; Gruesser, *Empire* ; Von Eschen, *Race*; Edwards, *Practice*; Stephens, *Black Empire*; Gaines, *American Africans*. This topic intersects as well as with the well-established push among many Americanists to rethink US culture and history in light of westward expansion and foreign policy, signaled in the early 1990s by Amy Kaplan and Pease, *Cultures*; Amy Kaplan, "Manifest Domesticity."

32. Studies that use the nineteenth century as a backstory toward the twentieth-century flowering of a radical position include books as varied as Gilroy's *Black Atlantic* and Von Eschen's *Race*. Roderick Ferguson offers some interesting challenges to the way African Americanists have constructed and framed the historical narrative of their subject. See Roderick Ferguson, "Lateral Moves"; Roderick Ferguson, *Reorder*. See especially Goyal, "We Need New Diasporas"; Goyal, *Runaway Genres*.

33. See, for example, studies that trace West African travel back and forth across the Atlantic Ocean in the seventeenth and eighteenth centuries, including Law and Mann, "West Africa"; Berlin, "From Creole to African"; Smallwood, *Saltwater Slavery*; Sweet, *Domingos Álvares*.

34. For Christianized West Africans as diary writers, see Karin Barber, *Africa's Hidden Histories*.

1. MARY SEACOLE'S WEST INDIAN HOSPITALITY

An earlier version of chapter 1 appeared as "Traveling with Her Mother's Tastes: The Negotiation of Gender, Race, and Location in *Wonderful Adventures of Mrs. Seacole in Many Lands*," *Signs* 26, no. 4 (Summer 2001): 949–81.

1. In the autobiography, Seacole styles herself a "Creole," and she also embraces her mulatto identity. As Kamau Brathwaite argues, *Creole* is a term that had and still retains a variety of meanings across time and space. For the children of white settlers, it was a specific reference to birth outside of England in the British West Indian colonies. Was Seacole appropriating the term to align herself with Afro-Jamaicans and against Africans? Throughout this chapter, I use the term *colored* or *mixed race* to refer to West Indian–born individuals such as Seacole who were a product of Black-white sexual relations, in line with Caribbean scholars who employ the same term. See Brathwaite, *Development*; Heuman, *Between Black and White*; Beckles, "On the Backs"; Cox, *Free Coloreds*; Sio, "Marginality." For possible shifts in the meaning of *colored* to *brown*, see most recently Edmondson, "'Most Intensely Jamaican.'" For a discussion of the US context, see Horton, *Free People*.

2. There have been a number of scholarly biographical essays covering Seacole, such as the introductions by Alexander and Dewjee and by Salih to Seacole, *Wonderful Adventures*. Seacole's reputation is currently enjoying a strong revival, sparking Jane Robinson's popular 2004 biography *Mary Seacole: The Most Famous Black Woman of the Victorian Age*. Though Robinson's research is thorough, she avoids anything even mildly controversial. In addition to Robinson, see Anionwu, *Short History*. Anionwu is a highly distinguished nurse, public health professor, and community health advocate who has tirelessly championed for full recognition of Seacole's achievements.

3. Alexander, "Let It Lie," 49n.

4. Jamaica Information Service, "Mary Seacole."

5. For a report on the installation of the statue, see BBC News, "Mary Seacole Statue." In 2004, well before the statue, Seacole was voted the most famous black Briton of all time. See Fernando, *Mary Seacole*; Matthew Taylor, "Nurse." For a summary of complaints about Seacole, see Gander, "Mary Seacole Statue."

6. For an example of the racist sensationalizing of Seacole's skin color and origins, see McDonald, "Lessons."

7. See, for example, Frazier, "Two Nurses." For an example of the ways Seacole's name is becoming more well known in nursing circles across the world, see Sleeth, "Mary Seacole." For a popular recognition of the role of Caribbean nurses, see BBC, *Black Nurses*. See also Godfrey, "Jamaican."

8. Continual scholarly interest in Seacole's *Wonderful Adventures* has resulted in many fine studies: Paquet, "Enigma"; McKenna, "'Fancies'"; Amy Robinson, "Authority"; Judd, *Bedside Seductions*; Hawthorne, "Self-Writing"; Baggett, "Caught between Home"; Paravisini-Gebert, "Mrs. Seacole's *Wonderful Adventures*"; Frederick, "Creole Performance"; Fish, *Black and White Women's Travel Narratives*; Fluhr, "Their Calling Me 'Mother'"; Rupprecht, "*Wonderful Adventures*"; Poon, "Comic Acts"; Chancy, "Subjectivity"; Damian, "Novel Speculation."

9. See Mary Prince [and Pringle], *History*; Moira Ferguson, *Hart Sisters*; Marilyn Richardson, *Maria W. Stewart*; Harriet Jacobs, *Incidents* ; Lee, *Life and Religious Experience*; Nancy Prince, *Narrative*.

10. Paquet, "Enigma," 651.

11. Faith Smith, "Coming Home," 906.

12. Gikandi, *Maps*, 124.

13. As Kathleen Wilson has convincingly argued, "Within imperial and colonial settings . . . historical actors were defined in multiple ways; and different genders, classes, ethnicities and races all participated, albeit in varied and unequal measure, in the creation of their history." Wilson, *Island Race*, 15.

14. See Senior, "Panama Railway"; Daley, "Watermelon Riot"; Bushnell, *Making*; Safford and Palacios, *Columbia*; Newton, *Silver Men*.

15. See Lalumia, "Realism"; Poovey, *Uneven Developments*; Dereli, "Gender Issues"; Small, *Florence Nightingale*; Royle, *Crimea*.

16. See Clifford, "Traveling Cultures"; Grewal, *Home*; Caren Kaplan, *Questions of Travel*.

17. Beckles, *Centering Woman*, 191–92.

18. Poovey, *Uneven Developments*, 168; Dereli, "Gender Issues," 65.

19. For important context on the intersection of gender and class with respect to the recruitment of Nightingale's Crimean nurses, see Rupprecht, "*Wonderful Adventures*."

20. Beckles, "On the Backs," 179.

21. Alexander and Dewjee, introduction, 28.

22. Soyer, *Soyer's Culinary Campaign*, 231, 435.

23. Soyer, *Soyer's Culinary Campaign*, 436, 269. See also Fluhr, "Loss Made Literal," 135, 125. In her family correspondence, Nightingale confirmed Soyer's identification of Sally as Seacole's daughter, claiming that she was fathered illegitimately by one Colonel

Bunbury. With no solid evidence for or against a union between Seacole and Bunbury, the truth behind Sally's parentage is, as they say, lost to history. See Jane Robinson, *Mary Seacole*, 155.

24. Josephs, "Mary Seacole," 50–51.

25. Bush, "White 'Ladies,'" 258. Beckles offers a similar assessment of life during slavery: "Black women, whether slave or free, were generally not as successful in extricating socio-economic benefits from propertied white males as were coloured women. Data for Bridgetown [Barbados] suggest that whereas black women remained in the 'small-time' fringes of this illicit social culture, large numbers of coloured women successfully fashioned their socio-ideological vision around the need to entertain white males, in return for social and material betterment. As free persons, coloured women's opportunities were severely limited, so this realization encouraged them to adopt a professional attitude towards the sex industry that brought them into intimate contact with propertied white males." Beckles, *Centering Women*, 32. See also Kerr, "Victims or Strategists?"; Welch, "'Unhappy and Afflicted Women?'"

26. For the full story of Pringle-Polgreen, see Handler, "Joseph Rachell"; Candlin and Pybus, *Enterprising Women*. For an important new reading of Rachel Pringle-Polgreen, see Fuentes, *Dispossessed Lives*.

27. Kerr, "Victims or Strategists?," 198, 202.

28. Kerr, "Victims or Strategists?," 201.

29. Seacole, *Wonderful Adventures*, ed. Alexander and Dewjee, 56. Unless otherwise indicated, all references to the 1857 autobiography are to this edition and are cited parenthetically in the text.

30. Small, *Florence Nightingale*, 17.

31. "Our Very Own Vivandière," 221. As Nicole Fluhr points out, the text accompanying the *Punch* illustration seems to be drawn from a letter written by Seacole. However, despite the magazine's support for Seacole, the illustration is parodic. See Fluhr, "Their Calling Me 'Mother.'"

32. Gikandi, *Maps*, 140.

33. Hawthorne, "Self-Writing," 314.

34. See, for instance, Russell, *Blessings*; Mills, *Discourses*; Lawrence, *Penelope Voyages*.

35. Rosemary George, *Politics*, 186.

36. Antoinette Burton, *At the Heart*, 10. For a related argument in the US context, see Amy Kaplan's classic essay "Manifest Domesticity."

37. Paquet, "Enigma," 659.

38. Senior, "Panama Railway"; Newton, *Silver Men*.

39. Mills, *Discourses*, 96–97.

40. Mills, *Discourses*, 96–97.

41. Catherine Hall, *White, Male and Middle Class*, 222–23.

42. See especially Damian, "Novel Speculation."

43. We might think here of Homi Bhabha's well-known theorization of the subversive nature of what he calls colonial mimicry. Bhabha, "Of Mimicry."

44. Paquet, "Enigma," 652.

45. Carlyle, *Occasional Discourse*, 4.

46. Schuler, *"Alas, Alas, Poor Kongo,"* 44.

47. Conniff, *Panama*, 20.

48. Garnet and Delany, of course, were among those African American leaders who also agitated at various times for Black immigration to Africa. For a standard history of African American nationalist and Black separatist movements in the nineteenth century, see Moses, *Golden Age*.

49. Bushnell, *Making*, 106–8.

50. Senior, "Panama Railway," 76; see also Daley, "Watermelon Riot."

51. Lalumia, "Realism," 26.

52. Blackwood, *Narrative*, 262–63.

53. Bamfield, *On the Strength*. According to Bamfield, on average in the Crimea there were six soldiers' wives to every one hundred men. These women were allowed to travel "on the strength" of their regiments, providing services to the soldiers such as cooking, cleaning, mending, and nursing.

54. Indeed, as Paravisini-Gebert argues, "Seacole . . . cleverly weaves Nightingale into her text, creating a mirror image that in many ways subverts Nightingale and allows Seacole, if not to displace Nightingale . . . at least to share her Crimean space." Paravisini-Gebert, "Mrs. Seacole's *Wonderful Adventures*," 77.

55. Kerr, "Victims or Strategists?," 201.

56. Dereli, "Gender Issues," 71.

57. Blackwood, *Narrative*, 56–57.

58. Goodman, *Fields*, 200.

59. Tisdall, *Mrs. Duberly's Campaigns*, 129, 144.

60. Hodge, *"Little Hodge,"* 110.

61. For more information on Fenton's photographic tour of the front, see Gernsheim and Gernsheim, *Roger Fenton*.

62. Faith Smith, "Coming Home," 905; Alexander and Dewjee, introduction, 38.

63. Damian, "'Novel Speculation,'" 17, 23; Jane Robinson, *Mary Seacole*.

2. HOME AND BELONGING FOR NANCY PRINCE

An earlier version of this chapter appeared as "Nancy Prince and the Politics of Mobility, Home, and Diasporic (Mis)Identification," *American Quarterly* 53, no. 1 (March 2001): 32–69.

1. For the story of Prince's Smith Court activity, see Sterling, *We Are Your Sisters*, 222; Barthelemy, introduction, 38.

2. Stanton, Anthony, and Gage, *History*, 384. For brief but useful references to Prince's life in Boston, see also Yee, *Black Women Abolitionists*.

3. Prince is comparable to other free Black American women in this period. For example, Mary Ann Shadd Cary immigrated to the Black Canadian town of Buxton, where she was the first Black woman in North America to publish a newspaper, the *Provincial Freeman*. According to Carla Peterson, Cary set out to "penetrate the male public sphere of the black press and convention movement" (Peterson, "Doers," 99). As biographer Jane Rhodes demonstrates, though Cary was a deeply committed activist in the service of

Black community development, she was also critical of the shortcomings of those communities, which resulted in some uneasy alliances with men and women in her circle. See Rhodes, *Mary Ann Shadd Cary*. Prince was similarly committed but also similarly critical of those reformers (Black and white) with whom she labored, and therefore her relationships with other activists were frequently tense.

4. See Marilyn Richardson, *Maria W. Stewart*.

5. Holly, *Vindication*, 3.

6. See Pratt, *Imperial Eyes*. In their work, Peterson and Cheryl Fish have both stressed the multiple identities of mobility that inhere uneasily within Prince's autobiography: that of privileged tourist, disparaged second-class black traveler, missionary, and expatriate. See Fish, *Black and White Women's Travel Narratives*.

7. Lawrence, *Penelope Voyages*, 18. For discussions of women and the politics of travel writing, see Grewal, *Home*; Bohls, *Women Travel Writers*; Chaudhuri and Strobel, *Western Women*; Mills, *Discourses*.

8. Amy Kaplan, "Manifest Domesticity," 582. According to Kaplan, "understanding the imperial reach of domesticity and its relation to the foreign should help re-map the critical terrain upon which women's domestic fiction has been constructed" (600). Kaplan makes clear that she is referring to domesticity as constructed in white middle-class female culture.

9. Amy Kaplan, "Manifest Domesticity," 582.

10. Afro-Europe, of course, provides the perfect example of African diaspora subjects outside of slavery. See, for example, Campt, *Other Germans*; Jacqueline Brown, *Dropping Anchor*.

11. Stuart Hall, "Cultural Identity," 233.

12. Nancy Prince, *Black Woman's Odyssey*, 3. Unless otherwise indicated, all references to the 1853 *Narrative of the Life and Travels of Mrs. Nancy Prince* are to this edition and are cited parenthetically in the text.

13. For a study of early Native-Black relations, see Jack Forbes, *Africans*. For groundbreaking recent work on the same topic, see Miles, *Ties That Bind*; Miles, *House on Diamond Hill*.

14. For a discussion of the social conditions for Black migratory labor, see Nash, *Forging Freedom*, 3–49.

15. Blakely, *Russia*.

16. Porter, *Haunted Journeys*, 188, 196. See also Stowe, *Going Abroad*, 165.

17. Peterson, "Doers," 94.

18. Bolster, *Black Jacks*, 2.

19. Stowe, *Going Abroad*, 55–56.

20. Stowe, *Going Abroad*, 73.

21. For a different reading of maternity in Prince's narrative, see Fish, *Black and White Women's Travel Narratives*.

22. Buzard, "Continent," 32.

23. For example, while slavery did not become a consistent feature of Russian life and culture, Black servants were considered important "embellishments" for the aristocracy and royal families. In recognition of Blacks' peripheral status as exotic curiosities in Rus-

sia, Prince never describes herself as merging with the Russian community she inhabits, a community that in terms of religion, language, race, and culture she would have no doubt found alien. For a general account of the Black presence in Russia, see Blakely, *Russia*.

24. Buzard, *Beaten Track*, 81–82.

25. Hansen, "Boston Female Anti-Slavery Society." According to Hansen, the BFASS was a radical feminist organization of white and Black "elite" women reformers. The Black women of the BFASS—such as Susan Paul, the daughter of the Reverend Thomas Paul Sr.—may have "represented the upper echelons of Boston's black community," but they were certainly not as wealthy as the white female members of Boston's Brahmin class. In a Black Boston community composed of runaway slaves, domestic workers, and tradespeople, Prince undoubtedly achieved a particular kind of community leadership consistent with the transformative role she occupied in Russia, and the story of her routing of a slave catcher in Smith Court (which is mentioned nowhere in the text by Prince herself) would support this view. See also Horton and Horton, *Black Bostonians*, 65.

26. Frances Foster, *Written by Herself*, 85.

27. Andrews, *Sisters*, 9. For a discussion of Stewart, see Marilyn Richardson, *Maria W. Stewart*, 3–27; Romero, *Home Fronts*.

28. See Midgley, "Can Women Be Missionaries?"

29. See, for instance, Peterson, *"Doers,"* 97.

30. For an extremely useful reading of Jamaica as one of a number of failed "utopias" in *Life and Travels*, see Amber Foster, "Nancy Prince's Utopias."

31. Schor, *Henry Highland Garnet*, 21.

32. For a discussion of Garnet's time in Jamaica, see, for example, Schor, *Henry Highland Garnet*. For more about Ward, See Watson, *Caribbean Culture*, chap. 3; Kerr-Ritchie, "Samuel Ward." For more about Webb, See Gardner, "Gentleman."

33. Schor, *Henry Highland Garnet*, 22.

34. For information on the long history of Black Americans working in overseas missions, see Martin, "Spelman's Emma B. Delany"; Sylvia Jacobs, *Black Americans*; Sylvia Jacobs "Give a Thought to Africa"; Sylvia Jacobs, "African-American Women Missionaries"; Wills and Newman, *Black Apostles*. In 1824, Prince's minister, Thomas Paul Sr., served as a missionary to Haiti, and Henry Highland Garnet served as a missionary to Jamaica during the 1860s. See Paul, "Letter," 57–59; Schor, *Henry Highland Garnet*. For information on Ingraham, see Clifton Johnson, "American Missionary Association."

35. Beaver, *All Loves Excelling*, 67. See also Welter, "She Hath Done."

36. Clifton Johnson, "American Missionary Association," 61–62. See also DeBoer, *Be Jubilant My Feet*. The Oberlin Congregationalist missionaries found no relief until 1847, when their missions fell under the jurisdiction of the American Missionary Association. See the Jamaican Mission, microfilm reels 1–6, American Missionary Association Archives.

37. See Kenny, *Contentious Liberties*, 81–82.

38. See Amber Foster, "Nancy Prince's Utopias."

39. Mary Turner, *Slaves and Missionaries*; Curtin, *Two Jamaicas*, 37–38.

40. See "Quarterly Record of the Missions in Connection to the United Secession Church for January 1844," papers of the American Missionary Association, microfilm reel 1.

41. Nancy Prince, *West Indies*, 14–15.

42. As the few post-1840 documentary traces of Nancy Prince demonstrate, a return to a New England Black community automatically registers the old tensions. Indeed, in a letter appearing after her first return from Jamaica in the September 17, 1841, issue of William Lloyd Garrison's *Liberator*, Prince describes her maltreatment on board the steamboat *Massachusetts* traveling from New York to Providence not only by the ship's white captain but also by two Black female chambermaids. Furious over the whole event, but even more so because of her betrayal at the hands of Black women, Prince writes to "caution . . . colored people to beware of that boat," but also "to show the recreant conduct of the colored girls, who deserve exposure for pursuing such a course." In a letter appearing in the May 25, 1843, issue of the *National Anti-Slavery Standard*, Prince outlines to those who had contributed funds to the founding of the Jamaican orphanage how the whole venture in Jamaica had finally failed, leaving her in financial distress. Her description of the Black Jamaicans in this letter is curiously less ambiguous and ambivalent that would later be the case in *Life and Travels*. In the *National Anti-Slavery Standard* letter, Prince suggests that Jamaican ex-slaves "are not the idle people some represent them to be. Most of them have bought land, and built homes. They raise all kinds of vegetables, and many of them cultivate sugar cane and coffee for themselves. They have no need to let themselves on the plantations. They are extremely kind to each other, and have shown an excellent capacity to take care of themselves." While she was unwavering in her support for Black emancipation, in many respects Prince clearly revised this view in the autobiographical remembering of her last trip to Jamaica.

43. Peterson, "Doers," 97.

44. Gilroy, *Black Atlantic*, 37.

45. See Mavis Campbell, *Maroons*; Carey Robinson, *Fighting Maroons*.

46. Price, *Maroon Societies*, 22; Heuman,"*Killing Time*." Nevertheless, as historian Michael Mullin hastens to add, "a variety of types of sources support the recognition by contemporaries, officials, and ordinary people, that treaty provisions notwithstanding, Maroons were not reliable allies; that they were not the slaves' police; and most important, when the chips were down and war against the whites was raised, they were joined by significant numbers of plantation slaves." Mullin, *Africa in America*, 293.

47. Bethel, *Roots*, 105; Mavis Campbell, *Back to Africa*, xi–xii.

48. Amber Foster, "Nancy Prince's Utopias," 344.

3. THE REPATRIATION OF SAMUEL AJAYI CROWTHER

1. Although capture by the Royal Navy was the first step toward freedom, there was a dark side to the entire enterprise. As John McCoubrey reminds us, British Navy captains could receive their prize money only if slavers were captured in open sea, prompting some officers to chase their intended targets beyond the port before taking them into custody. However, according to McCoubrey, "when pursued, slavers often cast

their human cargo overboard to lighten their ships for greater speed." See McCoubrey, "Turner's Slave Ship," 325.

Additionally, Crowther notes in his slave narrative that when he and his fellow slaves were put under the care of CMS missionaries, many read the requirement that they leave the mission settlement in order to testify against the captain and crew of their slave ship as a secret plot to re-enslave them. According to Crowther, "as time passed away, and our consent could not be got, we were compelled to go [to the Court of Mixed Commission] by being whipped." See Schön and Crowther, *Journals*, 384. For comparison's to "liberated" slaves taken by US naval ships to Liberia, see Fett, "Middle Passages."

2. The rest of the plaque reads "Erected AC MDCCCXVIII by Lieut. Col. McCarthy, Gov."

3. Ryan, "'Very Extensive System.'"

4. On the resistance of free Black migrants to white control in the colony, see Pybus, "'Less Favorable Specimen.'"

5. Spitzer, *Lives*, 56.

6. Spitzer, *Lives*, 56.

7. On the labeling of ex-slaves in Sierra Leone, see Fyfe, *History*, 114–15. Kopytoff's *Preface* provides a complete history of the migration, but extensive discussions are also to be found in Fyfe, *History*; Ajayi, *Christian Missions*; Ayandele, *Missionary Impact*.

8. Though the term *Saro* quickly came into widespread use, reactions to the immigrants varied from place to place. According to Kopytoff, "Lagos itself was the port from which many of them had been shipped as slaves. Indigenous Lagosians were virtually unrepresented among the Sierra Leonians, and since the primary economic activity in the town was still the slave trade, the emigrants found hostility there." On the other hand, "they were well received in Abeokuta, the new Egba town which had drawn together refugees from the entire countryside." Kopytoff, *Preface*, 268; see also 86–87, 130.

9. Basch, Schiller, and Blanc, *Nations Unbound*, 269; Jacqueline Brown, "Black Liverpool," 292.

10. Stuart Hall, "Cultural Identity," 224.

11. On retentions and the "memory" of Africa in the New World, see, for example, Herskovits, *Myth of the Negro Past* ; Mintz and Price, *Birth*; Robert Thompson, *Flash of the Spirit*; Holloway, *Africanisms*; Gwendolyn Hall, *Africans*; Gomez, *Exchanging Our Country Marks*; Warner-Lewis, *Central Africa*. For important studies of the politics of transnationality and racial identity among peoples of African descent in the Americas, see Gilroy, *Black Atlantic*; Winston James, *Holding Aloft the Banner*; Laguerre, *Diasporic Citizenship*; Carr, *Black Nationalism*; Nuñes, *Cannibal Democracy*. For an earlier history of African diaspora studies as a field, see Shepperson, "African Diaspora"; Patterson and Kelley, "Unfinished Migrations"; Edwards, "Uses of *Diaspora*." For examples of scholarship that documents African, Caribbean, and African American alliances in the early moments of Pan-Africanism, see Lemelle and Kelley, *Imagining Home*; Von Eschen, *Race*; Edwards, *Practice*.

12. Piot, "Atlantic Aporias," 156, 159. See also, for example, Matory, "English Professors."

13. Roberts, "Construction," 182, 188; emphasis added. Alpers calls for a complete decentering of the Atlantic basin as the focus of diaspora studies, so that more scholarly attention might be given to slavery and Black dispersal from the east coast of Africa, throughout the Indian Ocean basin, and even as far as Iraq and India. See Alpers, "Defining the African Diaspora"; Alpers, "Recollecting Africa," 86, 84. See also Joseph Harris, "Expanding the Scope." More recently, from a literary point of view, Goyal sounds a similar call, not so much to expand the study of slavery beyond the Atlantic world but to acknowledge the multiple forms of migration that have made the African diaspora a global phenomenon, especially for twenty-first-century writers. See Goyal, "We Need New Diasporas"; Goyal, *Runaway Genres*.

For an excellent summary of the challenges posed by Africanists working on Black Atlantic cultures, see Mann, "Shifting Paradigms." In particular, Mann points out the goals of the diaspora from the Nigerian Hinterland Project, whose organizers maintain that "persons born in Africa carried with them into slavery not only their cultures but also their history, and that if we understand the experience of slaves and the histories of the societies from which they came, then we will be able to trace these influences into the diaspora." Mann, "Shifting Paradigms," 5. Thus, instead of focusing solely upon the cultural aftermath of the Middle Passage once slaves reached the Americas, many Africanists argue that the study of dispersal can really be achieved only by taking a closer look at Africa itself.

14. Piot, "Atlantic Aporias," 156.

15. See, for instance, Peters, "Exile"; Clifford, "Diasporas."

16. See Lorenzo Turner, "Some Contacts"; Lindsay, "'To Return to the Bosom'"; Law and Mann, "West Africa"; Matory, "English Professors"; Blyden, *West Indians*; Mann and Bay, *Rethinking the African Diaspora*.

17. There has been little discussion of this migration of nineteenth-century Jamaicans to Ghana. For some information, see Jon Miller, *Social Control*, 116, 121, 122–24.

18. See, for instance, Clegg, *Price*; Mitchell, *Righteous Propagation*, chap. 2. On the health impact of emigration to Liberia for US Blacks, see McDaniel, *Swing Low, Sweet Chariot*.

19. Peters, "Exile," 20. On the history and complex politics of early "return" movements from the Americas to Africa, see Staudenraus, *African Colonization Movement*; Stein, *World*; Thomas, *Rise to Be a People*; Sundiata, *Brothers*. Two illuminating discussions of Black heritage tours taken by affluent African Americans and Afro-Europeans who want to "return" to the scene of African slavery are Bruner, "Tourism," and Hartman, *Lose Your Mother*. On diasporic community building, gender, and Black nationalism, see Bair, "Pan-Africanism"; Dorsey, *Reforming Men*, chap. 5; Ula Taylor, *Veiled Garvey*; McPherson, "Colonial Matriarchs."

20. Gaines, "Black Americans' Racial Uplift Ideology"; Gaines, *Uplifting the Race*; Gaines, *American Africans*; Mitchell, *Righteous Propagation*; Commander, *Afro-Atlantic Flight*.

21. A number of historians and anthropologists have stressed that the nineteenth-century Brazilian repatriation had a transformative effect upon West African populations, especially in what is now Nigeria. See, for example, Matory, "English Professors"; Mann and Bay, *Rethinking the African Diaspora;* Law and Mann, "West Africa."

22. Piot, "Atlantic Aporias," 156.

23. A number of the rescued slaves were themselves Muslim. See Cole, "Liberated Slaves."

24. See Kopytoff, *Preface*; Lynn, "Technology." As both Kopytoff and Lynn argue, after the 1860s Saro merchants would face stiff competition from European commercial houses that felt the wealth of West Africa should be managed by whites.

25. Matory, "English Professors," 96–97, 85.

26. Mann, "Shifting Paradigms," 5.

27. See Karin Barber, "Introduction." For two scholars of postcolonial literature who have addressed West African colonial culture and writing of this period, see Gikandi, "Embarrassment"; Olakunle George, "'Native' Missionary." To properly describe a nineteenth-century literary history of the Saro, one would have to think of Sierra Leone as a whole, since even writing generated by those who did not "return" to the Niger Valley would fall under the category of a literature of repatriation. One might also include the prose of other diasporic Blacks in Sierra Leone, some of whom hailed from the West Indies, Canada, the United States, and Britain, and a few of whom joined the Saro migration, albeit for a variety of different reasons. Using this framework, one could (as David Northrup has argued) include the numerous oral slave narratives recorded as contextualizing material in missionary language studies, such as Koelle, *Polyglotta Africana*, and first-person slave narratives, such as Wright, "Life." For a biography based on "autobiographical conversion statements," see Samuel Johnson, *History*. On Koelle's text, see Northrup, *Africa's Discovery*, chap. 2.

28. For a reading that treats Samuel Ajayi Crowther's nineteenth-century mission writings as literature, see Olakunle George, "'Native' Missionary."

29. For more on Crowther and Wright, see Spitzer, *Lives*.

30. Sanneh, *Abolitionists*, 148. There is no truly comprehensive biography of Samuel Crowther. Students of mission and West African history have generally consulted Page, *Black Bishop*, which served as the official CMS biography. Crowther is also featured in the official CMS institutional history; see Stock, "History." A useful account of Crowther's career as a bishop can also be found in Yates, *Venn*. See also Ajayi, *Christian Mission*; Ajayi, *Patriot*.

31. See Fyfe, *Sierra Leone Inheritance*, 149.

32. An early and important articulation of these ideas in the European colonization of the Americas can be found in Kolodny, *Lay of the Land*. See also Pratt, *Imperial Eyes*; Stepan, *Picturing Tropical Nature*.

33. Cornwall and Lindisfarne, *Dislocating Masculinity*; Lindsay and Miescher, *Men and Masculinities*; Lindsay, *Working with Gender*; Miescher, *Making Men*.

34. See, for instance, Dixon-Fyle and Cole, *New Perspectives*; Cole, *Krio*.

35. Fyfe, *History*, 85.

36. On West Indian migration to Sierra Leone, see Blyden, *West Indians*.

37. Kopytoff, *Preface*, 86.

38. Kolapo, "CMS Missionaries," 89, 95.

39. Walls, "Africa," 160–64.

40. Yates, *Venn*, 147.

41. Peel does not indicate whether white missionaries used genres in the same way.

42. Peel, "For Who Hath Despised the Day," 591–92. See also Peel, "Problems and Opportunities."

43. Peel, "For Who Hath Despised," 587, 595. See also Comaroff and Comaroff, *Of Revelation*; Peel, *Religious Encounter*.

44. Irvine, "Genres," 81n57.

45. Johnston, *Missionary Writing*. 6–7.

46. "Meeting," *Church Missionary Gleaner*, 63–64.

47. My thanks to Jennifer Wenzel for pressing me to develop my reading along these lines.

48. Peel, "For Who Hath Despised the Day," 597.

49. Crowther, journal entry for August 21, in extracts for July 27 to Sept. 25, 1846, CA 2 M 1, Church Missionary Society Archive.

50. Vance, *Sinews*, 3, 7. For a discussion of gender and religious activism among British mission society members in the nineteenth century, see Thorne, *Congregational Missions*.

51. Given Judith Irvine's observation that the missionary journal was not the place for articulating strong emotions, it is notable as well that Crowther uses a narrative form devised for relating mission business to dramatize what must have been an incredibly personal experience. When the same incident is reported by Crowther's white colleague the Reverend Henry Townsend, the event is relegated to the level of a postscript. In his letter to Henry Venn, Townsend barely mentions Crowther but spends a great deal of time on Afala: "The mother was almost overcome with surprise and joy; and as soon as she could recollect herself she blessed the English repeatedly, in the name of God, and poured out her thanks to me and Mrs. Townsend as their representatives." For Townsend, the reunion demonstrates "how powerful a means is now put into [the Parent Committee's] hands for the spread of the gospel in this part, when they know how many a lone mother's heart is gladdened by the return of the lost ones." Using the same zealous but formulaic phrasing that characterizes Crowther's account, Townsend operates on a much more pragmatic level, driven by the need to convince the Parent Committee that the mission is heading for success. See Henry Townsend to Henry Venn, August 18, 1846, CA 3 M 1, Church Missionary Society Archive.

52. Crowther, journal entry for August 21, 1846, CA 2 M 1, Church Missionary Society Archive.

53. Crowther, journal entry for August 21, 1846, CA 2 M 1, Church Missionary Society Archive.

54. Yates, *Venn*, 146.

55. Jon Miller, *Social Control*, chap. 2; on the CMS in particular, see 42, 195n44.

56. According to Miller, the seminary students from Basel were even more extreme than the CMS in their desire to control both the actions and the minds of their missionaries.

57. Heanley, *Memoir*, 299.

58. See C. P. Williams, "'Not Quite Gentlemen'"; Jenkins, "Church Missionary Society"; Zemka, "Holy Books"; Johnston, *Missionary Writing*; Jon Miller, *Social Control*; Predelli and Miller, "Piety and Patriarchy," 37–38

59. As Predelli and Miller demonstrate in their essay "Piety and Patriarchy," marriage between whites and Blacks—whether Africans or Blacks who had emigrated from the Americas—was not unheard of. An early Basel-trained CMS missionary, the Reverend Gustavus Nylander, married an African American woman when he arrived in West Africa. One of his two mixed-race daughters married Frederick Schön, the Basel-trained missionary who accompanied Crowther on the 1841 expedition. Also, the CMS archive contains accounts of white male agents dismissed or disgraced because of sexual relations with African women.

60. Charles Haensel to CMS clerical secretary Edward Bickersteth, February 12, 1828, CA 10 108, Church Missionary Society Archive.

61. Homi Bhabha's formulation of colonial mimicry comes to mind, of course, where the native's seemingly obedient reproduction of the colonizer's ways and values provides a haunting dissonance. However, even as African CMS missionaries seemed to be a threat to their white colleagues, there would probably have been internal stresses among the former, as well, based on status. In his discussion of the liberated African turned Wesleyan minister the Reverend Joseph May, Leo Spitzer notes that after the death of his white missionary mentors in 1831, the young May approached Samuel Crowther, now a liberated African with some standing in his community, requesting to be part of the household as a servant and "ward." This was a common enough relationship in the colony, thought to encourage more extensive acculturation for the newcomers. However, according to Spitzer's biographical discussion of May, Crowther was "concerned with the advancement of his own career, [and] showed no interest in helping the young man." Accordingly, May "left Crowther's household and proceeded to Freetown on his own to seek work and establish new connections." It was in Freetown that May discovered the Methodists, to whom he later transferred his religious allegiances. See Spitzer, *Lives*, 61–64.

62. It was under Haensel that the young Samuel was first introduced to the politics of journal writing as a form of autobiography. As one of Haensel's pupils, he was required to write daily about his activities in boarding school, in the third person no less, while also referencing the minister as "master." (And as an analogue to the CMS Parent Committee's scrutiny of the missionary's journals, Haensel made it his business to inspect and then sign off on each of Crowther's entries.) All Crowther's literary juvenilia are housed in the Church Missionary Society Archive, but a sample of his childhood journals can be found in Fyfe, *Sierra Leone Inheritance*, 138–40.

63. Fabian, *Language*, 27. See also his later study, *Out of Our Minds*.

64. For a modern account of the expedition, see Temperley, *White Dreams*.

65. Schön and Crowther, *Journals*, 275. Subsequent references to the expedition journals are cited parenthetically in the text.

66. Indeed, since Landon died mysteriously—some felt that she had been murdered by the unloving Maclean, others that she had died by suicide to escape being trapped in Africa, still others that she may have been poisoned by Maclean's African lover—her demise glamorized her lately tarnished life and initiated a sustained surge of interest in her work. See Stephenson, *Letitia Landon*.

67. The official expedition account (Allen and Thomson, *Narrative of the Expedition*) also ponders the grave markers, though the focus is on Landon, the Victorian poet, not Quaque.

68. See Priestly, "Philip Quaque."

69. Crowther to secretaries, November 2, 1841, in Schön and Crowther, *Journals*, 350.

70. In their appended letters to the journals, both Crowther and Schön stress the importance of Christian missionaries learning the language. This was more easily said than done, since white missionaries were often drawn from the working and lower middle classes and lacked the necessary linguistic education. See Zemka, "Holy Books"; Moira Ferguson, "Hannah Kilham."

71. Birtwhistle, *Thomas Birch Freeman*.

72. For Jones's biography, see Hanciles, "Reverend Edward Jones."

73. See Northrup, "Becoming African."

4. MARTIN R. DELANY AND ROBERT CAMPBELL IN WEST AFRICA

1. Felix, "Slave Petition."

2. "Bestes, Peter."

3. Stiles and Hopkins, "To the Public."

4. For standard accounts of Cuffee's biography and the events leading up to his 1815 journey to Sierra Leone, see Sheldon Harris, "American's Impressions." Though the American Colonization Society is often cited as the main organization, several states including Virginia, Massachusetts, Maryland, and Pennsylvania set up their own local colonization societies. Classic studies of the ACS, Black repatriation activism, and the creation of Liberia include Staudenraus, *African Colonization Movement*; Floyd Miller, *Search*; Shick, *Behold the Promised Land*; Dorsey, *Reforming Men*; Clegg, *Price of Liberty*; Tyler-McGraw, *African Republic*.

5. See Staudenraus, *African Colonization Movement*.

6. See especially Fairhead et al., *African-American Exploration*.

7. In 1858, the ex-slave minister and abolitionist Henry Highland Garnet established another ACS in New York—the Black-led African Civilization Society—to offer what Ousmane K. Power-Greene has recently called "a broader race redemption mission" dedicated to Black American resettlement in the same territory. Garnet's organization envisioned educated Black settlers spread across Nigeria, fighting the slave trade by bringing the message of Christianity and civilization. To address the practical problem of replacing revenue earned by slaves with revenue earned by an alternate commodity, Garnet and like-minded Black abolitionists argued for the establishment of widespread cotton production in West Africa: as with many reformers in Britain and the United States, Garnet believed that such production among Africans currently reliant on the slave trade would foster legitimate trade with textile producers in Europe and the American North. Additionally, this shift from the African export of people to the African export of cotton might have the potential to render slavery in the American South obsolete. With these goals in mind, Garnet sought to ally his society with like-minded philanthropists, such as Britain's Sir Thomas Fowell Buxton, and even with the infamous American Colonization Society. Given the distaste of American abolitionists for the white ACS, this latter connection alone earned Garnet a number of critics, including Delany—which was ironic, since both men envisioned the same plan for a Nigerian settlement of Black Americans. See Power-Greene, *Against Wind and Tide*, 158.

8. Delany, *Official Report*, 39 (hereafter cited parenthetically in the text as OR).

9. See especially Blackett, "Martin R. Delany"; Blackett, *Beating against the Barriers*; Blackett, *Building an Antislavery Wall*.

10. See, for instance, the work of Blackett.

11. Pratt, *Imperial Eyes*; Craciun, "What Is an Explorer?"; Cavell, "Making Books."

12. Levine, *Martin Delany, Frederick Douglass*, 14.

13. See Pratt, *Imperial Eyes*.

14. Craciun, "What Is an Explorer?," 30.

15. See Driver, *Geography Militant*, 104–8. Reade's map proffered the continent's history through the archives of white male exploration narratives, the contribution of Samuel Ajayi Crowther to the 1841 Niger expedition notwithstanding.

16. Driver, *Geography Militant*, 104.

17. See Craciun, "What Is an Explorer?"

18. See Blackett, "Martin R. Delany."

19. Robert Campbell, *Pilgrimage*, 248–49 (hereafter cited parenthetically in the text as P). Clearly, neither Delany nor Campbell understood West African concepts of land tenure, where the individual's access to land was based on the size of their household. Additionally, the concept of selling or possessing land did not translate across the cultural divide. In the minds of West Africans, since land was not a portable commodity, it could not be owned.

20. [Knight], *New Republic*, 66–67.

21. Randall Miller, *"Dear Master,"* 75.

22. Working for the Maryland State Colonization Society in the capacity of governor of Maryland-in-Africa, the Jamaican John Brown Russwurm recognized that while both sides had been aggressive, the indigenous populations had legitimate complaints against the settlers. Unfortunately he had little success mediating between the two sides. He died in 1851. For a full discussion of Russwurm's efforts, see Winston James, *Struggles*.

23. Levine, *Martin R. Delany: A Documentary Reader*, 321.

24. Levine, *Martin R. Delany: A Documentary Reader*, 323-324.

25. Levine, *Martin R. Delany: A Documentary Reader*, 321, 323, 322.

26. Levine, *Martin R. Delany: A Documentary Reader*, 320. In *Black Empire*, Michelle Ann Stephens makes similar arguments about later figures such as Marcus Garvey, Claude McKay, and C. L. R. James.

27. For the story of Buxton, Ontario, see Hepburn, *Crossing the Border*.

28. Rusert, "Delany's Comet," 805. Also see Rusert, *Fugitive Science*.

29. See Marsters, introduction, 1–3, 16–17.

30. Kark, "Contribution." For a broader discussion of the same phenomenon, see Jones and Voigt, "'Just a First Sketchy Makeshift.'"

31. Cary, *Plea for Emigration*, ii.

32. Delany, introduction, 85–86.

33. David Anderson, "Dying of Nostalgia," 250.

34. Though spelled differently, the ship was of course named for the Mende. Cinque, the leader of the *Amistad* shipboard revolt, was reportedly Mende. For a detailed reading of the *Amistad* revolt, see Sale, *Slumbering Volcano*.

35. See Biobaku, "Madame Tinubu."

36. Campbell obviously visited Lagos before Britain claimed the city state as a crown colony in March of 1862.

37. See Blyden, *West Indians*.

38. Monk, *Dr. Livingstone's Cambridge Lectures*, 31.

39. Monk, *Dr. Livingstone's Cambridge Lectures*, 38–39.

40. African Civilization Society, *Constitution*, 8.

41. African Civilization Society, *Constitution*, 34.

42. Venn, "West Africa," 394.

43. Always looking for ways to scandalize Victorian sensibilities, Burton, among other things, created the infamous Cannibal Club in 1863, composed of England's elite white male professionals, writers, and politicians. Though members were sworn to secrecy about club proceedings, Burton was hardly upset about the circulating rumor that as president he began each meeting by parading about the room with a mace fashioned to represent "an African head gnawing on a thighbone." See Kennedy, *Highly Civilized Man*, 168.

44. Richard Burton, *Abeokuta*, 1:85, 79–80.

45. Richard Burton, *Abeokuta*, 1:97–98.

46. Richard Burton, *Abeokuta*, 1:ix.

47. Levine, *Martin R. Delany: A Documentary Reader*, 363.

48. Levine, *Martin R. Delany: A Documentary Reader*, 374.

49. Levine, *Martin R. Delany: A Documentary Reader*, 374.

50. Levine, *Martin R. Delany: A Documentary Reader*, 375.

51. Levine, *Martin R. Delany: A Documentary Reader*, 373.

52. Levine, *Martin R. Delany: A Documentary Reader*, 373.

53. Levine, *Martin R. Delany: A Documentary Reader*, 374.

54. Roy, "Oriental Exhibits," 197.

5. SARAH FORBES BONETTA AND TRAVEL AS SOCIAL CAPITAL

1. Karin Barber, "Introduction," 3.

2. Karin Barber, "Introduction," 8.

3. Karin Barber, "Introduction," 3.

4. See Myers, *At Her Majesty's Request*, a young adult biography of Bonetta that has done a great deal to enable her rediscovery.

5. Bonetta's marriage to Davies produced four children—Victoria, Alice, Arthur, and Stella—though Alice died before her second birthday. An obituary appeared in the Yoruba-language newspaper edited by Henry Townsend, *Iwe Irohin*, on November 3, 1866. The notice reads: "Died at Lagos, on 3rd October, 18[6]6 aged one year and seven months, Alice Adelaide Ester Henrietha, infant daughter of Mrs. & Mrs. JPL Davies. *Of such is the kingdom of Heaven.*" I am deeply grateful to Josiah Olubowale for finding the death notice and translating it into English for me.

6. Dandeson Coates to James Schön, December 3, 1840, CA 1 L 3, Church Missionary Society Archive.

7. Buxton, *African Slave Trade*, 376.

8. Henry Townsend to Henry Venn, February 28, 1860, CA 2 O 85, Church Missionary Society Archive.

9. For a detailed discussion of the nineteenth-century recruitment and training of Protestant missionaries, see Jon Miller, *Social Control*.

10. Julia Sass to Henry Venn, December 18, 1856, Sass to Venn, July 14, 1868, Sass to Venn, June 7, 1856, Sass to Venn, May 13, 1859, CA 1 M 15, Church Missionary Society Archive.

11. Julia Sass to Henry Venn, May 13, 1859, CA 1 M 15, Church Missionary Society Archive.

12. "Female Education in Lagos."

13. "Our Miniature Handel Festival"; emphasis added;

14. "Entertainment."

15. Frederick Forbes, *Dahomey*, 1:207.

16. Perhaps Forbes or the Reverend Owen Emeric Vidal, who baptized her at Badagry, came up with the idea of the biblical Sarah. As Abraham's wife, Sarah was the recipient of God's grace with the birth of Isaac. Additionally, in Hebrew, *Sarah* roughly translates as *princess* or *queen.*

17. Anim-Addo, "Queen Victoria's Black 'Daughter,'" 13.

18. See McCoubrey, "Turner's Slave Ship."

19. Elebute, *Life*, 238 n24.

20. Charles Beaumont Phipps to Henry Venn, January 25, 1851, PP Vic A38a, Royal Archives.

21. See, for example, the itemized list dated November 17, 1852, PP 2 1 3000, Royal Archives.

22. Henry Venn to Charles Beaumont Phipps, January 7, 1853, PP 2 1 3000, Royal Archives.

23. Henry Venn to Charles Beaumont Phipps, January 7, 1853, PP 2 1 3000, Royal Archives.

24. See Jon Miller, *Social Control*. Missionaries were in fact reprimanded for not being detailed enough in their reports. For examples of what happened when missionaries held back information or simply lied, see especially Zemka, "Holy Books."

25. Julia Sass to Henry Venn, June 7, 1852, CA 1 M 15, Church Missionary Society Archive, emphasis added.

26. Charles Beaumont Phipps to James Davies, July 10, 1862, Myers Collection.

27. This is the same James Frederick Schön who supervised the young Samuel Ajayi Crowther on the 1841 Niger Expedition (see chapter 3).

28. Sarah Bonetta to Catherine Schön, May 9, 1861, Myers Collection.

29. Sarah Bonetta to Catherine Schön, May 16, 1861, Myers Collection.

30. Mann, *Slavery*, 5; see also chapter 3 for its specific relevance to Lagos at the time Bonetta arrived in 1862. Additionally, see Lynn, *Commerce*.

31. *Anglo-African*, October 3, 1863.

32. Mann, *Marrying Well*, 58.

33. While this arrangement was standard, some elite women developed their own businesses or worked with their husbands to maintain and then expand their income, such

that they were able to control their own funds. See Chuku, "Petty Traders." Though the women profiled by Chuku were not from Lagos, they were Western-educated Christians presumably bound by the Victorian idea that men controlled money and commerce, while women stayed at home. However, they redefined their Christian womanhood to include commercial enterprises which they ran and controlled with or without their husbands.

34. Adolphus Mann to Henry Venn, September 6, 1865, CA 2 O 66, Church Missionary Society Archive.

35. Sarah Forbes Bonetta travel diary, July–September, 1867, Coker Papers, Nigerian National Archives (hereafter cited as SFB Diary); Myers, *At Her Majesty's Request*, 125–27.

36. For a useful discussion of the mundane in everyday diary entries, see Sinor, *Extraordinary Work*.

37. SFB Diary, July 23, 1867.

38. SFB Diary, July 24, 1867.

39. SFB Diary, July 31, 1867.

40. SFB Diary, August 7, 1867. Bonetta refers to the Schön residence variously as "Palm House" and "Palm Hall."

41. SFB Diary, August 13, 1867.

42. SFB Diary, August 14–15, 1867.

43. SFB Diary, August 19, 1867.

44. SFB Diary, September 3, 1867.

45. James Davies to Sarah Bonetta, November 28, 1875, Coker Papers.

46. Elebute, *Life*, 143–52.

47. Elebute, *Life*, 165–66.

48. James Davies to Sarah Bonetta, December 6, 1875, Coker Papers.

49. SFB Diary, September 4, 1867.

50. Myers, *At Her Majesty's Request*, 126–27.

51. J. A. Maser to Charles Foresythe, May 30, 1873, CA 2 O 11, Church Missionary Society Archive.

52. J. A. Maser to the CMS Lagos Finance Committee, October 29, 1873, CA 2 O 11, Church Missionary Society Archive.

53. Charles Foresythe to J. A. Maser, September 29, 1873, CA 2 O 11, Church Missionary Society Archive.

54. Sarah Bonetta to Edward Hutchinson, August 7, 1873, CA 2 M 7, Church Missionary Society Archive.

55. Sarah Bonetta to Henry Wright, August 14, 1873, CA 2 M 7, Church Missionary Society Archive.

56. Sarah Bonetta to Henry Wright, August 14, 1873, CA 2 M 7, Church Missionary Society Archive.

57. Edward Hutchinson to James Davies, October 3, 1873, CA 2 L 4, Church Missionary Society Archive. Regardless of Hutchinson's quasisupportive comments, as the 1870s progressed, CMS officials—beginning with Hutchinson and Wright—worked consistently to undermine African Christian authority throughout British West Africa, and by the end of the nineteenth century, white ministers held an almost complete monopoly over local native churches.

58. This is most likely the William Reid connected to the Palace Hotel later in the nineteenth century. If so, the Royal Edinburgh Hotel was the forerunner of the today's luxurious Reid's Palace Hotel in Funchal.

59. Myers, *At Her Majesty's Request*, 134-135.

60. Sarah Bonetta to James Davies, May 13, 1880, Coker Papers.

61. George Heyward to H. F. Ponsonby, August 31, 1880. PP Vic 1882 12279, Royal Archives.

62. Harriet Phipps to Henry Ponsonby, November 18, 1880, PP 3 7 3a, Royal Archives. The queen also covered the unpaid tuition for Bonetta's daughter Victoria and the bills for her remaining years of education, while also providing her with an allowance.

63. James Davies to Princess Beatrice, March 31, 1884, PP 3 32, Royal Archives.

64. "Memorandum: Mrs. Victoria Randle (nee Davies)," n.d., PP 3 7 47, Royal Archives.

65. Henry Johnson, "In Memoriam," September 19, 1880, PP Vic 1882/12279, Royal Archives.

CODA

1. For a detailed story of Campbell's life after he moved to Lagos, see Blackett, *Beating against the Barriers*.

2. Both in the past (Edward Alpers) and more recently (Yogita Goyal), scholars have consistently pushed for a revisioning of the African diaspora.

3. See Hatfield, "Olaudah Equiano."

4. See, for instance, Craciun, "What Is an Explorer?"

5. Lowe, *Intimacies*, 35.

6. See Totten, *African American Travel*, chap. 3.

7. The story of Henson, Peary, their Inuit wives, and their Inuit children and great-grandchildren has become legendary. See, for example, LeMoine, "Elatu's Funeral," 341; Evans, "Forgotten Indigenous Women."

8. Matthew Henson, *Negro Explorer*, 6–7.

9. Matthew Henson, *Negro Explorer*, 189–200.

10. Matthew Henson is hardly a household name, so attempts by teachers and scholars to bring even the most basic aspects of his story to light remain an ongoing project.

11. For the story of Henson's Inuit descendants, see "World Away"; Buchanan, "Eskimo Goes to Harvard."

12. See Rediker and Linebaugh, *Many-Headed Hydra*; Scott, *Common Wind*; Bolster, *Black Jacks*; Schoeppner, *Moral Contagion*.

13. Two exceptions—one could also call them starting places—include the work of Tiya Miles, as in the case of *Ties That Bind*, about Cherokee enslavement of Black Americans, and Toni Morrison's *Home*, which follows the journey of a Black veteran troubled by his participation in atrocities against civilians during the Korean War.

Bibliography

ARCHIVES AND MANUSCRIPT COLLECTIONS

American Missionary Association Archives, Amistad Research Center, Tulane University, New Orleans

Church Missionary Society Archives, the University of Birmingham, Birmingham, United Kingdom

Coker Papers Nigerian National Archives, Ibadan, Nigeria

Myers, Walter Dean, Collection (private), Jersey City, New Jersey

Royal Archives, Windsor, United Kingdom

OTHER SOURCES

African Civilization Society, *Constitution of the African Civilization Society*. New Haven, CT: Stafford, 1861.

Ajayi, J. F. Ade. *Christian Missions in Nigeria, 1841–1891: The Making of a New Élite*. London: Longmans, 1965.

Ajayi, J. F. Ade. *A Patriot to the Core: Bishop Ajayi Crowther*. Ibadan, Nigeria: Anglican Diocese of Ibadan, 1992.

Ajayi, J. F. Ade. "Samuel Ajayi Crowther of Oyo." In *Africa Remembered: Narratives by West Africans from the Era of the Slave Trade*, edited by Philip D. Curtin, 289–98. Madison: University of Wisconsin Press, 1965.

Alexander, Ziggi. "'Let It Lie upon the Table': The Status of Black Women." *Gender and History* 2, no. 1 (1990): 22–33.

Alexander, Ziggi, and Audrey Dewjee. Introduction to *Wonderful Adventures of Mrs. Seacole in Many Lands*, 9–45. Bristol, UK: Falling Wall Press, 1984.

Allen, William, and T. R. H. Thomson. *A Narrative of the Expedition Sent by Her Majesty's Government to the Niger River in 1841*. London: Bentley, 1848.

Alpers, Edward A. "Defining the African Diaspora." Paper presented at the Center for Comparative Social Analysis Workshop, October 25, 2001. https://www.ces.uc.pt/formacao/materiais_racismo_pos_racismo/alpers.pdf.

Alpers, Edward A. "Recollecting Africa: Diasporic Memory in the Indian Ocean." *African Studies Review* 43, no. 1 (2000): 83–99.

Anderson, Benjamin J. K. "Narrative of a Journey to Musardu, the Capital of the Western Mandingoes." 1870. In *African-American Exploration in West Africa: Four Nineteenth-Century Diaries*, edited by James Fairhead, Tim Geysbeek, Svend E. Holsoe, and Melissa Leach, 157–239. Bloomington: Indiana University Press, 2003.

Anderson, David. "Dying of Nostalgia: Homesickness in the Union Army during the Civil War." *Civil War History* 56, no. 3 (2010): 247–82.

Anderson, Gerald H., ed. *Biographical Dictionary of Christian Missions*. New York: Macmillan Reference, 1998.

Andrews, William. *Sisters of the Spirit: Three Black Women's Autobiographies of the Nineteenth Century*. Bloomington: Indiana University Press, 1986.

Anim-Addo, Joan. "Queen Victoria's Black 'Daughter.'" In *Black Victorians/Black Victoriana*, edited by Gretchen Holbrook Gerzina, 11–19. New Brunswick, NJ: Rutgers University Press, 2003.

Anionwu, Elizabeth N. *A Short History of Mary Seacole: A Resource for Nurses and Teachers*. London: Royal College of Nursing, 2005.

Aptheker, Herbert, ed. *A Documentary History of the Negro People in the United States*. New York: Citadel, 1952.

Arac, Jonathan, and Harriet Ritvo, eds. *Macropolitics of Nineteenth-Century Literature: Nationalism, Exoticism, Imperialism*. Philadelphia: University of Pennsylvania Press, 1991.

Ayandele, Emmanuel Ayankanmi. *The Missionary Impact on Modern Nigeria, 1842–1914: A Political and Social Analysis*. London: Longmans, 1966.

Baggett, Paul. "Caught between Homes: Mary Seacole and the Question of Cultural Identity." *MaComère: Journal of the Association of Caribbean Women Writers and Scholars* 3 (2000): 45–56.

Bair, Barbara. "Pan-Africanism as Process: Adelaide Casley Hayford, Garveyism, and the Cultural Roots of Nationalism." In *Imagining Home: Class, Culture and Nationalism in the African Diaspora*, edited by Sidney J. Lemelle and Robin D. G. Kelley, 121–44. London: Verso, 1994.

Baker, Houston A., Jr. "Figuration of a New American Literary History." In *Ideology and Classic American Literature*, edited by Sacvan Bercovitch and Myra Jehlen, 145–71. Cambridge: Cambridge University Press, 1986.

Bamfield, Veronica. *On the Strength: The Story of the British Army Wife*. London: C. Knight, 1974.

Baraw, Charles. "William Wells Brown, 'Three Years in Europe,' and Fugitive Tourism." *African American Review* 4, no. 2 (Fall 2011): 453–70.

Barber, Karin, ed. *Africa's Hidden Histories: Everyday Literacy and Making the Self*. Bloomington: Indiana University Press, 2006.

Barber, Karin. "Introduction: Hidden Innovators in Africa." In *Africa's Hidden Histories: Everyday Literacy and Making the Self*, edited by Karin Barber, 1–24. Bloomington: Indiana University Press, 2006.

Barber, Mary Ann Serret. *Oshielle; or, Village Life in the Yoruba Country*. London: Nisbet, 1857.

Barthelemy, Anthony G. Introduction to *Collected Black Women's Narratives*, xxix–xlviii. New York: Oxford University Press, 1990.

Basch, Linda, Nina Glick Schiller, and Cristina Szanton Blanc. *Nations Unbound: Transnational Projects, Postcolonial Predicaments and Deterritorialized Nation States*. New York: Routledge, 1994.

Bassett, Thomas J. "Cartography and Empire Building in Nineteenth-Century West Africa." *Geographical Review* 84, no. 3 (July 1994): 316–35.

BBC. *Black Nurses: The Women Who Saved the NHS*. BBC Four, November 24, 2016. https://www.bbc.co.uk/programmes/p04hjnd9/player.

BBC News. "Mary Seacole Statue Unveiled in London." June 30, 2016. https://www.bbc.com/news/uk-england-london-36663206.

Beaver, R. Pierce. *All Loves Excelling: American Protestant Women in World Mission*. Grand Rapids, MI: Eerdmans, 1968.

Beckles, Hilary McD. *Centering Woman: Gender Discourses in Caribbean Slave Societies*. Kingston, Jamaica: Randle, 1998.

Beckles, Hilary McD. "On the Backs of Blacks: The Barbados Free-Coloureds' Pursuit of Civil Rights and the 1816 Slave Rebellion." *Immigrants and Minorities* 3, no. 2 (1994): 167–88.

Beckles, Hilary McD., and Verene Shepherd, eds. *Caribbean Slave Society and Economy: A Student Reader*. Kingston, Jamaica: Randle, 1991.

Bell, Gertrude [Lowthian]. *Amurath to Amurath*. 1911. Cambridge: Cambridge University Press, 2014.

Bercovitch, Sacvan, and Myra Jehlen, eds. *Ideology and Classic American Literature*. Cambridge: Cambridge University Press, 1986.

Berlin, Ira. "From Creole to African: Atlantic Creoles and the Origins of African-American Society in Mainland North America." *William and Mary Quarterly* 53, no. 2 (April 1996): 251–88.

"Bestes, Peter and Other Slaves Petition for Freedom." April 20, 1773. In *A Documentary History of the Negro People in the United States*, vol. 1, *From the Colonial Times through the Civil War*, edited by Herbert Aptheker, 7–8. New York: Citadel, 1952.

Bethel, Elizabeth Rauh. *The Roots of African-American Identity: Memory and History in Free Antebellum Communities*. New York: St. Martin's, 1997.

Bhabha, Homi K. "Of Mimicry and Man: The Ambivalence of Colonial Discourse." In *The Location of Culture*, 85–92. London: Routledge, 1994.

Bickers, Robert A., and Rosemary Seton, eds. *Missionary Encounters: Sources and Issues*. Richmond, UK: Curzon, 1996.

Biobaku, S. O. "Madame Tinubu." In *Eminent Nigerians in the Nineteenth Century*, edited by K. O. Dike, 33–41. London: Oxford University Press, 1966.

Bird, Dúnlaith. *Travelling in Different Skins: Gender Identity in European Women's Oriental Travel Narratives*. Oxford: Oxford University Press, 2012.

Bird, Isabella L. *The Hawaiian Archipelago: Six Months among the Palms Groves, Coral Reefs, and Volcanos of the Sandwich Islands*. London: Murray, 1875.

Bird, Isabella L. *Unbeaten Tracks in Japan: An Account of Travels on Horseback in the Interior*. London: Murray, 1880.

Birtwhistle, Allan. *Thomas Birch Freeman: West African Pioneer.* London: Cargate, 1950.

Blackett, R. J. M. *Beating against the Barriers: Biographical Essays in Afro-American History.* Baton Rouge: Louisiana State University Press, 1986.

Blackett, R. J. M. *Building an Antislavery Wall: Black Americans in the Atlantic Abolitionist Movement, 1830–1860.* Baton Rouge: Louisiana State University Press, 1983.

Blackett, R. J. M. "Martin R. Delany and Robert Campbell: Black Americans in Search of an African Colony." *Journal of Negro History* 62, no. 1 (1977): 1–25.

Blackwood, Alicia. *A Narrative of Personal Experiences and Impressions during a Residence in the Bosphorus throughout the Crimean War.* London: Hatchard, 1881.

Blakely, Allison. *Russia and the Negro: Blacks in Russian History and Thought.* Washington, DC: Howard University Press, 1986.

Blunt, Alison. *Travel, Gender and Imperialism: Mary Kingsley and West Africa.* New York: Guilford, 1994.

Blyden, Nemata Amelia. *West Indians in West Africa, 1808–1880: The African Diaspora in Reverse.* Rochester, NY: University of Rochester Press, 2000.

Bohls, Elizabeth. *Slavery and the Politics of Place: Representing the Colonial Caribbean, 1770–1833.* Cambridge: Cambridge University Press, 2016.

Bohls, Elizabeth. *Women Travel Writers and the Language of Aesthetics, 1716–1819.* Cambridge: Cambridge University Press, 1995.

Bolster, W. Jeffrey. *Black Jacks: African American Seamen in the Age of Sail.* Cambridge, MA: Harvard University Press, 1998.

Booth, William. *In Darkest England, and The Way Out.* 1890. N.p.: Pantianos, 2018.

Bowen, T. J. *Central Africa: Adventures and Missionary Labors.* Charleston, SC: Southern Baptist Publication Society, 1857.

Brathwaite, Kamau. *The Development of Creole Society in Jamaica.* Oxford: Clarendon, 1972.

Brawley, Lisa C. "Frederick Douglass's *My Bondage and My Freedom* and the Fugitive Tourist Industry." *Novel* 30, no. 1 (Autumn 1996): 98–128.

Brawley, Lisa C. "Fugitive Nation: Slavery, Travel and Technologies of American Identity." PhD diss., University of Chicago, 1995.

Brown, Henry Box. *Narrative of the Life of Henry Box Brown, Written by Himself.* 1851. Edited by John Ernest. Chapel Hill: University of North Carolina Press, 2008.

Brown, Jacqueline Nassy. "Black Liverpool, Black America, and the Gendering of Diasporic Space." *Cultural Anthropology* 13, no. 3 (August 1998): 291–325.

Brown, Jacqueline Nassy. *Dropping Anchor, Settling Sail: Geographies of Race in Black Liverpool.* Princeton, NJ: Princeton University Press, 2005.

Bruner, Edward M. "Tourism in Ghana: The Representation of Slavery and the Return of the Black Diaspora." *American Anthropologist* 98, no. 2 (June 1996): 290–304.

Brusky, Sarah. "The Travels of William and Ellen Craft: Race and Travel Literature in the 19th Century." *Prospects* 25 (October 2000): 177–92.

Buchanan, Leo H. "An Eskimo Goes to Harvard." *Bay State Banner,* August 16, 2011. https://www.baystatebanner.com/2011/08/16/an-eskimo-goes-to-harvard/.

Burton, Antoinette. *At the Heart of Empire: Indians and the Colonial Encounter in Late-Victorian Britain.* Berkeley: University of California Press, 1998.

Burton, Richard Francis. *Abeokuta and the Camaroons Mountains: An Exploration.* 2 vols. 1863. Cambridge: Cambridge University Press, 2011.

Burton, Richard Francis. *Personal Narrative of a Pilgrimage to Al-Madinah and Meccah.* London: Longman, 1855–56.

Bush, Barbara. "White 'Ladies,' Coloured 'Favorites' and Black 'Wenches': Some Considerations of Sex, Race and Class Factors in Social Relations in White Creole Society in the British Caribbean." *Slavery and Abolition* 2, no. 3 (1981): 245–62.

Bushnell, David. *The Making of Modern Colombia: A Nation in Spite of Itself.* Berkeley: University of California Press, 1993.

Buxton, Thomas Fowell. *The African Slave Trade.* London: Murray, 1839.

Buzard, James. *The Beaten Track: European Tourism, Literature, and the Ways to "Culture," 1800–1918.* Oxford: Oxford University Press, 1993.

Buzard, James. "A Continent of Pictures: Reflections on the 'Europe' of Nineteenth-Century Tourists." *PMLA* 108, no. 1 (January 1993): 30–44.

Campbell, J. T. *Middle Passages: African American Journeys to Africa, 1787–2005.* New York: Penguin, 2006.

Campbell, Mavis C. *Back to Africa: George Ross and the Maroons: From Nova Scotia to Sierra Leone.* Trenton, NJ: Africa World, 1993.

Campbell, Mavis C. *The Maroons of Jamaica, 1655–1796: A History of Resistance, Collaboration, and Betrayal.* Granby, MA: Bergin and Garvey, 1988.

Campbell, Robert. *A Pilgrimage to My Motherland.* 1861. In *Search for a Place: Separatism and Africa, 1860,* by M. R. Delany and Robert Campbell, edited by Howard Bell, 149–250. Ann Arbor: University of Michigan Press, 1969.

Campt, Tina M. *Other Germans: Black Germans and the Politics of Race, Gender, and Memory in the Third Reich.* Ann Arbor: University of Michigan Press, 2005.

Candlin, Kit, and Cassandra Pybus. *Enterprising Women: Gender, Race, and Power in the Revolutionary Atlantic.* Athens: University of Georgia Press, 2015.

Caretta, Vincent. "Does Equiano Still Matter?" *Historically Speaking* 7, no. 3 (January–February 2006): 2–7.

Carlyle, Thomas. *Occasional Discourse on the Nigger Question.* London: Bosworth, 1853.

Carr, Robert. *Black Nationalism in the New World: Reading the African American and West Indian Experience.* Durham, NC: Duke University Press, 2002.

Cary, Mary Ann Shadd. *A Plea for Emigration; or, Notes of Canada West, in Its Moral, Social, and Political Aspect, with Suggestions Respecting Mexico, West Indies, and Vancouver's Island, for the Information of Colored Emigrants.* Edited by Phanuel Antwi. 1852. Calgary, AB: Broadview, 2016.

Cavell, Janice. "Making Books for Mr. Murray: The Case of William Edward Parry's Third Arctic Narrative." *The Library: Transactions of the Bibliographical Society* 14, no. 1 (2013): 45–49.

Chancy, Mariam J. A. "Subjectivity in Motion: Caribbean Women's Articulations of Being from Fanon/Capécia to *The Wonderful Adventures of Mrs. Seacole in Many Lands.*" *Hypatia* 30, no. 2 (2015): 434–49.

Chaney, Michael A. "Traveling Harlem's Europe: Vagabondage from Slave Narratives to Gwendolyn Bennett's 'Wedding Day' and Claude McKay's *Banjo*." *Journal of Narrative Theory* 32, no. 1 (Winter 2002): 52–76.

Chaudhuri, Nupur, and Margaret Strobel. *Western Women and Imperialism: Complicity and Resistance*. Bloomington: Indiana University Press, 1992.

Chuku, Gloria Ifeoma. "From Petty Traders to International Merchants: A Historic Account of Three Igbo Women in Trade and Commerce, 1886 to 1970." *African Economic History* 27 (1999): 1–22.

Clapperton, Hugh. *Journal of a Second Expedition into the Interior, from the Bight of Benin to Soccatoo*. London: Murray, 1829.

Clegg, Claude. *The Price of Liberty: African Americans and the Making of Liberia*. Chapel Hill: University of North Carolina Press, 2004.

Clifford, James. "Diasporas." In *Routes: Travel and Translation in the Late Twentieth Century*, 244–78. Cambridge, MA: Harvard University Press, 1997.

Clifford, James. "Traveling Cultures." In *Routes: Travel and Translation in the Late Twentieth Century*, 17–46. Cambridge, MA: Harvard University Press, 1997.

Cole, Gibril R. *The Krio of West Africa: Islam, Culture, Creolization, and Colonialism in the Nineteenth Century*. Athens: Ohio University Press, 2013.

Cole, Gibril R. "Liberated Slaves and Islam in Nineteenth-Century West Africa." In *The Yoruba Diaspora in the Atlantic World*, edited by Toyin Falola and Matt D. Childs, 383–403. Bloomington: Indiana University Press, 2004.

Comaroff, Jean, and John L. Comaroff. *Of Revelation and Revolution*. Vol. 1, *Christianity, Colonialism, and Consciousness in South Africa*. Chicago: University of Chicago Press, 1992.

Commander, Michelle D. *Afro-Atlantic Flight: Speculative Returns and the Black Fantastic*. Durham, NC: Duke University Press, 2017.

Conniff, Michael L. *Panama and the United States: The Forced Alliance*. Athens: University of Georgia Press, 2001.

Cooper, James Fenimore. *Notions of the Americans: Picked Up by a Travelling Bachelor*. Philadelphia: Carey, Lea and Carey, 1828.

Cornwall, Andrea, and Nancy Lindisfarne, eds. *Dislocating Masculinity: Comparative Ethnographies*. London: Routledge, 1994.

Cox, Edward L. *Free Coloreds in the Slave Societies of St. Kitts and Grenada, 1763–1833*. Knoxville: University of Tennessee Press, 1984.

Craciun, Adriana. "What Is an Explorer?" *Eighteenth-Century Studies* 45, no. 1 (2011): 29–51.

Craft, William, and Ellen Craft. *Running a Thousand Miles for Freedom; or, The Escape of William and Ellen Craft from Slavery*. 1860. Mineola, NY: Dover, 2014.

Crowther, Samuel Ajayi. *Journal of an Expedition up the Niger and Tshadda Rivers*. London: Church Missionary House, 1855.

Crowther, Samuel Ajayi. *Niger Mission: Bishop Crowther's Report of the Overland Journey from Lokoja to Bida, on the River Niger, and Thence to Lagos, on the Sea Coast*. London: Church Missionary House, 1872.

Curtin, Philip D., ed. *Africa Remembered: Narratives by West Africans from the Era of the Slave Trade*. Madison: University of Wisconsin Press, 1965.

Curtin, Philip D. *Two Jamaicas: The Role of Ideas in a Tropical Colony, 1830–1865*. Cambridge, MA: Harvard University Press, 1955.

Daley, Mercedes Chen. "The Watermelon Riot: Cultural Encounters in Panama City, April 15, 1856." *Hispanic American Historical Review* 70, no. 1 (February 1990): 85–108.

Damian, Jessica. "A Novel Speculation: Mary Seacole's Ambitious Adventures in the New Granada Gold Mining Company." *Journal of West Indian Literature* 16, no. 1 (November 2007): 15–36.

DeBoer, Clara Merritt. *Be Jubilant My Feet: African-Americans in the American Missionary Association, 1839–1861*. New York: Garland, 1994.

Delany, Martin R. *Blake: or, The Huts of America*. Edited by Jerome McGann. Cambridge, MA: Harvard University Press, 2017. Originally published in the *Anglo-African Magazine*, 1859–60; *Weekly Anglo-African*, 1861–62.

Delany, Martin R. Introduction to *Four Months in Liberia*, by William Nesbit. In *Liberian Dreams: Back-to-Africa Narratives from the 1850s*, edited by Wilson Jeremiah Moses, 81–86. University Park: Pennsylvania State University Press, 1998.

Delany, Martin R. *Official Report of the Niger Valley Exploring Party*. 1861. In *Search for a Place: Separatism and Africa, 1860*, by M. R. Delany and Robert Campbell, edited by Howard Bell, 23–148. Ann Arbor: University of Michigan Press, 1969.

Delany, Martin R., and Robert Campbell. *Search for a Place: Black Separatism and Africa, 1860*. Edited by Howard Bell. Ann Arbor: University of Michigan Press, 1969.

Denham, Dixon, Hugh Clapperton, and Walter Oudney. *Narrative of Travels and Discoveries in Northern and Central Africa in the Years 1822, 1823, and 1824*. London: Murray, 1826.

Dereli, Cynthia. "Gender Issues and the Crimean War: Creating Roles for Women?" In *Gender Roles and Sexuality in Victorian Literature*, edited by Christopher Parker, 57–83. Aldershot, UK: Scolar, 1995.

Dixon-Fyle, Mac, and Gibril Cole, eds. *New Perspectives on Sierra Leone Krio*. New York: Lang, 2006.

Dorsey, Bruce. *Reforming Men and Women: Gender in the Antebellum City*. Ithaca, NY: Cornell University Press, 2006.

Douglass, Frederick. *Narrative of the Life of Frederick Douglass, an American Slave. Written by Himself*. 1845. Edited by Houston A. Baker Jr. New York: Penguin, 1982.

Driver, Felix. *Geography Militant: Cultures of Exploration and Empire*. Oxford: Blackwell, 2001.

Eberhardt, Isabelle. *In the Shadow of Islam*. 1906. London: Owen, 2014.

Edmondson, Belinda. "'Most Intensely Jamaican': The Rise of Brown Identity in Jamaica." In *Victorian Jamaica*, edited by Tim Barringer and Wayne Modest, 553–76. Durham, NC: Duke University Press, 2018.

Edwards, Brent Hayes. *The Practice of Diaspora: Literature, Translation, and the Rise of Black Internationalism*. Cambridge, MA: Harvard University Press, 2003.

Edwards, Brent Hayes. "The Uses of *Diaspora*." *Social Text* 66, no. 1 (Spring 2001): 45–73.

Elebute, Adeyemo. *The Life of James Pinson Labulo Davies: A Colossus of Victorian Lagos.* Lagos, Nigeria: Kachifo, 2013.

"The Entertainment of the 1st Instant." *Lagos Observer*, September 14, 1882.

Equiano, Olaudah. *The Interesting Narrative and Other Writings.* Edited by Vincent Caretta. New York: Penguin, 2003.

Evans, Ian. "The Forgotten Indigenous Women of Robert Peary's Arctic Expeditions." *Arctic Deeply*, July 31, 2017. https://www.newsdeeply.com/arctic/community/2017/07/31/the-forgotten-indigenous-women-of-robert-pearys-arctic-expeditions.

Fabian, Johannes. *Language and Colonial Power: The Appropriation of Swahili in the Former Belgian Congo, 1880–1938.* Berkeley: University of California Press, 1991.

Fabian, Johannes. *Out of Our Minds: Reason and Madness in the Exploration of Central Africa.* Berkeley: University of California Press, 2000.

Fabian, Johannes. *Time and the Other: How Anthropology Makes Its Object.* New York: Columbia University Press, 1983.

Fairhead, James, Tim Geysbeek, Svend E. Holsoe, and Melissa Leach, eds. *African-American Exploration in West Africa: Four Nineteenth-Century Diaries.* Bloomington: Indiana University Press, 2003.

Falola, Toyin, and Matt D. Childs, eds. *The Yoruba Diaspora in the Atlantic World.* Bloomington: Indiana University Press, 2004.

Felix. "Slave Petition for Freedom, January 6, 1773." In *A Documentary History of the Negro People in the United States*, vol. 1, *From the Colonial Times through the Civil War*, edited by Herbert Aptheker, 6–7. New York: Citadel, 1952.

"Female Education in Lagos." *Eagle*, June 30, 1883.

Ferguson, Moira. "Hannah Kilham: Gender, the Gambia, and the Politics of Language." In *Romanticism, Race and Imperial Culture, 1780–1834*, edited by Sonia Hofkosh and Alan Richardson, 114–48. Bloomington: University of Indiana Press, 1996.

Ferguson, Moira, ed. *The Hart Sisters: Early African Caribbean Writers, Evangelicals, and Radicals.* Lincoln: University of Nebraska Press, 1993.

Ferguson, Roderick A. "The Lateral Moves of African American Studies in a Period of Migration." In *Strange Affinities: The Gender and Sexual Politics of Comparative Racialization*, edited by Grace Kyungwon Hong and Roderick A. Ferguson, 113–30. Durham, NC: Duke University Press, 2011.

Ferguson, Roderick A. *The Reorder of Things: The University and Its Pedagogy of Minority Difference.* Minneapolis: University of Minnesota Press, 2012.

Fernando, Sonali, dir. *Mary Seacole: The Real Angel of the Crimea.* October Films, Channel 4 Television Corporation, 2005. https://vimeo.com/60935252.

Fett, Sharla M. "Middle Passages and Forced Migrations: Liberated Africans in U.S. Ships and Camps." *Slavery and Abolition* 30, no. 1 (2010): 75–98.

Field, Emily Donaldson. "'Excepting Himself': Olaudah Equiano, Native Americans, and the Civilizing Mission." *MELUS* 34, no. 4 (December 2009): 15–38.

Fish, Cheryl J. *Black and White Women's Travel Narratives: Antebellum Explorations.* Gainesville: University Press of Florida, 2004.

Fluhr, Nicole M. "Loss Made Literal: Nineteenth-Century Maternal Figures." PhD diss., University of Michigan, 1999.

Fluhr, Nicole M. "'Their Calling Me "Mother" Was Not, I Think, Altogether Unmeaning': Mary Seacole's Maternal Personae." *Victorian Literature and Culture* 34 (2006): 95–113.

Forbes, Frederick E. *Dahomey and the Dahomans: Being the Journals of Two Missions to the King of Dahomey, and Residence at His Capital, in the Year 1849 and 1850.* 2 vols. London: Longman, Brown, Green and Longmans, 1851.

Forbes, Frederick E. *Six Months' Service in the African Blockade.* 1849. London: Dawsons, 1969.

Forbes, Jack D. *Africans and Native Americans: The Language of Race and the Evolution of Red-Black Peoples.* Urbana: University of Illinois Press, 1993.

Foster, Amber. "Nancy Prince's Utopias: Reimagining the African American Utopian Tradition." *Utopian Studies* 24, no. 2 (2013): 329–48.

Foster, Frances Smith. *Written by Herself: Literary Production of African American Women, 1746–1892.* Bloomington: Indiana University Press, 1993.

Franklin, John. *Narrative of a Journey to the Shores of the Polar Sea.* London: Murray, 1823.

Frazier, Ian. "Two Nurses." *New Yorker*, April 25, 2011. https://www.newyorker.com /magazine/2011/04/25/two-nurses.

Frederick, Rhonda. "Creole Performance in *Wonderful Adventures of Mrs. Seacole in Many Lands.*" In *Dialogues of Dispersal: Gender, Sexuality, and African Diaspora*, edited by Sandra Gunning, Tera W. Hunter, and Michele Mitchell, 91–110. London: Blackwell, 2004.

Freeman, Thomas Birch, and John Beecham. *Journal of Various Visits to the Kingdoms of Ashanti, Aku, and Dahomi, in Western Africa.* 1844. New York: Cambridge University Press, 2010.

Fuentes, Marisa J. *Dispossessed Lives: Enslaved Women, Violence, and the Archive.* Philadelphia: University of Pennsylvania Press, 2016.

Fyfe, Christopher. *A History of Sierra Leone.* New York: Oxford University Press, 1962.

Fyfe, Christopher. *Sierra Leone Inheritance.* New York: Oxford University Press, 1964.

Gaines, Kevin K. *American Africans in Ghana: Black Expatriates and the Civil Rights Era.* Chapel Hill: University of North Carolina Press, 2012.

Gaines, Kevin K. "Black Americans' Racial Uplift Ideology as 'Civilizing Mission': Pauline E. Hopkins on Race and Imperialism." In *Cultures of United States Imperialism*, edited by Amy Kaplan and Donald Pease, 433–55. Durham, NC: Duke University Press, 1993.

Gaines, Kevin K. *Uplifting the Race: Black Leadership, Politics, and Culture in the Twentieth Century.* Chapel Hill: University of North Carolina Press, 1996.

Gander, Kashmira. "Mary Seacole Statue: Why Nightingale Fans Are Angry the Crimean War Nurse Is Being Commemorated." *Independent*, June 24, 2016. https://www .independent.co.uk/arts-entertainment/florence-vs-mary-the-big-nurse-off-a7100676 .html.

Gardner, Eric. "A Gentleman of Superior Cultivation and Refinement: Recovering the Biography of Frank J. Webb." *African American Review* 50, no. 4 (Winter 2017): 1043–54.

George, Olakunle. "The 'Native' Missionary, the African Novel, and In-Between." *Novel* 36, no. 1 (2002): 5–25.

George, Rosemary Marangoly. *The Politics of Home: Postcolonial Relocation and Twentieth-Century Fiction*. Berkeley: University of California Press, 1999.

Gernsheim, Helmut, and Alison Gernsheim. *Roger Fenton: Photographer of the Crimean War: His Photographs and His Letters from the Crimea*. London: Secker and Warburg, 1954.

Gerzina, Gretchen Holbrook, ed. *Black Victorians/Black Victoriana*. New Brunswick, NJ: Rutgers University Press, 2003.

Gikandi, Simon. "The Embarrassment of Victorianism: Colonial Subjects and the Lure of Englishness." In *Victorian Afterlife: Postmodern Culture Rewrites the Nineteenth Century*, edited by John Kucich and Dianne F. Sadoff, 157–85. Minneapolis: University of Minnesota Press, 2000.

Gikandi, Simon. *Maps of Englishness: Writing Identity in the Culture of Colonialism*. New York: Columbia University Press, 1997.

Gilroy, Paul. *The Black Atlantic: Modernity and Double Consciousness*. Cambridge, MA: Harvard University Press, 1993.

Godfrey, Tom. "Jamaican 'Helped Make Canada's Health Care More Inclusive.'" *Share*, July 6, 2017, 7–8. https://www.sharenews.com/july-6-2017-vol-40-no-15/.

Gomez, Michael. *Exchanging Our Country Marks: The Transformation of African Identities in the Colonial and Antebellum South*. Chapel Hill: University of North Carolina Press, 1998.

Goodman, Temple. *The Fields of War: A Young Cavalryman's Crimea Campaign*. Edited by Philip Warner. London: Murray, 1977.

Gordon-Reed, Annette. *The Hemingses of Monticello: An American Family*. New York: Norton, 2008.

Goyal, Yogita. *Runaway Genres: The Global Afterlives of Slavery*. New York: New York University Press, 2019.

Goyal, Yogita. "We Need New Diasporas." *American Literary History* 29, no. 4 (Winter 2017): 640–63.

Grewal, Inderpal. *Home and Harem: Nation, Gender, Empire, and the Cultures of Travel*. Durham, NC: Duke University Press, 1996.

Griffin, Farah J., and Cheryl J. Fish, eds. *A Stranger in the Village: Two Centuries of African-American Travel Writing*. Boston: Beacon, 1998.

Gruesser, John Cullen. *The Empire Abroad and the Empire at Home: African American Literature and the Era of Overseas Expansion*. Athens: University of Georgia Press, 2012.

Gunning, Sandra, Tera W. Hunter, and Michele Mitchell, eds. *Dialogues of Dispersal: Gender, Sexuality, and African Diasporas*. London: Blackwell, 2004.

Hall, Catherine. *White, Male and Middle Class: Explorations in Feminism and History*. Cambridge: Polity, 1992.

Hall, Gwendolyn Midlo. *Africans in Colonial Louisiana: The Development of Afro-Creole Culture in the Eighteenth Century*. Baton Rouge: Louisiana State University Press, 1992.

Hall, Stuart. "Cultural Identity and Diaspora." In *Identity, Community, Culture, Difference*, edited by Jonathan Rutherford, 222–37. London: Lawrence and Wishart, 1990.

Hanciles, Jehu J. "The Reverend Edward Jones." In *Biographical Dictionary of Christian Missions*, edited by Gerald H. Anderson, 340. New York: Macmillan Reference, 1998.

Handler, Jerome S. "Joseph Rachell and Rachael Pringle-Polgreen: Petty Entrepreneurs." In *Struggle and Survival in Colonial America*, edited by D. G. Sweet and Gary B. Nash, 376–92. Berkeley: University of California Press, 1981.

Hansen, Debra Gold. "The Boston Female Anti-Slavery Society and the Limits of Gender Politics." In *The Abolitionist Sisterhood: Women's Political Culture in Antebellum America*, edited by Jean Fagan Yellin and John C. Van Horne, 45–65. Ithaca, NY: Cornell University Press, 1994.

Harris, Joseph E. "Expanding the Scope of African Diaspora Studies: The Middle East and India, a Research Agenda." *Radical History Review* 87 (October 2003): 157–68.

Harris, Sheldon H. "An American's Impressions of Sierra Leone, 1811." *Journal of Negro History* 47, no. 1 (January 1962): 35–41.

Hartman, Saidiya. *Lose Your Mother: A Journey Along the Atlantic Slave Route.* New York: Farrar, Straus and Giroux, 2007.

Hatfield, Philip. "Olaudah Equiano and the Draw of the Arctic." *American Collections* (blog of the British Library). October 9, 2014. https://blogs.bl.uk/americas/2014/10/olaudah-equiano-and-the-draw-of-the-arctic.html.

Hawthorne, Evelyn. "Self-Writing, Literary Traditions, and Post-Emancipation Identity: The Case of Mary Seacole." *Biography* 23, no. 2 (Spring 2000): 309–31.

Heanley, R. M. *A Memoir of Edward Steere, DD, LLD, Third Missionary Bishop in Central Africa.* London: George Bell and Sons, 1888.

Henson, Josiah. *The Life of Josiah Henson, Formerly a Slave, Now an Inhabitant of Canada, as Narrated by Himself.* Boston: Phelps, 1849.

Henson, Matthew. *A Negro Explorer at the North Pole.* New York: Stokes, 1912.

Hepburn, Sharon A. Roger. *Crossing the Border: A Free Black Community in Canada.* Urbana: University of Illinois Press, 2007.

Herskovits, Melville J. *The Myth of the Negro Past.* 1941. Boston: Beacon, 1958.

Heuman, Gad J. *Between Black and White: Race, Politics, and the Free Coloreds in Jamaica, 1792–1865.* Westport, CT: Greenwood, 1981.

Heuman, Gad J. *"The Killing Time": The Morant Bay Rebellion in Jamaica.* Knoxville: University of Tennessee Press, 1994.

Hinds, Elizabeth Jane Wall. "The Spirit of Trade: Olaudah Equiano's Conversion, Legalism, and the Merchant's Life." *African American Review* 32, no. 4 (Winter 1998): 635–47.

Hodge, Edward Cooper. *"Little Hodge" Being Extracts from the Diaries and Letters of Colonel Edward Cooper Hodge, Written during the Crimean War, 1854–1856.* Edited by the Marquess of Anglesey. London: Cooper, 1971.

Hofkosh, Sonia, and Alan Richardson, eds. *Romanticism, Race and Imperial Culture, 1780–1834.* Bloomington: University of Indiana Press, 1996.

Holloway, Joseph E., ed. *Africanisms in American Culture.* Bloomington: Indiana University Press, 1991.

Holly, James Theodore. *A Vindication of the Capacity of the Negro Race for Self-Government, and Civilized Progress, As Demonstrated by Historical Events of the Haytian Revolution; and the Subsequent Acts of That People since Their National Independence.* New Haven, CT: Stanley, 1857.

Hong, Grace Kyungwon, and Roderick A. Ferguson, eds. *Strange Affinities: The Gender and Sexual Politics of Comparative Racialization.* Durham, NC: Duke University Press, 2011.

Horton, James Oliver. *Free People of Color: Inside the African American Community.* Washington, DC: Smithsonian Institution Press, 1993.

Horton, James Oliver, and Lois E. Horton. *Black Bostonians: Family Life and Community Struggle in the Antebellum North.* New York: Holmes and Meier, 1979.

Irvine, Judith T. "Genres of Conquest: From Literature to Science in Colonial African Linguistics." In *Verbal Arts across Cultures: The Aesthetics and Proto-Aesthetics of Communication,* edited by Hubert Knoblauch and Helga Kotthoff, 63–90. Tübingen, Germany: Narr, 2001.

Jacobs, Harriet. *Incidents in the Life of a Slave Girl, Written by Herself.* Edited by Jean Fagan Yellin. 1861. Cambridge, MA: Harvard University Press, 1998.

Jacobs, Sylvia M. "African-American Women Missionaries and European Imperialism in Southern Africa, 1880–1920." *Women's Studies International Forum* 13, no. 4 (1990): 381–94.

Jacobs, Sylvia M., ed. *Black Americans and the Missionary Movement in Africa.* Westport, CT: Greenwood, 1982.

Jacobs, Sylvia M. "Give a Thought to Africa: Black Women Missionaries in Southern Africa." In *Western Women and Imperialism,* edited by Nupur Chaudhuri and Margaret Strobel, 207–28. Bloomington: Indiana University Press, 1992.

Jamaica Information Service. "Mary Seacole: Caring for the Wounded." February 14, 2017. https://jis.gov.jm/information/get-the-facts/marcy-seacole-caring-wounded/.

James, Winston. *Holding Aloft the Banner of Ethiopia: Caribbean Radicalism in Early Twentieth-Century America.* London: Verso, 1998.

James, Winston. *The Struggles of John Brown Russwurm: The Life and Writings of a Pan-Africanist Pioneer, 1799–1851.* New York: New York University Press, 2010.

Jenkins, Paul. "The Church Missionary Society and the Basel Mission: An Early Experiment in Inter-European Cooperation." In *The Church Missionary Society and World Christianity, 1799–1999,* edited by Kevin Ward and Brian Stanley, 43–65. Grand Rapids, MI: Eerdmans, 2000.

Johnson, Clifton Herman. "The American Missionary Association, 1846–1861: A Study of Christian Abolitionism." PhD diss., University of North Carolina, Chapel Hill, 1959.

Johnson, Samuel. *A Journey to the Western Islands of Scotland.* London: Strahan and Cadell, 1775.

Johnson, Samuel. *The History of the Yorubas.* Edited by Obadiah Johnson. 1921. Cambridge: Cambridge University Press, 2010.

Johnston, Anna. *Missionary Writing and Empire, 1800–1860.* New York: Cambridge University Press, 2003.

Jones, Adam, and Isabel Voigt. "'Just a First Sketchy Makeshift': German Travellers and Their Cartographic Encounters in Africa, 1850–1914." *History of Africa* 39 (2012): 9–39.

Josephs, Aleric. "Mary Seacole: Jamaican Nurse and 'Doctress' 1805/10–1881." *Jamaican Historical Review* 17 (1991): 48–65.

Judd, Catherine. *Bedside Seductions: Nursing and the Victorian Imagination, 1830–1880.* Basingstoke, UK: Macmillan, 1998.

Kaplan, Amy. "Manifest Domesticity." *American Literature* 70, no. 3 (September 1998): 581–606.

Kaplan, Amy, and Donald Pease, eds. *Cultures of United States Imperialism.* Durham, NC: Duke University Press, 1994.

Kaplan, Caren. *Questions of Travel: Post-Modern Discourses of Displacement.* Durham, NC: Duke University Press, 1996.

Kark, Ruth. "The Contribution of Nineteenth-Century Protestant Missionary Societies to Historical Cartography." *Imago Mundi* 45, no. 1 (January 1993): 112–19.

Kelleter, Frank. "Ethnic Self-Dramatization and Technologies of Travel in *The Interesting Narrative of Olaudah Equiano or Gustavus Vassa, the African, Written by Himself* (1789)." *Early American Literature* 39, no. 1 (2004): 67–84.

Kelley, Joyce. "Increasingly 'Imaginative Geographies': Excursions in Otherness, Fantasy, and Modernism in Early Twentieth-Century Women's Travel Writing." *Journal of Narrative Theory* 35, no. 3 (2005): 357–73.

Kennedy, Dane. *The Highly Civilized Man: Richard Burton and the Victorian Mind.* Cambridge, MA: Harvard University Press, 2007.

Kenny, Gale L. *Contentious Liberties: American Abolitionists and Post-Emancipation Jamaica, 1834–1866.* Athens: University of Georgia Press, 2011.

Kerr, Paulette A. "Victims or Strategists? Female Lodging-House Keepers in Jamaica." In *Engendering History: Caribbean Women in Historical Perspective,* edited by Verene Shepherd, Bridget Brereton, and Barbara Bailey, 197–212. New York: St. Martin's, 1995.

Kerr-Ritchie, Jeffery. "Samuel Ward and the Making of an Imperial Subject." *Slavery and Abolition* 33, no. 2 (June 2012): 205–19.

Kingsley, Mary H. *Travels in West Africa: Congo Français, Corisco and Cameroons.* London: Macmillan, 1897.

[Knight, Helen Cross]. *The New Republic.* Boston: Massachusetts Sabbath School Society, 1851.

Knoblauch, Hubert, and Helga Kotthoff, eds. *Verbal Arts across Cultures: The Aesthetics and Proto-Aesthetics of Communication.* Tübingen, Germany: Narr, 2001.

Koelle, Sigismund. *Polyglotta Africana: A Comparative Vocabulary.* London: Church Missionary House, 1854.

Kolapo, Femi J. "CMS Missionaries of African Origin and Extra-Religious Encounters at the Niger-Benue Confluence, 1858–1880." *African Studies Review* 43, no. 2 (September 2000): 87–115.

Kolodny, Annette. *The Lay of the Land: Metaphor as Experience and History in American Life and Letters.* Chapel Hill: University of North Carolina Press, 1984.

Kopytoff, Jean Herskovitz. *A Preface to Modern Nigeria: The "Sierra Leonians" in Yoruba, 1830–1890.* Madison: University of Wisconsin Press, 1965.

Laguerre, Michel S. *Diasporic Citizenship: Haitian Americans in Transnational America.* London: Palgrave Macmillan, 1998.

Lalumia, Matthew. "Realism and Anti-Aristocratic Sentiment in Victorian Depictions of the Crimean War." *Victorian Studies* 21, no. 1 (1981): 25–51.

Law, Robin, and Kristin Mann. "West Africa in the Atlantic Community: The Case of the Slave Coast." *William and Mary Quarterly* 56, no. 2 (April 1999): 307–34.

Lawrence, Karen R. *Penelope Voyages: Women and Travel in the British Literary Tradition.* Ithaca, NY: Cornell University Press, 1994.

Lee, Jarena. *The Life and Religious Experience of Jarena Lee, a Colored Lady: Giving an Account of the Call to Preach the Gospel.* 1839. In *Sisters of the Spirit: Three Black Women's Autobiographies of the Nineteenth Century*, edited by William L. Andrews, 25–48. Bloomington: Indiana University Press, 1986.

Lemelle, Sidney J., and Robin D. G. Kelley, eds. *Imagining Home: Class, Culture and Nationalism in the African Diaspora.* London: Verso, 1994.

LeMoine, Genevieve. "Elatu's Funeral: A Glimpse at Inughuit-American Relations on Robert E. Peary's 1898–1902 Expedition." *Arctic* 67, no. 3 (September 2014): 340–46:

Levine, Robert S. *Martin Delany, Frederick Douglass, and the Politics of Representative Identity.* Chapel Hill: University of North Carolina Press, 1997.

Levine, Robert S., ed. *Martin R. Delany: A Documentary Reader.* Chapel Hill: University of North Carolina Press, 2003.

Lindsay, Lisa A. "'To Return to the Bosom of their Fatherland': Brazilian Immigrants in Nineteenth-Century Lagos." *Slavery and Abolition* 15, no. 1 (1994): 22–50.

Lindsay, Lisa A. *Working with Gender: Wage Labor and Social Change in Southwestern Nigeria.* London: Heinemann, 2003.

Lindsay, Lisa A., and Stephan Miescher, eds. *Men and Masculinities in Modern Africa.* London: Heinemann, 2003.

Livingstone, David. *Missionary Travels and Researches in South Africa.* London: Murray, 1857.

Loth, Laura. "Writing and Traveling in Colonial Algeria after Isabelle Eberhardt: Henrietta Celarié's French (Cross) Dressing." *Tulsa Studies in Women's Literature* 36, no. 1 (Spring 2017): 75–98.

Lovejoy, Paul E. "Construction of Identity: Olaudah Equiano or Gustavus Vassa?" *Historically Speaking* 7, no. 3 (2006): 8–9.

Lowe, Lisa. *The Intimacies of Four Continents.* Durham, NC: Duke University Press, 2015.

Lucasi, Stephen. "William Wells Brown's *Narrative* and Telling Subjectivity." *African American Review* 41, no. 3 (Fall 2007): 405–25.

Lynn, Martin. *Commerce and Economic Change in West Africa: The Palm Oil Trade in the Nineteenth Century.* Cambridge: Cambridge University Press, 1997.

Lynn, Martin. "Technology, Trade, and 'A Race of Native Capitalists': The Krio Diaspora in West Africa and the Steamship, 1852–95." *Journal of African History* 33 (1992): 421–40.

Mann, Kristin. *Marrying Well: Marriage, Status and Social Change among the Educated Elite in Colonial Lagos.* Cambridge: Cambridge University Press, 1985.

Mann, Kristin. "Shifting Paradigms in the Study of the African Diaspora and of Atlantic History and Culture." *Slavery and Abolition* 22, no. 1 (2001): 3–21.

Mann, Kristin. *Slavery and the Birth of an African City: Lagos, 1760–1900.* Bloomington: Indiana University Press, 2010.

Mann, Kristin, and Mia G. Bay, eds. *Rethinking the African Diaspora: The Making of a Black Atlantic World in the Bight of Benin and Brazil.* New York: Routledge, 2001.

Marsters, Kate Ferguson. Introduction to *Travels in the Interior District of Africa,* by Mungo Park, 1–28. Durham, NC: Duke University Press, 2000.

Martin, Sandy D. "Spelman's Emma B. Delany and the African Mission." In *This Far by Faith: Readings in African-American Women's Religious Biography,* edited by Judith Weisenfeld and Richard Newman, 220–39. New York: Routledge, 1995.

Matory, J. Lorand. "The English Professors of Brazil: On the Diasporic Roots of the Yoruba Nation." *Comparative Studies in Society and History* 41, no. 1 (January 1999): 72–103.

McCoubrey, John. "Turner's Slave Ship: Abolition, Ruskin, and Reception," *Word and Image* 14, no. 4 (1998): 319–353.

McDaniel, Antonio. *Swing Low, Sweet Chariot: The Mortality Cost of Colonizing Liberia in the Nineteenth Century.* Chicago: University of Chicago Press, 1994.

McDonald, Lynn. "Lessons in Lies: How the BBC, School Text Books and Even Exam Boards Have Twisted History to Smear Florence Nightingale and Make a Saint of This Woman." *Daily Mail,* July 31, 2014. http://www.dailymail.co.uk/femail/article -2712683/Mary-Seacole-saint-Florence-Nightingake-smeared-twisting-history.html.

McKenna, Bernard. "'Fancies of Exclusive Possession': Validation and Disassociation in Mary Seacole's England and Caribbean." *Philological Quarterly* 76, no. 2 (Spring 1997): 219–39.

McPherson, Anne. "Colonial Matriarchs: Garveyism, Maternalism, and Belize's Black Cross Nurses, 1920–1952." *Gender and History* 15, no. 3 (2004): 507–27.

"Meeting of the Friends of African Civilization." In *Constitution of the African Civilization Society,* edited by Joseph P. Thompson, 9–39. New Haven, CT: Stafford, 1861.

"Meeting of the Rev. Samuel Crowther with His Mother." *Church Missionary Gleaner* 8 (1847): 63–65.

Midgley, Claire. "Can Women Be Missionaries? Envisioning Female Agency in the Early Nineteenth-Century British Empire." *Journal of British Studies* 45, no. 2 (April 2006): 335–58.

Miescher, Stephan F. *Making Men in Ghana.* Bloomington: Indiana University Press, 2005.

Miles, Tiya. *The House on Diamond Hill: A Cherokee Plantation Story.* Chapel Hill: University of North Carolina Press, 2010.

Miles, Tiya. *Ties That Bind: The Story of an Afro-Cherokee Family in Slavery and in Freedom.* Berkeley: University of California Press, 2006.

Miller, Floyd J. *The Search for a Black Nationality: Black Emigration and Colonization, 1787–1863.* Urbana: University of Illinois Press, 1975.

Miller, Jon. *The Social Control of Religious Zeal: A Study of Organizational Contradictions.* New Brunswick, NJ: Rutgers University Press, 1994.

Miller, Randall M. *"Dear Master": Letters of a Slave Family.* Athens: University of Georgia Press, 2006.

Mills, Sara. *Discourses of Difference: An Analysis of Women's Travel Writing and Colonialism.* London: Routledge, 1991.

Mintz, Sydney W., and Richard Price. *The Birth of African-American Culture: An Anthropological Perspective*. Boston: Beacon, 1992.

Mitchell, Michele. *Righteous Propagation: African American and the Politics of Racial Destiny after Reconstruction*. Chapel Hill: University of North Carolina Press, 2004.

Monk, William, ed. *Dr. Livingstone's Cambridge Lectures, Together with a Prefatory Letter by the Reverend Professor Sedgwick*. Cambridge: Deighton and Bell, 1858.

Montagu, Mary Wortley. *The Turkish Embassy Letters*. Introduction by Anita Desai. London: Virago, 1993.

Morrison, Toni. *Home*. New York: Vintage, 2013.

Moses, Wilson Jeremiah. *The Golden Age of Black Nationalism, 1850–1925*. New York: Oxford University Press, 1978.

Moses, Wilson Jeremiah, ed. *Liberian Dreams: Back-to-Africa Narratives from the 1850s*. University Park: Pennsylvania State University Press, 1998.

Mullin, Michael. *Africa in America: Slave Acculturation and Resistance in the American South and the British Caribbean 1736–1831*. Urbana: University of Illinois Press, 1995.

Murphy, Geraldine. "Olaudah Equiano, Accidental Tourist." *Eighteenth-Century Studies* 27, no. 4 (Summer 1994): 551–68.

Myers, Walter Dean. *At Her Majesty's Request: An African Princess in Victorian England*. New York: Scholastic, 1999.

Nash, Gary B. *Forging Freedom: The Formation of Philadelphia's Black Community, 1720–1840*. Cambridge, MA: Harvard University Press, 1988.

Nesbit, William. "Four Months in Liberia: Or African Colonization Exposed." 1851. In *Liberian Dreams: Back-to-Africa Narratives from the 1850s*, edited by Wilson Jeremiah Moses, 79–125. University Park: Pennsylvania State University Press, 1998.

Newton, Velma. *The Silver Men: West Indian Labour Migration to Panama, 1850–1914*. Kingston, Jamaica: University of the West Indies Press, 1997.

Northrup, David. *Africa's Discovery of Europe: 1450–1859*. New York: Oxford University Press, 2002.

Northrup, David. "Becoming African: Identity Formation among Liberated Slaves in Nineteenth-Century Sierra Leone." *Slavery and Abolition* 27 (2006): 1–21.

Nuñes, Zita. *Cannibal Democracy: Race and Representation in the Literature of the Americas*. Minneapolis: University of Minnesota Press, 2008.

Olmsted, Frederick Law. *The Cotton Kingdom: A Traveller's Observations on Cotton and Slavery in the American Slave States*. New York: Mason Brothers, 1861.

"Our Miniature Handel Festival." *Lagos Observer*, November 9, 1883.

"Our Very Own Vivandière." *Punch*, May 30, 1857.

Page, Jesse. *The Black Bishop: Samuel Ajayi Crowther*. London: Hodder and Stoughton, 1908.

Paquet, Sandra Pouchet. "The Enigma of Arrival: *The Wonderful Adventures of Mrs. Seacole in Many Lands*." *African American Review* 26, no. 4 (1992): 651–63.

Paravisini-Gebert, Lizabeth. "Mrs. Seacole's *Wonderful Adventures in Many Lands* and the Consciousness of Transit." In *Black Victorians/Black Victoriana*, edited by Gretchen Holbrook Gerzina, 71–87. New Brunswick, NJ: Rutgers University Press, 2003.

Park, Mungo. *Travels in the Interior Districts of Africa*. 1799. Edited by Kate Ferguson Marsters. Durham, NC: Duke University Press, 2000.

Patterson, Tiffany, and Robin D. G. Kelley. "Unfinished Migrations: Reflections on the African Diaspora and the Making of the Modern World." *African Studies Review* 43, no. 1 (April 2000): 11–45.

Paul, Thomas, Sr. "Letter to the Editor." 1824. In *A Stranger in the Village: Two Centuries of African-American Travel Writing*, edited by Farah J. Griffin and Cheryl J. Fish, 57–59. Boston: Beacon, 1998.

Peel, J. D. Y. "For Who Hath Despised the Day of Small Things: Missionary Narratives and Historical Anthropology." *Comparative Studies in Society and History* 37, no. 3 (July 1995): 581–607.

Peel, J. D. Y. "Problems and Opportunities in an Anthropologist's Use of a Missionary Archives." In *Missionary Encounters: Sources and Issues*, edited by Robert A. Bickers and Rosemary Seton, 70–94. Richmond, UK: Curzon, 1996.

Peel, J. D. Y. *Religious Encounter and the Making of the Yoruba*. Bloomington: Indiana University Press, 2003.

Peters, John Durham. "Exile, Nomadism, and Diaspora: The Stakes of Mobility in the Western Canon." In *Home, Exile, Homeland: Film, Media, and the Politics of Place*, edited by Hamid Naficy, 17–44. New York: Routledge, 1999.

Peterson, Carla L. *"Doers of the Word": African American Women Speakers and Writers in the North (1830–1880)*. New York: Oxford University Press, 1995.

Piot, Charles. "Atlantic Aporias: Africa and Gilroy's Black Atlantic." *South Atlantic Quarterly* 100, no. 1 (Winter 2001): 155–70.

Poon, Angela. "Comic Acts of (Be)longing: Performing Englishness in *Wonderful Adventures of Mrs. Seacole in Many Lands*." *Victorian Literature and Culture* 35 (2007): 501–16.

Poovey, Mary. *Uneven Developments: The Ideological Work of Gender in Mid-Victorian England*. Chicago: University of Chicago Press, 1988.

Porter, Dennis. *Haunted Journeys: Desire and Transgression in European Travel Writing*. Princeton, NJ: Princeton University Press, 2014.

Power-Greene, Ousmane K. *Against Wind and Tide: The African American Struggle against the Colonization Movement*. New York: New York University Press, 2014.

Pratt, Mary Louise. *Imperial Eyes: Travel Writing and Transculturation*. New York: Routledge, 1992.

Predelli, Line, and Jon Miller. "Piety and Patriarchy: Contested Gender Regimes in Nineteenth-Century Evangelical Missions." In *Gendered Missions: Women and Men in Missionary Discourse and Practice*, edited by Mary Taylor Huber and Nancy C. Lutkehaus, 67–111. Ann Arbor: University of Michigan Press, 1999.

Price, Richard, ed. *Maroon Societies: Rebel Slave Communities in the Americas*. Baltimore: Johns Hopkins University Press, 1996.

Priestly, Margaret. "Philip Quaque of Cape Coast." In *Africa Remembered: Narratives by West Africans from the Era of the Slave Trade*, edited by Philip Curtin, 99–139. Madison: University of Wisconsin Press, 1965.

Prince, Mary [and Thomas Pringle]. *The History of Mary Prince, a West Indian Slave. Related by Herself. With a Supplement by the Editor. To Which is Added the Narrative of Asa-Asa, a Captured African*. London, 1831.

Prince, Nancy. *A Black Woman's Odyssey through Russia and Jamaica: The Narrative of Nancy Prince*. Edited by Ronald G. Walters. New York: Wiener, 1989.

Prince, Nancy. *Narrative of the Life and Travels of Mrs. Nancy Prince*. Boston: William A. Hall, 1850.

Prince, Nancy. *The West Indies: Being a Description of the Islands, Progress of Christianity, Education, and Liberty among the Colored Population Generally*. Boston: Dow and Jackson, 1841.

Pryor, Elizabeth Stordeur. *Colored Travelers: Mobility and the Fight for Citizenship before the Civil War*. Chapel Hill: University of North Carolina Press, 2016.

Pudaloff, Ross J. "No Change without Purchase: Olaudah Equiano and the Economies of Self and Market." *Early American Literature* 40, no. 3 (2005): 499–527.

Pybus, Cassandra. "'A Less Favorable Specimen': The Abolitionist Response to Self-Emancipated Slaves in Sierra Leone." *Parliamentary History* 26 (2007): 97–112.

Reade, Winwood. *The African Sketch-Book*. 2 vols. London: Smith, Elder, 1873.

Rediker, Marcus, and Peter Linebaugh. *The Many-Headed Hydra: Sailors, Slaves, Commoners, and the Hidden History of the Revolutionary Atlantic*. London: Verso, 2000.

Rhodes, Jane. *Mary Ann Shadd Cary: The Black Press and Protest in the Nineteenth Century*. Bloomington: Indiana University Press, 2001.

Richardson, Marilyn, ed. *Maria W. Stewart, America's First Black Woman Political Writer*. Bloomington: Indiana University Press, 1987.

Richardson, Samuel. *Pamela; or, Virtue Rewarded*. 1740. New York: Penguin, 1981.

Roberts, Richard. "The Construction of Cultures in Diaspora: African and African New World Experiences." *South Atlantic Quarterly* 98, nos. 1–2 (Winter 1999): 177–90.

Robinson, Amy. "Authority and the Public Display of Identity: *Wonderful Adventures of Mrs. Seacole in Many Lands*." *Feminist Studies* 20, no. 3 (1994): 537–57.

Robinson, Carey. *The Fighting Maroons of Jamaica*. Kingston, Jamaica: Collins and Sangster, 1969.

Robinson, Jane. *Mary Seacole: The Most Famous Black Woman of the Victorian Age*. New York: Carroll and Graf, 2004.

Romero, Lora. *Home Fronts: Domesticity and Its Critics in the Antebellum United States*. Durham, NC: Duke University Press, 1997.

Roy, Parama. "Oriental Exhibits: Englishmen and Natives in Burton's *Personal Narrative of a Pilgrimage to Al-Madinah and Meccah*." *boundary 2* 22, no. 1 (1991): 185–210.

Royle, Trevor. *Crimea: The Great Crimean War, 1854–1856*. New York: St. Martin's, 2000.

Rupprecht, Anita. "*Wonderful Adventures of Mrs. Seacole in Many Lands* (1857): Colonial Identity and the Geographical Imagination." In *Colonial Lives across the British Empire: Imperial Careering in the Long Nineteenth Century*, edited by David Lambert and Alan Lester, 176–203. Cambridge: Cambridge University Press, 2006.

Rusert, Britt. "Delany's Comet: Fugitive Science and the Speculative Imaginary of Emancipation." *American Quarterly* 65, no. 4 (2013): 799–829.

Rusert, Britt. *Fugitive Science: Empiricism and Freedom in Early African American Culture.* New York: New York University Press, 2017.

Russell, Mary. *The Blessings of a Good Thick Skirt: Women Travelers and Their World.* London: Harper Collins, 1994.

Ryan, Maeve. "A 'Very Extensive System of Peculation and Jobbing': The Liberated African Department of Sierra Leone, Humanitarian Governance and the Fraud Inquiry of 1848." *Journal of Colonialism and Colonial History* 17, no. 3 (Winter 2016). https://muse.jhu.edu/article/639507.

Safford, Frank, and Marco Palacios. *Colombia: Fragmented Land, Divided Society.* New York: Oxford University Press, 2001.

Sale, Maggie. *The Slumbering Volcano: American Slave Ship Revolts and the Production of Rebellious Masculinity.* Durham, NC: Duke University Press, 1997.

Samuels, Ellen. *Fantasies of Identification: Disability, Gender, Race.* New York: New York University Press, 2014.

Sanneh, Lamin. *Abolitionists Abroad: American Blacks and the Making of Modern West Africa.* Cambridge, MA: Harvard University Press, 1999.

Schoeppner, Michael A. *Moral Contagion: Black Atlantic Sailors, Citizenship, and Diplomacy in Antebellum America.* Cambridge: Cambridge University Press, 2019.

Schön, James Frederick, and Samuel A. Crowther. *Journals of the Rev. James Frederick Schön and Mr. Samuel Crowther: Who . . . Accompanied the Expedition up the Niger, in 1841 on Behalf of the Church Missionary Society.* London: Hatchard, 1842.

Schor, Joel. *Henry Highland Garnet: A Voice in Black Radicalism in the Nineteenth Century.* Westport, CT: Greenwood, 1977.

Schuler, Monica. *"Alas, Alas, Poor Kongo": A Social History of Indentured African Immigration into Jamaica, 1841–1865.* Baltimore: Johns Hopkins University Press, 1980.

Scott, Julius. *A Common Wind: Afro-American Currents in the Age of Haitian Revolution.* London: Verso, 2018.

Seacole, Mary. *Wonderful Adventures of Mrs. Seacole in Many Lands.* Edited by Sara Salih. 1857. London: Penguin, 2005.

Seacole, Mary. *Wonderful Adventures of Mrs. Seacole in Many Lands.* Edited by Ziggi Alexander and Audrey Dewjee. 1857. Bristol, UK: Falling Wall Press, 1984.

Senior, Olive. "The Panama Railway." *Jamaica Journal* 14, no. 44 (1980): 66–77.

Shepherd, Verene A., ed. *Maharani's Misery: Narratives of a Passage from India to the Caribbean.* Kingston, Jamaica: University of the West Indies Press, 2002.

Shepperson, George. "African Diaspora: Concept and Context." In *Global Dimensions of the African Diaspora*, edited by Joseph E. Harris, 41–50. Washington, DC: Howard University Press, 1982.

Shick, Tom. *Behold the Promised Land: A History of Afro-American Settler Society in Nineteenth-Century Liberia.* Baltimore: Johns Hopkins University Press, 1980.

Simmons, K. Merinda. "Beyond 'Authenticity': Migration and Epistemology of 'Voice' in Mary Prince's *History of Mary Prince* and Maryse Condé's *I, Tituba.*" *College English* 36, no. 4 (Fall 2009): 75–99.

Sims, James L. "Scenes in the Interior of Liberia: Being a Tour through the Countries of the Dey, Goulah, Pessah, Barlain, Kpellay, Suloany and King Boatswain's Tribes, in

1858." 1858. In *African-American Exploration in West Africa: Four Nineteenth-Century Diaries*, edited by James Fairhead, Tim Geysbeek, Svend E. Holsoe, and Melissa Leach, 93–123. Bloomington: Indiana University Press, 2003.

Sinor, Jennifer. *The Extraordinary Work of Ordinary Writing: Annie Ray's Diary*. Iowa City: University of Iowa Press, 2002.

Sio, Arnold. "Marginality and Free Colored Identity in Caribbean Slave Society." In *Caribbean Slave Society and Economy: A Student Reader*, edited by Hilary Beckles and Verene Shepherd, 150–59. Kingston, Jamaica: Randle, 1991.

Sleeth, Peter. "Mary Seacole: Disease and Care of the Wounded, from Jamaica to the Crimea." *Nursing Clio* (blog), March 22, 2018. https://nursingclio.org/2018/03/22/mary-seacole-care-jamaica-to-the-crimea/.

Small, Hugh. *Florence Nightingale: Avenging Angel*. London: Constable and Robinson, 1999.

Smallwood, Stephanie E. *Saltwater Slavery: A Middle Passage from African to American Diaspora*. Cambridge, MA: Harvard University Press, 2008.

Smith, Amanda Berry. *An Autobiography: The Story of the Lord's Dealings with Mrs. Amanda Smith, the Colored Evangelist: Containing an Account of Her Life Work of Faith, and Her Travels in America, England, Ireland, Scotland, India, and Africa as an Independent Missionary*. 1893. New York: Oxford University Press, 1988.

Smith, Faith. "Coming Home to the Real Thing: Gender and Intellectual Life in the Anglophone Caribbean." *South Atlantic Quarterly* 93, no. 4 (1994): 895–923.

Soyer, Alexis. *Soyer's Culinary Campaign; Being Historical Reminiscences of the Late War*. London: Routledge, 1857.

Spitzer, Leo. *Lives In Between: Assimilation in Austria, Brazil, West Africa, 1790–1945*. New York: Columbia University Press, 1990.

Stanley, Henry M. *How I Found Livingstone: Travels, Adventures and Discoveries in Central Africa*. New York: Scribner's, 1872.

Stanley, Henry M. *In Darkest Africa on the Quest, Rescue, and Retreat of Emin, Governor of Equatoria*. London: Sampson Low, 1890.

Stanton, Elizabeth Cady, Susan B. Anthony, and Matilda Joslyn Gage, eds. *History of Woman Suffrage*. Vol 1. 1881. Salem, NH: Ayer, 1985.

Staudenraus, P. J. *The African Colonization Movement, 1816–1865*. New York: Columbia University Press, 1961.

Stein, Judith. *The World of Marcus Garvey: Race and Class in Modern Society*. Baton Rouge: Louisiana State University Press, 1991.

Stepan, Nancy Leys. *Picturing Tropical Nature*. Chicago: University of Chicago Press, 2006.

Stephens, Michelle Ann. *Black Empire: The Masculine Global Imaginary of Caribbean Intellectuals in the United States, 1914–1962*. Durham, NC: Duke University Press, 2005.

Stephenson, Glennis. *Letitia Landon: The Woman behind L. E. L.* Manchester: Manchester University Press, 1995.

Sterling, Dorothy, ed. *We Are Your Sisters: Black Women in the Nineteenth Century*. New York: Norton, 1984.

Stiles, Ezra, and Samuel Hopkins. "To the Public." Circular letter, Newport, RI, April 10, 1776. https://en.wikisource.org/wiki/To_the_Public._There_Has_Been_a_Design _Formed_ . . . _to_Send_the_Gospel_to_Guinea.

St. John de Crèvecoeur, J. Hector. *Letters from an American Farmer: Describing Certain Provincial Situations, Manners, and Customs, Not Generally Known; and Conveying Some Idea of the Late and Present Interior Circumstances of the British Colonies of North America.* 1782. New York: Penguin, 1981.

Stock, Eugene. *The History of the Church Missionary Society: Its Environment, Its Men and Its Work. In Three Volumes.* London: Church Missionary Society, 1899.

Stowe, William W. *Going Abroad: European Travel in Nineteenth-Century American Culture.* Princeton, NJ: Princeton University Press, 1994.

Sundiata, Ibrahim. *Brothers and Strangers: Black Zion, Black Slavery, 1914–1940.* Durham, NC: Duke University Press, 2003.

Sweet, James H. *Domingos Álvares, African Healing, and the Intellectual History of the Atlantic World.* Chapel Hill: University of North Carolina Press, 2013.

Taylor, Matthew. "Nurse Is Most Famous Black Briton." *Guardian,* February 10, 2004. https://www.theguardian.com/uk/2004/feb/10/britishidentity.artsandhumanities.

Taylor, Ula Yvette. *The Veiled Garvey: The Life and Times of Amy Jacques Garvey.* Chapel Hill: University of North Carolina Press, 2003.

Temperley, Howard. *White Dreams, Black Africa: The British Antislavery Expedition to the River Niger, 1841–1842.* New Haven, CT: Yale University Press, 1991.

Thomas, Lamont D. *Rise to Be a People: A Biography of Paul Cuffee.* Urbana: University of Illinois Press, 1986.

Thompson, Joseph P. "Anniversary Address: African Civilization and the Cotton Trade." In *Constitution of the African Civilization Society,* 9–39. New Haven, CT: Stafford, 1861.

Thompson, Robert Farris. *Flash of the Spirit: African and Afro-American Art and Philosophy.* New York: Vintage, 1984.

Thorne, Susan. *Congregational Missions and the Making of Imperial Culture in Nineteenth-Century England.* Stanford, CA: Stanford University Press, 1999.

Tisdall, E. E. P. *Mrs. Duberly's Campaigns: An Englishwoman's Experiences in the Crimean War and Indian Mutiny.* London: Rand McNally, 1963.

Totten, Gary. *African American Travel Narratives from Abroad: Mobility and Cultural Work in the Age of Jim Crow.* Amherst: University of Massachusetts Press, 2015.

Trollope, [Frances]. *Domestic Manners of the Americans.* London: Whittaker, Treacher, 1832.

Tucker, [Sarah]. *Abbeokuta; or, Sunrise within the Tropics.* London: Nisbet, 1853.

Turner, Lorenzo D. "Some Contacts of Brazilian Ex-Slaves with Nigeria, West Africa." *Journal of African American History* 27, no. 1 (January 1942): 55–67.

Turner, Mary. *Slaves and Missionaries: The Disintegration of Jamaican Slave Society, 1787–1834.* Kingston, Jamaica: University of the West Indies Press, 1998.

Tyler-McGraw, Marie. *An African Republic: Black and White Virginians in the Making of Liberia.* Chapel Hill: University of North Carolina Press, 2009.

Vance, Norman. *The Sinews of the Spirit: The Ideal of Christian Manliness in Victorian Literature and Religious Thought.* Cambridge: Cambridge University Press, 1985.

Venn, Henry. "West Africa: Viewed in Connexion with Slavery, Christianity, and the Supply of Cotton." *Christian Observer*, May 1861, 389–403.

Von Eschen, Penny. *Race against Empire: Black Americans and Anticolonialism, 1937–1957.* Ithaca, NY: Cornell University Press, 1997.

Walls, Andrew F. "Africa as the Theatre of Christian Engagement with Islam in the Nineteenth Century." *Journal of Religion in Africa* 29 (1993): 155–74.

Ward, Kevin, and Brian Stanley, eds. *The Church Missionary Society and World Christianity, 1799–1999.* Grand Rapids, MI: Eerdmans, 2000.

Warner-Lewis, Maureen. *Central Africa in the Caribbean: Transcending Time, Transcending Cultures.* Kingston, Jamaica: University of the West Indies Press, 2003.

Watson, Tim. *Caribbean Culture and British Fiction in the Atlantic World, 1780–1870.* Cambridge: Cambridge University Press, 2008.

Weisenfeld, Judith, and Richard Newman, eds. *This Far by Faith: Readings in African-American Women's Religious Biography.* New York: Routledge, 1995.

Welch, Pedro L. V. "'Unhappy and Afflicted Women?' Free Colored Women in Barbados, 1780–1834." *Revista/Review Interamericana* 29 (1999). http://cai.sg.inter.edu/revista-ciscla/volume29/welsh.html.

Welter, Barbara. "She Hath Done What She Could: Protestant Women's Missionary Careers in Nineteenth-Century America." *American Quarterly* 30, no. 5 (Winter 1978): 624–38.

Williams, C. P. "'Not Quite Gentlemen': An Examination of 'Middling Class' Protestant Missionaries from Britain, c. 1850–1900." *Journal of Ecclesiastical History* 31, no. 3 (July 1980): 301–15.

Williams, George Washington. *An Open Letter to His Serene Majesty Leopold II, King of the Belgians and Sovereign of the Independent State of Congo.* 1890. Accessed February 24, 2021. doi:10.2307/60225491.

Wills, David W., and Richard Newman. *Black Apostles at Home and Abroad: Afro-Americans and the Christian Mission from the Revolution to Reconstruction.* Boston: Hall, 1992.

Wilson, Kathleen. *The Island Race: Englishness, Empire and Gender in the Eighteenth Century.* London: Routledge, 2003.

Wong, Edlie L. *Neither Fugitive nor Free: Atlantic Slavery, Freedom Suits, and the Legal Culture of Travel.* New York: New York University Press, 2009.

"A World Away, Explorer's Kin Meet." *New York Times*, June 7, 1987, 47.

Wright, Joseph. "The Life of Joseph Wright." In *Africa Remembered: Narratives by West Africans from the Era of the Slave Trade*, edited by Philip Curtin, 322–33. Madison: University of Wisconsin Press, 1965.

Yates, T. E. *Venn and the Victorian Bishops Abroad: The Missionary Policies of Henry Venn and Their Repercussions on the Anglican Episcopate of the Colonial Period, 1841–1872.* London: SPCK, 1978.

Yee, Shirley J. *Black Women Abolitionists: A Study in Activism, 1828–1860.* Knoxville: University of Tennessee Press, 1992.

Yellin, Jean Fagan, and John C. Van Horne, eds. *The Abolitionist Sisterhood: Women's Political Culture in Antebellum America.* Ithaca, NY: Cornell University Press, 1994.

Youngs, Tim. *The Cambridge Introduction to Travel Writing*. New York: Cambridge University Press, 2013.

Zeleza, Paul Tiyambe. "Rewriting the African Diaspora: Beyond the Black Atlantic." *African Affairs* 104, no. 414 (2005): 35–68.

Zemka, Sue. "The Holy Books of Empire: Translations of the British and Foreign Bible Society." In *Macropolitics of Nineteenth-Century Literature: Nationalism, Exoticism, Imperialism*, edited by Jonathan Arac and Harriet Ritvo, 102–37. Philadelphia: University of Pennsylvania Press, 1991.

Abbeokuta (Tucker), 153
Abbott, Thomas, 75–76
Abeokuta, 21, 101, 104–6, 117, 129–30, 142–43, 150, 153
Abeokuta and the Cameroon Mountains (Burton), 153
abolitionism, 42, 57, 70, 126, 131, 169, 179. *See also* slavery: abolition of
academic knowledge, 17–18. *See also* interdisciplinarity
activist genealogy, 17
Africa: as a home, 4, 59, 88, 124, 138, 149; and the justification of civilization, 139; natural resources of, 137, 141; perceptions of, 12, 14, 101, 113–14, 133, 135–36, 153, 215n11; white narratives of, 127. *See also specific nations;* Mother Africa, idea of
African, as terminology, 13, 99
African Aid Society, 152
African American studies, 89
African Civilization Society, 152, 220n7
African diasporic identity, 1, 5, 31, 62, 96, 150. *See also* diaspora
Africanists, 205n18, 216n13
African male passivity, 107
Africans: stereotypes of, 135; white expectations of, 175
African Sketchbook (Driver), 127
African slave trade, 88, 121–22
agency, 9, 55–56, 64–66, 100, 105, 107, 112, 181, 199
Ajayi, Jacob, 102

Albert, Prince, 93
Alexander I (Russian czar), 63–64
American Antislavery Society (AAS), 69–70
American Civil War, 6, 16–17, 58
American Colonization Society (ACS), 3, 14, 59, 89, 121, 129–30, 220n7
American Revolution, 65, 121
Amurath to Amurath (Bell), 9
Anderson, Benjamin J. K., 3
Anderson, David, 138
Anglo-African (Lagos), 174
Anglophone diaspora, 10–11
Anim-Addo, Joan, 169–70
anticolonialism, 42, 129. *See also* colonialism
anti-Semitism, 21, 45, 153
Appeal to the Colored Citizens of the World (Walker), 204
Aray, Amos, 122
Aroloya Church, 187
Association for Promoting Educational and Religious Matters in Lagos, 188, 191
Atlantic African diaspora, 5, 14, 20, 118. *See also* diaspora
Atlantic Creole identity, 13–14
Atlantic slave trade, 88, 149, 153, 206n20. *See also* slavery
Ayres, Eli, 129

Barber, Karin, 92, 160
Barber, Mary Ann Serret, 153
Basel Missionary Society, 110–11
Beadslee, J. S. O., 78

Beaver, R. Pierce, 75
Beckles, Hilary McD., 29, 31
Bell, Gertrude, 9
belonging, 9, 120, 176, 183; flexibility, 167.
    See also dislocation; home
Berlin, Ira, 13
Bestes, Peter, 120
Bhabha, Homi, 219n61
Bird, Isabella, 9
Black American audience, 136
Black Atlantic cultures, 13, 62, 206n18, 216n13
Black diasporic identity, 62, 75, 142. See also
    diaspora
Blackett, R. J. J., 198
Black masculinity, 65, 135
Black Nationalism, 16, 60, 124, 142, 198
Black nationhood, 132, 141
Blackness: and gender, 10, 58, 66; and immobil-
    ity, 6; perceptions of, 5, 199. See also race;
    whiteness
Black Panthers, 124
Blackwood, Lady Alicia, 45, 48–49
Blake (Delany), 204
Blyden, Nemata, 145–46
Bonetta, Sarah Forbes, 17, 21–22, 161; and
    Church Missionary Society (CMS), 188–89;
    death of, 192–94; and the denial of home,
    198; early life of, 163, 168–71; freedom
    for, 181–82; legacy of, 195–96; and local
    allegiances, 16; and making travel meaning-
    ful, 167; marriage of, 161–63, 172–73, 222n5;
    and motherhood, 179; and motivations for
    writing, 163; perceptions of, 5, 163, 168–69,
    171–72, 175–76, 181; public image of, 167,
    174–75, 184–85; social status of, 178, 186–87,
    189–91, 198–99. See also James P. L. Davies;
    Queen Victoria
Boston Female Anti-Slavery Society (BFASS),
    70, 213n25
Botswana, 146
Bowen, Thomas Jefferson, 135, 153
Brawley, Lisa, 6
British Baptists, 75–76
Brooks, Richard, 74
Brown, Henry "Box," 6
Burton, Richard Francis, 2, 21, 128, 153–54, 156,
    222n43
Bush, Barbara, 33

Buxton (Canada), 134, 211n3, 221n7
Buxton, Lady, 183–84, 192
Buxton, Sir Thomas Fowell, 164, 220n7
Buzard, James, 67–68

Campbell, Mary, 179
Campbell, Mavis, 82
Campbell, Robert, 157; and Abeokuta, 122–23,
    129–30; and civilization, 148–49; and the
    Crowther brothers, 150–51; home for, 125,
    198; identity of, 131, 145–48; and Islam,
    157–58; and malaria, 137; migration of, 17,
    152; and ocular proof, 125; perceptions of, 3,
    126, 153; travel patterns of, 145; writing style
    of, 21, 128, 143. See also Martin R. Delany
Canada, 59
capitalism, 12, 18, 35. See also colonialism;
    imperialism
Caretta, Vincent, 13
Caribbean: economic depression in, 78; and
    economic opportunity, 28; literature of, 3;
    white women in, 33. See also specific nations
Carlyle, Thomas, 42
Cary, Mary Ann Shadd, 59, 138
Cavell, Janice, 126
Central Africa (Bowen), 135, 153
Chaney, Michael A., 6
Charge of the Light Brigade, 37, 50
Christianity: and control of churches, 224n57;
    conversion to, 14–15, 86–87, 100, 106,
    146, 149; expansion of, 14, 17, 40, 95, 126;
    interpretations of, 63, 76–77, 101; and native
    control of churches, 190; perceived necessity
    of, 136; and rebirth, 169; and travel, 11; and
    womanhood, 223–24n33. See also missionary
    work; religion
Christianization, 20, 91, 111, 121–22, 144–45,
    153, 170
Christian Observer, 152
Church Missionary Gleaner, 104–5, 107–8
Church Missionary Record, 15
Church Missionary Society (CMS): and control,
    86, 171, 187–88; and Samuel Ajayi Crowther,
    99; and masculine identity, 102; and na-
    tive missionaries, 165; obligations to, 142;
    presence of, 85, 125, 144; and recruitment,
    109–10; representatives of, 20, 93–94, 101;
    and Sarah Forbes Bonetta, 162; and Saro

migration, 164; tensions with, 187; and white leaders, 198

Church Missionary Society Parent Committee, 96, 103, 109–10, 187–88, 191

citizenship, 6–7, 9, 27, 83, 198

civilization: perceived need of, 136, 139, 158; promoters of, 90, 111, 154; as status, 148–49; threats to, 114; and whiteness, 130

civilizing mission, 14, 16–17, 205n1

Clapperton, Hugh, 2, 135–36

class: hierarchies of, 79, 110; importance of, 45; modalities of, 16, 52; privilege of, 22, 180–81; as a subject position, 58. *See also* elite social status; race; sexuality

Clegg, Thomas, 152

Cleveland Colored Convention, 133–34

clothing, 158. *See also* cross-dressing

Coates, Dandeson, 164

Cocke, James Hartwell, 130

Cole, Mary, 179

colonialism: as context of missionary work, 107; and diaspora, 52; and elitism, 151; and emancipation, 84; and exploration, 201–2; and masculinity, 96; opposition to, 42, 129; practices of, 3–4, 28–29, 33, 88, 156; promotion of, 15, 27; and racial politics, 148; relations of, 38; return to, 125. *See also* anticolonialism; capitalism

colonial mimicry, 219n61

colonial subjectivities, 25, 150, 199

complicity, 4. *See also* resistance

Congregationalist church, 75

contact zones (Pratt), 16, 207n29

Cornwall, Andrea, 96

Court of Mixed Commission, 86

Craciun, Adriana, 126–28

Craft, Ellen, 6–9

Craft, William, 6–8

creole identity, 12–15, 200, 208n1. *See also* krio identity

Crimean War: aftermath of, 44; effects of, 45; and gender, 28–31, 45, 48; literature of, 37–39, 50; public perception of, 23–24, 32, 37, 45

cross-dressing, 6–9. *See also* clothing

Crowther, Samuel, Jr., 150–51

Crowther, Samuel Ajayi, 20, 94; childhood of, 170; and his mother, 104–8; and home, 101, 198; identities of, 17, 84–85, 97–100, 102,

112, 115; on the importance of language, 116–17; and local allegiances, 16; and missionary work, 15, 19–20, 99, 111, 117–18, 149, 219n61; perceptions of, 2–3, 93–95, 101, 109, 153, 188; self-presentation of, 96, 102, 112–13; slave narrative of, 108, 214–15n1. *See also* James Frederick Schön

Crowther, Susan, 100

Crummell, Alexander, 59

Cuffee, Paul, 89, 121, 220n4

Culinary Campaign (Soyer), 32, 35, 46

Curtin, Philip, 77

Dahomey and the Dahomans (Forbes), 167

Daily Morning Post (Cleveland), 133

Damian, Jessica, 53

Davies, James P. L., 21, 161–63, *162*, 170, 172–73, 184–85, 188, 191–95, 199. *See also* Sarah Forbes Bonetta

Davies, Paulina, 166

Davies, Victoria, 162–63, 177, 195–96

Delany, Martin R., *123*; and Abeokuta, 129–30; and Black Nationalism, 3, 142; as counterpart to Mary Seacole, 43; and the emigration debate, 59, 122, 131–32; and the exploration narrative, 128; and identity, 131, 151, 200; and imperialism, 16–17, 136; and Islam, 157–58; and Liberia, 139–40; and malaria, 137–38, 141, 148; and masculinity, 135; and ocular proof, 125; perceptions of, 21, 126, 137, 139, 155–56, 198; travel patterns of, 145; and the United States Civil War, 155. *See also* Robert Campbell

Denham, Dixon, 2

diaspora: and colonialism, 52; communities of, 3–4, 43, 81, 132; and gender, 5, 89, 100–119; and identity, 13–16, 83, 95, 100–109, 151; and literature, 100–109, 199; sites of, 84, 92. *See also* Atlantic African diaspora; Black diasporic identity; identity

Dickens, Charles, 114

disease, 31, 38

dislocation, 70. *See also* belonging; home

domesticity, 19, 38, 49, 57, 61, 67

Domestic Manners of the Americans (Trollope), 9

Donsunmu, King, 185

Douglass, Frederick, 6, 204

Douglass, Robert, 122

Dred Scott v. Sandford, 6
Driver, Felix, 127
Duberly, Frances, 49–52

Eagle (Lagos), 166
East Africa, 132–33
Eberhardt, Isabelle, 9
economic conditions, 19, 27–28, 33, 55–56, 66, 71, 78. *See also* poverty
education, 20, 150, 160, 163, 165, 174, 188
Edward VII, King, 195
Elaw, Zilpha, 11, 59
Elebute, Adeyemo, 170
elite social status, 1–2, 17, 150–51, 162, 174, 179, 187, 223–24n33. *See also* class; nonelite population; social status
emigration debate, 57, 59–60, 80, 83–84, 89, 121–22, 131, 133, 211n48. *See also* home; migration; repatriation
empire: African American responses to, 207–8n31; expansiveness of, 150; and the exploration narrative, 128; margins of, 26; rhetoric of, 62. *See also* imperialism
English Heritage blue plaque, 25
English identity, 27, 36, 40, 52, 87, 115. *See also* United Kingdom
English–West Indian relations, 36
Enlightenment (European), 127, 201
Equiano, Olaudah, 12–13, 200, 204, 206n20
European values, 4, 66–67, 91, 97–98
exploration: as colonizing practice, 201–2; and fantasies, 143; and heroism, 126, 131; and identity, 126, 131, 201; labor of, 114; politics of, 112–13; public anxieties of, 112–13, 115; and superiority, 133; tradition of, 153
exploration narrative genre, 4, 9, 125, 128, 139, 201–2

Fabian, Johannes, 112
family separation, 6, 10
Female Institution of Freetown, 165, 171, 174
feminism, 26, 38
Fenton, Roger, 50
54th Massachusetts Colored Infantry Regiment, 123, 155, 198
First African Baptist Church, 69–70
flight, as theme, 6
Fluhr, Nicole, 210n31

Foote, Julia, 71
Forbes, Frederick E., 163, 167, 169–70, 179, 196
Foresythe, Charles, 187–88
Foster, Amber, 83
Franklin, John, 2
freedom: achievement of, 61, 65; assumptions of, 26; costs of, 10; and enslavement, 120; and gender, 8, 38; and home, 61; and informality, 182; and marriage, 8, 19, 163, 194. *See also* marriage
Freeman, John Birch, 116–17
Freeman, Sambo, 120
Fugitive Slave Law, 6–7, 9
Fyfe, Christopher, 98

Gardiner, Nancy. *See* Prince, Nancy
Garnet, Henry Highland, 43, 59, 73, 152, 220n7
Garvey, Marcus, 89–90, 124
gender: and diaspora, 5, 89, 100–119; modalities of, 52; and race, 8; and social status, 92–93, 111. *See also* masculinity
gender roles, 9, 22, 29, 40, 48–49, 52, 61, 87, 126, 175
George, Rosemary M., 38
Gezo, King, 168
Gikandi, Simon, 28
Gilroy, Paul, 13, 82
global and local binary, 37
Gold Coast, as migration destination, 121
Gollmer, C. A., 109, 111
Goodman, Temple, 49
Gordon-Reed, Annette, 10

Haensel, Charles, 111–12
Haiti, 60, 121, 207n30
Hall, Catherine, 40
Harris, J. Dennis, 43
Harvey, Thomas, 73–74
Hausa identity, 99
Hawaiian Archipelago, The (Bird), 9
Hawthorne, Evelyn, 37
Hayward, George, 193
Hemings, Sally, 10
hemispheric anticolonialism, 42
Hennessey, John Pope, 185, 191
Henson, Josiah, 6
Henson, Matthew, 201–2, 225n10
heroism, 49, 51, 126–28, 131

Hinderer, David, 109, 111
Hodge, Edward, 49
Holbrook, Felix, 120
Holly, James Theodore, 43, 59
home: Africa as, 4, 59, 124, 138, 149; and
    agency, 199; as an imaginary, 2, 138, 183;
    birthplace, 16; conceptions of, 138; establish-
    ment of, 125; flexibility of, 39, 167, 176–77,
    187; and freedom, 61; locations of, 59, 67,
    72–82, 98, 167; loss of, 7, 9, 62–72, 198; mul-
    tiple meanings of, 64; as a physical domicile,
    197; routines of, 161, 181; and transatlantic
    migration, 89. See also belonging; disloca-
    tion; emigration debate
How I Found Livingstone (Stanley), 127
Hutchinson, Edward, 189

Ibadan-Ijaye War, 136
identity, 3, 14, 20, 60, 92, 99, 156, 160. See also
    diaspora
Illustrated London News, 32
immobility, 6. See also mobility
imperial eyes, 2
imperialism: acceptance of, 37; and diasporic
    travel, 89; as discursive, 5, 61–62; and
    expansion, 15, 40; forms of, 133, 173; and the
    frontier, 36; and identity, 156; opposition to,
    4, 7, 41, 43; power of, 26, 40; and race, 148;
    visions of, 154; as worldview, 2, 136. See also
    capitalism; empire
Incidents in the Life of a Slave Girl (Jacobs), 6, 8
indigenous people: conflicts with, 121–22; con-
    flict with, 3, 28, 41, 98, 129; knowledge of,
    147; religion of, 90–91; respect for, 144, 157
Ingraham, David, 74
Institute for Colored Youth, 21
interdisciplinarity, 18, 127. See also academic
    knowledge
Interesting Narrative, The (Equiano), 12–13,
    200, 204
Intimacies of Four Continents, The (Lowe), 200
Inuit, 201–2
Ipson, Robert, 203–4
Irvine, Judith, 103, 218n51
Islam, 100, 157–58, 173

Jacobs, Harriet, 6, 8–9, 68, 206
Jamaica, 26, 40, 58, 62, 72–82

Jefferson, Thomas, 10
Johnson, Anna, 104
Johnson, Henry, 196
Joie, Chester, 120
Jonas, Simon, 114
Jones, Edward, 117
Josephs, Aleric, 33
Journal Kept during the Russian War (Duberly), 49
Journal of an Expedition up the Niger and Tshadda
    Rivers (Crowther), 3
Journal of a Second Expedition (Clapperton), 135
Journals of the Rev. James Frederick Schön and
    Mr. Samuel Crowther (Crowther), 2–3, 20,
    100–101, 112–16, 152
Journals of Various Visits (Freeman), 117

Kaplan, Amy, 61
Kark, Ruth, 136
Kenny, Gale L., 75
Kerr, Paulette A., 34
Kimball, Joseph Horace, 73–74
Kingsley, Mary H., 9
Kingston Public Hospital, 24–25
Kolapo, Femi J., 99
Kopytoff, Jean, 99, 215n8
krio identity, 97. See also creole identity

Lagos, 17, 91, 122–23, 131, 161, 166–67, 173, 185,
    187–88, 199
Lagos Philharmonic Club, 187, 191–92
Landon, Letita Elizabeth, 114–15, 219n66
land tenure, 221n19
language: colonization of, 156; loss of, 116; of
    missionary communities, 110; power of, 87,
    116–17, 220n70; preservation of, 87, 100;
    scholarship on, 94
Lawrence, Karen, 60
Lee, Jarena, 10–11, 68, 71
Leopold, Prince, 195
Levine, Robert, 126, 156
Liberator, 71, 79, 155–56, 158, 198, 214n42
Liberia, 3, 13–15, 59, 89–90, 121, 129–30, 132,
    136, 139–41, 143
Life and Travels (Prince), 19, 55–56, 59, 61,
    63–65, 72, 74, 77, 79–81, 83–84
Life of Josiah Henson, The (Henson), 6
Lindisfarne, Nancy, 96
literacy, 91–92, 95

literary canons, 17–18, 27

literature: African, 143; African American, 3

Livingston, David, 136

Livingstone, David, 2, 127, 135, 146–47

locality, 16, 37, 77–78, 82

Lodder, Edward Francis, 144–45

London General Gazetteer, 74

London Missionary Society, 104, 127

Lovejoy, Paul, 13

Lowe, Lisa, 200–201

Lucasi, Stephen, 6

Maclean, George, 114

Maharani's Misery (Shepherd), 202–3

malaria, 2–3, 28, 89–90, 101, 114, 137–38, 148.
   See also tropical fevers

Malcolm X, 124

Mammy stereotype, 30

Mann, Adolphus, 175, 188–89

Mann, Kristin, 173

Maroons migration, 81–82, 84, 98

marriage, 8, 19, 22, 56, 64, 112, 163, 181, 194,
   196, 219n59. *See also* freedom; miscegenation; polygamy

Maryland-in-Africa, 130

masculinity, 4, 29, 60, 65, 96–97, 101–2,
   108–19, 126, 135–36, 185, 204. *See also* gender; patriarchy

Maser, J. A., 187–88

masquerade, 158–59

Matory, J. Lorand, 88, 91–92

May, Joseph, 219n61

McCoubrey, John, 214n1

memory, 83, 93, 108, 117, 170, 216n11. *See also*
   nostalgia

Methodist Missionary Society, 125

Middle Passage, 6, 12, 27, 65, 88, 206n20.
   See also triangle trade

Midgley, Claire, 72

Miescher, Stephan, 96

migration: and colonialism, 15; and creolization, 12; as involuntary, 118, 154; patterns of,
   98–99. *See also* emigration debate; *specific
   nations*

Miller, Jon, 109–10, 171

miscegenation, 33–34, 112. *See also* marriage

missionary institutions, 76–77, 110, 171. *See also*
   specific institutions

missionary journals, 102–5, 107, 115, 119, 152,
   218n51

missionary map, 136

missionary narratives, 61–62

Missionary Travels and Researches in South Africa
   (Livingstone), 2, 127, 135

missionary work: and authority, 19–20, 61,
   188–89; and diaspora, 84; and education,
   166; financing of, 106; and gender, 95; as
   identity, 60; by natives, 150, 166; perceptions
   of, 2–3, 55, 143–44; and race, 15, 110–11,
   213n34; recruitment for, 74, 109–10; as travel
   opportunity, 11, 55. *See also* Christianity;
   Christianization; paternalism

mission hierarchy, 93

mixed-race identity, 13, 26, 28–29, 31, 36, 46,
   52, 219n59. *See also* race

mobile colonies, 112

mobility, 6–7, 52–53, 64, 107, 112, 118, 145, 200.
   See also immobility

Montagu, Lady Mary Wortley, 9

moral ideals, 10, 35, 41, 49, 61, 77, 141

Moses, 196

Mother Africa, idea of, 88, 124, 149. *See also*
   Africa

motherhood, 27, 30, 67, 107–8, 178–79

Mrs. Rogers, 50, 51

Mullin, Michael, 214n46

My Bondage and My Freedom (Douglass), 6

Myers, Walter Dean, 195–96

names, 127, 169–71, 178, 223n16

"Narrative of a Journey to Musardu" (Anderson), 3

*Narrative of a Journey to the Shores of the Polar
   Sea* (Franklin), 2

Narrative of Personal Experiences (Blackwood), 45

Narrative of the Life of Frederick Douglass (Douglass), 6

Narrative of the Life of Henry Box Brown
   (Brown), 6

*Narrative of Travels and Discoveries in Northern
   and Central Africa* (Denham, Clapperton, and
   Oudney), 2

National Anti-Slavery Standard letter, 214n42

National Association of Colored Women, 57–58

National Women's Rights Convention, 57

Negro Explorer at the North Pole, A (Henson),
   201–2

New Granada, 42

New York Herald, 127

Nicholson, Lancelot, 188–89, 192

Nigeria, 3, 20–21, 118, 123, 129, 136; British control of, 3; founders of, 87; landscape of, 147–48; and migration, 91, 131, 164; and nationalism, 92; perceptions of, 135, 140–41, 143, 152, 157–58

Niger Mission (Crowther), 3

Niger Valley: Christianity in, 95; and industrial opportunity, 113–14; and Saro migration, 90

Niger Valley expedition of 1841, 100–101, 112–16, 152

Nightingale, Florence, 19, 23–24, 29–30, 32–33, 35, 41, 44, 46, 48. *See also* Mary Seacole

nonelite population, 160. *See also* elite social status

Northrup, David, 14, 118

nostalgia, 138. *See also* memory

Nupe identity, 99

nursing profession, 25–26, 35

Nylander, Gustavus, 219n59

Observer (Lagos), 166

"Occasional Discourse on the Nigger Question" (Carlyle), 42

ocular proof, 125

Official Report of the Niger Valley Exploring Party (Delany), 3, 21, 124, 126, 133–41, 143, 148, 152, 200, 205n3

Open Letter to His Serene Majesty Leopold II, An (Williams), 3–4

Oshielle (Barber), 153

Osumosa, Efunporoye Osuntinubu, 142

Ottoman Empire letters (Montagu), 9

Oudney, Walter, 2

Oyo, Kingdom of, 97, 101

Palmerston, Lord, 93

Panama, 28–29, 40, 42–43, 78

Park, Mungo, 2, 126–27, 155

paternalism, 84, 142, 179, 201–2. *See also* missionary work

patriarchy, 65. *See also* masculinity

patriotism, 35, 44–45, 51

Paul, Susan, 213n25

Paul, Thomas, 69, 213n25, 213n34

Peary, Robert, 201

Peel, J. D. Y., 102–3, 105–6, 112

Personal Narrative (Burton), 2

Phillippo, James, 73

Phipps, Charles Beaumont, 171–72, 190

Phipps, Julia. *See* Tebbs, Julia

Pilgrimage to My Motherland, A (Campbell), 3, 21, 124, 126, 137, 143, 152–54, 157, 158

Piot, Charles, 88, 90

Plea for Emigration, A (Cary), 59

polygamy, 100, 108, 155. *See also* marriage

Porter, Dennis, 54

poverty, 10, 19, 23, 65. *See also* economic conditions

Power-Greene, Ousmane K., 220n7

Pratt, Mary Louise, 2, 4, 96, 126, 128

Price, Richard, 82–83

Prince, Mary, 10

Prince, Nancy: alienation of, 69–70, 83; as counterpart to Mary Seacole, 43; early life of, 55–57, 65; fundraising efforts of, 79; and gender, 63; and home, 61–72; marriage of, 63–64; and migration, 59–60, 80, 98; missionary work of, 75–77; perceptions of, 5, 19, 73, 75, 82–83; precarious life of, 197; as public figure, 57–58, 67–68, 74; travel of, 64, 66, 71–74, 78, 80; in the United States, 68–69, 78, 81–82, 214n42

Prince, Nero, 56–57, 63–64, 68

Principia of Ethnology (Delany), 134

Pringle-Polgreen, Rachel, 33–34, 47

"Project for an Expedition" (Delany), 139

Punch, 32, 35, 210n31

Purnell, James W., 122

Quamine, John, 120–21

Quaque, Philip, 115–16, 118

race: commonalities of, 62, 84, 131; hierarchies of, 52, 79; and missionary work, 110–11; and passing, 6–8; politics of, 77, 148; representatives of, 126; stereotypes of, 47; as a subject position, 58. *See also* Blackness; class; mixed-race identity; sexuality; whiteness

racism, 7, 16–17, 21, 42, 56, 83, 90, 109, 144, 151, 153–54, 199, 201–2

Randle, Victoria. *See* Davies, Victoria

Reade, Winwood, 127, 143

Reid, Douglas, A., 32

Reid, William, 193, 225n58
religion, 10–11, 61, 84, 95. *See also* Christianity
repatriation, 12, 14–15, 90, 119–20, 123, 216n21, 217n27. *See also* emigration debate; return
resistance, 4. *See also* complicity
return: and colonialism, 123–24; diasporic fantasies of, 132; as discursive, 92; as emotional, 183; flexibility of, 2, 118, 167; and missionary work, 101; narratives of, 105; as nostalgic, 15; strategies of, 3, 87, 89, 196. *See also* repatriation
Richardson, Samuel, 8–9
Roberts, Richard, 88
Robinson, Damian, 53
Robinson, Jane, 53
Rowlandson, Thomas, 33–34, 46
Roy, Parama, 156
Royal Geographical Society, 94, 128, 152
Royal Navy blockade, 20, 86, 93, 97, 170, 214n1. *See also* slave trade
Running a Thousand Miles for Freedom (Craft and Craft), 6
Rusert, Britt, 134
Russell, William H., 32
Russia, 56–57, 67–68, 212n23
Russwurm, John Brown, 59, 221n22

Said, Edward, 156
Samaritan Asylum for African American Children, 70
Sanneh, Lamin, 95
Saro identity, 87, 97–100, 112, 215n8, 217n27
Saro migration, 87–90, 92, 95, 98, 112, 118, 160, 164
Sass, Julia, 165–66, 171–72, 174, 185, 188
Scenes in the Interior of Liberia (Sims), 3
Schoeppner, Michael A., 204
Schön, James Frederick, 2–3, 100–101, 172–73, 219. *See also* Samuel Ajayi Crowther
Schuler, Monica, 42
Seacole, Mary, 17, 24; and English identity, 38, 40–43, 52; and exclusion, 202; family of, 209–10n23; financial status of, 23, 197; legacy of, 25, 28, 43; and mixed-race identity, 29; and motherhood, 30–33; nursing work of, 19, 41; perceptions of, 5, 18, 23–26, 30, 32–34, 36–37, 45, 49–50, 53, 208n2; rejection of, 35, 44–45; self-presentation of, 27,

30, 44, 46–47, 51; travel of, 39–40, 44, 64. *See also* Florence Nightingale
Seacole, Sally, 32–33
Seacole Fund, 23, 52
self-determination, 38, 90, 134–35, 166
Senior, Olive, 43
sexual exploitation, 33–34, 203–4
sexual innuendo, 33, 48
sexuality, 33–34, 47, 52, 158. *See also* class; race
Shadow of Islam, In the (Eberhardt), 9
Shepherd, Verene A., 202–3
Sierra Leone, 12, 15, 81–84, 86–87, 89, 97–98, 117–18, 121, 164, 169–70, 204, 217n27
Sierra Leone Company, 14
Sims, James L., 3
Six Months' Service in the African Blockade (Forbes), 170
Skipwith, Peyton, 130
slave narrative, 6, 12, 20, 108
slavery: abolition of, 6–7, 10, 14, 28, 42, 57, 76, 84, 97, 204, 207n30; attitudes toward, 12, 93; escape from, 5–6, 63; life after, 26, 78, 87; opposition to, 3–4, 57; practices of, 118, 169–70; in Russia, 212n23; sexual power dynamics of, 33; threats of, 149; in the United States, 120; white accounts of, 33–34. *See also* abolitionism; Atlantic slave trade
slave trade: across the Atlantic, 88, 149, 153, 206n20; ending of, 167–68; internal to Africa, 88, 97, 101. *See also* Royal Navy blockade; triangle trade
Smith, Amanda Berry, 11, 71
Smith, Faith, 27, 52
Smith Court incident, 58
social status, 22, 26, 33, 56, 64, 72, 92–93, 98, 111, 162–63, 176, 200. *See also* elite social status
Somerset v. Stewart, 10
Soyer, Alexis, 32, 34–35, 47
Spitzer, Leo, 219n61
Stanley, Henry Morton, 127
Steere, Edward, 110
Stewart, Maria W., 59, 71
Stockton, Betsy, 75
Stockton Robert, 129
Stowe, William, 66
St. Thomas' Hospital, 25
Sturge, Joseph, 73–74

Tebbs, Julia (née Phibbs), 190
Thome, James Armstrong, 73–74
Thompson, Joseph Parrish, 152
Times (London), 32
Tinubu, Madame, 142
Totten, Gary, 8
tourism, 9, 44, 67, 161, 180
Townsend, Henry, 109, 111, 144, 153, 165, 188
translations, 20
travel: freedom to, 6–7, 10–11, 29; as leisure, 161; meanings of, 6, 18, 166–67; motivations for, 11, 40, 53, 56, 200; praise of, 164; and public identity, 197; resistance to, 165; as social prestige, 22; and survival, 13
Travels in the Interior Districts of Africa (Park), 2, 126–27
Travels in West Africa (Kingsley), 9
travel writing, 1, 5, 16, 40, 60, 72, 125, 176
treaties, 129
triangle trade, 12, 206n20. *See also* Middle Passage; slave trade
Trollope, Anthony, 34
Trollope, Frances, 9
tropical fevers, 2–3, 28, 89–90, 98, 121, 139–40. *See also* malaria
tuberculosis, 192
Tucker, Sarah, 153
Turner, Mary, 77

Unbeaten Tracks in Japan (Bird), 9
United Kingdom, 10, 14, 25, 28, 38, 73, 97, 170, 207. *See also* English identity
Universal Negro Improvement Association, 89
University of the West Indies, 24–25
United States: abolition of slavery in, 7, 14, 57, 72, 204; compared to Russia, 68; compared to the West Indies, 84; cultural citizenship of, 83; and the emigration debate, 89; as home, 63, 67; and imperialism, 29, 43; and Panama, 28, 40; perceptions of, 73, 132, 138; racism in, 21, 56, 90; Reconstruction era, 198; slavery in, 120
United States Civil War, 123, 155, 198

Vance, Norman, 107
Venn, Henry, 20, 128, 152–53, 165–66, 171–72, 175, 185, 188, 190, 198
Verney, Sir Henry, 23–24

Victoria, Queen: and Sarah Forbes Bonetta, 21–22, 161, 163, 167, 170–71, 173–74, 182, 186–87, 192–94, 199; and Samuel Ajayi Crowther, 93; death of, 195; and Frances Duberly, 52; and Mary Seacole, 197. *See also* Sarah Forbes Bonetta
Victorian era conventions, 9, 25, 31, 51, 126, 142, 175
Vidal, Owen Emeric, 223n16
Vindication of the Capacity of the Negro Race for Self-Government, A (Holly), 60
Vose, Money, 63, 65

Walker, David, 63
Walker's Appeal (Walker), 63
War of 1812, 63
Wentworth, Trelawny, 47
Wesleyan Missionary Notices (Freeman), 117
Wesleyan Parent Committee, 117
West Africa: climate of, 90; and land tenure, 221n19; as migration destination, 152; perceptions of, 4, 59, 92, 131, 154–56; repatriation to, 120; women in, 100
West African Affairs Committee, 191
Western values, 11, 41, 165
West Indian-English relations, 36
West Indian identity, 27, 38, 47, 60, 73, 79, 99, 124, 146
West Indies: communities of, 145; compared to the United States, 84; and home, 98; legal status of, 31; migration to, 72, 133; and miscegenation, 33; missionary organizations in, 74–75
West Indies, The (Prince), 58–59, 72, 80
West Indies emancipation, 57
Wharton, Tobias, 62, 65
White, Charlotte H., 75
whiteness, 9, 29, 33, 38, 49, 74, 77, 126–27, 144–45, 151, 154. *See also* Blackness; race
Williams, George Washington, 3–4, 148
Wilson, Harriet, 68
women: activism by, 70; and authority, 70–71; financial power of, 33; and freedom, 38; as missionaries, 95–96; and self-determination, 38; travel by, 11, 60; in West Africa, 100
women's roles, 61–62, 87, 155–56, 175
women's suffrage, 197–98

Wonderful Adventures of Mrs. Seacole in Many Lands (Seacole), 18–19, 23–26, 29, 32, 34–35, 36, 37–39, 43, 46–50, 52–53, 202
World War II nation-building, 88
Wright, Henry, 188–90
Wright, James, 93

Yamma, Bristol, 120–21
Yates, T. E., 100
Yoruba identity, 2, 90–91, 99–100, 108, 142
Yorubaland, 122
Yoruba Mission, 85, 189
Youngs, Tim, 5